Charles Lamb, Mary Lamb

Mrs. Leicester's School and Other Writings in Prose and Verse

Charles Lamb, Mary Lamb

Mrs. Leicester's School and Other Writings in Prose and Verse

ISBN/EAN: 9783337075323

Printed in Europe, USA, Canada, Australia, Japan

Cover: Foto ©Paul-Georg Meister /pixelio.de

More available books at **www.hansebooks.com**

MRS. LEICESTER'S SCHOOL

AND

OTHER WRITINGS IN PROSE AND VERSE

BY

CHARLES LAMB

WITH INTRODUCTION AND NOTES BY

ALFRED AINGER

London

MACMILLAN AND CO.

1885

INTRODUCTION.

IN addition to the Stories for Children with which it opens, the present volume contains a selection from various prose papers of Lamb's, printed in his lifetime, but not collected into book-form until long after his death. It was an enthusiastic lover of Charles Lamb in the United States to whom is due the credit of searching for and identifying his many outlying contributions to periodical literature, and this gentleman has as yet received scant justice from Lamb's editors in this country.

It was in the year 1863 that the late Mr. J. E. Babson of Chelsea, U.S., began publishing in the pages of the *Atlantic Monthly Magazine* a series of Lamb's papers and essays that had remained apparently unrecognised in the various magazines and newspapers where they originally appeared. In prosecuting his researches Mr. Babson afterwards received the assistance of Mr. Alexander Ireland of Manchester, whose knowledge of the writings of Lamb and Lamb's intimate friends is probably greater than that of any other Englishman. The series was re-issued by Mr. Babson at Boston in the following year, under the title of "*Eliana*, being the hitherto uncollected writings of Charles Lamb." The volume was at once reprinted in England, and, I believe, without any recognition of its origin, or the labours of Mr. Babson. During the twenty years that have elapsed, a few fresh pieces by Lamb have been identified and added to Mr. Babson's collection, and have appeared in various English editions. The shorter prose papers in the present volume are therefore, for the most part, from Mr. Babson's volume, but in every case they have been compared with the originals in Leigh Hunt's Periodicals, Hone's Tablebooks, and other publications to which they were first contributed.

While gratefully acknowledging my obligation to Mr. Babson, I have not been able to adopt his theory of the responsibilities of an editor. "The admirers of Elia," he boldly declares in the preface to his volume, "want to possess every scrap and fragment of his inditing. They cannot let oblivion have the least 'notelet' or 'essaykin' of his." I hope that I may still be reckoned among the admirers of Elia, though I refuse assent to this proposition. The truth is, that every writer of mark leaves behind him shreds and remnants of stuff, some of which are characteristic and worthy of preservation, and some are otherwise; and it is, in my deliberate opinion, an injustice to any such writer to dilute his reputation by publishing every scrap of writing that he is known to have produced, merely because the necessity of making a choice may expose the editor to the risk of censure.

I have ventured, then, to omit some half dozen prose pieces that have appeared in the recent editions of Lamb's complete works. In the first place, there are among these certain fragments, which were left fragments not by accident, but because Lamb tired of his task or found he had misconceived his powers. He began a story called *Juke Judkins*, and wrote only a single chapter. He began turning into prose, under the title of "The Defeat of Time," Thomas Hood's graceful poem, the *Plea of the Midsummer Fairies*, but left it half finished. He once produced a weak string of conceits on an unsavoury subject, called *A Vision of Horns*, of which he confessed himself, in a letter to a correspondent, thoroughly ashamed, and which it would have cut him to the quick to think might be permanently associated with his name. Again, most recent editions have included a letter of the poet Thomson's, which Lamb had discovered in a newspaper of the last century and published in the *London Magazine*.

As the letter has long ago been included in standard biographies of Thomson (for instance, the one prefixed to the Aldine Edition of his poems) there seems to be no possible reason for reprinting it once more. A version in prose of the story of Beaumont and Fletcher's tragedy, *Cupid's Revenge*, and a farce, called *The Pawnbroker's Daughter*, based upon one of Lamb's early essays in Leigh Hunt's *Reflector*, I have also accepted the responsibility of omitting.

In taking this course I have not acted merely upon personal preference, but on a principle that I think may be claimed as sound. I have not willingly excluded any fragment, however short, which exhibited Lamb's peculiar vein of humour or his unique faculty of criticism. No lack of these will be found in the shorter papers here given. I would point to the remarks on De Foe's Secondary Novels and on Wordsworth's *Excursion;* to the delightful autobiographical details in *Captain Starkey;* to the comments on the acting of Miss Kelly and Dowton; to the amazing parody on a certain well-known style of polite biography in the imaginary memoir of Liston; to the rare and almost Shakspearian vein of imagination in the speculation on the Religion of Actors, with its wonderful image of Munden "making mouths at the invisible event;" and lastly, to the noble tenderness of parts of the letter to Southey, and, above all, to the pathetic words upon the death of Coleridge. We should be the poorer in our knowledge and appreciation of Charles Lamb without these and other side-lights upon his mind and character.

The two contributions to Godwin's Library for Children which open the volume have been often reprinted since their first appearance early in the century. The Story of Ulysses was probably the first serious attempt to give literary form to the finest of the world's fairy tales, for the benefit of the young. In passing through Lamb's hands the classic touch must inevitably have given place to the romantic, and it was therefore a gain, rather than the reverse, that he should have chiefly used the version of George Chapman, whose fine Elizabethan cadence may everywhere be traced. Perhaps the *Adventures of Ulysses* may yet again one day be found among the standard books of the nursery. It certainly seems a pity that incidents, characters, and images that are part of the current coin of the world's intercourse should not become familiar in the years when imagination is keenest and freshest.

I make no apology for printing *Mrs. Leicester's School* as a whole. Three of the stories composing it are by Charles Lamb, the others by his sister. He always loyally upheld the superior value of his sister's contribution; and indeed she exhibits in them qualities of humour and observation quite as notable as any corresponding gift of her brother's. "It is now several days," wrote Walter Savage Landor to Crabb Robinson in 1831, "since I read the book you recommended to me—*Mrs. Leicester's School*—and I feel as if I owed a debt in deferring to thank you for many hours of exquisite delight. Never have I read anything in prose so many times over, within so short a space of time, as *The Father's Wedding-Day*. Most people, I understand, prefer the first tale—in truth a very admirable one—but others could have written it. Show me the man or woman, modern or ancient, who could have written this one sentence—'When I was dressed in my new frock I wished poor mamma was alive, to see how fine I was on papa's wedding-day; and I ran to my favourite station at her bedroom door.' How natural in a little girl is this incongruity—this impossibility! Richardson would have given his *Clarissa* and Rousseau his *Heloise* to have imagined it. A fresh source of the pathetic bursts out before us, and not a bitter one. If your Germans can show us anything comparable to what I have transcribed, I would almost undergo a year's gurgle of their language for it. The story is admirable throughout—incomparable, inimitable!"

Of course we recognise here Landor's well-known accent of extravagant generosity, but he was not losing his critical balance. And there are others of Mary Lamb's stories that he might have instanced with enthusiasm. The *Young Mahometan*, delightful for its renewed memories of Blakesware House, abounds in felicities of phrase. The little girl, spending lonely hours in the library of the old mansion, finds a volume called *Mahometanism Explained*, and greedily devours it. "The book said that those who believed all the wonderful stories which were related of Mahomet were called Mahometans and True Believers;—I concluded that I must be a Mahometan, for I believed every word I read." The child broods over her newly-discovered revelation, and yearns that her near relatives should awake to the truth. She becomes so feverish with excitement that her mother comes to sleep in her room. "In the middle of the night I could not resist the strong desire I felt to tell her what preyed so on my mind. I awoke her out of a sound sleep, *and begged she would be so kind as to be a Mahometan.*" This is exquisite; even more so are the particulars that follow of the doctor who was called in, to whom the case was, however, new, "he never having attended a little Mahometan before." The sagacious old doctor is not, however, baffled, but carries off the young lady to spend a few days with himself and his wife, that he may study the case at leisure. "In a few days he fetched me away. His wife was in the carriage with him. Having heard what he said about her prescriptions, I expected, between the doctor and his lady, to undergo a severe course of medicine, especially as I heard him very formally ask her advice what was good for a Mahometan fever; the moment after he had handed me into the carriage. She studied a little while, and then she said a ride to Harlow Fair would not be amiss. He said he was entirely of her opinion, *because it suited him to go there to buy a horse.*" The Mahometan fever, as the reader will anticipate, soon passes away.

It is the sweet humour of Steele and Goldsmith that is here manifest, and the old-fashioned formality of some of the writing, due to the example of Richardson and his school, need be no obstacle to these stories keeping their place among the cherished volumes of the nursery. Mrs. Cowden Clarke tells us how she once heard Charles Lamb address his sister, "with his peculiar mood of tenderness beneath blunt, abrupt speech—'You must die first, Mary.' She nodded with her little quiet nod and sweet smile: 'Yes, I must die first, Charles.'" It was ordered otherwise, as we know; but in the history of faithful love and duty, as well as in that of English literature, there will be no survivorship. Should Charles and Mary Lamb ever die from the memories of men, it will be on the self-same day.

In bringing to a conclusion this collection of Lamb's writings, to be followed, as I hope, by a uniform edition of his correspondence, I have once more to thank the many friends who have aided me by information and suggestion, and notably Mr. Alexander Ireland, who never wearies in the service of literary good-fellowship, and whose great knowledge of Lamb's contemporaries has been continually of advantage to me.

ALFRED AINGER.

TOR CASTLE, FORT-WILLIAM,
 August 1885.

CONTENTS.

	PAGE
Mrs. Leicester's School	1
The Sailor Uncle	5
The Farmhouse	15
The Changeling	22
The Father's Wedding-Day	42
The Young Mahometan	46
Visit to the Cousins	54
*The Witch Aunt	64
The Merchant's Daughter	71
*First Going to Church	75
*The Sea-Voyage	82
The Adventures of Ulysses	89
Guy Faux	180
On the Ambiguities arising from Proper Names	190
On the Custom of Hissing at the Theatres	192
The Good Clerk, a Character	200
The Reynolds Gallery	207
Wordsworth's "Excursion"	210
Theatrical Notices	225

* The tales marked with an asterisk are by Charles Lamb; the others by his sister Mary.

CONTENTS.

	PAGE
First Fruits of Australian Poetry	235
The Gentle Giantess	238
On a Passage in "The Tempest"	242
Letter to an old Gentleman whose Education has been neglected	246
Biographical Memoir of Mr. Liston	253
Autobiography of Mr. Munden	262
Reflections in the Pillory	266
The Last Peach	271
The Illustrious Defunct	274
The Religion of Actors	281
The Months	285
Reminiscence of Sir Jeffery Dunstan	290
Captain Starkey	293
The Ass	298
In re Squirrels	302
Estimate of Defoe's Secondary Novels	304
Recollections of a Late Royal Academician	307
Remarkable Correspondent	315
The Humble Petition of an Unfortunate Day	318
Mrs. Gilpin riding to Edmonton	320
Saturday Night	322
Thoughts on Presents of Game	325
A Popular Fallacy, that a Deformed Person is a Lord	328
Charles Lamb's Autobiography	331
Letter of Elia to Robert Southey, Esq.	333
Table-Talk and Fragments of Criticism	348
Elia to his Correspondents	361
On the Death of Coleridge	365

PROLOGUES, EPILOGUES, AND MISCELLANEOUS VERSE.

	PAGE
Prologue to Coleridge's "Remorse"	367
Prologue to Godwin's "Antonio"	369
Prologue to Godwin's "Faulkener"	371
Epilogue to Sheridan Knowles' "Wife"	372
To Thomas Stothard, R.A.	373
To Clara N.	373
To my Friend the Indicator	374
Saint Crispin to Mr. Gifford	374
On Haydon's Picture of Christ's Entry into Jerusalem	375
Translation	375

POLITICAL SQUIBS, EPIGRAMS, ETC.

To Sir James Mackintosh	377
The Triumph of the Whale	377
The Three Graves	379
Epigram written in the Last Reign	379
Lines suggested by a Sight of Waltham Cross	380
"One Dip"	380
Satan in Search of a Wife	381

MRS. LEICESTER'S SCHOOL:

OR,

THE HISTORY OF SEVERAL YOUNG LADIES,

RELATED BY THEMSELVES.

Dedication.

TO THE
YOUNG LADIES AT AMWELL SCHOOL.

MY DEAR YOUNG FRIENDS,—Though released from the business of the school, the absence of your governess confines me to Amwell during the vacation. I cannot better employ my leisure hours than in contributing to the amusement of you, my kind pupils, who, by your affectionate attentions to my instructions, have rendered a life of labour pleasant to me.

On your return to school I hope to have a fair copy, ready to present to each of you, of your own biographical conversations last winter.

Accept my thanks for the approbation you were pleased to express when I offered to become your amanuensis. I hope you will find I have executed the office with a tolerably faithful pen, as you know I took notes each day during those conversations, and arranged my materials after you were retired to rest.

I begin from the day our school commenced. It was opened by your governess for the first time on the——

day of February. I pass over your several arrivals on the morning of that day. Your governess received you from your friends in her own parlour.

Every carriage that drove from the door I knew had left a sad heart behind. Your eyes were red with weeping, when your governess introduced me to you as the teacher she had engaged to instruct you. She next desired me to show you into the room which we now call the playroom. "The ladies," said she, "may play and amuse themselves, and be as happy as they please this evening, that they may be well acquainted with each other before they enter the schoolroom to-morrow morning."

The traces of tears were on every cheek, and I also was sad; for I, like you, had parted from my friends, and the duties of my profession were new to me, yet I felt that it was improper to give way to my own melancholy thoughts. I knew that it was my first duty to divert the solitary young strangers; for I considered that this was very unlike the entrance to an old-established school, where there is always some good-natured girl who will show attentions to a new scholar, and take pleasure in initiating her into the customs and amusements of the place. These, thought I, have their own amusements to invent; their own customs to establish. How unlike, too, is this forlorn meeting to old schoolfellows returning after the holidays, when mutual greetings soon lighten the memory of parting sorrow.

I invited you to draw near a bright fire which blazed in the chimney, and looked the only cheerful thing in the room.

During our first solemn silence, which, you may remember, was only broken by my repeated requests that you would make a smaller and still smaller circle, till I saw the fireplace fairly enclosed round, the idea came into my mind, which has since been a source of amusement to you in the recollection, and to myself in particular has been of essential benefit, as it enabled me to form a just estimate of the dispositions of you, my young pupils, and

DEDICATION.

assisted me to adopt my plan of future instructions to each individual temper.

An introduction to a point we wish to carry, we always feel to be an awkward affair, and generally execute it in an awkward manner; so I believe I did then; for when I imparted this idea to you, I think I prefaced it rather too formally for such young auditors; for I began with telling you that I had read in old authors, that it was not unfrequent in former times, when strangers were assembled together, as we might be, for them to amuse themselves with telling stories—either of their own lives, or the adventures of others. "Will you allow me, ladies," I continued, "to persuade you to amuse yourselves in this way? You will not then look so unsociably upon each other; for we find that these strangers, of whom we read, were as well acquainted before the conclusion of the first story as if they had known each other many years. Let me prevail upon you to relate some little anecdotes of your own lives. Fictitious tales we can read in books, and they were therefore better adapted to conversation in those times when books of amusement were more scarce than they are at present."

After many objections of not knowing what to say or how to begin, which I overcame by assuring you how easy it would be, for that every person is naturally eloquent when they are the hero or heroine of their own tale;—the *Who should begin?* was next in question.

I proposed to draw lots, which formed a little amusement of itself. Miss Manners, who till then had been the saddest of the sad, began to brighten, and said it was just like drawing king and queen; and began to tell us where she passed last Twelfth-day; but as her narration must have interfered with the more important business of the lottery, I advised her to postpone it till it came to her turn to favour us with the history of her life, when it would appear in its proper order. The first number fell to the share of Miss Villiers, whose joy at drawing what we called the *first prize* was tempered with shame at appearing as the first historian in the company. She wished she had not been the very first:—she had passed all her life in a retired village, and had nothing to relate of herself that could give the least entertainment; she had not the least idea in the world where to begin.

"Begin," said I, "with your name, for that at present is unknown to us. Tell us the first thing you can remember; relate whatever happened to make a great impression on you when you were very young; and if you find you can connect your story till your arrival here to-day, I am sure we shall listen to you with pleasure; and if you like to break off, and only treat us with a part of your history, we will excuse you, with many thanks for the amusement which you have afforded us; and the young lady who has drawn the second number will, I hope, take her turn with the same indulgence, to relate either all, or any part of the events of her life, as best pleases her own fancy, or as she finds she can manage it with the most ease to herself." Encouraged by this offer of indulgence, Miss Villiers began.

If in my report of her story, or in any which follow, I shall appear to make her or you speak an older language than it seems probable that you should use, speaking in your own words, it must be remembered that what is very proper and becoming when spoken, requires to be arranged with some little difference before it can be set down in writing. Little inaccuracies must be pared away, and the whole must assume a more formal and correct appearance. My own way of thinking, I am sensible, will too often intrude itself; but I have endeavoured to preserve, as exactly as I could, your own words and your own peculiarities of style and manner, and to approve myself

Your faithful historiographer,
as well as true friend,
M. B.

ELIZABETH VILLIERS.

My father is the curate of a village church about five miles from Amwell. I was born in the parsonage-house, which joins the churchyard. The first thing I can remember was my father teaching me the alphabet from the letters on a tombstone that stood at the head of my mother's grave. I used to tap at my father's study door; I think I now hear him say, "Who is there?—What do you want, little girl?" "Go and see mamma. Go and learn pretty letters." Many times in the day would my father lay aside his books and his papers to lead me to this spot, and make me point to the letters, and then set me to spell syllables and words: in this manner, the epitaph on my mother's tomb being my primer and my spelling-book, I learned to read.

I was one day sitting on a step placed across the churchyard stile, when a gentleman, passing by, heard me distinctly repeat the letters which formed my mother's name, and then say *Elizabeth Villiers*, with a firm tone, as if I had performed some great matter. This gentleman was my uncle James, my mother's brother; he was a lieutenant in the Navy, and had left England a few weeks after the marriage of my father and mother, and now, returned home from a long sea-voyage, he was coming to visit my mother—no tidings of her decease having reached him, though she had been dead more than a twelvemonth.

When my uncle saw me sitting on the stile, and heard me pronounce my mother's name, he looked earnestly in my face, and began to fancy a resemblance to his sister, and to think I might be her child. I was too intent on my employment to observe him, and went spelling on. "Who has taught you to spell so prettily, my little maid?" said my uncle. "Mamma," I replied; for I had an idea that the words on the tombstone were somehow a part of mamma, and that she had taught me. "And who is mamma?" asked my uncle. "Elizabeth Villiers," I replied; and then my uncle called me his dear little niece, and said he would go with me to mamma; he took hold of my hand, intending to lead me home, delighted that he had found out who I was, because he imagined it would be such a pleasant surprise to his sister to see her little daughter bringing home her long-lost sailor uncle.

I agreed to take him to mamma, but we had a dispute about the way thither. My uncle was for going along the road which led directly up to our house; I pointed to the churchyard, and said that was the way to mamma. Though impatient of any delay, he was not willing to contest the point with his new relation; therefore he lifted me over the stile, and was then going to take me along the path to a gate he knew was at the end of our garden; but no, I would not go that way neither; letting go his hand, I said, "You do not know the way,—I will show you;" and making what haste I could among the long grass and thistles, and jumping over the low graves, he said, as he followed what he called my *wayward steps*, "What a positive soul this little niece of mine is! I knew the way to your mother's house before you were born, child." At last I stopped at my mother's grave, and pointing to the tombstone said, "Here is mamma!" in a voice of exultation, as if I had now convinced him that I knew the way best. I looked up in his face to see him acknowledge his mistake; but oh! what a face of sorrow did I see! I was so frightened, that I have but an imperfect recollection of what followed. I remember I pulled his coat, and cried "Sir, sir!" and tried to move him. I knew not what to do. My mind was in a strange confusion; I thought I had done something wrong in bringing the gentleman to mamma, to make him cry so sadly; but what it was I could not tell. This grave had always been a scene of delight to me. In the house my father would often be weary of my prattle, and send me from him; but here he was all my own. I might say anything, and be as frolicsome as I pleased here; all was cheerfulness and good-humour in our visits to mamma, as we called it. My father would tell me how quietly mamma slept there, and that he and his little Betsy would one day sleep beside mamma in that grave; and when I went to bed, as I laid my little head on the pillow, I used to wish I was sleeping in the grave with my papa and mamma; and in my childish dreams I used to fancy myself there; and it was a place within the ground, all smooth, and soft, and green. I never made out any figure of mamma, but still it was the tombstone, and papa, and the smooth green grass, and my head resting upon the elbow of my father.

How long my uncle remained in this agony of grief I know not—to me it seemed a very long time; at last he took me in his arms, and held me so tight that I began to cry, and ran home to my father and told him that a gentleman was crying about mamma's pretty letters.

No doubt it was a very affecting meeting between my father and my uncle. I remember that it was the very first day I ever saw my father weep—that I was in sad trouble, and went into the kitchen and told Susan, our servant, that papa was crying; and she wanted to keep me with her, that I might not disturb the conversation; but I would go back to the parlour to *poor papa*, and I went in softly and crept between my father's knees. My uncle offered to take me in his arms, but I turned sullenly from him, and clung closer to my father, having conceived a dislike to my uncle because he had made my father cry.

Now I first learned that my mother's death was a heavy affliction; for I heard my father tell a melancholy story of her long illness, her death, and what he had suffered from her loss. My uncle said what a sad thing it was for my father to be left with such a young child; but my father replied, his little Betsy was all his comfort, and that, but for me, he should have died with grief. How I could be any comfort to my father, struck me with wonder. I knew I was pleased when he played and talked with me; but I thought that was all goodness and favour done to me, and I had no notion how I could make any part of his happiness. The sorrow I now heard he had suffered was as new and strange to me. I had no idea that he had ever been unhappy; his voice was always kind and cheerful; I had never before seen him weep, or show any such signs of grief as those in which I used to express my little troubles. My thoughts on these subjects were confused and childish; but from that time I never ceased pondering on the sad story of my dead mamma.

The next day I went, by mere habit, to the study door, to call papa to the beloved grave; my mind misgave me, and I could not tap at the door. I went backwards and forwards between the kitchen and the study, and what to do with myself I did not know. My uncle met me in the passage, and said, "Betsy, will you come and walk with me in the garden?" This I refused, for this was not what I wanted, but the old amusement of sitting on the grave and talking to papa. My uncle tried to persuade me, but still I said, "No, no," and ran crying into the kitchen. As he followed me in there, Susan said, "This child is so fretful to-day, I do not know what to do with her." "Ay," said my uncle, "I suppose my poor brother spoils her, having but one." This reflection on my papa made me quite in a little passion of anger, for I had not forgot that with this new uncle sorrow had first come into our dwelling; I screamed loudly, till my father came out to know what it was all about. He sent my uncle into the parlour, and said he would manage the little wrangler by himself. When my uncle was gone I ceased crying; my father forgot to lecture me for my ill-humour, or to inquire into the cause, and we were soon seated by the side of the tombstone. No lesson went on that day; no talking of pretty mamma sleeping in the green grave; no jumping from the tombstone to the ground; no merry jokes or pleasant stories. I sat upon my father's knee, looking up in his face and thinking, "*How sorry papa looks*," till having been fatigued with crying, and now oppressed with thought, I fell fast asleep.

My uncle soon learned from Susan that this place was our constant haunt; she told him she did verily believe her master would never get the better of the death of her mistress while he continued to teach the child to read at the tombstone; for though it might soothe his grief, it kept it for ever fresh in his memory. The sight of his sister's grave had been such a shock to my uncle, that he readily entered into Susan's apprehensions; and concluding that if I were set to study by some other means, there would no longer be a pretence for these visits to the grave, away my kind uncle hastened to the nearest market-town to buy me some books.

I heard the conference between my uncle and Susan, and I did not approve of his interfering in our pleasure. I saw him take his hat and walk out, and I secretly hoped he was gone *beyond seas again*, from whence Susan had told me he had come. Where *beyond seas* was, I could not tell; but I concluded it was somewhere a great way off. I took my seat on the churchyard stile, and kept looking down the road, and saying, "I hope I shall not see my uncle again. I hope my uncle will not come from *beyond seas* any more;" but I said this very softly, and had a kind of notion that I was in a perverse ill-humoured fit. Here I sat till my uncle returned from the market-town with his new purchases. I saw him come walking very fast, with a parcel under his arm. I was very sorry to see him, and I frowned and tried to look very cross. He untied his parcel, and said, "Betsy, I have brought you a pretty book." I turned my head away, and said, "I don't want a book;" but I could not help peeping again to look at it. In the hurry of opening the parcel, he had scattered all the books upon the ground, and there I saw fine gilt covers and gay pictures all fluttering about. What a fine sight! All my resentment vanished, and I held up my face to kiss him, that being my way of thanking my father for any extraordinary favour.

My uncle had brought himself into rather a troublesome office; he had heard me spell so well, that he thought there was nothing to do but to put books into my hand and I should read; yet notwithstanding I spelt tolerably well, the letters in my new library were so much smaller than I had been accustomed to; they were like Greek characters to me; I could make nothing at all of them. The honest sailor was not to be discouraged by this difficulty; though unused to play the schoolmaster, he taught me to read the small print with unwearied diligence and patience; and whenever he saw my father and me look as if we wanted to resume our visits to the grave, he would propose some pleasant walk; and if my father said it was too far for the child to walk, he would set me on his shoulder and say, "Then Betsy shall ride!" and in this manner has he carried me many, many miles.

In these pleasant excursions my uncle seldom forgot to make Susan furnish him with a luncheon, which, though it generally happened every day, made a constant surprise to my papa and me, when, seated under some shady tree, he pulled it out of his pocket, and began to distribute his little store; and then I used to peep into the other pocket, to see if there were not some currant wine there, and the little bottle of water for me; if, perchance, the water was forgot, then it made another joke,—that poor Betsy must be forced to drink a little drop of wine. These are childish things to tell of; and, instead of my own silly history, I wish I could remember the entertaining stories my uncle used to relate of his voyages and travels, while we sat under the shady trees eating our noontide meal.

The long visit my uncle made us was such an important event in my life, that I fear I shall tire your patience with talking of him; but when he is gone, the remainder of my story will be but short.

The summer months passed away, but not swiftly;—the pleasant walks and the charming stories of my uncle's adventures made them seem like years to me. I remember the approach of winter by the warm great-coat he bought for me, and how proud I was when I first put it on; and that he called me Little Red Riding Hood, and bade me beware of wolves; and that I laughed, and said there were no such things now; then he told me how many wolves, and bears, and tigers, and lions he had met with in uninhabited lands that were like Robinson Crusoe's island. Oh, these were happy days!

In the winter our walks were shorter and less frequent. My books were now my chief amusement, though my studies were often interrupted by a game of romps with my uncle, which too often ended in a quarrel, because he played so roughly; yet long before this I dearly loved my uncle, and the improvement I made while he was with us was very great indeed. I could now read very well, and the continual habit of listening to the conversation of my father and my uncle made me a little woman in understanding; so that my father said to him, "James, you have made my child quite a companionable little being!"

My father often left me alone with my uncle; sometimes to write his sermons; sometimes to visit the sick, or give counsel to his poor neighbours; then my uncle used to hold long conversations with me, telling me how I should strive to make my father happy, and endeavour to improve myself when he was gone. Now I began justly to understand why he had taken such pains to keep my father from visiting my mother's grave,—that

grave which I often stole privately to look at; but now
never without awe and reverence, for my uncle used to
tell me what an excellent lady my mother was; and I
now thought of her as having been a real mamma, which
before seemed an ideal something, no way connected with
life. And he told me that the ladies from the Manor-
house, who sat in the best pew in the church, were not
so graceful, and the best women in the village were not
so good, as was my sweet mamma; and that if she had
lived, I should not have been forced to pick up a little
knowledge from him, a rough sailor, or to learn to knit
and sew of Susan, but that she would have taught me
all ladylike fine works, and delicate behaviour, and
perfect manners, and would have selected for me proper
books, such as were most fit to instruct my mind, and
of which he nothing knew. If ever in my life I shall
have any proper sense of what is excellent or becoming
in the womanly character, I owe it to these lessons of
my rough unpolished uncle; for, in telling me what my
mother would have made me, he taught me what to wish
to be; and when, soon after my uncle left us, I was
introduced to the ladies at the Manor-house, instead of
hanging down my head with shame, as I should have
done before my uncle came, like a little village rustic, I
tried to speak distinctly, with ease and a modest gentleness, as my uncle had said my mother used to do; instead
of hanging down my head abashed, I looked upon them,
and thought what a pretty sight a fine lady was, and
how well my mother must have appeared, since she was
so much more graceful than these high ladies were; and
when I heard them compliment my father on the admirable behaviour of his child, and say how well he had
brought me up, I thought to myself, "Papa does not
much mind my manners, if I am but a good girl; but it
was my uncle that taught me to behave like mamma."
I cannot now think my uncle was so rough and unpolished as he said he was, for his lessons were so
good and so impressive that I shall never forget them,

and I hope they will be of use to me as long as I live. He would explain to me the meaning of all the words he used, such as grace and elegance, modest diffidence and affectation, pointing out instances of what he meant by those words, in the manners of the ladies and their young daughters who came to our church; for, besides the ladies of the Manor-house, many of the neighbouring families came to our church, because my father preached so well.

It must have been early in the spring when my uncle went away, for the crocuses were just blown in the garden, and the primroses had begun to peep from under the young budding hedgerows. I cried as if my heart would break, when I had the last sight of him through a little opening among the trees as he went down the road. My father accompanied him to the market-town, from whence he was to proceed in the stage-coach to London. How tedious I thought all Susan's endeavours to comfort me were. The stile where I first saw my uncle came into my mind, and I thought I would go and sit there, and think about that day; but I was no sooner seated there, than I remembered how I had frightened him by taking him so foolishly to my mother's grave, and then again how naughty I had been when I sat muttering to myself at this same stile, wishing that he who had gone so far to buy me books might never come back any more; all my little quarrels with my uncle came into my mind now that I could never play with him again, and it almost broke my heart. I was forced to run into the house to Susan for that consolation I had just before despised.

Some days after this, as I was sitting by the fire with my father, after it was dark, and before the candles were lighted, I gave him an account of my troubled conscience at the church-stile, when I remembered how unkind I had been to my uncle when he first came, and how sorry I still was whenever I thought of the many quarrels I had had with him.

My father smiled, and took hold of my hand, saying, "I will tell you all about this, my little penitent. This is the sort of way in which we all feel when those we love are taken from us. When our dear friends are with us, we go on enjoying their society, without much thought or consideration of the blessing we are possessed of, nor do we too nicely weigh the measure of our daily actions—we let them freely share our kind or our discontented moods; and, if any little bickerings disturb our friendship, it does but the more endear us to each other when we are in a happier temper. But these things come over us like grievous faults when the object of our affection is gone for ever. Your dear mamma and I had no quarrels; yet in the first days of my lonely sorrow how many things came into my mind that I might have done to have made her happier. It is so with you, my child. You did all a child could do to please your uncle, and dearly did he love you; and these little things which now disturb your tender mind, were remembered with delight by your uncle; he was telling me in our last walk, just perhaps as you were thinking about it with sorrow, of the difficulty he had in getting into your good graces when he first came; he will think of these things with pleasure when he is far away. Put away from you this unfounded grief; only let it be a lesson to you to be as kind as possible to those you love; and remember, when they are gone from you, you will never think you had been kind enough. Such feelings as you have now described are the lot of humanity. So you will feel when I am no more, and so will your children feel when you are dead. But your uncle will come back again, Betsy, and we will now think of where we are to get the cage to keep the talking parrot in, he is to bring home; and go and tell Susan to bring the candles, and ask her if the nice cake is almost baked that she promised to give us for our tea."

At this point, my dear Miss Villiers, you thought fit to break off your story, and the wet eyes of your young auditors seemed to confess that you had succeeded in moving their feelings with your pretty narrative. It now fell by lot to the turn of Miss Manners to relate her story, and we were all sufficiently curious to know what so very young an historian had to tell of herself. I shall continue the narratives for the future in the order in which they followed, without mentioning any of the interruptions which occurred from the asking of questions, or from any other cause, unless materially connected with the stories. I shall also leave out the apologies with which you severally thought fit to preface your stories of yourselves, though they were very seasonable in their place, and proceeded from a proper diffidence, because I must not swell my work to too large a size.

LOUISA MANNERS.

My name is Louisa Manners; I was seven years of age last birthday, which was on the first of May. I remember only four birthdays. The day I was four years old was the first that I recollect. On the morning of that day, as soon as I awoke, I crept into mamma's bed, and said, "Open your eyes, mamma, for it is my birthday. Open your eyes and look at me!" Then mamma told me I should ride in a post-chaise, and see my grandmamma and my sister Sarah. Grandmamma lived at a farmhouse in the country, and I had never in all my life been out of London; no, nor had I ever seen a bit of green grass, except in the Drapers' Garden, which is near my papa's house in Broad Street; nor had I ever rode in a carriage before that happy birthday.

I ran about the house talking of where I was going,

and rejoicing so that it was my birthday, that when I got into the chaise I was tired, and fell asleep.

When I awoke, I saw the green fields on both sides of the chaise, and the fields were full, quite full, of bright shining yellow flowers, and sheep and young lambs were feeding in them. I jumped, and clapped my hands together for joy, and I cried out, "This is

" ' Abroad in the meadows to see the young lambs,' "

for I knew many of Watts's hymns by heart.

The trees and hedges seemed to fly swiftly by us, and one field, and the sheep, and the young lambs, passed away; and then another field came, and that was full of cows; and then another field, and all the pretty sheep returned; and there was no end of these charming sights till we came quite to grandmamma's house, which stood all alone by itself, no house to be seen at all near it.

Grandmamma was very glad to see me, and she was very sorry that I did not remember her, though I had been so fond of her when she was in town but a few months before. I was quite ashamed of my bad memory. My sister Sarah showed me all the beautiful places about grandmamma's house. She first took me into the farmyard, and I peeped into the barn; there I saw a man thrashing, and as he beat the corn with his flail, he made such a dreadful noise that I was frightened, and ran away; my sister persuaded me to return; she said Will Tasker was very good-natured; then I went back, and peeped at him again; but as I could not reconcile myself to the sound of his flail, or the sight of his black beard, we proceeded to see the rest of the farmyard.

There was no end to the curiosities that Sarah had to show me. There was the pond where the ducks were swimming, and the little wooden houses where the hens slept at night. The hens were feeding all over the yard, and the prettiest little chickens, they were feeding too, and little yellow ducklings that had a hen for their mamma. She was so frightened if they went near the water! Grandmamma says a hen is not esteemed a very wise bird.

We went out of the farmyard into the orchard. Oh, what a sweet place grandmamma's orchard is! There were pear-trees, and apple-trees, and cherry-trees, all in blossom. These blossoms were the prettiest flowers that ever were seen; and among the grass under the trees there grew buttercups, and cowslips, and daffodils, and blue-bells. Sarah told me all their names, and she said I might pick as many of them as ever I pleased.

I filled my lap with flowers, I filled my bosom with flowers, and I carried as many flowers as I could in both my hands; but as I was going into the parlour to show them to my mamma, I stumbled over a threshold which was placed across the parlour, and down I fell with all my treasure.

Nothing could have so well pacified me for the misfortune of my fallen flowers as the sight of a delicious syllabub which happened at that moment to be brought in. Grandmamma said it was a present from the red cow to me because it was my birthday; and then, because it was the first of May, she ordered the syllabub to be placed under the May-bush that grew before the parlour-door, and when we were seated on the grass round it, she helped me the very first to a large glass full of the syllabub, and wished me many happy returns of that day, and then she said I was myself the sweetest little May-blossom in the orchard.

After the syllabub, there was the garden to see, and a most beautiful garden it was;—long and narrow, a straight gravel walk down the middle of it; at the end of the gravel walk there was a green arbour with a bench under it.

There were rows of cabbages and radishes, and pease and beans. I was delighted to see them, for I never saw so much as a cabbage growing out of the ground before.

On one side of this charming garden there were a great many beehives, and the bees sung so prettily.

Mamma said, "Have you nothing to say to these pretty bees, Louisa?" Then I said to them—

> "How doth the little busy bee improve each shining hour,
> And gather honey all the day from every opening flower."

They had a most beautiful flower-bed to gather it from, quite close under the hives.

I was going to catch one bee, till Sarah told me about their stings, which made me afraid for a long time to go too near their hives; but I went a little nearer, and a little nearer every day, and before I came away from grandmamma's, I grew so bold, I let Will Tasker hold me over the glass windows at the top of the hives, to see them make honey in their own home.

After seeing the garden, I saw the cows milked, and that was the last sight I saw that day; for while I was telling mamma about the cows, I fell fast asleep, and I suppose I was then put to bed.

The next morning my papa and mamma were gone. I cried sadly, but was a little comforted at hearing they would return in a month or two, and fetch me home. I was a foolish little thing then, and did not know how long a month was. Grandmamma gave me a little basket to gather my flowers in. I went into the orchard, and before I had half-filled my basket I forgot all my troubles.

The time I passed at my grandmamma's is always in my mind. Sometimes I think of the good-natured pied cow that would let me stroke her while the dairy-maid was milking her. Then I fancy myself running after the dairy-maid into the nice clean dairy, and see the pans full of milk and cream. Then I remember the wood-house; it had once been a large barn, but being grown old, the wood was kept there. My sister and I used to peep about among the faggots, to find the eggs the hens sometimes left there. Birds' nests we might not look for. Grandmamma was very angry once, when Will Tasker brought home a bird's nest full of pretty speckled eggs for me. She sent him back to the hedge with it again. She said the little birds would not sing any more if their eggs were taken away from them.

A hen, she said, was a hospitable bird, and always laid more eggs than she wanted, on purpose to give her mistress to make puddings and custards with.

I do not know which pleased grandmamma best, when we carried her home a lapful of eggs, or a few violets; for she was particularly fond of violets.

Violets' were very scarce; we used to search very carefully for them every morning round by the orchard hedge, and Sarah used to carry a stick in her hand to beat away the nettles; for very frequently the hens left their eggs among the nettles. If we could find eggs and violets too, what happy children we were!

Every day I used to fill my basket with flowers, and for a long time I liked one pretty flower as well as another pretty flower; but Sarah was much wiser than me, and she taught me which to prefer.

Grandmamma's violets were certainly best of all, but they never went in the basket, being carried home, almost flower by flower, as soon as they were found, therefore blue-bells might be said to be the best, for the cowslips were all withered and gone before I learned the true value of flowers. The best blue-bells were those tinged with red; some were so very red that we called them red blue-bells, and these Sarah prized very highly indeed. Daffodils were so very plentiful, they were not thought worth gathering unless they were double ones; and buttercups I found were very poor flowers indeed, yet I would pick one now and then, because I knew they were the very same flowers that had delighted me so in the journey; for my papa had told me they were.

I was very careful to love best the flowers which Sarah praised most, yet sometimes, I confess, I have even picked a daisy, though I knew it was the very worst flower of all, because it reminded me of London, and the Drapers' Garden; for, happy as I was at grandmamma's,

I could not help sometimes thinking of my papa and mamma, and then I used to tell my sister all about London; how the houses stood all close to each other; what a pretty noise the coaches made; and what a great many people there were in the streets. After we had been talking on these subjects, we generally used to go into the old wood-house and play at being in London. We used to set up bits of wood for houses; our two dolls we called papa and mamma; in one corner we made a little garden with grass and daisies, and that was to be the Drapers' Garden. I would not have any other flowers here than daisies, because no other grew among the grass in the real Drapers' Garden. Before the time of hay-making came, it was very much talked of. Sarah told me what a merry time it would be, for she remembered everything which had happened for a year or more. She told me how nicely we should throw the hay about. I was very desirous, indeed, to see the hay made.

To be sure, nothing could be more pleasant than the day the orchard was mowed: the hay smelled so sweet, and we might toss it about as much as ever we pleased; but, dear me, we often wish for things that do not prove so happy as we expected; the hay, which was at first so green and smelled so sweet, became yellow and dry, and was carried away in a cart to feed the horses; and then, when it was all gone, and there was no more to play with, I looked upon the naked ground, and perceived what we had lost in these few merry days. Ladies, would you believe it, every flower, blue-bells, daffodils, buttercups, daisies, all were cut off by the cruel scythe of the mower. No flower was to be seen at all, except here and there a short solitary daisy, that a week before one would not have looked at.

It was a grief, indeed, to me, to lose all my pretty flowers; yet when we are in great distress, there is always, I think, something which happens to comfort us; and so it happened now that gooseberries and currants were almost ripe, which was certainly a very pleasant

THE FARMHOUSE. 21

prospect. Some of them began to turn red, and as we never disobeyed grandmamma, we used often to consult together, if it was likely she would permit us to eat them yet; then we would pick a few that looked the ripest, and run to ask her if she thought they were ripe enough to eat, and the uncertainty what her opinion would be made them doubly sweet if she gave us leave to eat them.

When the currants and gooseberries were quite ripe, grandmamma had a sheep-shearing. All the sheep stood under the trees to be sheared. They were brought out of the field by old Spot, the shepherd. I stood at the orchard-gate and saw him drive them all in. When they had cropped off all their wool, they looked very clean, and white, and pretty; but, poor things, they ran shivering about with cold, so that it was a pity to see them. Great preparations were making all day for the sheep-shearing supper. Sarah said a sheep-shearing was not to be compared to a harvest-home, *that* was so much better, for that then the oven was quite full of plum-pudding, and the kitchen was very hot indeed with roasting beef; yet I can assure you there was no want at all of either roast-beef or plum-pudding at the sheep-shearing.

My sister and I were permitted to sit up till it was almost dark, to see the company at supper. They sat at a long oak table, which was finely carved, and as bright as a looking-glass.

I obtained a great deal of praise that day, because I replied so prettily when I was spoken to. My sister was more shy than me; never having lived in London was the reason of that. After the happiest day bed-time will come! We sat up late; but at last grandmamma sent us to bed; yet though we went to bed, we heard many charming songs sung; to be sure, we could not distinguish the words, which was a pity, but the sound of their voices was very loud, and very fine indeed.

The common supper that we had every night was very cheerful. Just before the men came out of the field, a large faggot was flung on the fire; the wood used to crackle and blaze, and smell delightfully; and then the crickets, for they loved the fire, they used to sing; and old Spot, the shepherd, who loved the fire as well as the crickets did, he used to take his place in the chimney corner; after the hottest day in summer, there old Spot used to sit. It was a seat within the fireplace, quite under the chimney, and over his head the bacon hung.

When old Spot was seated, the milk was hung in a skillet over the fire, and then the men used to come and sit down at the long white table.

Pardon me, my dear Louisa, that I interrupted you here. You are a little woman now to what you were then; and I may say to you, that though I loved to hear you prattle of your early recollections, I thought I perceived some ladies present were rather weary of hearing so much of the visit to grandmamma. You may remember I asked you some questions concerning your papa and mamma, which led you to speak of your journey home; but your little town-bred head was so full of the pleasures of a country life, that you first made many apologies that you were unable to tell what happened during the harvest, as unfortunately you were fetched home the very day before it began.

ANN WITHERS.

My name you know is Withers, but as I once thought I was the daughter of Sir Edward and Lady Harriot Lesley, I shall speak of myself as Miss Lesley, and call Sir Edward and Lady Harriot my father and mother during the period I supposed them entitled to those beloved names. When I was a little girl, it was the perpetual subject of my contemplation that I was an heiress, and the daughter of a baronet; that my mother was the Honourable Lady Harriot; that we had a nobler mansion, infinitely finer pleasure grounds, and equipages more splendid than any of the neighbouring families. Indeed, my good friends, having observed nothing of this error of mine in either of the lives which have hitherto been related, I am ashamed to confess what a proud child I once was. How it happened I cannot tell, for my father was esteemed the best bred man in the country, and the condescension and affability of my mother were universally spoken of.

"Oh, my dear friend," said Miss ———, "it was very natural indeed, if you supposed you possessed these advantages. We make no comparative figure in the county, and my father was originally a man of no consideration at all; and yet I can assure you, both he and mamma had a prodigious deal of trouble to break me off this infirmity when I was very young."—"And do reflect for a moment," said Miss Villiers, "from whence could proceed any pride in me—a poor curate's daughter;—at least any pride worth speaking of; for the difficulty my father had to make me feel myself on an equality with a miller's little daughter who visited me, did not seem an anecdote worth relating. My father, from his profession, is accustomed to look into these things, and whenever he has observed any tendency to this fault in me, and has made me sensible of my error, I, who am rather a weak-spirited girl, have been so much distressed at his reproofs, that to restore me to my own good opinion he would make me sensible that pride is a defect inseparable from human nature; showing me, in our visits to the poorest labourers, how pride would, as he expressed it, 'prettily peep out from under their ragged garbs.' My father dearly loved the poor. In persons of a rank superior to our own humble one, I wanted not much assistance from my father's nice discernment to know that it existed there; and for these latter he would always claim that toleration from me, which he said he observed I was less willing to allow than to the former instances. 'We are told in Holy Writ,' he would say, 'that it is easier for a camel to go through the eye of a needle, than for a rich man to enter into the kingdom of heaven. Surely this is not meant alone to warn the affluent; it must also be understood as an expressive illustration, to instruct the lowly-fortuned man, that he should bear with those imperfections, inseparable from that dangerous prosperity from which he is happily exempt.' But we sadly interrupt your story."

"You are very kind, ladies, to speak with so much indulgence of my foible," said Miss Withers, and was going to proceed, when little Louisa Manners asked, "Pray, are not equipages carriages?"—"Yes, Miss Manners, an equipage is a carriage."—"Then I am sure if my papa had but one equipage I should be very proud; for once when my papa talked of keeping a one-horse chaise, I never was so proud of anything in my life; I used to dream of riding in it, and imagine I saw my playfellows walking past me in the streets."

"Oh, my dear Miss Manners," replied Miss Withers, "Your young head might well run on a thing so new to you; but you have preached a useful lesson to me in your own pretty rambling story, which I shall not easily forget. When you were speaking with such delight of the pleasure the sight of a farmyard, an orchard, and a narrow slip of kitchen-garden gave you, and could for years preserve so lively the memory of one short ride, and that probably through a flat uninteresting country, I remembered how early I learned to disregard the face of Nature, unless she were decked in picturesque scenery; how wearisome our parks and grounds became to me, unless some improvements were going forward which I thought would attract notice; but those days are gone!"

—I will now proceed in my story, and bring you acquainted with my real parents.

Alas! I am a changeling, substituted by my mother for the heiress of the Lesley family; it was for my sake she did this naughty deed; yet, since the truth has been known, it seems to me as if I had been the only sufferer by it; remembering no time when I was not Harriot Lesley, it seems as if the change had taken from me my birthright.

Lady Harriot had intended to nurse her child herself; but being seized with a violent fever soon after its birth, she was not only unable to nurse it, but even to see it for several weeks. I was not quite a month old at this time, when my mother was hired to be Mrs. Lesley's nurse—she had once been a servant in the family—her husband was then at sea.

She had been nursing Miss Lesley a few days, when a girl who had the care of me brought me into the nursery to see my mother. It happened that she wanted something from her own home, which she despatched the girl to fetch, and desired her to leave me till her return. In her absence she changed our clothes; then keeping me to personate the child she was nursing, she sent away the daughter of Sir Edward to be brought up in her own poor cottage.

When my mother sent away the girl, she affirmed she had not the least intention of committing this bad action; but after she was left alone with us, she looked on me, and then on the little lady-babe, and she wept over me, to think she was obliged to leave me to the charge of a careless girl, debarred from my own natural food, while she was nursing another person's child.

The laced cap and the fine cambric robe of the little Harriot were lying on the table ready to be put on: in these she dressed me, only just to see how pretty her own dear baby would look in missy's fine clothes. When she saw me thus adorned, she said to me, "Oh, my dear Ann, you look as like Missy as anything can be. I am sure my lady herself, if she were well enough to see you, would not know the difference." She said these words aloud, and while she was speaking, a wicked thought came into her head—how easy it would be to change these children! On which she hastily dressed Harriot in my coarse raiment. She had no sooner finished the transformation of Miss Lesley into the poor Ann Withers, than the girl returned and carried her away, without the least suspicion that it was not the same infant that she had brought thither.

It was wonderful that no one discovered that I was not the same child. Every fresh face that came into the room filled the nurse with terror. The servants still continued to pay their compliments to the baby in the same form as usual, saying, how like it is to its papa! Nor did Sir Edward himself perceive the difference, his lady's illness probably engrossing all his attention at the time; though, indeed, gentlemen seldom take much notice of very young children.

When Lady Harriot began to recover, and the nurse saw me in her arms caressed as her own child, all fears of detection were over; but the pangs of remorse then seized her; as the dear sick lady hung with tears of fondness over me, she thought she should have died with sorrow for having so cruelly deceived her.

When I was a year old Mrs. Withers was discharged; and because she had been observed to nurse me with uncommon care and affection, and was seen to shed many tears at parting from me, to reward her fidelity, Sir Edward settled a small pension on her, and she was allowed to come every Sunday to dine in the housekeeper's room, and see her little lady.

When she went home, it might have been expected she would have neglected the child she had so wickedly stolen; instead of which she nursed it with the greatest tenderness, being very sorry for what she had done; all the ease she could ever find for her troubled conscience, was in her extreme care of this injured child; and in the weekly visits to its father's house she constantly brought it with her. At the time I have the earliest recollection of her, she was become a widow, and with the pension Sir Edward allowed her, and some plain work she did for our family, she maintained herself and her supposed daughter. The doting fondness she showed for her child was much talked of; it was said she waited upon it more like a servant than a mother; and it was observed its clothes were always made, as far as her slender means would permit, in the same fashion, and her hair cut and curled in the same form as mine. To this person, as having been my faithful nurse, and to her child, I was always taught to show particular civility, and the little girl was always brought into the nursery to play with me. Ann was a little delicate thing, and remarkably well-behaved; for though so much indulged in every other respect, my mother was very attentive to her manners.

As the child grew older, my mother became very uneasy about her education. She was so very desirous of having her well-behaved, that she feared to send her to school, lest she should learn ill manners among the village children, with whom she never suffered her to play; and she was such a poor scholar herself, that she could teach her little or nothing. I heard her relate this her distress to my own maid, with tears in her eyes, and I formed a resolution to beg of my parents that I might have Ann for a companion, and that she might be allowed to take lessons with me of my governess.

My birthday was then approaching, and on that day I was always indulged in the privilege of asking some peculiar favour.

"And what boon has my annual petitioner to beg to-day?" said my father, as he entered the breakfast-room on the morning of my birthday. Then I told him of the great anxiety expressed by Nurse Withers concerning her daughter; how much she wished it was in her power to give her an education that would enable her to get her living without hard labour. I set the good qualities of Ann Withers in the best light I could, and in conclusion, I begged she might be permitted to partake with me in education, and become my companion. "This is a very serious request indeed, Harriot," said Sir Edward; "your mother and I must consult together on the subject." The result of this conversation was favourable to my wishes; in a few weeks my foster-sister was taken into the house, and placed under the tuition of my governess.

To me, who had hitherto lived without any companions of my own age except occasional visitors, the idea of a playfellow constantly to associate with was very pleasant; and after the first shyness of feeling her altered situation was over, Ann seemed as much at her ease as if she had always been brought up in our house. I became very fond of her, and took pleasure in showing her all manner of attentions; which so far won on her affections, that she told me she had a secret intrusted to her by her mother, which she had promised never to reveal as long as her mother lived, but that she almost wished to confide it to me, because I was such a kind friend to her; yet, having promised never to tell it till the death of her mother, she was afraid to tell it to me. At first I assured her that I would never press her to the disclosure, for that promises of secrecy were to be held sacred; but whenever we fell into any confidential kind of conversation, this secret seemed always ready to come out. Whether she or I were most to blame, I know not, though I own I could not help giving frequent hints how well I could keep a secret. At length she told me what I have before related, namely, that she was in truth the daughter of Sir Edward and Lady Lesley, and I the child of her supposed mother.

When I was first in possession of this wonderful secret, my heart burned to reveal it. I thought how praiseworthy it would be in me to restore to my friend the rights of her birth; yet I thought only of becoming her patroness, and raising her to her proper rank; it never occurred to me that my own degradation must necessarily follow. I endeavoured to persuade her to let me tell this important affair to my parents: this she positively refused. I expressed wonder that she should so faithfully keep this secret for an unworthy woman, who in her infancy had done her such an injury.

"Oh!" said she, "you do not know how much she loves me, or you would not wonder that I never resent that. I have seen her grieve and be so very sorry on my account, that I would not bring her into more trouble for any good that could happen to myself. She has often told me, that since the day she changed us, she has never known what it is to have a happy moment; and when she returned home from nursing you, finding me very thin and sickly, how her heart smote her for what she had done; and then she nursed and fed me with such anxious care, that she grew much fonder of me than if I had been her own; and that on the Sundays, when she used to bring me here, it was more pleasure to her to see me in my own father's house, than it was to her to see you, her real child. The shyness you showed towards her while you were very young, and the forced civility you seemed to affect as you grew older, always appeared like ingratitude towards her who had done so much for you. My mother has desired me to disclose this after her death, but I do not believe I shall ever mention it then, for I should be sorry to bring any reproach even on her memory."

In a short time after this important discovery, Ann was sent home to pass a few weeks with her mother, on the occasion of the unexpected arrival of some visitors to our house; they were to bring children with them, and these I was to consider as my own guests.

In the expected arrival of my young visitants, and in making preparations to entertain them, I had little leisure to deliberate on what conduct I should pursue with regard to my friend's secret. Something must be done, I thought, to make her amends for the injury she had sustained, and I resolved to consider the matter attentively on her return. Still my mind ran on conferring favours. I never considered myself as transformed into the dependent person. Indeed, Sir Edward at this time set me about a task which occupied the whole of my attention; he proposed that I should write a little interlude, after the manner of the French *Petites Pieces;* and to try my ingenuity, no one was to see it before the representation, except the performers, myself, and my little friends, who, as they were all younger than me, could not be expected to lend me much assistance. I have already told you what a proud girl I was. During the writing of this piece, the receiving of my young friends, and the instructing them in their several parts, I never felt myself of so much importance. With Ann, my pride had somewhat slumbered; the difference of our rank left no room for competition; all was complacency and good-humour on my part, and affectionate gratitude, tempered with respect, on hers. But here I had full room to show courtesy, to affect those graces, to imitate that elegance of manners practised by Lady Harriot to their mothers. I was to be their instructress in action and in attitudes, and to receive their praises and their admiration of my theatrical genius. It was a new scene of triumph for me, and I might then be said to be in the very height of my glory.

If the plot of my piece, for the invention of which they so highly praised me, had been indeed my own, all would have been well; but unhappily I borrowed from a source which made my drama end far differently from what I intended it should. In the catastrophe I lost not only the name I personated in the piece, but with it my own name also; and all my rank and consequence in the world fled from me for ever. My father presented me with a beautiful writing-desk for the use of my new authorship; my silver standish was placed upon it; a quire of gilt paper was before me. I took out a parcel of my best crow quills, and down I sat in the greatest form imaginable.

I conjecture I have no talent for invention; certain it is, that when I sat down to compose my piece, no story would come into my head, but the story which Ann had so lately related to me. Many sheets were scrawled over in vain, I could think of nothing else; still the babies and the nurse were before me in all the *minutiæ* of description Ann had given them. The costly attire of the lady-babe—the homely garb of the cottage-infant—the affecting address of the fond mother to her own offspring—then the charming *équivoque* in the change of the children; it all looked so dramatic;—it was a play ready-made to my hands. The invalid mother would form the pathetic, the silly exclamations of the servants the ludicrous, and the nurse was nature itself. It is true, I had a few scruples that it might, should it come to the knowledge of Ann, be construed into something very like a breach of confidence. But she was at home, and might never happen to hear of the subject of my piece, and if she did, why, it was only making some handsome apology. To a dependent companion, to whom I had been so very great a friend, it was not necessary to be so very particular about such a trifle.

Thus I reasoned as I wrote my drama, beginning with the title, which I called "The Changeling," and ending with these words: *The curtain drops, while the lady clasps the baby in her arms, and the nurse sighs audibly.* I invented no new incident; I simply wrote the story as Ann had told it to me, in the best blank verse I was able to compose.

By the time it was finished, the company had arrived. The casting the different parts was my next care. The Honourable Augustus M——, a young gentleman of five years of age, undertook to play the father. He was only to come in and say, *How does my little darling do to-day?* The three Miss ——s were to be the servants; they too had only single lines to speak.

As these four were all very young performers, we made them rehearse many times over, that they might walk in and out with proper decorum; but the performance was stopped before their entrances and their exits arrived. I complimented Lady Elizabeth, the sister of Augustus, who was the eldest of the young ladies, with the choice of the lady mother or the nurse. She fixed on the former; she was to recline on a sofa, and, affecting ill health, speak some eight or ten lines, which began with—*O that I could my precious baby see!* To her cousin Miss Emily ——, was given the girl who had the care of the nurse's child; two dolls were to personate the two children; and the principal character of the nurse I had the pleasure to perform myself. It consisted of several speeches, and a very long soliloquy during the changing of the children's clothes.

The elder brother of Augustus, a gentleman of fifteen years of age, who refused to mix in our childish drama, yet condescended to paint the scenes; and our dresses were got up by my own maid.

When we thought ourselves quite perfect in our several parts, we announced it for representation. Sir Edward and Lady Harriot, with their visitors, the parents of my young troop of comedians, honoured us with their presence. The servants were also permitted to go into a music-gallery, which was at the end of a ball-room we had chosen for our theatre.

As author and principal performer, standing before a noble audience, my mind was too much engaged with the arduous task I had undertaken, to glance my eyes towards the music-gallery, or I might have seen two more spectators there than I expected. Nurse Withers and her daughter Ann were there; they had been invited by the housekeeper to be present at the representation of Miss Lesley's play.

In the midst of the performance, as I, in the character of the nurse, was delivering the wrong child to the girl, there was an exclamation from the music-gallery of "Oh! it's all true! it's all true!" This was followed by a bustle among the servants, and screams as of a person in an hysteric fit. Sir Edward came forward to inquire what was the matter. He saw it was Mrs. Withers who had fallen into a fit. Ann was weeping over her, and crying out, "O Miss Lesley, you have told all in the play!"

Mrs. Withers was brought out into the ball-room; there, with tears and in broken accents, with every sign of terror and remorse, she soon made a full confession of her so-long-concealed guilt.

The strangers assembled to see our childish mimicry of passion were witnesses to a highly-wrought dramatic scene in real life. I had intended they should see the curtain drop without any discovery of the deceit; unable to invent any new incident, I left the conclusion imperfect as I found it; but they saw a more strict poetical justice done; they saw the rightful child restored to its parents, and the nurse overwhelmed with shame, and threatened with the severest punishment.

"Take this woman," said Sir Edward, "and lock her up, till she be delivered into the hands of justice."

Ann, on her knees, implored mercy for her mother. Addressing the children, who were gathered round her, "Dear ladies," said she, "help me, on your knees help me, to beg forgiveness for my mother." Down the young ones all dropped—even Lady Elizabeth bent on her knee. "Sir Edward, pity her distress, Sir Edward, pardon her!" All joined in the petition, except one whose voice ought to have been loudest in the appeal. No word, no accent came from me. I hung over Lady Harriot's chair, weeping as if my heart would break; but I wept for my own fallen fortunes, not for my mother's sorrow.

I thought within myself, "If in the integrity of my heart, refusing to participate iu this unjust secret, I had boldly ventured to publish the truth, I might have had some consolation in the praises which so generous an action would have merited; but it is through the vanity of being supposed to have written a pretty story that I have meanly broken my faith with my friend, and unintentionally proclaimed the disgrace of my mother and myself." While thoughts like these were passing through my mind, Ann had obtained my mother's pardon. Instead of being sent away to confinement and the horrors of a prison, she was given by Sir Edward into the care of the housekeeper, who had orders from Lady Harriot to see her put to bed and properly attended to, for again this wretched woman had fallen into a fit.

Ann would have followed my mother, but Sir Edward brought her back, telling her that she should see her when she was better. He then led her towards Lady Harriot, desiring her to embrace her child; she did so, and I saw her, as I had phrased it in the play, *clasped in her mother's arms.*

This scene had greatly affected the spirits of Lady Harriot; through the whole of it, it was with difficulty she had been kept from fainting, and she was now led into the drawing-room by the ladies. The gentlemen followed, talking with Sir Edward of the astonishing instance of filial affection they had just seen in the earnest pleadings of the child for her supposed mother.

Ann, too, went with them, and was conducted by her whom I had always considered as my own particular friend. Lady Elizabeth took hold of her hand and said, "Miss Lesley, will you permit me to conduct you to the drawing-room?"

I was left weeping behind the chair where Lady Harriot had sat, and, as I thought, quite alone. A something had before twitched my frock two or three times so slightly I had scarcely noticed it; a little head now peeped round, and looking up in my face, said, "She is not Miss Lesley!" It was the young Augustus; he had been sitting at my feet, but I had not observed him. He then started up, and taking hold of my hand with one of his, with the other holding fast by my clothes, he led, or rather dragged me, into the midst of the company assembled in the drawing-room. The vehemence of his manner, his little face as red as fire, caught every eye. The ladies smiled, and one gentleman laughed in a most unfeeling manner. His elder brother patted him on the head, and said, "Your are a humane little fellow : Elizabeth, we might have thought of this."

Very kind words were now spoken to me by Sir Edward, and he called me Harriot, precious name now grown to me. Lady Harriot kissed me, and said she would never forget how long she had loved me as her child. These were comfortable words; but I heard echoed round the room, "Poor thing, *she* cannot help it—I am sure *she* is to be pitied. Dear Lady Harriot, how kind, how considerate you are!" Ah! what a deep sense of my altered condition did I then feel!

"Let the young ladies divert themselves in another room," said Sir Edward; "and, Harriot, take your new sister with you, and help her to entertain your friends." Yes, he called me Harriot again, and afterwards invented new names for his daughter and me, and always called us by them, apparently in jest; yet I knew it was only because he would not hurt me with hearing our names reversed. When Sir Edward desired us to show the children into another room, Ann and I walked towards the door. A new sense of humiliation arose—how could I go out at the door before Miss Lesley?—I stood irresolute; she drew back. The elder brother of my friend Augustus assisted me in this perplexity; pushing us all forward, as if in a playful mood, he drove us indiscriminately before him, saying, "I will make one among you to-day." He had never joined in our sports before.

My luckless play, that sad instance of my duplicity, was never once mentioned to me afterwards, not even by any one of the children who had acted in it; and I must also tell you how considerate an old lady was at the time about our dresses. As soon as she perceived things growing very serious, she hastily stripped off the upper garments we wore to represent our different characters. I think I should have died with shame if the child had led me into the drawing-room in the mummery I had worn to represent a nurse. This good lady was of another essential service to me; for perceiving an irresolution in every one how they should behave to us, which distressed me very much, she contrived to place Miss Lesley above me at table, and called her Miss Lesley, and me Miss Withers; saying at the same time in a low voice, but as if she meant I should hear her, "It is better these things should be done at once, then they are over." My heart thanked her, for I felt the truth of what she said.

My poor mother continued very ill for many weeks; no medicine could remove the extreme dejection of spirits she laboured under. Sir Edward sent for the clergyman of the parish to give her religious consolation. Every day he came to visit her, and he would always take Miss Lesley and me into the room with him. I think, Miss Villiers, your father must be just such another man as Dr. Wheelding, our worthy rector; just so I think he would have soothed the troubled conscience of my repentant mother. How feelingly, how kindly he used to talk of mercy and forgiveness!

My heart was softened by my own misfortunes and the sight of my penitent suffering mother. I felt that she was now my only parent; I strove, earnestly strove to love her; yet ever when I looked in her face, she would seem to me to be the very identical person whom I should have once thought sufficiently honoured by a slight inclination of the head, and a civil "How do you do, Mrs. Withers?" One day, as Miss Lesley was hanging over her with her accustomed fondness, Dr. Wheelding reading in a prayer-book, and, as I thought, not at that moment regarding us, I threw myself on my knees and silently prayed that I too might be able to love my mother.

Dr. Wheelding had been observing me; he took me into the garden, and drew from me the subject of my petition.

"Your prayers, my good young lady," said he, "I hope are heard; sure I am they have caused me to adopt a resolution which, as it will enable you to see your mother frequently, will, I hope, greatly assist your pious wishes. I will take your mother home with me to superintend my family. Under my roof, doubtless, Sir Edward will often permit you to see her. Perform your duty towards her as well as you possibly can. Affection is the growth of time. With such good wishes in your young heart, do not despair that in due time it will assuredly spring up."

With the approbation of Sir Edward and Lady Harriot, my mother was removed in a few days to Dr. Wheelding's house. There she soon recovered; there she at present resides. She tells me she loves me almost as well as she did when I was a baby, and we both wept at parting when I came to school.

Here, perhaps, I ought to conclude my story, which I fear has been a tedious one; permit me, however, to say a few words concerning the time which elapsed since the discovery of my birth until my arrival here.

It was on the fifth day of —— that I was known to be Ann Withers, and the daughter of my supposed nurse. The company who were witness to my disgrace departed in a few days, and I felt relieved from some part of the mortification I hourly experienced. For every fresh instance even of kindness or attention I experienced went to my heart, that I should be forced to feel thankful for it.

Circumstanced as I was, surely I had nothing justly to complain of. The conduct of Sir Edward and Lady Harriot was kind in the extreme; still preserving every appearance of a parental tenderness for me, but ah! I might no longer call them by the dear names of father and mother. Formerly, when speaking of them, I used, proud of their titles, to delight to say, "Sir Edward or Lady Harriot did this, or this;" now I would give worlds to say, "My father or my mother."

I should be perfectly unkind if I were to complain of Miss Lesley—indeed, I have not the least cause of complaint against her. As my companion, her affection and her gratitude had been unbounded; and now that it was my turn to be the humble friend, she tried by every means in her power to make me think she felt the same respectful gratitude which in her dependent station she had so naturally displayed.

Only in a few rarely constituted minds does that true attentive kindness spring up, that delicacy of feeling, which enters into every trivial thing, is ever awake and keeping watch lest it should offend. Myself, though educated with the extremest care, possessed but little of this virtue. Virtue I call it, though among men it is termed politeness; for since the days of my humiliating reverse of fortune I have learned its value.

I feel quite ashamed to give instances of any deficiency I observed, or thought I have observed, in Miss Lesley. Now I am away from her, and dispassionately speaking of it, it seems as if my own soreness of temper had made me fancy things. I really believe now that I was mistaken; but Miss Lesley had been so highly praised for her filial tenderness, I thought at last she seemed to make a parade about it, and used to run up to my mother, and affect to be more glad to see her than she really was after a time; and I think Dr. Wheelding thought so by a little hint he once dropped. But he, too, might be mistaken, for he was very partial to me.

I am under the greatest obligation in the world to this good Dr. Wheelding. He has made my mother quite a respectable woman, and I am sure it is owing a great deal to him that she loves me so well as she does.

And here, though it may seem a little out of place, let me stop to assure you, that if I ever could have had any doubt of the sincerity of Miss Lesley's affection towards me, her behaviour on the occasion of my coming here ought completely to efface it. She entreated with many tears, and almost the same energy with which she pleaded for forgiveness for my mother, that I might not be sent away. But she was not alike successful in her supplications.

Miss Lesley had made some progress in reading and writing during the time she was my companion only; it was highly necessary that every exertion should be now made—the whole house was, as I may say, in requisition for her instruction; Sir Edward and Lady Harriot devoted great part of the day to this purpose. A well-educated young person was taken under our governess to assist her in her labours, and to teach Miss Lesley music. A drawing-master was engaged to reside in the house.

At this time I was not remarkably forward in my education. My governess being a native of France, I spoke French very correctly, and I had made some progress in Italian; but I had had the instruction of masters only during the few months in the year we usually passed in London.

Music I never had the least ear for; I could scarcely be taught my notes. This defect in me was always particularly regretted by my mother, she being an excellent performer herself, both on the piano and on the harp. I think I have some taste for drawing; but as Lady Harriot did not particularly excel in this, I lost so much time in the summer months, practising only under my governess, that I made no great proficiency even in this my favourite art. But Miss Lesley, with all these advantages which I have named,—everybody so eager to instruct her, she so willing to learn—everything so new and delightful to her, how could it happen otherwise? she in a short time became a little prodigy. What best pleased Lady Harriot was, after she had conquered the first difficulties, she discovered a wonderful talent for music. Here she was her mother's own girl indeed—she had the same sweet-toned voice—the same delicate finger. Her musical governess had little now to do; for as soon as Lady Harriot perceived this excellence in her, she gave up all company and devoted her whole time to instructing her daughter in this science.

Nothing makes the heart ache with such a hopeless, heavy pain, as envy.

I had felt deeply before, but till now I could not be said to envy Miss Lesley. All day long the notes of the harp or the piano spoke sad sounds to me of the loss of a loved mother's heart.

To have in a manner two mothers, and Miss Lesley to engross them both, was too much indeed.

It was at this time that one day I had been wearied with hearing Lady Harriot play one long piece of Haydn's music after another to her enraptured daughter. We were to walk with our governess to Dr. Wheelding's that morning; and after Lady Harriot had left the room, and we were quite ready for our walk, Miss Lesley would not leave the instrument for I know not how long.

It was on that day that I thought she was not quite honest in her expressions of joy at the sight of my poor mother, who had been waiting at the garden-gate near two hours to see her arrive; yet she might be, for the music had put her in remarkably good spirits that morning.

Oh, the music quite, quite won Lady Harriot's heart! Till Miss Lesley began to play so well, she often lamented the time it would take before her daughter would have the air of a person of fashion's child. It was my part of the general instruction to give her lessons on this head. We used to make a kind of play of it, which we called lectures on fashionable manners: it was a pleasant amusement to me, a sort of keeping up the memory of past times. But now the music was always in the way. The last time it was talked of, Lady Harriot said her daughter's time was too precious to be taken up with such trifling.

I must own that the music had that effect on Miss Lesley, as to render these lectures less necessary, which I will explain to you; but first let me assure you that Lady Harriot was by no means in the habit of saying things of this kind. It was almost a solitary instance; I could give you a thousand instances the very reverse of this, in her as well as in Sir Edward. How kindly, how frequently, would they remind me, that to me alone it was owing that they ever knew their child! calling the day on which I was a petitioner for the admittance of Ann into the house, the blessed birthday of their generous girl.

Neither dancing, nor any foolish lectures, could do much for Miss Lesley; she remained for some time wanting in gracefulness of carriage; but all that is usually attributed to dancing, music finally effected. When she was sitting before the instrument, a resemblance to her mother became apparent to every eye. Her attitudes and the expression of her countenance were the very same. This soon followed her into everything; all was ease and natural grace; for the music, and with it the idea of Lady Harriot, was always in her thoughts. It was a pretty sight to see the daily improvement in her person, even to me, poor envious girl that I was.

Soon after Lady Harriot had hurt me by calling my little efforts to improve her daughter trifling, she made me large amends in a very kind and most unreserved conversation that she held with me.

She told me all the struggles she had had at first to feel a maternal tenderness for her daughter; and she frankly confessed, that she had now gained so much on her affections that she feared she had too much neglected the solemn promise she had made me, *Never to forget how long she had loved me as her child.*

Encouraged by her returning kindness, I owned how much I had suffered; and ventured to express my fears that I had hardly courage enough to bear the sight of my former friends under a new designation, as I must now appear to them on our removal to London, which was expected to take place in a short time.

A few days after this she told me in the gentlest manner possible that Sir Edward and herself were of opinion it would conduce to my happiness to pass a year or two at school.

I knew that this proposal was kindly intended to spare me the mortification I so much dreaded; therefore I endeavoured to submit to my hard fate with cheerfulness, and prepared myself, not without reluctance, to quit a mansion which had been the scene of so many enjoyments, and latterly of such very different feelings.

ELINOR FORESTER.

WHEN I was very young, I had the misfortune to lose my mother. My father very soon married again. The morning of the day on which that event took place, my father set me on his knee, and as he often used to do after the death of my mother, he called me his dear little orphaned Elinor; and then he asked me if I loved Miss Saville. I replied "Yes." Then he said, this dear lady was going to be so kind as to be married to him, and that she was to live with us and be my mamma. My father told me this with such pleasure in his looks, that I thought it must be a very fine thing indeed to have a new mamma; and on his saying it was time for me to be dressed against his return from church, I ran in great spirits to tell the good news in the nursery. I found my maid and the housemaid looking out of the window to see my father get into his carriage, which was newly painted; the servants had new liveries and fine white ribands in their hats; and then I perceived my father had left off his mourning. The maids were dressed in new coloured gowns and white ribands. On the table I saw a new muslin frock trimmed with fine lace, ready for me to put on. I skipped about the room quite in an ecstasy.

When the carriage drove from the door, the housekeeper came in to bring the maids new white gloves. I repeated to her the words I had just heard, that that dear lady, Miss Saville, was going to be married to papa, and that she was to live with us and be my mamma.

The housekeeper shook her head, and said, "Poor thing! how soon children forget everything!"

I could not imagine what she meant by my forgetting everything, for I instantly recollected poor mamma used to say I had an excellent memory.

The women began to draw on their white gloves, and the seams rending in several places, Ann said, "This is just the way our gloves served us at my mistress's funeral." The other checked her, and said "Hush!" I was then thinking of some instances in which my mamma had praised my memory, and this reference to her funeral fixed her idea in my mind.

From the time of her death no one had ever spoken to me of my mamma, and I had apparently forgotten her; yet I had a habit, which perhaps had not been observed, of taking my little stool, which had been my mamma's footstool, and a doll which my mamma had dressed for me while she was sitting in her elbow-chair, her head supported with pillows. With these in my hands, I used to go to the door of the room in which I had seen her in her last illness; and after trying to open it, and peeping through the keyhole, from whence I could just see a glimpse of the crimson curtains, I used to sit down on the stool before the door, and play with my doll, and sometimes sing to it mamma's pretty song of "Balow my babe;" imitating as well as I could the weak voice in which she used to sing it to me. My mamma had a very sweet voice. I remember now the gentle tone in which she used to say my prattle did not disturb her.

When I was dressed in my new frock, I wished poor mamma was alive to see how fine I was on papa's wedding-day, and I ran to my favourite station at her bedroom door. There I sat thinking of my mamma, and trying to remember exactly how she used to look; because I foolishly imagined that Miss Saville was to be changed into something like my own mother, whose pale and delicate appearance in her last illness was all that I retained of her remembrance.

When my father returned home with his bride, he walked upstairs to look for me, and my new mamma followed him. They found me at my mother's door, earnestly looking through the keyhole. I was thinking so intently on my mother, that when my father said, "Here is your new mamma, my Elinor," I turned round and began to cry, for no other reason than because she had a very high colour, and I remembered my mamma was very pale; she had bright black eyes, my mother's were mild blue eyes; and that instead of the wrapping gown and close cap in which I remembered my mamma, she was dressed in all her bridal decorations.

I said, "Miss Saville shall not be my mamma," and I cried till I was sent away in disgrace.

Every time I saw her for several days, the same notion came into my head that she was not a bit more like mamma than when she was Miss Saville. My father was very angry when he saw how shy I continued to look at her; but she always said, "Never mind! Elinor and I shall soon be better friends."

One day, when I was very naughty indeed, for I would not speak one word to either of them, my papa took his hat and walked out, quite in a passion. When he was gone, I looked up at my new mamma, expecting to see her very angry too; but she was smiling and looking very good-naturedly upon me; and she said, "Now we are alone together, my pretty little daughter, let us forget papa is angry with us, and tell me why you were peeping through that door the day your papa brought me home, and you cried so at the sight of me." "Because mamma used to be there," I replied. When she heard me say this, she fell a-crying very sadly indeed; and I was so very sorry to hear her cry so, that I forgot I did not love her, and I went up to her and said, "Don't cry, I won't be naughty any more, I won't peep through the door any more."

Then she said I had a little kind heart, and I should not have any occasion, for she would take me into the room herself; and she rang the bell, and ordered the key of that room to be brought to her; and the housekeeper brought it, and tried to persuade her not to go. But she said, "I must have my own way in this;" and she carried me in her arms into my mother's room.

Oh, I was so pleased to be taken into mamma's room. I pointed out to her all the things that I remembered to have belonged to mamma, and she encouraged me to tell her all the little incidents which had dwelt on my memory concerning her. She told me that she went to school with mamma when she was a little girl, and that I should come into this room with her every day when papa was gone out, and she would tell me stories of mamma when she was a little girl no bigger than me.

When my father came home we were walking in a garden at the back of our house, and I was showing her mamma's geraniums, and telling her what pretty flowers they had when mamma was alive.

My father was astonished; and he said, "Is this the sullen Elinor? what has worked this miracle?" "Ask no questions," she replied, "or you will disturb our new-born friendship. Elinor has promised to love me, and she says, too, that she will call me 'mamma.'" "Yes, I will,—mamma, mamma, mamma," I replied, and hung about her with the greatest fondness.

After this she used to pass great part of the mornings with me in my mother's room, which was now made the repository of all my playthings, and also my schoolroom. Here my new mamma taught me to read. I was a sad little dunce, and scarcely knew my letters. My own mamma had often said, when she got better she would hear me read every day, but as she never got better, it was not her fault. I now began to learn very fast, for when I said my lesson well, I was always rewarded with some pretty story of my mother's childhood; and these stories generally contained some little hints that were instructive to me, and which I greatly stood in want of; for, between improper indulgence and neglect, I had many faulty ways.

In this kind manner my mother-in-law has instructed and improved me, and I love her because she was my mother's friend when they were young. She has been my only instructress, for I never went to school till I came here. She would have continued to teach me, but she has not time, for she has a little baby of her own now, and that is the reason I came to school.

MARGARET GREEN.

My father has been dead nearly three years. Soon after his death, my mother being left in reduced circumstances, she was induced to accept the offer of Mrs. Beresford, an elderly lady of large fortune, to live in her house as her companion and the superintendent of her family. This lady was my godmother, and as I was my mother's only child, she very kindly permitted her to have me with her.

Mrs. Beresford lived in a large old family mansion; she kept no company, and never moved except from the breakfast-parlour to the eating-room, and from thence to the drawing-room to tea.

Every morning when she first saw me, she used to nod her head very kindly, and say, "How do you do, little Margaret?" But I do not recollect she ever spoke to me during the remainder of the day: except, indeed, after I had read the psalms and the chapters, which was my daily task; then she used constantly to observe that I improved in my reading, and frequently added, "I never heard a child read so distinctly."

She had been remarkably fond of needlework, and her conversation with my mother was generally the history of some pieces of work she had formerly done; the dates when they were begun, and when finished; what had retarded their progress, and what had hastened their completion. If occasionally any other events were spoken of, she had no other chronology to reckon by, than in the recollection of what carpet, what sofa-cover, what set of chairs, were in the frame at that time.

I believe my mother is not particularly fond of needlework; for in my father's lifetime I never saw her amuse herself in this way; yet, to oblige her kind patroness, she undertook to finish a large carpet which the old lady had just begun when her eyesight failed her. All day long my mother used to sit at the frame, talking of the shades of the worsted, and the beauty of the colours—Mrs. Beresford seated in a chair near her, and, though her eyes were so dim she could hardly distinguish one colour from another, watching through her spectacles the progress of the work.

When my daily portion of reading was over, I had a taste of needlework, which generally lasted half an hour. I was not allowed to pass more time in reading or work, because my eyes were very weak, for which reason I was always set to read in the large-print family Bible. I was very fond of reading; and when I could, unobserved, steal a few minutes as they were intent on their work, I used to delight to read in the historical part of the Bible; but this, because of my eyes, was a forbidden pleasure; and the Bible never being removed out of the room, it was only for a short time together that I dared softly to lift up the leaves and peep into it.

As I was permitted to walk in the garden, or wander about the house whenever I pleased, I used to leave the parlour for hours together, and make out my own solitary amusement as well as I could. My first visit was always to a very large hall, which, from being paved with marble, was called the marble hall. In this hall, while Mrs.

Beresford's husband was living, the tenants used to be feasted at Christmas.

The heads of the twelve Cæsars were hung round the hall. Every day I mounted on the chairs to look at them, and to read the inscriptions underneath, till I became perfectly familiar with their names and features.

Hogarth's prints were below the Cæsars: I was very fond of looking at them, and endeavouring to make out their meaning.

An old broken battledore and some shuttlecocks, with most of the feathers missing, were on a marble slab in one corner of the hall, which constantly reminded me that there had once been younger inhabitants here than the old lady and her gray-headed servants. In another corner stood a marble figure of a satyr; every day I laid my hand on his shoulder to feel how cold he was.

This hall opened into a room full of family portraits. They were all in the dresses of former times: some were old men and women, and some were children. I used to long to have a fairy's power to call the children down from their frames to play with me. One little girl in particular, who hung by the side of a glass door which opened into the garden, I often invited to walk there with me, but she still kept her station—one arm round a little lamb's neck, and in her hand a large bunch of roses. From this room I usually proceeded to the garden.

When I was weary of the garden I wandered over the rest of the house. The best suite of rooms I never saw by any other light than what glimmered through the tops of the window-shutters, which, however, served to show the carved chimney-pieces, and the curious old ornaments about the rooms; but the worked furniture and carpets of which I heard such constant praises I could have but an imperfect sight of, peeping under the covers which were kept over them, by the dim light; for I constantly lifted up a corner of the envious cloth that hid these highly-praised rarities from my view.

The bedrooms were also regularly explored by me, as

well to admire the antique furniture, as for the sake of contemplating the tapestry hangings, which were full of Bible history. The subject of the one which chiefly attracted my attention was Hagar and her son Ishmael. Every day I admired the beauty of the youth, and pitied the forlorn state of him and his mother in the wilderness. At the end of the gallery into which these tapestry rooms opened, was one door which, having often in vain attempted to open, I concluded to be locked; and finding myself shut out, I was very desirous of seeing what it contained; and though still foiled in the attempt, I every day endeavoured to turn the lock, which—whether by constantly trying I loosened, being probably a very old one, or that the door was not locked but fastened tight by time, I know not—to my great joy, as I was one day trying the lock as usual, it gave way, and I found myself in this so-long-desired room.

It proved to be a very large library. This was indeed a precious discovery. I looked round on the books with the greatest delight. I thought I would read them every one. I now forsook all my favourite haunts, and passed all my time here. I took down first one book, then another.

If you never spent whole mornings alone in a large library, you cannot conceive the pleasure of taking down books in the constant hope of finding an entertaining book among them; yet, after many days, meeting with nothing but disappointment, it becomes less pleasant. All the books within my reach were folios of the gravest cast. I could understand very little that I read in them, and the old dark print and the length of the lines made my eyes ache.

When I had almost resolved to give up the search as fruitless, I perceived a volume lying in an obscure corner of the room. I opened it. It was a charming print; the letters were almost as large as the type of the family Bible. In the first page I looked into I saw the name of my favourite Ishmael, whose face I knew so well from the tapestry, and whose history I had often read in the Bible.

I sat myself down to read this book with the greatest eagerness. The title of it was *Mahometanism Explained.* It was a very improper book, for it contained a false history of Abraham and his descendants.

I shall be quite ashamed to tell you the strange effect it had on me. I know it was very wrong to read any book without permission to do so. If my time were to come over again, I would go and tell my mamma that there was a library in the house, and ask her to permit me to read a little while every day in some book that she might think proper to select for me. But unfortunately I did not then recollect that I ought to do this: the reason of my strange forgetfulness might be that my mother, following the example of her patroness, had almost wholly discontinued talking to me. I scarcely ever heard a word addressed to me from morning to night. If it were not for the old servants saying, "Good morning to you, Miss Margaret!" as they passed me in the long passages, I should have been the greatest part of the day in as perfect a solitude as Robinson Crusoe. It must have been because I was never spoken to at all that I forgot what was right and what was wrong, for I do not believe that I ever remembered I was doing wrong all the time I was reading in the library. A great many of the leaves in *Mahometanism Explained* were torn out, but enough remained to make me imagine that Ishmael was the true son of Abraham; I read here that the true descendants of Abraham were known by a light which streamed from the middle of their foreheads. It said that Ishmael's father and mother first saw this light streaming from his forehead as he was lying asleep in the cradle. I was very sorry so many of the leaves were torn out, for it was as entertaining as a fairy tale. I used to read the history of Ishmael, and then go and look at him in the tapestry, and then read his history again. When I had almost learned the history of Ishmael by heart, I read the rest of the book, and then I came to the history of Mahomet, who was there said to be the last descendant of Abraham.

If Ishmael had engaged so much of my thoughts, how much more so must Mahomet? His history was full of nothing but wonders from the beginning to the end. The book said that those who believed all the wonderful stories which were related of Mahomet were called Mahometans, and True Believers:—I concluded that I must be a Mahometan, for I believed every word I read.

At length I met with something which I also believed, though I trembled as I read it. This was, that after we are dead we are to pass over a narrow bridge, which crosses a bottomless gulf. The bridge was described to be no wider than a silken thread; and it is said that all who were not Mahometans would slip on one side of this bridge, and drop into the tremendous gulf that had no bottom. I considered myself as a Mahometan, yet I was perfectly giddy whenever I thought of passing over this bridge.

One day, seeing the old lady totter across the room, a sudden terror seized me, for I thought how would she ever be able to get over the bridge? Then too it was that I first recollected that my mother would also be in imminent danger; for I imagined she had never heard the name of Mahomet, because I foolishly conjectured this book had been locked up for ages in the library, and was utterly unknown to the rest of the world.

All my desire was now to tell them the discovery I had made; for I thought, when they knew of the existence of *Mahometanism Explained*, they would read it, and become Mahometans, to ensure themselves a safe passage over the silken bridge. But it wanted more courage than I possessed to break the matter to my intended converts; I must acknowledge that I had been reading without leave; and the habit of never speaking, or being spoken to, considerably increased the difficulty.

My anxiety on this subject threw me into a fever. I

was so ill that my mother thought it necessary to sleep in the same room with me. In the middle of the night I could not resist the strong desire I felt to tell her what preyed so much on my mind.

I awoke her out of a sound sleep, and begged she would be so kind as to be a Mahometan. She was very much alarmed, for she thought I was delirious, which I believe I was; for I tried to explain the reason of my request, but it was in such an incoherent manner that she could not at all comprehend what I was talking about.

The next day a physician was sent for, and he discovered, by several questions that he put to me, that I had read myself into a fever. He gave me medicines, and ordered me to be kept very quiet, and said he hoped in a few days I should be very well; but as it was a new case to him, he never having attended a little Mahometan before, if any lowness continued after he had removed the fever, he would, with my mother's permission, take me home with him to study this extraordinary case at his leisure; and added, that he could then hold a consultation with his wife, who was often very useful to him in prescribing remedies for the maladies of his younger patients.

In a few days he fetched me away. His wife was in the carriage with him. Having heard what he said about her prescriptions, I expected, between the doctor and his lady, to undergo a severe course of medicine, especially as I heard him very formally ask her advice what was good for a Mahometan fever, the moment after he had handed me into the carriage. She studied a little while, and then she said, a ride to Harlow Fair would not be amiss. He said he was entirely of her opinion, because it suited him to go there to buy a horse.

During the ride they entered into conversation with me, and in answer to their questions, I was relating to them the solitary manner in which I had passed my time; how I found out the library, and what I had read in the fatal book which had so heated my imagination —when we arrived at the fair; and Ishmael, Mahomet, and the narrow bridge vanished out of my head in an instant.

Oh! what a cheerful sight it was to me to see so many happy faces assembled together, walking up and down between the rows of booths that were full of showy things; ribands, laces, toys, cakes, and sweetmeats! While the doctor was gone to buy his horse, his kind lady let me stand as long as I pleased at the booths, and gave me many things which she saw I particularly admired. My needle-case, my pincushion, indeed, my work-basket and all its contents, are presents which she purchased for me at this fair. After we returned home she played with me all the evening at a geographical game, which she also bought for me at this cheerful fair.

The next day she invited some young ladies of my own age to spend the day with me. She had a swing put up in the garden for us, and a room cleared of the furniture, that we might play at blindman's buff. One of the liveliest of the girls, who had taken on herself the direction of our sports, she kept to be my companion all the time I stayed with her, and every day contrived some new amusement for us.

Yet this good lady did not suffer all my time to pass in mirth and gaiety. Before I went home she explained to me very seriously the error into which I had fallen. I found that so far from *Mahometanism Explained* being a book concealed only in this library, it was well known to every person of the least information.

The Turks, she told me, were Mahometans, and that, if the leaves of my favourite book had not been torn out, I should have read that the author of it did not mean to give the fabulous stories here related as true, but only wrote it as giving a history of what the Turks, who are a very ignorant people, believe concerning the impostor Mahomet, who feigned himself to be a descendant of Ishmael. By the good offices of the physician and his lady, I was carried home at the end of a month, perfectly cured of the error into which I had fallen, and very much ashamed of having believed so many absurdities.

EMILY BARTON.

When I was a very young child, I remember residing with an uncle and aunt who live in ———shire. I think I remained there near a twelvemonth. I am ignorant of the cause of my being so long left there by my parents, who, though they were remarkably fond of me, never came to see me during all that time. As I did not know I should ever have occasion to relate the occurrences of my life, I never thought of inquiring the reason.

I am just able to recollect that when I first went there I thought it was a fine thing to live in the country, and play with my little cousins in the garden all day long; and I also recollect that I soon found that it was a very dull thing to live in the country with little cousins who have a papa and mamma in the house, while my own dear papa and mamma were in London, many miles away.

I have heard my papa observe, girls who are not well managed are a most quarrelsome race of little people. My cousins very often quarrelled with me, and then they always said, "I will go and tell my mamma, cousin Emily;" and then I used to be very disconsolate, because I had no mamma to complain to of my grievances.

My aunt always took Sophia's part because she was so young; and she never suffered me to oppose Mary or Elizabeth, because they were older than me.

The playthings were all the property of one or other of my cousins. The large dolls belonged to Mary or Elizabeth, and the pretty little wax dolls were dressed on purpose for Sophia, who always began to cry the instant I touched them. I had nothing that I could call my own but one pretty book of stories; and one day, as Sophia was endeavouring to take it from me, and I was trying to keep it, it was all torn to pieces; and my aunt would not be angry with her. She only said, Sophia was a little baby and did not know any better. My uncle promised to buy me another book, but he never remembered it. Very often when he came home in the evening he used to say, "I wonder what I have got in my pocket;" and then they all crowded round him, and I used to creep towards him, and think, maybe it is my book that my uncle has got in his pocket. But, no; nothing ever came out for me. Yet the first sight of a plaything, even if it be not one's own, is always a cheerful thing, and a new toy would put them in a good humour for a while, and they would say, "Here, Emily, look what I have got. You may take it in your own hand and look at it." But the pleasure of examining it was sure to be stopped in a short time by the old story of "Give that to me again; you know that is mine." Nobody could help, I think, being a little out of humour if they were always served so; but if I showed any signs of discontent, my aunt always told my uncle I was a little peevish fretful thing, and gave her more trouble than all her own children put together. My aunt would often say, what a happy thing it was to have such affectionate children as hers were. She was always praising my cousins because they were affectionate; that was sure to be her word. She said I had not one atom of affection in my disposition, for that no kindness ever made the least impression on me. And she would say all this with Sophia seated on her lap, and the two eldest perhaps hanging round their papa, while I was so dull to see them taken so much notice of, and so sorry that I was not affectionate, that I did not know what to do with myself.

Then there was another complaint against me; that I was so shy before strangers. Whenever any strangers spoke to me, before I had time to think what answer I should give, Mary or Elizabeth would say, "Emily is so shy, she will never speak." Then I, thinking I was very shy, would creep into a corner of the room, and be ashamed to look up while the company stayed.

Though I often thought of my papa and mamma, by degrees the remembrance of their persons faded out of my mind. When I tried to think how they used to look, the faces of my cousins' papa and mamma only came into my mind.

One morning my uncle and aunt went abroad before breakfast, and took my cousins with them. They very often went out for whole days together and left me at home. Sometimes they said it was because they could not take so many children; and sometimes they said it was because I was so shy, it was no amusement to me to go abroad.

That morning I was very solitary indeed, for they had even taken the dog Sancho with them, and I was very fond of him. I went all about the house and garden to look for him. Nobody could tell me where Sancho was, and then I went into the front court and called, "Sancho, Sancho." An old man that worked in the garden was there, and he said Sancho was gone with his master. Oh! how sorry I was; I began to cry, for Sancho and I used to amuse ourselves for hours together when everybody was gone out. I cried till I heard the mail-coachman's horn, and then I ran to the gate to see the mail-coach go past. It stopped before our gate, and a gentleman got out, and the moment he saw me he took me in his arms, and kissed me, and said I was Emily Barton, and asked me why the tears were on my little pale cheeks; and I told him the cause of my distress. The old man asked him to walk into the house, and was going to call one of the servants; but the gentleman would not let him, and he said, "Go on with your work, I want to talk to this little girl before I go into the house." Then he sat down on a bench which was in the court, and asked me many questions; and I told him all my little troubles, for he was such a good-natured looking gentleman that I prattled very freely to him. I told him all I have told you, and more, for the unkind treatment I met with was more fresh in my mind than it is now. Then he called to the old man, and desired him to fetch a post-chaise, and gave him money that he should make haste, and I never saw the old man walk so fast before. When he had been gone a little while, the gentleman said, "Will you walk with me down the road to meet the chaise, and you shall ride in it a little way along with me." I had nothing on, not even my old straw bonnet that I used to wear in the garden; but I did not mind that, and I ran by his side a good way, till we met the chaise, and the old man riding with the driver. The gentleman said, "Get down and open the door," and then he lifted me in. The old man looked in a sad fright, and said "Oh! sir, I hope you are not going to take the child away?" The gentleman threw out a small card, and bid him give that to his master, and calling to the post-boy to drive on, we lost sight of the old man in a minute.

The gentleman laughed very much and said, "We have frightened the old man, he thinks I am going to run away with you;" and I laughed, and thought it a very good joke, and he said, "So you tell me you are very shy;" and I replied, "Yes, sir, I am, before strangers." He said, "So I perceive you are," and then he laughed again, and I laughed, though I did not know why. We had such a merry ride, laughing all the way at one thing or another, till we came to a town where the chaise stopped, and he ordered some breakfast. When I got out I began to shiver a little, for it was the latter end of autumn; the leaves were falling off the trees, and the air blew very cold. Then he desired the waiter to go and order a straw hat and a little warm coat for me; and when the milliner came, he told her he had stolen a little heiress, and we were going to Gretna Green in such a hurry that the young lady had no time to put on her bonnet before she came out. The milliner said I was a pretty little heiress, and she wished us a pleasant journey. When we had breakfasted, and I was equipped in my new coat and bonnet, I jumped into the chaise again as warm and as lively as a little bird.

When it grew dark we entered a large city; the chaise began to roll over the stones, and I saw the lamps ranged along London streets.

Though we had breakfasted and dined upon the road, and I had got out of one chaise into another many times, and was now riding on in the dark, I never once considered where I was, or where I was going to. I put my head out of the chaise window, and admired those beautiful lights. I was sorry when the chaise stopped, and I could no longer look at the brilliant rows of lighted lamps.

Taken away by a stranger under a pretence of a short ride, and brought quite to London, do you not expect some perilous end of this adventure? Ah! it was my papa himself, though I did not know who he was till after he had put me into my mamma's arms, and told her how he had run away with his own little daughter. "It is your papa, my dear, that has brought you to your own home."—"This is your mamma, my love," they both exclaimed at once. Mamma cried for joy to see me, and she wept again when she heard my papa tell what a neglected child I had been at my uncle's. This he had found out, he said, by my own innocent prattle, and that he was so offended with his brother, my uncle, that he would not enter his house. And then he said what a little, happy, good child I had been all the way, and that when he found I did not know him, he would not tell me who he was, for the sake of the pleasant surprise it would be to me. It was a surprise and a happiness indeed, after living with unkind relations, all at once to know I was at home with my own dear papa and mamma.

My mamma ordered tea. Whenever I happen to like my tea very much, I always think of the delicious cup of tea mamma gave us after our journey. I think I see the urn smoking before me now, and papa wheeling the sofa round, that I might sit between them at the table.

Mamma called me Little Runaway, and said it was very well it was only papa. I told her how we frightened the old gardener, and opened my eyes to show her how he stared, and how my papa made the milliner believe we were going to Gretna Green. Mamma looked grave, and said she was almost frightened to find I had been so fearless; but I promised her another time I would not go into a post-chaise with a gentleman without asking him who he was: and then she laughed, and seemed very well satisfied.

Mamma, to my fancy, looked very handsome. She was very nicely dressed, quite like a fine lady. I held up my head, and felt very proud that I had such a papa and mamma. I thought to myself, "O dear, my cousins' papa and mamma are not to be compared to mine!"

Papa said, "What makes you bridle and simper so, Emily?" Then I told him all that was in my mind. Papa asked if I did not think him as pretty as I did mamma. I could not say much for his beauty, but I told him he was a much finer gentleman than my uncle, and that I liked him the first moment I saw him, because he looked so good-natured. He said, "Well, then, he must be content with that half praise; but he had always thought himself very handsome." "O dear!" said I, and fell a-laughing, till I spilt my tea, and mamma called me a little awkward girl.

The next morning my papa was going to the Bank to receive some money, and he took mamma and me with him, that I might have a ride through London streets. Every one that has been in London must have seen the Bank, and therefore you may imagine what an effect the fine large rooms, and the bustle and confusion of people had on me, who was grown such a little wondering rustic that the crowded streets and the fine shops alone kept me in continual admiration.

As we were returning home down Cheapside, papa

said, "Emily shall take home some little books. Shall we order the coachman to the corner of St. Paul's Churchyard, or shall we go to the Juvenile Library in Skinner Street?" Mamma said she would go to Skinner Street, for she wanted to look at the new buildings there. Papa bought me seven new books, and the lady in the shop persuaded him to take more, but mamma said that was quite enough at present.

We went home by Ludgate Hill, because mamma wanted to buy something there; and while she went into a shop, papa heard me read in one of my new books, and said he was glad to find I could read so well, for I had forgot to tell him my aunt used to hear me read every day.

My papa stopped the coach opposite to St. Dunstan's Church, that I might see the great iron figures strike upon the bell, to give notice that it was a quarter of an hour past two. We waited some time that I might see this sight, but just at the moment they were striking, I happened to be looking at a toy-shop that was on the other side of the way, and unluckily missed it. Papa said, "Never mind; we will go into the toy-shop, and I dare say we shall find something that will console you for your disappointment." "Do," said mamma, "for I knew Miss Pearson, who keeps this shop, at Weymouth, when I was a little girl, not much older than Emily. Take notice of her,—she is a very intelligent old lady." Mamma made herself known to Miss Pearson, and showed me to her, but I did not much mind what they said; no more did papa—for we were busy among the toys.

A large wax-doll, a baby-house completely furnished, and several other beautiful toys, were bought for me. I sat and looked at them with an amazing deal of pleasure as we rode home—they quite filled up one side of the coach.

The joy I discovered at possessing things I could call my own, and the frequent repetition of the words,

My own, my own, gave my mamma some uneasiness. She justly feared that the cold treatment I had experienced at my uncle's had made me selfish, and therefore she invited a little girl to spend a few days with me, to see, as she has since told me, if I should not be liable to fall into the same error from which I had suffered so much at my uncle's.

As my mamma had feared, so the event proved; for I quickly adopted my cousins' selfish ideas, and gave the young lady notice that they were my own playthings, and she must not amuse herself with them any longer than I permitted her. Then presently I took occasion to begin a little quarrel with her, and said, "I have got a mamma now, Miss Frederica, as well as you, and I will go and tell her, and she will not let you play with my doll any longer than I please, because it is my own doll." And I very well remember I imitated, as nearly as I could, the haughty tone in which my cousins used to speak to me.

"Oh, fie! Emily," said my mamma; "can you be the little girl who used to be so distressed because your cousins would not let you play with their dolls? Do you not see you are doing the very same unkind thing to your playfellow that they did to you?" Then I saw as plain as could be what a naughty girl I was, and I promised not to do so any more.

A lady was sitting with mamma, and mamma said, "I believe I must pardon you this once, but I hope never to see such a thing again. This lady is Miss Frederica's mamma, and I am quite ashamed that she should be witness to your inhospitality to her daughter, particularly as she was so kind to come on purpose to invite you to a share in her *own* private box at the theatre this evening. Her carriage is waiting at the door to take us, but how can we accept of the invitation after what has happened?"

The lady begged it might all be forgotten; and mamma consented that I should go, and she said,

"But I hope, my dear Emily, when you are sitting in the playhouse, you will remember that pleasures are far more delightful when they are shared among numbers. If the whole theatre were your own, and you were sitting by yourself to see the performance, how dull it would seem to what you will find it, with so many happy faces around us, all amused with the same thing!" I hardly knew what my mamma meant, for I had never seen a play; but when I got there, after the curtain drew up, I looked up towards the galleries, and down into the pit, and into all the boxes, and then I knew what a pretty sight it was to see a number of happy faces. I was very well convinced that it would not have been half so cheerful, if the theatre had been my own, to have sat there by myself. From that time, whenever I felt inclined to be selfish, I used to remember the theatre where the mamma of the young lady I had been so rude to gave me a seat in her own box. There is nothing in the world so charming as going to a play. All the way there I was as dull and as silent as I used to be in ——shire, because I was so sorry mamma had been displeased with me. Just as the coach stopped, Miss Frederica said, "Will you be friends with me, Emily?" and I replied, "Yes, if you please, Frederica;" and we went hand-in-hand together into the house. I did not speak any more till we entered the box, but after that I was as lively as if nothing at all had happened.

I shall never forget how delighted I was at the first sight of the house. My little friend and I were placed together in the front, while our mammas retired to the back part of the box to chat by themselves, for they had been so kind as to come very early, that I might look about me before the performance began.

Frederica had been very often at a play. She was very useful in telling me what everything was. She made me observe how the common people were coming bustling down the benches in the galleries, as if they were afraid they should lose their places. She told me what a crowd these poor people had to go through before they got into the house. Then she showed me how leisurely they all came into the pit, and looked about them before they took their seats. She gave me a charming description of the king and queen at the play, and showed me where they sat, and told me how the princesses were dressed. It was a pretty sight to see the remainder of the candles lighted; and so it was to see the musicians come up from under the stage. I admired the music very much, and I asked if that was the play. Frederica laughed at my ignorance, and then she told me, when the play began the green curtain would draw up to the sound of soft music and I should hear a lady, dressed in black, say,

"Music hath charms to soothe the savage breast;"

and those were the very first words the actress, whose name was Almeria, spoke. When the curtain began to draw up, and I saw the bottom of her black petticoat, and heard the soft music, what an agitation I was in! But before that we had long to wait. Frederica told me we should wait till all the dress-boxes were full, and then the lights would pop up under the orchestra; the second music would play, and then the play would begin.

This play was the Mourning Bride. It was a very moving tragedy; and after that, when the curtain dropped, and I thought it was all over, I saw the most diverting pantomime that ever was seen. I made a strange blunder the next day, for I told papa that Almeria was married to Harlequin at last; but I assure you I meant to say Columbine, for I knew very well that Almeria was married to Alphonso; for she said she was in the first scene. She thought he was dead, but she found him again, just as I did my papa and mamma, when she least expected it.

MARIA HOWE.

I was brought up in the country. From my infancy I was always a weak and tender-spirited girl, subject to fears and depressions. My parents, and particularly my mother, were of a very different disposition. They were what is usually called gay: they loved pleasure, and parties, and visiting; but as they found the turn of my mind to be quite opposite, they gave themselves little trouble about me, but upon such occasions generally left me to my choice, which was much oftener to stay at home and indulge myself in my solitude, than to join in their rambling visits. I was always fond of being alone, yet always in a manner afraid. There was a book closet which led into my mother's dressing-room. Here I was eternally fond of being shut up by myself, to take down whatever volumes I pleased, and pore upon them, no matter whether they were fit for my years or no, or whether I understood them. Here, when the weather would not permit my going into the dark walk, *my walk*, as it was called, in the garden; here, when my parents have been from home, I have stayed for hours together, till the loneliness which pleased me so at first, has at length become quite frightful and I have rushed out of the closet into the inhabited parts of the house, and sought refuge in the lap of some one of the female servants, or of my aunt, who would say, seeing me look pale, that Maria had been frightening herself with some of those *nasty books:* so she used to call my favourite volumes, which I would not have parted with, no, not with one of the least of them, if I had had the choice to be made a fine princess, and to govern the world. But my aunt was no reader. She used to excuse herself, and say that reading hurt her eyes. I have been naughty enough to think that this was only an excuse, for I found that my aunt's weak eyes did not prevent her from poring ten hours a day upon her prayer-book, or her favourite *Thomas à Kempis*. But this was always her excuse for not reading any of the books I recommended. My aunt was my father's sister. She had never been married. My father was a good deal older than my mother, and my aunt was ten years older than my father. As I was often left at home with her, and as my serious disposition so well agreed with hers, an intimacy grew up between the old lady and me, and she would often say that she loved only one person in the world and that was me. Not that she and my parents were on very bad terms; but the old lady did not feel herself respected enough. The attention and fondness which she showed to me, conscious as I was that I was almost the only being she felt anything like fondness to, made me love her, as it was natural; indeed, I am ashamed to say, that I fear I almost loved her better than both my parents put together. But there was an oddness, a silence about my aunt, which was never interrupted but by her occasional expressions of love to me, that made me stand in fear of her. An odd look from under her spectacles would sometimes scare me away when I had been peering up in her face to make her kiss me. Then she had a way of muttering to herself, which, though it was good words and religious words that she was mumbling, somehow I did not like. My weak spirits, and the fears I was subject to, always made me afraid of any personal singularity or oddness in any one. I am ashamed, ladies, to lay open so many particulars of our family; but indeed it is necessary to the understanding of what I am going to tell you, of a very great weakness, if not wickedness, which I was guilty of towards my aunt. But I must return to my studies, and tell you what books I found in the closet, and what reading I chiefly admired. There was a great *Book of Martyrs* in which I used to read, or rather I used to spell out meanings; for I was too ignorant to make out many words; but there it was written all about those good men who chose to be burned alive rather than forsake their religion and become naughty Papists. Some words I could make out, some I could not; but I made out enough to fill my little head with vanity, and I used to think I was so courageous I could be burned too, and I would put my hands upon the flames which were pictured in the pretty pictures which the book had, and feel them; but you know, ladies, there is a great difference between the flames in a picture and real fire, and I am now ashamed of the conceit which I had of my own courage, and think how poor a martyr I should have made in those days. Then there was a book not so big; but it had pictures in it; it was called Culpepper's *Herbal;* it was full of pictures of plants and herbs, but I did not much care for that. Then there was Salmon's *Modern History*, out of which I picked a good deal. It had pictures of Chinese gods, and the great hooded serpent, which ran strangely in my fancy. There were some law books too, but the old English frightened me from reading them. But above all, what I relished was Stackhouse's *History of the Bible,* where there was the picture of the ark, and all the beasts getting into it. This delighted me, because it puzzled me, and many an aching head have I got with poring into it, and contriving how it might be built, with such and such rooms to hold all the world if there should be another flood, and sometimes settling what pretty beasts should be saved and what should not, for I would have no ugly or deformed beast in my pretty ark. But this was only a piece of folly and vanity that a little reflection might cure me of. Foolish girl that I was! to suppose that any creature is really ugly that has all its limbs contrived with heavenly wisdom, and was doubtless formed to some beautiful end, though a child cannot comprehend it. Doubtless a frog or a toad is not uglier in itself than a squirrel or a pretty green lizard; but we want understanding to see it.

[*Here I must remind you, my dear Miss Howe, that one of the young ladies smiled and two or three were seen to titter at this part of your narration, and you seemed, I thought, a little too angry for a girl of your sense and reading; but you will remember, my dear, that young heads are not always able to bear strange and unusual assertions; and if some elder person, possibly, or some book which you had found, had not put it into your head, you would hardly have discovered by your own reflection that a frog or a toad was equal in real loveliness to a frisking squirrel, or a pretty green lizard, as you called it; not remembering that at this very time you gave the lizard the name of* pretty, *and left it out to the frog—so liable we are all to prejudices. But you went on with your story.*]

These fancies, ladies, were not so very foolish or naughty, perhaps, but they may be forgiven in a child of six years old; but what I am going to tell, I shall be ashamed of, and repent, I hope, as long as I live. It will teach me not to form rash judgments. Besides the picture of the ark, and many others which I have forgot, Stackhouse contained one picture which made more impression upon my childish understanding than all the rest. It was the picture of the raising up of Samuel, which I used to call the Witch of Endor picture. I was always very fond of picking up stories about witches. There was a book called *Glanvil on Witches*, which used to lie about in this closet; it was thumbed about, and showed it had been much read in former times. This was my treasure. Here I used to pick out the strangest stories. My not being able to read them very well probably made them appear more strange and out of the way to me. But I could collect enough to understand that witches were old women who gave themselves up to do mischief—how by the help of spirits as bad as themselves they lamed cattle, and made the corn not grow; and how they made images of wax to stand for people that had done them any injury, or they thought had done them injury; and how they burned the images before a slow fire, and stuck pins in them; and the persons which these waxen images represented, however far distant, felt all the pains and torments in good earnest, which were inflicted in show upon these images; and such a horror I had of these wicked witches, that though I am now better instructed, and look upon all these stories as mere idle tales, and invented to fill people's heads with nonsense, yet I cannot recall to mind the horrors which I then felt without shuddering, and feeling something of the old fit return.

[*Here, my dear Miss Howe, you may remember that Miss M———, the youngest of our party, showing some more curiosity than usual, I winked upon you to hasten to your story, lest the terrors which you were describing should make too much impression upon a young head, and you kindly understood my sign, and said less upon the subject of your fears than I fancy you first intended.*]

This foolish book of witch stories had no pictures in it, but I made up for them out of my own fancy, and out of the great picture of the raising up of Samuel in Stackhouse. I was not old enough to understand the difference there was between these silly improbable tales, which imputed such powers to poor old women, who are the most helpless things in the creation, and the narrative in the Bible, which does not say that the witch, or pretended witch, raised up the dead body of Samuel by her own power; but, as it clearly appears, he was permitted by the divine will to appear to confound the presumption of Saul; and that the witch herself was really as much frightened and confounded at the miracle as Saul himself, not expecting a real appearance; but probably having prepared some juggling, sleight-of-hand tricks and sham appearance to deceive the eyes of Saul: whereas she, nor any one living, had never the power to raise the dead to life, but only He who made them from the first. These reasons I might have read in Stackhouse itself if I had been old enough, and have read them in that very book since I was older, but at that time I looked at little beyond the picture.

THE WITCH AUNT.

These stories of witches so terrified me, that my sleeps were broken, and in my dreams I always had a fancy of a witch being in the room with me. I know now that it was only nervousness; but though I can laugh at it now as well as you, ladies, if you knew what I suffered, you would be thankful that you have had sensible people about you to instruct you and teach you better. I was let grow up wild like an ill weed, and thrived accordingly. One night that I had been terrified in my sleep with my imaginations, I got out of bed and crept softly to the adjoining room. My room was next to where my aunt usually sat when she was alone. Into her room I crept for relief from my fears. The old lady was not yet retired to rest, but was sitting with her eyes half-open, half-closed; her spectacles tottering upon her nose; her head nodding over her prayer-book; her lips mumbling the words as she read them, or half-read them in her dozing posture; her grotesque appearance; her old-fashioned dress, resembling what I had seen in that fatal picture in Stackhouse; all this, with the dead time of night, as it seemed to me (for I had gone through my first sleep), joined to produce a wicked fancy in me, that the form which I had beheld was not my aunt, but some witch. Her mumbling of her prayers confirmed me in this shocking idea. I had read in Glanvil of those wicked creatures reading their prayers *backwards*, and I thought that this was the operation which her lips were at this time employed about. Instead of flying to her friendly lap for that protection which I had so often experienced when I have been weak and timid, I shrunk back terrified and bewildered to my bed, where I lay in broken sleeps and miserable fancies till the morning, which I had so much reason to wish for, came. My fancies a little wore away with the light, but an impression was fixed, which could not for a long time be done away. In the daytime, when my father and mother were about the house, when I saw them familiarly speak to my aunt, my fears all vanished; and when the good creature has taken me upon her knees and shown me any kindness more than ordinary, at such times I have melted into tears and longed to tell her what naughty foolish fancies I had had of her. But when night returned, that figure which I had seen recurred—the posture, the half-closed eyes, the mumbling and muttering which I had heard—a confusion was in my head, *who* it was I had seen that night :—it was my aunt, and it was not my aunt :—it was that good creature, who loved me above all the world, engaged at her good task of devotions—perhaps praying for some good to me. Again, it was a witch—a creature hateful to God and man, reading backwards the good prayers; who would perhaps destroy me. In these conflicts of mind I passed several weeks, till, by a revolution in my fate, I was removed to the house of a female relation of my mother's, in a distant part of the country, who had come on a visit to our house, and observing my lonely ways, and apprehensive of the ill effect of my mode of living upon my health, begged leave to take me home to her house to reside for a short time. I went with some reluctance at leaving my closet, my dark walk, and even my aunt, who had been such a source of both love and terror to me. But I went, and soon found the grand effects of a change of scene. Instead of melancholy closets and lonely avenues of trees, I saw lightsome rooms and cheerful faces; I had companions of my own age; no books were allowed me but what were rational and sprightly; that gave me mirth or gave me instruction. I soon learned to laugh at witch stories; and when I returned after three or four months' absence to our own house, my good aunt appeared to me in the same light in which I had viewed her from my infancy, before that foolish fancy possessed me, or rather, I should say, more kind, more fond, more loving than before. It is impossible to say how much good that lady, the kind relation of my mother's that I spoke of, did to me by changing the scene. Quite a new turn of ideas was given to me; I became sociable and companionable; my parents soon discovered a change in me, and I have found a similar alteration in them. They have been plainly more fond of me since that change, as from that time I learned to conform myself more to their way of living. I have never since had that aversion to company and going out with them which used to make them regard me with less fondness than they would have wished to show. I impute almost all that I had to complain of in their neglect to my having been a little, unsociable, uncompanionable mortal. I lived in this manner for a year or two, passing my time between our house and the lady's who so kindly took me in hand, till, by her advice, I was sent to this school;—where I have told you, ladies, what for fear of ridicule I never ventured to tell any person besides, the story of my foolish and naughty fancy.

CHARLOTTE WILMOT.

UNTIL I was eleven years of age my life was one continued series of indulgence and delight. My father was a merchant, and supposed to be in very opulent circumstances, at least I thought so, for at a very early age I perceived that we lived in a more expensive way than any of my father's friends did. It was not the pride of birth, of which, Miss Withers, you once imagined you might justly boast, but the mere display of wealth that I was early taught to set an undue value on. My parents spared no cost for masters to instruct me; I had a French governess, and also a woman-servant whose sole business it was to attend on me. My playroom was crowded with toys, and my dress was the admiration of all my youthful visitors, to whom I gave balls and entertainments as often as I pleased. I looked down on all my young companions as my inferiors; but I chiefly assumed airs of superiority over Maria Hartley, whose father was a clerk in my father's counting-house, and therefore I concluded she would regard the fine show I made with more envy and admiration than any other of my companions. In the days of my humiliation, which I too soon experienced, I was thrown on the bounty of her father for support. To be a dependant on the charity of her family seemed the heaviest evil that could have befallen me; for I remembered how often I had displayed my finery and my expensive ornaments, on purpose to enjoy the triumph of my superior advantages; and, with shame I now speak it, I have often glanced at her plain linen frock, when I showed her my beautiful ball-dresses. Nay, I once gave her a hint, which she so well understood that she burst into tears, that I could not invite her to some of my parties because her mamma once sent her on my birthday in a coloured frock. I cannot now think of my want of feeling without excessive pain; but one day I saw her highly amused with some curious toys, and on her expressing the pleasure the sight of them gave her, I said, "Yes, they are very well for those who are not accustomed to these things; but, for my part, I have so many, I am tired of them, and I am quite delighted to pass an hour in the empty closet your mamma allows you to receive your visitors in, because there is nothing there to interrupt the conversation."

Once, as I have said, Maria was betrayed into tears; now that I insulted her by calling her own small apartment an empty closet, she turned quick upon me, but not in anger, saying, "Oh, my dear Miss Wilmot, how very sorry I am"—— Here she stopped; and though I knew not the meaning of her words, I felt it as a reproof. I hung down my head abashed; yet perceiving that she was all that day more kind and obliging than ever, and being conscious of not having merited this kindness, I thought she was mean-spirited, and therefore I consoled myself with having discovered this fault in her, for I thought my arrogance was full as excusable as her meanness.

In a few days I knew my error; I learned why Maria

had been so kind, and why she had said she was sorry. It was for me, proud disdainful girl that I was, that she was sorry; she knew, though I did not, that my father was on the brink of ruin; and it came to pass, as she feared it would, that in a few days my playroom was as empty as Maria's closet, and all my grandeur was at an end.

My father had what is called an execution in the house; everything was seized that we possessed. Our splendid furniture, and even our wearing apparel, all my beautiful ball-dresses, my trinkets, and my toys, were taken away by my father's merciless creditors. The week in which this happened was such a scene of hurry, confusion, and misery, that I will not attempt to describe it.

At the end of a week I found that my father and mother had gone out very early in the morning. Mr. Hartley took me home to his own house, and I expected to find them there; but, oh! what anguish did I feel, when I heard him tell Mrs. Hartley they had quitted England, and that he had brought me home to live with them. In tears and sullen silence I passed the first day of my entrance into this despised house. Maria was from home. All the day I sat in a corner of the room grieving for the departure of my parents; and if for a moment I forgot that sorrow, I tormented myself with imagining the many ways which Maria might invent to make me feel in return the slights and airs of superiority which I had given myself over her. Her mother began the prelude to what I expected, for I heard her freely censure the imprudence of my parents. She spoke in whispers; yet, though I could not hear every word, I made out the tenor of her discourse. She was very anxious, lest her husband should be involved in the ruin of our house. He was the chief clerk in my father's counting-house. Towards evening he came in and quieted her fears by the welcome news that he had obtained a more lucrative situation than the one he had lost.

At eight in the evening Mrs. Hartley said to me, "Miss Wilmot, it is time for you to be in bed, my dear;" and ordered the servant to show me upstairs, adding that she supposed she must assist me to undress, but that when Maria came home, she must teach me to wait on myself. The apartment in which I was to sleep was at the top of the house. The walls were white-washed, and the roof was sloping. There was only one window in the room, a small casement, through which the bright moon shone, and it seemed to me the most melancholy sight I had ever beheld. In broken and disturbed slumbers I passed the night. When I awoke in the morning, she whom I most dreaded to see, Maria, who I supposed had envied my former state, and who I now felt certain would exult over my present mortifying reverse of fortune, stood by my bedside. She awakened me from a dream, in which I thought she was ordering me to fetch her something; and on my refusal, she said I must obey her, for I was now her servant. Far differently from what my dreams had pictured did Maria address me! She said in the gentlest tone imaginable, "My dear Miss Wilmot, my mother begs you will come down to breakfast; will you give me leave to dress you?" My proud heart would not suffer me to speak, and I began to attempt to put on my clothes; but never having been used to do anything for myself, I was unable to perform it, and was obliged to accept of the assistance of Maria. She dressed me, washed my face, and combed my hair; and as she did these services for me, she said in a most respectful manner, "Is this the way you like to wear this, Miss Wilmot?" or, "Is this the way you like this done?" and courtesied as she gave me every fresh article to put on. The slights I expected to receive from Maria would not have distressed me more than the delicacy of her behaviour did. I hung down my head with shame and anguish.

In a few days Mrs. Hartley ordered her daughter to instruct me in such useful works and employments as

Maria knew. Of everything which she called useful I was most ignorant. My accomplishments I found were held in small estimation here, by all indeed, except Maria. She taught me nothing without the kindest apologies for being obliged to teach me, who, she said, was so excellent in all elegant arts ; and was for ever thanking me for the pleasure she had formerly received from my skill in music and pretty fancy works. The distress I was in made these complimentary speeches not flatteries, but sweet drops of comfort to my degraded heart, almost broken with misfortune and remorse.

I remained at Mr. Hartley's but two months ; for at the end of that time my father inherited a considerable property by the death of a distant relation, which has enabled him to settle his affairs. He established himself again as a merchant ; but as he wished to retrench his expenses, and begin the world again on a plan of strict economy, he sent me to this school to finish my education.

SUSAN YATES.

I was born and brought up in a house in which my parents had all their lives resided, which stood in the midst of that lonely tract of land called the Lincolnshire Fens. Few families besides our own lived near the spot, both because it was reckoned an unwholesome air, and because its distance from any town or market made it an inconvenient situation. My father was in no very affluent circumstances, and it was a sad necessity which he was put to of having to go many miles to fetch anything from the nearest village, which was full seven miles distant, through a sad miry way that at all times made it heavy walking, and after rain was almost impassable. But he had no horse or carriage of his own.

The church which belonged to the parish in which

our house was situated stood in this village; and its distance being, as I said before, seven miles from our house, made it quite an impossible thing for my mother or me to think of going to it. Sometimes, indeed, on a fine dry Sunday my father would rise early, and take a walk to the village, just to see how *goodness thrived*, as he used to say; but he would generally return tired, and the worse for his walk. It is scarcely possible to explain to any one who has not lived in the Fens what difficult and dangerous walking it is. A mile is as good as four, I have heard my father say, in those parts. My mother, who in the early part of her life had lived in a more civilised spot, and had been used to constant church-going, would often lament her situation. It was from her I early imbibed a great curiosity and anxiety to see that thing which I had heard her call a church, and so often lament that she could never go to. I had seen houses of various structures, and had seen in pictures the shapes of ships and boats, and palaces and temples, but never rightly anything that could be called a church, or that could satisfy me about its form. Sometimes I thought it must be like our house, and sometimes I fancied it must be more like the house of our neighbour, Mr. Sutton, which was bigger and handsomer than ours. Sometimes I thought it was a great hollow cave, such as I have heard my father say the first inhabitants of the earth dwelt in. Then I thought it was like a waggon, or a cart, and that it must be something movable. The shape of it ran in my mind strangely, and one day I ventured to ask my mother what was that foolish thing she was always longing to go to, and which she called a church. Was it anything to eat or drink, or was it only like a great huge plaything to be seen and stared at?—I was not quite five years of age when I made this inquiry.

This question, so oddly put, made my mother smile; but in a little time she put on a more grave look, and informed me that a church was nothing that I had supposed it, but it was a great building, far greater than any house which I had seen, where men and women and children came together twice a day on Sundays, to hear the Bible read, and make good resolutions for the week to come. She told me that the fine music which we sometimes heard in the air came from the bells of St. Mary's Church, and that we never heard it but when the wind was in a particular point. This raised my wonder more than all the rest; for I had somehow conceived that the noise which I heard was occasioned by birds up in the air, or that it was made by the angels, whom (so ignorant I was till that time) I had always considered to be a sort of birds; for before this time I was totally ignorant of anything like religion, it being a principle of my father that young heads should not be told too many things at once, for fear they should get confused ideas and no clear notions of anything. We had always indeed so far observed Sundays, that no work was done upon that day, and upon that day I wore my best muslin frock, and was not allowed to sing or to be noisy; but I never understood why that day should differ from any other. We had no public meetings: indeed, the few straggling houses which were near us would have furnished but a slender congregation; and the loneliness of the place we lived in, instead of making us more sociable, and drawing us closer together, as my mother used to say it ought to have done, seemed to have the effect of making us more distant and averse to society than other people. One or two good neighbours indeed we had, but not in numbers to give me an idea of church attendance.

But now my mother thought it high time to give me some clearer instruction in the main points of religion, and my father came readily into her plan. I was now permitted to sit up half an hour later on a Sunday evening that I might hear a portion of Scripture read, which had always been their custom, though by reason of my tender age, and my father's opinion on the impropriety of children being taught too young, I had never till now been an auditor. I was taught my prayers, and those things which you, ladies, I doubt not, had the benefit of being instructed in at a much earlier age.

The clearer my notions on these points became, they only made me more passionately long for the privilege of joining in that social service, from which it seemed that we alone, of all the inhabitants of the land, were debarred; and when the wind was in that point which enabled the sound of the distant bells of St. Mary's to be heard over the great moor which skirted our house, I have stood out in the air to catch the sounds, which I almost devoured; and the tears have come into my eyes when sometimes they seemed to speak to me almost in articulate sounds, to *come to church*, and because of the great moor which was between me and them, I could not come; and the too tender apprehensions of these things have filled me with a religious melancholy. With thoughts like these I entered into my seventh year.

And now the time was come when the great moor was no longer to separate me from the object of my wishes and of my curiosity. My father having some money left him by the will of a deceased relation, we ventured to set up a sort of a carriage—no very superb one, I assure you, ladies; but in that part of the world it was looked upon with some envy by our poorer neighbours. The first party of pleasure which my father proposed to take in it was to the village where I had so often wished to go, and my mother and I were to accompany him; for it was very fit, my father observed, that little Susan should go to church and learn how to behave herself, for we might some time or other have occasion to live in London, and not always be confined to that out-of-the-way spot.

It was on a Sunday morning that we set out, my little heart beating with almost breathless expectation. The day was fine, and the roads as good as they ever are in those parts. I was so happy and so proud! I was lost in dreams of what I was going to see. At length the tall steeple of St. Mary's Church came in view. It was pointed out to me by my father, as the place from which that music had come, which I had heard over the moor, and had fancied to be angels singing. I was wound up to the highest pitch of delight at having visibly presented to me the spot from which had proceeded that unknown friendly music; and when it began to peal, just as we approached the village, it seemed to speak, *Susan is come*, as plainly as it used to invite me *to come*, when I heard it over the moor. I pass over our alighting at the house of a relation, and all that passed till I went with my father and mother to church.

St. Mary's Church is a great church for such a small village as it stands in. My father said it had been a cathedral, and that it had once belonged to a monastery, but the monks were all gone. Over the door there was stonework, representing saints and bishops, and here and there, along the sides of the church, there were figures of men's heads made in a strange grotesque way: I have since seen the same sort of figures in the round tower of the Temple Church in London. My father said they were very improper ornaments for such a place, and so I now think them; but it seems the people who built these great churches in old times gave themselves more liberties than they do now; and I remember that when I first saw them, and before my father had made this observation, though they were so ugly and out of shape, and some of them seem to be grinning and distorting their features with pain or with laughter, yet being placed upon a church, to which I had come with such serious thoughts, I could not help thinking they had some serious meaning; and I looked at them with wonder, but without any temptation to laugh. I somehow fancied they were the representation of wicked people set up as a warning.

When we got into the church, the service was not begun, and my father kindly took me round to show me the monuments and everything else remarkable. I remember seeing one of a venerable figure, which my father said had been a judge. The figure was kneeling, as if it was alive, before a sort of desk, with a book, I suppose the Bible, lying on it. I somehow fancied the figure had a sort of life in it, it seemed so natural, or that the dead judge that it was done for said his prayers at it still. This was a silly notion, but I was very young, and had passed my little life in a remote place, where I had never seen anything nor knew anything; and the awe which I felt at first being in a church took from me all power but that of wondering. I did not reason about anything; I was too young. Now I understand why monuments are put up for the dead, and why the figures which are put upon them are described as doing the actions which they did in their lifetimes, and that they are a sort of pictures set up for our instruction. But all was new and surprising to me on that day—the long windows with little panes, the pillars, the pews made of oak, the little hassocks for the people to kneel on, the form of the pulpit, with the sounding-board over it, gracefully carved in flower-work. To you, who have lived all your lives in populous places, and have been taken to church from the earliest time you can remember, my admiration of these things must appear strangely ignorant. But I was a lonely young creature, that had been brought up in remote places, where there was neither church nor church-going inhabitants. I have since lived in great towns, and seen the ways of churches and of worship, and I am old enough now to distinguish between what is essential in religion, and what is merely formal or ornamental.

When my father had done pointing out to me the things most worthy of notice about the church, the service was almost ready to begin; the parishioners had most of them entered and taken their seats; and we were shown into a pew where my mother was already seated. Soon after the clergyman entered, and the organ began to play what is called the voluntary. I had never seen so many people assembled before. At first I thought that all eyes were upon me, and that because I was a stranger. I was terribly ashamed and confused at first; but my mother helped me to find out the places in the prayer-book, and being busy about that took off some of my painful apprehensions. I was no stranger to the order of the service, having often read in the prayer-book at home, but my thoughts being confused, it puzzled me a little to find out the responses and other things, which I thought I knew so well; but I went through it tolerably well. One thing which has often troubled me since is, that I am afraid I was too full of myself and of thinking how happy I was, and what a privilege it was for one that was so young to join in the service with so many grown people, so that I did not attend enough to the instruction which I might have received. I remember I foolishly applied everything that was said to myself, so as it could mean nobody but myself, I was so full of my own thoughts. All that assembly of people seemed to me as if they were come together only to show me the way of a church. Not but I received some very affecting impressions from some things which I heard that day; but the standing up and sitting down of the people, the organ, the singing:—the way of all these things took up more of my attention than was proper; or I thought it did. I believe I behaved better, and was more serious when I went a second time, and a third time; for now we went as a regular thing every Sunday, and continued to do so, till, by a still further change for the better in my father's circumstances, we removed to London. Oh! it was a happy day for me my first going to St. Mary's Church; before that day I used to feel like a little outcast in the wilderness, like one that did not belong to the world of Christian people. I have never felt like a little outcast since. But I never can hear the sweet noise of bells, that I don't think of the angels singing, and what poor but pretty thoughts I had of angels in my uninstructed solitude.

ARABELLA HARDY.

I WAS born in the East Indies. I lost my father and mother young. At the age of five my relations thought it proper that I should be sent to England for my education. I was to be intrusted to the care of a young woman who had a character for great humanity and discretion; but just as I had taken leave of my friends, and we were about to take our passage, the young woman suddenly fell sick, and could not go on board. In this unpleasant emergency no one knew how to act. The ship was at the very point of sailing, and it was the last which was to sail for the season. At length the captain, who was known to my friends, prevailed upon my relation, who had come with us to see us embark, to leave the young woman on shore, and to let me embark separately. There was no possibility of getting any other female attendant for me in the short time allotted for our preparation; and the opportunity of going by that ship was thought too valuable to be lost. No other ladies happened to be going, and so I was consigned to the care of the captain and his crew—rough and unaccustomed attendants for a young creature delicately brought up as I had been; but indeed they did their best to make me not feel the difference. The unpolished sailors were my nursery-maids and my waiting-women. Everything was done by the captain and the men to accommodate me, and make me easy. I had a little room made out of the cabin, which was to be considered as my room, and nobody might enter into it. The first mate had a great character for bravery and all sailor-like accomplishments; but with all this he had a gentleness of manners, and a pale feminine cast of face, from ill health and a weakly constitution, which subjected him to some ridicule from the officers, and caused him to be named Betsy. He did not much like the appellation, but he submitted to it the better, saying that those who gave him a woman's name well knew that he had a man's heart, and that in the face of danger he would go as far as any man. To this young man, whose real name was Charles Atkinson, by a lucky thought of the captain, the care of me was especially intrusted. Betsy was proud of his charge, and, to do him justice, acquitted himself with great diligence and adroitness through the whole of the voyage. From the beginning I had somehow looked upon Betsy as a woman, hearing him so spoken of, and this reconciled me in some measure to the want of a maid which I had been used to. But I was a manageable girl at all times, and gave nobody much trouble.

I have not knowledge enough to give an account of my voyage, or to remember the names of the seas we passed through, or the lands which we touched upon in our course. The chief thing I can remember (for I do not recollect the events of the voyage in any order) was Atkinson taking me upon deck to see the great whales playing about in the sea. There was one great whale came bounding up out of the sea, and then he would dive into it again, and then would come up at a distance where nobody expected him, and another whale was following after him. Atkinson said they were at play, and that the lesser whale loved that bigger whale, and kept it company all through the wide seas; but I thought it strange play, and a frightful kind of love; for I every minute expected they would come up to our ship and toss it. But Atkinson said a whale was a gentle creature, and it was a sort of sea-elephant, and that the most powerful creatures in nature are always the least hurtful. And he told me how men went out to take these whales, and stuck long pointed darts into them; and how the sea was discoloured with the blood of these poor whales for many miles' distance; and I admired the courage of the men, but I was sorry for the inoffensive whale. Many other pretty sights he used to show me, when he was not on watch, or doing some duty for the ship. No one was more attentive to his duty than he; but at such times as he had leisure he would show me all pretty sea-sights:—the dolphins and porpoises that came before a storm, and all the colours which the sea changed to; how sometimes it was a deep blue and then a deep green, and sometimes it would seem all on fire; all these various appearances he would show me, and attempt to explain the reason of them to me, as well as my young capacity would admit of. There were a lion and a tiger on board, going to England as a present to the king; and it was a great diversion to Atkinson and me, after I got rid of my first terrors, to see the ways of these beasts in their dens, and how venturous the sailors were in putting their hands through the grates, and patting their rough coats. Some of the men had monkeys, which ran loose about, and the sport was for the men to lose them and find them again. The monkeys would run up the shrouds, and pass from rope to rope, with ten times greater alacrity than the most experienced sailor could follow them; and sometimes they would hide themselves in the most unthought-of places, and when they were found, they would grin and make mouths, as if they had sense. Atkinson described to me the ways of these little animals in their native woods, for he had seen them. Oh, how many ways he thought of to amuse me in that long voyage!

Sometimes he would describe to me the odd shapes and varieties of fishes that were in the sea, and tell me tales of the sea-monsters that lay hid at the bottom, and were seldom seen by men; and what a glorious sight it would be, if our eyes could be sharpened to behold all the inhabitants of the sea at once swimming in the great deeps, as plain as we see the gold and silver fish in a bowl of glass. With such notions he enlarged my infant capacity to take in many things.

When in foul weather I have been terrified at the motion of the vessel, as it rocked backwards and forwards, he would still my fears, and tell me that I used to be rocked so once in a cradle, and that the sea was God's bed, and the ship our cradle, and we were as safe in that greater motion as when we felt that lesser one in our little wooden sleeping-places. When the wind was up, and sang through the sails, and disturbed me with its violent clamours, he would call it music, and bid me hark to the sea-organ, and with that name he quieted my tender apprehensions. When I have looked around with a mournful face at seeing all *men* about me, he would enter into my thoughts, and tell me pretty stories of his mother and his sisters, and a female cousin that he loved better than his sisters, whom he called Jenny, and say that when we got to England I should go and see them, and how fond Jenny would be of his little daughter, as he called me; and with these images of women and females which he raised in my fancy, he quieted me for a while. One time, and never but once, he told me that Jenny had promised to be his wife if ever he came to England, but that he had his doubts whether he should live to get home, for he was very sickly. This made me cry bitterly.

That I dwell so long upon the attention of this Atkinson, is only because his death, which happened just before we got to England, affected me so much, that he alone of all the ship's crew has engrossed my mind ever since; though indeed the captain and all were singularly kind to me, and strove to make up for my uneasy and unnatural situation. The boatswain would pipe for my diversion, and the sailor-boy would climb the dangerous mast for my sport. The rough foremast-man would never willingly appear before me till he had combed his long black hair smooth and sleek, not to terrify me. The officers got up a sort of play for my amusement, and Atkinson, or, as they called him, Betsy, acted the heroine of the piece. All ways that could be contrived were thought upon to reconcile me to my lot. I was the universal favourite; I do not know how deservedly; but I suppose it was because I was alone, and there was no female in the ship besides me. Had I come over with female relations or attendants, I should have excited no particular curiosity; I should have required no uncommon attentions. I was one little woman among a crew of men; and I believe the homage which I have read that men universally pay to women, was in this case directed to me in the absence of all other womenkind. I do not know how that might be, but I was a little princess among them, and I was not six years old.

I remember the first drawback which happened to my comfort was Atkinson's not appearing the whole of one day. The captain tried to reconcile me to it by saying that Mr. Atkinson was confined to his cabin; that he was not quite well, but a day or two would restore him. I begged to be taken in to see him, but this was not granted. A day, and then another came, and another, and no Atkinson was visible, and I saw apparent solicitude in the faces of all the officers, who nevertheless strove to put on their best countenances before me, and to be more than usually kind to me. At length, by the desire of Atkinson himself, as I have since learned, I was permitted to go into his cabin and see him. He was sitting up, apparently in a state of great exhaustion; but his face lighted up when he saw me, and he kissed me and told me that he was going a great voyage, far longer than that which we had passed together, and he should never come back; and though I was so young, I understood well enough that he meant this of his death, and I cried sadly; but he comforted me, and told me that I must be his little executrix, and perform his last will, and bear his last words to his mother and his sisters, and to his cousin Jenny, whom I should see in a short time; and he gave me his blessing, as a father would bless his child, and he sent a last kiss by me to all his female relations, and he made me promise that I would go and see them when I got to England. And soon after this he died. But I was in another part of the ship when he died, and I was not told it till we got to shore, which was a few days after; but they kept telling me that he was better and better, and that I should soon see him, but that it disturbed him to talk with any one. Oh, what a grief it was when I learned that I had lost an old shipmate that had made an irksome situation so bearable by his kind assiduities; and to think that he was gone, and I could never repay him for his kindness!

When I had been a year and a half in England, the captain, who had made another voyage to India and back, thinking that time had alleviated a little the sorrow of Atkinson's relations, prevailed upon my friends who had the care of me in England to let him introduce me to Atkinson's mother and sisters. Jenny was no more; she had died in the interval, and I never saw her. Grief for his death had brought on a consumption, of which she lingered about a twelvemonth and then expired. But in the mother and the sisters of this excellent young man I have found the most valuable friends I possess on this side the great ocean. They received me from the captain as the little *protégée* of Atkinson, and from them I have learned passages of his former life; and this in particular, that the illness of which he died was brought on by a wound of which he never quite recovered, which he got in the desperate attempt, when he was quite a boy, to defend his captain against a superior force of the enemy which had boarded him, and which, by his premature valour inspiriting the men, they finally succeeded in repulsing. This was that Atkinson who, from his pale and feminine appearance, was called Betsy; this was he whose womanly care of me got him the name of a woman; who, with more than female attention, condescended to play the handmaid to a little unaccompanied orphan that fortune had cast upon the care of a rough sea-captain and his rougher crew.

THE ADVENTURES OF ULYSSES.

This work is designed as a supplement to the *Adventures of Telemachus*. It treats of the conduct and sufferings of Ulysses, the father of Telemachus. The picture which it exhibits is that of a brave man struggling with adversity; by a wise use of events, and with an inimitable presence of mind under difficulties, forcing out a way for himself through the severest trials to which human life can be exposed; with enemies natural and preternatural surrounding him on all sides. The agents in this tale, besides men and women, are giants, enchanters, sirens: things which denote external force or internal temptations, the twofold danger which a wise fortitude must expect to encounter in its course through this world. The fictions contained in it will be found to comprehend some of the most admired inventions of Grecian mythology.

The groundwork of the story is as old as the *Odyssey*, but the moral and the colouring are comparatively modern. By avoiding the prolixity which marks the speeches and the descriptions in *Homer*, I have gained a rapidity to the narration which I hope will make it more attractive and give it more the air of a romance to young readers, though I am sensible that by the curtailment I have sacrificed in many places the manners to the passion, the subordinate characteristics to the essential interest of the story. The attempt is not to be considered as seeking a comparison with any of the direct translations of the *Odyssey*, either in prose or verse, though if I were to state the obligations which I have had to one obsolete version,[1] I should have run the hazard of depriving myself of the very slender degree of reputation which I could hope to acquire from a trifle like the present undertaking.

Chapter I.

The Cicons—The fruit of the lotos-tree—Polyphemus and the Cyclops—The kingdom of the winds, and God Æolus's fatal present—The Læstrygonian man-eaters.

This history tells of the wanderings of Ulysses and his followers in their return from Troy, after the destruction of that famous city of Asia by the Grecians. He was inflamed with a desire of seeing again, after a ten years' absence, his wife and native country Ithaca. He was king of a barren spot, and a poor country, in comparison of the fruitful plains of Asia which he was leaving, or the wealthy kingdoms which he touched upon in his return; yet wherever he came, he could never see a soil which appeared in his eyes half so sweet or desirable as his country earth. This made him refuse the offers of the goddess Calypso to stay with her, and partake of her immortality, in the delightful island: and this gave him strength to break from the enchantments of Circe, the daughter of the Sun.

From Troy ill winds cast Ulysses and his fleet upon the coast of the Cicons, a people hostile to the Grecians. Landing his forces, he laid siege to their chief city Ismarus, which he took, and with it much spoil, and slew many people. But success proved fatal to him; for his soldiers, elated with the spoil and the good store of provisions which they found in that place, fell to eating and drinking, forgetful of their safety, till the Cicons, who inhabited the coast, had time to assemble their friends and allies from the interior, who mustering in prodigious force, set

[1] The translation of *Homer* by Chapman in the reign of James I.

upon the Grecians, while they negligently revelled and feasted, and slew many of them and recovered the spoil. They, dispirited and thinned in their numbers, with difficulty made their retreat good to the ships.

Thence they set sail, sad at heart, yet something cheered that with such fearful odds against them they had not all been utterly destroyed. A dreadful tempest ensued, which for two nights and two days tossed them about, but the third day the weather cleared, and they had hopes of a favourable gale to carry them to Ithaca; but as they doubled the Cape of Malea, suddenly a north wind arising, drove them back as far as Cythera. After that, for the space of nine days, contrary winds continued to drive them in an opposite direction to the point to which they were bound, and the tenth day they put in at a shore where a race of men dwell that are sustained by the fruit of the lotos-tree. Here Ulysses sent some of his men to land for fresh water, who were met by certain of the inhabitants, that gave them some of their country food to eat; not with any ill intention towards them, though in the event it proved pernicious; for, having eaten of this fruit, so pleasant it proved to their appetite, that they in a minute quite forgot all thoughts of home, or of their countrymen, or of ever returning back to the ships to give an account of what sort of inhabitants dwelt there, but they would needs stay and live there among them, and eat of that precious food for ever; and when Ulysses sent other of his men to look for them, and to bring them back by force, they strove, and wept, and would not leave their food for heaven itself, so much the pleasure of that enchanting fruit had bewitched them. But Ulysses caused them to be bound hand and foot, and cast under the hatches; and set sail with all possible speed from that baneful coast, lest others after them might taste the lotos, which had such strange qualities to make men forget their native country and the thoughts of home.

Coasting on all that night by unknown and out of the

way shores, they came by day-break to the land where the Cyclops dwell, a sort of giant shepherds that neither sow nor plough, but the earth untilled produces for them rich wheat and barley and grapes, yet they have neither bread nor wine, nor know the arts of cultivation, nor care to know them; for they live each man to himself, without laws or government, or anything like a state or kingdom, but their dwellings are in caves, on the steep heads of mountains, every man's household governed by his own caprice, or not governed at all, their wives and children as lawless as themselves, none caring for others, but each doing as he or she thinks good. Ships or boats they have none, nor artificers to make them, no trade or commerce, or wish to visit other shores; yet they have convenient places for harbours and for shipping. Here Ulysses with a chosen party of twelve followers landed, to explore what sort of men dwelt there, whether hospitable and friendly to strangers, or altogether wild and savage, for as yet no dwellers appeared in sight.

The first sign of habitation which they came to was a giant's cave rudely fashioned, but of a size which betokened the vast proportions of its owner, the pillars which supported it being the bodies of huge oaks or pines, in the natural state of the tree, and all about showed more marks of strength than skill in whoever built it. Ulysses, entering in, admired the savage contrivances and artless structure of the place, and longed to see the tenant of so outlandish a mansion; but well conjecturing that gifts would have more avail in extracting courtesy than strength could succeed in forcing it, from such a one as he expected to find the inhabitant, he resolved to flatter his hospitality with a present of Greek wine, of which he had store in twelve great vessels; so strong that no one ever drank it without an infusion of twenty parts of water to one of wine, yet the fragrance of it even then so delicious, that it would have vexed a man who smelled it to abstain from tasting it; but whoever tasted it, it was able to raise his courage to the height of heroic deeds.

Taking with them a goatskin flagon full of this precious liquor, they ventured into the recesses of the cave. Here they pleased themselves a whole day with beholding the giant's kitchen, where the flesh of sheep and goats lay strewed, his dairy where goat-milk stood ranged in troughs and pails, his pens where he kept his live animals; but those he had driven forth to pasture with him when he went out in the morning. While they were feasting their eyes with a sight of these curiosities, their ears were suddenly deafened with a noise like the falling of a house. It was the owner of the cave who had been abroad all day feeding his flock, as his custom was, in the mountains, and now drove them home in the evening from pasture. He threw down a pile of fire-wood, which he had been gathering against supper-time, before the mouth of the cave, which occasioned the crash they heard. The Grecians hid themselves in the remote parts of the cave, at sight of the uncouth monster. It was Polyphemus, the largest and savagest of the Cyclops, who boasted himself to be the son of Neptune. He looked more like a mountain crag than a man, and to his brutal body he had a brutish mind answerable. He drove his flock, all that gave milk, to the interior of the cave, but left the rams and the he-goats without. Then taking up a stone so massy that twenty oxen could not have drawn it, he placed it at the mouth of the cave, to defend the entrance, and sat him down to milk his ewes and his goats; which done, he lastly kindled a fire, and throwing his great eye round the cave (for the Cyclops have no more than one eye, and that placed in the midst of their forehead), by the glimmering light he discerned some of Ulysses' men.

"Ho, guests, what are you? merchants or wandering thieves?" he bellowed out in a voice which took from them all power of reply, it was so astounding.

Only Ulysses summoned resolution to answer, that they came neither for plunder nor traffic, but were Grecians who had lost their way, returning from Troy;

which famous city, under the conduct of Agamemnon, the renowned son of Atreus, they had sacked, and laid level with the ground. Yet now they prostrated themselves humbly before his feet, whom they acknowledged to be mightier than they, and besought him that he would bestow the rites of hospitality upon them, for that Jove was the avenger of wrongs done to strangers, and would fiercely resent any injury which they might suffer.

"Fool," said the Cyclop, "to come so far to preach to me the fear of the gods. We Cyclops care not for your Jove, whom you fable to be nursed by a goat, nor any of your blessed ones. We are stronger than they, and dare bid open battle to Jove himself, though you and all your fellows of the earth join with him." And he bade them tell him where their ship was, in which they came, and whether they had any companions. But Ulysses, with a wise caution, made answer, that they had no ship or companions, but were unfortunate men whom the sea, splitting their ship in pieces, had dashed upon his coast, and they alone had escaped. He replied nothing, but gripping two of the nearest of them, as if they had been no more than children, he dashed their brains out against the earth, and (shocking to relate) tore in pieces their limbs, and devoured them, yet warm and trembling, making a lion's meal of them, lapping the blood: for the Cyclops are *man-eaters*, and esteem human flesh to be a delicacy far above goat's or kid's; though by reason of their abhorred customs few men approach their coast except some stragglers, or now and then a shipwrecked mariner. At a sight so horrid Ulysses and his men were like distracted people. He, when he had made an end of his wicked supper, drained a draught of goat's milk down his prodigious throat, and lay down and slept among his goats. Then Ulysses drew his sword, and half resolved to thrust it with all his might in at the bosom of the sleeping monster; but wiser thoughts restrained him, else they had there without help all perished, for none but Polyphemus himself could have removed that mass of stone which he had placed to guard the entrance. So they were constrained to abide all that night in fear.

When day came the Cyclop awoke, and kindling a fire, made his breakfast of two other of his unfortunate prisoners, then milked his goats as he was accustomed, and pushing aside the vast stone, and shutting it again when he had done, upon the prisoners, with as much ease as a man opens and shuts a quiver's lid, he let out his flock, and drove them before him with whistlings (as sharp as winds in storms) to the mountains.

Then Ulysses, of whose strength or cunning the Cyclop seems to have had as little heed as of an infant's, being left alone, with the remnant of his men which the Cyclop had not devoured, gave manifest proof how far manly wisdom excels brutish force. He chose a stake from among the wood which the Cyclop had piled up for firing, in length and thickness like a mast, which he sharpened and hardened in the fire, and selected four men, and instructed them what they should do with this stake, and made them perfect in their parts.

When the evening was come, the Cyclop drove home his sheep; and as fortune directed it, either of purpose, or that his memory was overruled by the gods to his hurt (as in the issue it proved), he drove the males of his flock, contrary to his custom, along with the dams into the pens. Then shutting-to the stone of the cave, he fell to his horrible supper. When he had despatched two more of the Grecians, Ulysses waxed bold with the contemplation of his project, and took a bowl of Greek wine, and merrily dared the Cyclop to drink.

"Cyclop," he said, "take a bowl of wine from the hand of your guest; it may serve to digest the man's flesh that you have eaten, and show what drink our ship held before it went down. All I ask in recompense, if you find it good, is to be dismissed in a whole skin. Truly you must look to have few visitors, if you observe this new custom of eating your guests."

The brute took and drank, and vehemently enjoyed

the taste of wine, which was new to him, and swilled again at the flagon, and entreated for more, and prayed Ulysses to tell him his name, that he might bestow a gift upon the man who had given him such brave liquor. The Cyclops (he said) had grapes, but this rich juice (he swore) was simply divine. Again Ulysses plied him with the wine, and the fool drank it as fast as he poured out, and again he asked the name of his benefactor, which Ulysses cunningly dissembling, said: "My name is Noman; my kindred and friends in my own country call me Noman." "Then," said the Cyclop, "this is the kindness I will show thee, Noman; I will eat thee last of all thy friends." He had scarce expressed his savage kindness when the fumes of the strong wine overcame him, and he reeled down upon the floor and sank into a dead sleep.

Ulysses watched his time, while the monster lay insensible, and heartening up his men, they placed the sharp end of the stake in the fire till it was heated red-hot, and some god gave them a courage beyond that which they were used to have, and the four men with difficulty bored the sharp end of the huge stake, which they had heated red-hot, right into the eye of the drunken cannibal, and Ulysses helped to thrust it in with all his might, still farther and farther, with effort, as men bore with an augur, till the scalded blood gushed out, and the eye-ball smoked, and the strings of the eye cracked, as the burning rafter broke in it, and the eye hissed, as hot iron hisses when it is plunged into water.

He waking, roared with the pain so loud that all the cavern broke into claps like thunder. They fled, and dispersed into corners. He plucked the burning stake from his eye, and hurled the wood madly about the cave. Then he cried out with a mighty voice for his brethren the Cyclops, that dwelt hard by in caverns upon hills; they hearing the terrible shout came flocking from all parts to inquire what ailed Polyphemus? and what cause he had for making such horrid clamours in the night-time to break their sleeps? if his fright proceeded from any mortal? if strength or craft had given him his death's blow? He made answer from within that Noman had hurt him, Noman had killed him, Noman was with him in the cave. They replied, "If no man has hurt thee, and no man is with thee, then thou art alone, and the evil that afflicts thee is from the hand of heaven, which none can resist or help." So they left him and went their way, thinking that some disease troubled him. He, blind and ready to split with the anguish of the pain, went groaning up and down in the dark, to find the doorway, which when he found, he removed the stone, and sat in the threshold, feeling if he could lay hold on any man going out with the sheep, which (the day now breaking) were beginning to issue forth to their accustomed pastures. But Ulysses, whose first artifice in giving himself that ambiguous name, had succeeded so well with the Cyclop, was not of a wit so gross to be caught by that palpable device. But casting about in his mind all the ways which he could contrive for escape (no less than all their lives depending on the success), at last he thought of this expedient. He made knots of the osier twigs upon which the Cyclop commonly slept, with which he tied the fattest and fleeciest of the rams together, three in a rank, and under the belly of the middle ram he tied a man, and himself last, wrapping himself fast with both his hands in the rich wool of one, the fairest of the flock.

And now the sheep began to issue forth very fast; the males went first, the females unmilked stood by, bleating and requiring the hand of their shepherd in vain to milk them, their full bags sore with being unemptied, but he much sorer with the loss of sight. Still as the males passed, he felt the backs of those fleecy fools, never dreaming that they carried his enemies under their bellies: so they passed on till the last ram came loaded with his wool and Ulysses together. He stopped that ram and felt him, and had his hand once in the hair of Ulysses, yet knew it not, and he chid the ram for being last, and spoke to it as if it understood him, and asked it whether it did not wish that its master had his eye again, which that abominable Noman with his execrable rout had put out, when they had got him down with wine; and he willed the ram to tell him whereabouts in the cave his enemy lurked, that he might dash his brains and strew them about, to ease his heart of that tormenting revenge which rankled in it. After a deal of such foolish talk to the beast he let it go.

When Ulysses found himself free, he let go his hold, and assisted in disengaging his friends. The rams which had befriended them they carried off with them to the ships, where their companions with tears in their eyes received them, as men escaped from death. They plied their oars, and set their sails, and when they were got as far off from shore as a voice would reach, Ulysses cried out to the Cyclop: "Cyclop, thou should'st not have so much abused thy monstrous strength, as to devour thy guests. Jove by my hand sends thee requital to pay thy savage inhumanity." The Cyclop heard, and came forth enraged, and in his anger he plucked a fragment of a rock, and threw it with blind fury at the ships: it narrowly escaped lighting upon the bark in which Ulysses sat, but with the fall it raised so fierce an ebb, as bore back the ship till it almost touched the shore. "Cyclop," said Ulysses, "if any ask thee who imposed on thee that unsightly blemish in thine eye, say it was Ulysses, son of Laertes: the king of Ithaca am I called, the waster of cities." Then they crowded sail, and beat the old sea, and forth they went with a forward gale; sad for forepast losses, yet glad to have escaped at any rate; till they came to the isle where Æolus reigned, who is god of the winds.

Here Ulysses and his men were courteously received by the monarch, who showed him his twelve children which have rule over the twelve winds. A month they stayed and feasted with him, and at the end of the month he dismissed them with many presents, and gave to Ulysses at parting an ox's hide, in which were enclosed *all the winds:* only he left abroad the western wind, to play upon their sails and waft them gently home to Ithaca. This bag, bound in a glittering silver band, so close that no breath could escape, Ulysses hung up at the mast. His companions did not know its contents, but guessed that the monarch had given to him some treasures of gold or silver.

Nine days they sailed smoothly, favoured by the western wind, and by the tenth they approached so nigh as to discern lights kindled on the shores of their country earth; when, by ill fortune, Ulysses, overcome with fatigue of watching the helm, fell asleep. The mariners seized the opportunity, and one of them said to the rest: "A fine time has this leader of ours: wherever he goes he is sure of presents, when we come away empty-handed; and see, what king Æolus has given him, store no doubt of gold and silver." A word was enough to those covetous wretches, who quick as thought untied the bag, and instead of gold, out rushed with mighty noise *all the winds.* Ulysses with the noise awoke and saw their mistake, but too late, for the ship was driving with all the winds back far from Ithaca, far as to the island of Æolus from which they had parted, in one hour measuring back what in nine days they had scarcely tracked, and in sight of home too! Up he flew amazed, and raving doubted whether he should not fling himself into the sea for grief of his bitter disappointment. At last he hid himself under the hatches for shame. And scarce could he be prevailed upon, when he was told he was arrived again in the harbour of king Æolus, to go himself or send to that monarch for a second succour; so much the disgrace of having misused his royal bounty (though it was the crime of his followers and not his own) weighed upon him: and when at last he went, and took a herald with him, and came where the god sat on his throne, feasting with his children, he would not trust in among them at their meat, but set himself down like one unworthy in the threshold.

Indignation seized Æolus to behold him in that manner returned; and he said: "Ulysses, what has brought you back? are you so soon tired of your country? or did not our present please you? we thought we had given you a kingly passport." Ulysses made answer: "My men have done this ill mischief to me: they did it while I slept." "Wretch," said Æolus, "avaunt, and quit our shores: it fits not us to convoy men whom the gods hate, and will have perish."

Forth they sailed, but with far different hopes than when they left the same harbour the first time with all the winds confined, only the west-wind suffered to play upon their sails to waft them in gentle murmurs to Ithaca. They were now the sport of every gale that blew, and despaired of ever seeing home more. Now those covetous mariners were cured of their surfeit for gold, and would not have touched it if it had lain in untold heaps before them.

Six days and nights they drove along, and on the seventh day they put in to Lamos, a port of the Læstrygonians. So spacious this harbour was, that it held with ease all their fleet, which rode at anchor, safe from any storms, all but the ship in which Ulysses was embarked. He, as if prophetic of the mischance which followed, kept still without the harbour, making fast his bark to a rock at the land's point, which he climbed with purpose to survey the country. He saw a city with smoke ascending from the roofs, but neither ploughs going, nor oxen yoked, nor any sign of agricultural works. Making choice of two men, he sent them to the city to explore what sort of inhabitants dwelt there. His messengers had not gone far before they met a damsel, of stature surpassing human, who was coming to draw water from a spring. They asked her who dwelt in that land. She made no reply, but led them in silence to her father's palace. He was a monarch and named Antiphas. He and all his people were giants. When they entered the palace, a woman, the mother of the damsel, but far taller than she, rushed abroad and called for Antiphas. He came, and snatching up one of the two men, made as if he would devour him. The other fled. Antiphas raised a mighty shout, and instantly, this way and that, multitudes of gigantic people issued out at the gates, and making for the harbour, tore up huge pieces of the rocks, and flung them at the ships which lay there, all which they utterly overwhelmed and sank; and the unfortunate bodies of men which floated, and which the sea did not devour, these cannibals thrust through with harpoons, like fishes, and bore them off to their dire feast. Ulysses with his single bark that had never entered the harbour escaped; that bark which was now the only vessel left of all the gallant navy that had set sail with him from Troy. He pushed off from the shore, cheering the sad remnant of his men, whom horror at the sight of their countrymen's fate had almost turned to marble.

Chapter II.

The house of Circe—Men changed into beasts—The voyage to hell—The banquet of the dead.

On went the single ship till it came to the island of Æea, where Circe the dreadful daughter of the Sun dwelt. She was deeply skilled in magic, a haughty beauty, and had hair like the Sun. The Sun was her parent, and begot her and her brother Æetes (such another as herself) upon Perse, daughter to Oceanus.

Here a dispute arose among Ulysses' men, which of them should go ashore and explore the country; for there was a necessity that some should go to procure water and provisions, their stock of both being nigh spent: but their hearts failed them when they called to mind the shocking fate of their fellows whom the Læstrygonians had eaten, and those which the foul Cyclop Polyphemus had crushed between his jaws; which moved them so tenderly in the recollection that they wept. But tears never yet supplied any man's wants; this Ulysses knew full well, and dividing his men (all that were left) into two companies, at the head of one of which was himself, and at the head of the other Eurylochus, a man of tried courage, he cast lots which of them should go up into the country, and the lot fell upon Eurylochus and his company, two and twenty in number; who took their leave, with tears, of Ulysses and his men that stayed, whose eyes wore the same wet badges of weak humanity, for they surely thought never to see these their companions again, but that on every coast where they should come, they should find nothing but savages and cannibals.

Eurylochus and his party proceeded up the country, till in a dale they descried the house of Circe, built of bright stone, by the road's side. Before her gate lay many beasts, as wolves, lions, leopards, which, by her art, of wild she had rendered tame. These arose when they saw strangers, and ramped upon their hinder paws, and fawned upon Eurylochus and his men, who dreaded the effects of such monstrous kindness; and staying at the gate they heard the enchantress within, sitting at her loom, singing such strains as suspended all mortal faculties, while she wove a web, subtle and glorious, and of texture inimitable on earth, as all the housewiferies of the deities are. Strains so ravishingly sweet, provoked even the sagest and prudentest heads among the party to knock and call at the gate. The shining gate the enchantress opened, and bade them come in and feast. They unwise followed, all but Eurylochus, who stayed without the gate, suspicious that some train was laid for them. Being entered, she placed them in chairs of state, and set before them meal and honey, and Smyrna wine; but mixed with baneful drugs of powerful enchantment. When they had eaten of these, and drunk of her cup, she touched them with her charming-rod, and straight they were transformed into swine, having the bodies of swine, the bristles, and snout, and grunting noise of that animal; only they still retained the minds of men, which made them the more to lament their brutish transformation. Having changed them, she shut them up in her sty with many more whom her wicked sorceries had formerly changed, and gave them swine's food, mast, and acorns, and chestnuts, to eat.

Eurylochus, who beheld nothing of these sad changes from where he was stationed without the gate, only instead of his companions that entered (who he thought had all vanished by witchcraft) beheld a herd of swine, hurried back to the ship, to give an account of what he had seen: but so frightened and perplexed, that he could give no distinct report of anything, only he remembered a palace, and a woman singing at her work, and gates guarded by lions. But his companions, he said, were all vanished.

Then Ulysses suspecting some foul witchcraft, snatched his sword, and his bow, and commanded Eurylochus instantly to lead him to the place. But Eurylochus fell down, and embracing his knees, besought him by the name of a man whom the gods had in their protection, not to expose his safety, and the safety of them all, to certain destruction.

"Do thou then stay, Eurylochus!" answered Ulysses: "eat thou and drink in the ship in safety; while I go alone upon this adventure: necessity, from whose law is no appeal, compels me."

So saying he quitted the ship and went on shore, accompanied by none; none had the hardihood to offer to partake that perilous adventure with him, so much they dreaded the enchantments of the witch. Singly he pursued his journey till he came to the shining gates which stood before her mansion: but when he essayed to put his foot over her threshold, he was suddenly stopped by the apparition of a young man, bearing a golden rod in his hand, who was the god Mercury. He held Ulysses by the wrist, to stay his entrance; and "Whither wouldest thou go?" he said; "O, thou most erring of the sons of men! knowest thou not that this is the house of great Circe, where she keeps thy friends in a loathsome sty, changed from the fair forms of men into the detestable and ugly shapes of swine? art thou prepared to share their fate, from which nothing can ransom thee?" But neither his words, nor his coming from heaven, could stop the daring foot of Ulysses, whom compassion for the misfortune of his friends had rendered careless of danger: which when the god perceived, he had pity to see valour so misplaced, and gave him the flower of the herb *moly*, which is sovereign against enchantments. The moly is a small unsightly root, its virtues but little known, and in low estimation; the dull shepherd treads on it every day with his clouted shoes; but it bears a small white flower, which is medicinal against charms, blights, mildews, and damps.—"Take this in thy hand," said Mercury, "and with it boldly enter her gates: when she shall strike thee with her rod, thinking to change thee, as she has changed thy friends, boldly rush in upon her with thy sword, and extort from her the dreadful oath of the gods, that she will use no enchantments against thee: then force her to restore thy abused companions." He gave Ulysses the little white flower, and instructing him how to use it, vanished.

When the god was departed, Ulysses with loud knockings beat at the gate of the palace. The shining gates were opened, as before, and great Circe with hospitable cheer invited in her guest. She placed him on a throne with more distinction than she had used to his fellows, she mingled wine in a costly bowl, and he drank of it, mixed with those poisonous drugs. When he had drunk, she struck him with her charming-rod, and "To your sty," she cried; "out, swine; mingle with your companions." But those powerful words were not proof against the preservative which Mercury had given to Ulysses; he remained unchanged, and as the god had directed him, boldly charged the witch with his sword, as if he meant to take her life: which when she saw, and perceived that her charms were weak against the antidote which Ulysses bore about him, she cried out and bent her knees beneath his sword, embracing his, and said, "Who or what manner of man art thou? Never drank any man before thee of this cup, but he repented it in some brute's form. Thy shape remains unaltered as thy mind. Thou canst be none other than Ulysses, renowned above all the world for wisdom, whom the fates have long since decreed that I must love. This haughty bosom bends to thee. O Ithacan, a goddess woos thee to her bed."

"O Circe," he replied, "how canst thou treat of love or marriage with one whose friends thou hast turned into beasts? and now offerest him thy hand in wedlock, only that thou mightest have him in thy power, to live the life of a beast with thee, naked, effeminate, subject to thy will, perhaps to be advanced in time to the honour of a place in thy sty. What pleasure canst thou promise, which may tempt the soul of a reasonable man? thy meats, spiced with poison; or thy wines, drugged with death? Thou must swear to me, that thou wilt never attempt against me the treasons which thou hast practised upon my friends." The enchantress, won by the terror of his threats, or by the violence of that new love which she felt kindling in her veins for him, swore by Styx, the great oath of the gods, that she meditated no injury to him. Then Ulysses made show of gentler treatment, which gave her hopes of inspiring him with a passion equal to that which she felt. She called her handmaids, four that served her in chief, who were daughters to her silver fountains, to her sacred rivers, and to her consecrated woods, to deck her apartments, to spread rich carpets, and set out her silver tables with dishes of the purest gold, and meat as precious as that which the gods eat, to entertain her guest. One brought water to wash his feet, and one brought wine to chase away, with a refreshing sweetness, the sorrows that had come of late so thick upon him and hurt his noble mind. They strewed perfumes on his head, and after he had bathed in a bath of the choicest aromatics, they brought him rich and costly apparel to put on. Then he was conducted to a throne of massive silver, and a regale, fit for Jove when he banquets, was placed before him. But the feast which Ulysses desired was to see his friends (the partners of his voyage) once more in the shapes of men; and the food which could give him nourishment must be taken in at his eyes. Because he missed this sight, he sat melancholy and thoughtful, and would taste of none of the rich delicacies placed before him. Which when Circe noted, she easily divined the cause of his sadness, and leaving the seat in which she sat throned, went to her sty, and led abroad his men, who came in like swine, and filled the ample hall, where Ulysses sat, with gruntings. Hardly had he time to let his sad eye run over their altered forms and brutal metamorphosis, when with an ointment which she smeared over them, suddenly their bristles fell off, and they started up in their own shapes men as before. They knew their leader again, and clung about him with joy of their late restoration, and some shame for their late change; and wept so loud, blubbering out their joy in broken accents, that the palace was filled with a sound of pleasing mourning, and the witch herself, great Circe, was not unmoved at the sight. To make her atonement complete, she sent for the remnant of Ulysses' men who stayed behind at the ship, giving up their great commander for lost; who when they came, and saw him again alive, circled with their fellows, no expression can tell what joy they felt; they even cried out with rapture, and to have seen their frantic expressions of mirth, a man might have supposed that they were just in sight of their country earth, the cliffs of rocky Ithaca. Only Eurylochus would hardly be persuaded to enter that palace of wonders, for he remembered with a kind of horror how his companions had vanished from his sight.

Then great Circe spake, and gave order, that there should be no more sadness among them, nor remembering of past sufferings. For as yet they fared like men that are exiles from their country, and if a gleam of mirth shot among them, it was suddenly quenched with the thought of their helpless and homeless condition. Her kind persuasions wrought upon Ulysses and the rest, that they spent twelve months in all manner of delight with her in her palace. For Circe was a powerful magician, and could command the moon from her sphere, or unroot the solid oak from its place to make it dance for their diversion, and by the help of her illusions she could vary the taste of pleasures, and contrive delights, recreations, and jolly pastimes, to "fetch the day about from sun to sun, and rock the tedious year as in a delightful dream."

At length Ulysses awoke from the trance of the faculties into which her charms had thrown him, and the thought of home returned with tenfold vigour to goad and sting him; that home where he had left his virtuous wife Penelope, and his young son Telemachus. One day when Circe had been lavish of her caresses, and was in her kindest humour, he moved to her subtly, and as it were afar off, the question of his home-return; to which she answered firmly, "O Ulysses, it is not in my power to detain one whom the gods have destined to further trials. But leaving me, before you pursue your journey home, you must visit the house of Hades, or Death, to consult the shade of Tiresias the Theban prophet; to whom alone, of all the dead, Proserpine, queen of hell, has committed the secret of future events: it is he that must inform you whether you shall ever see again your wife and country." "O Circe," he cried; "that is impossible: who shall steer my course to Pluto's kingdom? Never ship had strength to make that voyage." "Seek no guide," she replied; "but raise you your mast, and hoist your white sails, and sit in your ship in peace: the north wind shall waft you through the seas, till you shall cross the expanse of the ocean, and come to where grow the poplar groves, and willows pale, of Proserpine : where Pyriphlegethon and Cocytus and Acheron mingle their waves. Cocytus is an arm of Styx, the forgetful river. Here dig a pit, and make it a cubit broad and a cubit long, and pour in milk, and honey, and wine, and the blood of a ram, and the blood of a black ewe, and turn away thy face while thou pourest in, and the dead shall come flocking to taste the milk and the blood; but suffer none to approach thy offering till thou hast inquired of Tiresias all which thou wishest to know."

He did as great Circe had appointed. He raised his mast, and hoisted his white sails, and sat in his ship in peace. The north wind wafted him through the seas, till he crossed the ocean, and came to the sacred woods of Proserpine. He stood at the confluence of the three floods, and digged a pit, as she had given directions, and poured in his offering; the blood of a ram, and the blood of a black ewe, milk, and honey, and wine; and the dead came to his banquet : aged men, and women, and youths, and children who died in infancy. But none of them would he suffer to approach, and dip their thin lips in the offering, till Tiresias was served, not though his own mother was among the number, whom now for the first time he knew to be dead, for he had left her living when he went to Troy, and she had died since his departure, and the tidings never reached him : though it irked his soul to use constraint upon her, yet in compliance with the injunction of great Circe, he forced her to retire along with the other ghosts. Then Tiresias, who bore a golden sceptre, came and lapped of the offering, and immediately he knew Ulysses, and began to prophecy: *he denounced woe to Ulysses, woe, woe, and many sufferings, through the anger of Neptune for the putting out of the eye of the sea-god's son. Yet there was safety after suffering, if they could abstain from slaughtering the oxen of the Sun after they landed in the Triangular island. For Ulysses, the gods had destined him from a king to become a beggar, and to perish by his own guests, unless he slew those who knew him not.*

This prophecy, ambiguously delivered, was all that Tiresias was empowered to unfold, or else there was no longer place for him; for now the souls of the other dead came flocking in such numbers, tumultuously demanding the blood, that freezing horror seized the limbs of the living Ulysses, to see so many, and all dead, and he the only one alive in that region. Now his mother came and lapped the blood, without restraint from her son, and now she knew him to be her son, and inquired of him why he had come alive to their comfortless habitations. And she said, that affliction for Ulysses' long absence had preyed upon her spirits, and brought her to the grave.

Ulysses' soul melted at her moving narration, and forgetting the state of the dead, and that the airy texture of disembodied spirits does not admit of the embraces of flesh and blood, he threw his arms about her to clasp her: the poor ghost melted from his embrace, and looking mournfully upon him vanished away.

Then saw he other females.—Tyro, who when she lived was the paramour of Neptune, and by him had Pelias and Neleus. Antiope, who bore two like sons to Jove, Amphion and Zethus, founders of Thebes. Alcmena, the mother of Hercules, with her fair daughter, afterwards her daughter-in-law, Megara. There also Ulysses saw Jocasta, the unfortunate mother and wife of Œdipus; who ignorant of kin wedded with her son, and when she had discovered the unnatural alliance, for shame and grief hanged herself. He continued to drag a wretched life above the earth, haunted by the dreadful Furies.—There was Leda, the wife of Tyndarus, the mother of the beautiful Helen, and of the two brave brothers, Castor and Pollux, who obtained this grace from Jove, that being dead, they should enjoy life alternately, living in pleasant places under the earth. For Pollux had prayed that his brother Castor, who was subject to death, as the son of Tyndarus, should partake of his own immortality, which he derived from an immortal sire: this the Fates denied; therefore Pollux was permitted to divide his immortality with his brother Castor, dying and living alternately.—There was Iphimedeia, who bore two sons to Neptune that were giants, Otus and Ephialtes: Earth in her prodigality never nourished bodies to such portentous size and beauty as these two children were of, except Orion. At nine years old they had imaginations of climbing to heaven to see what the gods were doing; they thought to make stairs of mountains, and were for piling Ossa upon Olympus, and setting Pelion upon that, and had perhaps performed it, if they had lived till they were striplings; but they were cut off by death in the infancy of their ambitious project.—Phædra was there, and Procris, and Ariadne, mournful for Theseus' desertion, and Mæra, and Clymene, and Eryphile, who preferred gold before wedlock faith.

But now came a mournful ghost, that late was Agamemnon, son of Atreus, the mighty leader of all the host of Greece and their confederate kings that warred against Troy. He came with the rest to sip a little of the blood at that uncomfortable banquet. Ulysses was moved with compassion to see him among them, and asked him what untimely fate had brought him there, if storms had overwhelmed him coming from Troy, or if he had perished in some mutiny by his own soldiers at a division of the prey.

"By none of these," he replied, "did I come to my death, but slain at a banquet to which I was invited by Ægisthus after my return home. He conspiring with my adulterous wife, they laid a scheme for my destruction, training me forth to a banquet as an ox goes to the slaughter, and there surrounding me they slew me with all my friends about me.

"Clytemnestra, my wicked wife, forgetting the vows which she swore to me in wedlock, would not lend a hand to close my eyes in death. But nothing is so heaped with impieties as such a woman, who would kill her spouse that married her a maid. When I brought her home to my house a bride, I hoped in my heart that she would be loving to me and to my children. Now, her black treacheries have cast a foul aspersion on her whole sex. Blest husbands will have their loving wives in suspicion for her bad deeds."

"Alas!" said Ulysses, "there seems to be a fatality in your royal house of Atreus, and that they are hated of Jove for their wives. For Helen's sake, your brother Menelaus' wife, what multitudes fell in the wars of Troy!"

Agamemnon replied, "For this cause be not thou more kind than wise to any woman. Let not thy words express to her at any time all that is in thy mind, keep still some secrets to thyself. But thou by any bloody contrivances of thy wife never need'st fear to fall. Exceeding wise she is, and to her wisdom she has a goodness as eminent: Icarius' daughter, Penelope the chaste: we left her a young bride when we parted from our wives to go to the wars, her first child suckling at her breast, the young Telemachus, whom you shall see grown up to manhood on your return, and he shall greet his father with befitting welcomes. My Orestes, my dear son, I shall never see again. His mother has deprived his father of the sight of him, and perhaps will slay him as she slew his sire. It is now no world to trust a woman in.—But what says fame? is my son yet alive? lives he in Orchomen, or in Pylus, or is he resident in Sparta, in his uncle's court? as yet, I see, divine Orestes is not here with me."

To this Ulysses replied that he had received no certain tidings where Orestes abode, only some uncertain rumours which he could not report for truth.

While they held this sad conference, with kind tears striving to render unkind fortunes more palatable, the soul of great Achilles joined them. "What desperate adventure has brought Ulysses to these regions," said Achilles, "to see the end of dead men and their foolish shades?"

Ulysses answered him that he had come to consult Tiresias respecting his voyage home. "But thou, O son of Thetis," said he, "why dost thou disparage the state of the dead? seeing that as alive thou didst surpass all men in glory, thou must needs retain thy pre-eminence here below: so great Achilles triumphs over death."

But Achilles made reply that he had much rather be a peasant-slave upon the earth than reign over all the dead: So much did the inactivity and slothful condition of that state displease his unquenchable and restless spirit. Only he inquired of Ulysses if his father Peleus were living, and how his son Neoptolemus conducted himself.

Of Peleus Ulysses could tell him nothing: but of Neoptolemus he thus bore witness: "From Scyros I convoyed your son by sea to the Greeks, where I can speak of him, for I knew him. He was chief in council and in the field. When any question was proposed, so quick was his conceit in the forward apprehension of any case, that he ever spoke first, and was heard with more attention than the older heads. Only myself and aged Nestor could compare with him in giving advice. In battle I cannot speak his praise, unless I could count all that fell by his sword. I will only mention one instance of his manhood. When we sat hid in the belly of the wooden horse, in the ambush which deceived the Trojans to their destruction, I, who had the management of that stratagem, still shifted my place from side to side to note the behaviour of our men. In some I marked their hearts trembling, through all the pains which they took to appear valiant, and in others tears, that in spite of manly courage would gush forth. And to say truth, it was an adventure of high enterprise, and as perilous a stake as was ever played in war's game. But in him I could not observe the least sign of weakness, no tears nor tremblings, but his hand still on his good sword, and ever urging me to set open the machine and let us out before the time was come for doing it; and when we sallied out he was still first in that fierce destruction and bloody midnight desolation of King Priam's city."

This made the soul of Achilles to tread a swifter pace, with high-raised feet, as he vanished away, for the joy which he took in his son being applauded by Ulysses.

A sad shade stalked by, which Ulysses knew to be the ghost of Ajax, his opponent, when living, in that famous dispute about the right of succeeding to the arms of the deceased Achilles. They being adjudged by the Greeks to Ulysses, as the prize of wisdom above bodily strength, the noble Ajax in despite went mad, and slew himself. The sight of his rival turned to a shade by his dispute, so subdued the passion of emulation in Ulysses, that for his sake he wished that judgment in that controversy had been given against himself, rather than so illustrious a chief should have perished for the desire of those arms, which his prowess (second only to Achilles in fight) so eminently had deserved. "Ajax," he cried, "all the Greeks mourn for thee as much as they lamented for Achilles. Let not thy wrath burn for ever, great son of Telamon. Ulysses seeks peace with thee, and will make any atonement to thee that can appease thy hurt spirit." But the shade stalked on, and would not exchange a word with Ulysses, though he prayed it with many tears and many earnest entreaties. "He might have spoke to me," said Ulysses, "since I spoke to him; but I see the resentments of the dead are eternal."

Then Ulysses saw a throne, on which was placed a judge distributing sentence. He that sat on the throne was Minos, and he was dealing out just judgments to the dead. He it is that assigns them their place in bliss or woe.

Then came by a thundering ghost, the large-limbed Orion, the mighty hunter, who was hunting there the ghosts of the beasts which he had slaughtered in desert hills upon the earth; for the dead delight in the occupations which pleased them in the time of their living upon the earth.

There was Tityus suffering eternal pains because he had sought to violate the honour of Latona as she passed from Pytho into Panopeus. Two vultures sat perpetually preying upon his liver with their crooked beaks, which as fast as they devoured is for ever renewed; nor can he fray them away with his great hands.

There was Tantalus, plagued for his great sins, standing up to the chin in water, which he can never taste, but still as he bows his head, thinking to quench his burning thirst, instead of water he licks up unsavoury dust. All fruits pleasant to the sight, and of delicious flavour, hang in ripe clusters about his head, seeming as though they offered themselves to be plucked by him; but when he reaches out his hand, some wind carries them far out of his sight into the clouds, so he is starved in the midst of plenty by the righteous doom of Jove, in memory of that inhuman banquet at which the sun turned pale, when the unnatural father served up the limbs of his little son in a dish, as meat for his divine guests.

There was Sisyphus, that sees no end to his labours. His punishment is, to be for ever rolling up a vast stone to the top of a mountain, which when it gets to the top, falls down with a crushing weight, and all his work is to be begun again. He was bathed all over in sweat, that reeked out a smoke which covered his head like a mist. His crime had been the revealing of state secrets.

There Ulysses saw Hercules: not that Hercules who enjoys immortal life in heaven among the gods, and is married to Hebe or Youth, but his shadow which remains below. About him the dead flocked as thick as bats, hovering around, and cuffing at his head: he stands with his dreadful bow, ever in the act to shoot.

There also might Ulysses have seen and spoken with the shades of Theseus, and Pirithous, and the old heroes; but he had conversed enough with horrors, therefore, covering his face with his hands, that he might see no more spectres, he resumed his seat in his ship, and pushed off. The barque moved of itself without the help of any oar, and soon brought him out of the regions of death into the cheerful quarters of the living, and to the island of Æea, whence he had set forth.

Chapter III.

The song of the Sirens—Scylla and Charybdis—The oxen of the Sun—The judgment—The crew killed by lightning.

"Unhappy man, who at thy birth wast appointed twice to die! others shall die once: but thou, besides that death that remains for thee, common to all men, hast in thy lifetime visited the shades of death. Thee Scylla, thee Charybdis, expect. Thee the deathful Sirens lie in wait for, that taint the minds of whoever listen to them with their sweet singing. Whosoever shall but hear the call of any Siren, he will so despise both wife and children through their sorceries, that the stream of his affection never again shall set homewards, nor shall he take joy in wife or children thereafter, or they in him."

With these prophetic greetings great Circe met Ulysses on his return. He besought her to instruct him in the nature of the Sirens, and by what method their baneful allurements were to be resisted.

"They are sisters three," she replied, "that sit in a mead (by which your ship must needs pass) circled with dead men's bones. These are the bones of men whom they have slain, after with fawning invitements they have enticed them into their fen. Yet such is the celestial harmony of their voice accompanying the persuasive magic of their words, that knowing this, you shall not be able to withstand their enticements. Therefore when you are to sail by them, you shall stop the ears of your companions with wax, that they may hear no note of that dangerous music; but for yourself, that you may hear, and yet live, give them strict command to bind you hand and foot to the mast, and in no case to set you free, till you are out of the danger of the temptation, though you should entreat it, and implore it ever so much, but to bind you rather the more for your requesting to be loosed. So shall you escape that snare."

Ulysses then prayed her that she would inform him what Scylla and Charybdis were, which she had taught him by name to fear. She replied: "Sailing from Æea to Trinacria, you must pass at an equal distance between two fatal rocks. Incline never so little either to the one side or the other, and your ship must meet with certain destruction. No vessel ever yet tried that pass without being lost, but the Argo, which owed her safety to the sacred freight she bore, the fleece of the golden-backed ram, which could not perish. The biggest of these rocks which you shall come to, Scylla hath in charge. There, in a deep whirlpool at the foot of the rock, the abhorred monster shrouds her face; who if she were to show her full form, no eye of man or god could endure the sight; thence she stretches out all her six long necks peering and diving to suck up fish, dolphins, dog-fish, and whales, whole ships, and their men, whatever comes within her raging gulf. The other rock is lesser, and of less ominous aspect; but there dreadful Charybdis sits, supping the black deeps. Thrice a day she drinks her pits dry, and thrice a day again she belches them all up: but when she is drinking, come not nigh, for being once caught, the force of Neptune cannot redeem you from her swallow. Better trust to Scylla, for she will but have for her six necks, six men: Charybdis in her insatiate draught will ask all."

Then Ulysses inquired, in case he should escape Charybdis, whether he might not assail that other monster with his sword: to which she replied that he must not think that he had an enemy subject to death, or wounds, to contend with: for Scylla could never die. Therefore, his best safety was in flight, and to invoke none of the gods but Cratis, who is Scylla's mother, and might perhaps forbid her daughter to devour them. For his conduct after he arrived at Trinacria she referred him to the admonitions which had been given him by Tiresias.

Ulysses having communicated her instructions, as far as related to the Sirens, to his companions, who had not been present at that interview; but concealing from them the rest, as he had done the terrible predictions of Tiresias, that they might not be deterred by fear from pursuing their voyage: the time for departure being come, they set their sails, and took a final leave of great Circe; who by her art calmed the heavens, and gave them smooth seas, and a right fore wind (the seaman's friend) to bear them on their way to Ithaca.

They had not sailed past a hundred leagues before the breeze which Circe had lent them suddenly stopped. It was stricken dead. All the sea lay in prostrate slumber. Not a gasp of air could be felt. The ship stood still. Ulysses guessed that the island of the Sirens was not far off, and that they had charmed the air so with their devilish singing. Therefore he made him cakes of wax, as Circe had instructed him, and stopped the ears of his men with them: then causing himself to be bound hand and foot, he commanded the rowers to ply their oars and row as fast as speed could carry them past that fatal shore. They soon came within sight of the Sirens, who sang in Ulysses' hearing:

> Come here, thou, worthy of a world of praise,
> That dost so high the Grecian glory raise;
> Ulysses! stay thy ship; and that song hear
> That none pass'd ever, but it bent his ear,
> But left him ravish'd, and instructed more
> By us, than any, ever heard before.
> For we know all things, whatsoever were
> In wide Troy labour'd: whatsoever there
> The Grecians and the Trojans both sustain'd:
> By those high issues that the gods ordain'd:
> And whatsoever all the earth can show
> To inform a knowledge of desert, we know.

These were the words, but the celestial harmony of the voices which sang them no tongue can describe: it took the ear of Ulysses with ravishment. He would have broke his bonds to rush after them; and threatened, wept, sued, entreated, commanded, crying out with tears and passionate imprecations, conjuring his men by all the ties of perils past which they had endured in common, by fellowship and love, and the authority which he retained among them, to let him loose; but at no rate would they obey him. And still the Sirens sang. Ulysses made signs, motions, gestures, promising mountains of gold if they would set him free; but their oars only moved faster. And still the Sirens sung. And still the more he adjured them to set him free, the faster with cords and ropes they bound him; till they were quite out of hearing of the Sirens' notes, whose effect great Circe had so truly predicted. And well she might speak of them, for often she had joined her own enchanting voice to theirs, while she has sat in the flowery meads, mingled with the Sirens and the Water Nymphs, gathering their potent herbs and drugs of magic quality: their singing altogether has made the gods stoop, and "heaven drowsy with the harmony."

Escaped that peril, they had not sailed yet an hundred leagues farther, when they heard a roar afar off, which Ulysses knew to be the barking of Scylla's dogs, which surround her waist, and bark incessantly. Coming nearer they beheld a smoke ascend, with a horrid murmur, which arose from that other whirlpool, to which they made nigher approaches than to Scylla. Through the furious eddy, which is in that place, the ship stood still as a stone, for there was no man to lend his hand to an oar, the dismal roar of Scylla's dogs at a distance, and the nearer clamours of Charybdis, where everything made an echo, quite taking from them the power of exertion. Ulysses went up and down encouraging his men, one by one, giving them good words, telling them that they were in greater perils when they were blocked up in the Cyclop's cave, yet, heaven assisting his counsels, he had delivered them out of that extremity. That he could not believe but they remembered it; and wished them to give the same trust to the same care which he had now for their welfare. That they must exert all the strength and wit which they had, and try if Jove would not grant them an escape even out of this peril. In particular he cheered up the pilot who sat at the helm, and told him that he must show more firmness than other men, as he had more trust committed to him, and had the sole management by his skill of the vessel in which all their safeties were embarked. That a rock lay hid within those boiling whirlpools which he saw, on the outside of which he must steer, if he would avoid his own destruction, and the destruction of them all.

They heard him, and like men took to the oars; but little knew what opposite danger, in shunning that rock, they must be thrown upon. For Ulysses had concealed from them the wounds, never to be healed, which Scylla was to open: their terror would else have robbed them all of all care to steer, or move an oar, and have made them hide under the hatches for fear of seeing her, where he and they must have died an idle death. But even then he forgot the precautions which Circe had given him to prevent harm to his person; who had willed him not to arm, or show himself once to Scylla: but disdaining not to venture life for his brave companions, he could not contain, but armed in all points, and taking a lance in either hand, he went up to the fore deck, and looked when Scylla would appear.

She did not show herself as yet, and still the vessel steered closer by her rock, as it sought to shun that other more dreaded: for they saw how horribly Charybdis' black throat drew into her all the whirling deep, which she disgorged again, that all about her boiled like a kettle, and the rock roared with troubled waters; which when she supped in again, all the bottom turned up, and disclosed far under shore the swart sands naked, whose whole stern sight frayed the startled blood from their faces, and made Ulysses turn his to view the wonder of whirlpools. Which when Scylla saw, from out her black den, she darted out her six long necks, and swoopt up as many of his friends: whose cries Ulysses heard, and saw them too late, with their heels turned up, and their hands thrown to him for succour, who had been their help in all extremities, but could not deliver them now; and he heard them shriek out, as she tore them, and to the last they continued to throw their hands out to him for sweet life. In all his sufferings he never had beheld a sight so full of miseries.

Escaped from Scylla and Charybdis, but with a diminished crew, Ulysses, and the sad remains of his followers, reached the Trinacrian shore. Here landing, he beheld oxen grazing of such surpassing size and beauty, that both from them, and from the shape of the island (having three promontories jutting into the sea) he judged rightly that he was come to the Triangular island, and the oxen of the Sun, of which Tiresias had forewarned him.

So great was his terror lest through his own fault, or that of his men, any violence or profanation should be offered to the holy oxen, that even then, tired as they were with the perils and fatigues of the day past, and unable to stir an oar, or use any exertion, and though night was fast coming on, he would have them re-embark immediately, and make the best of their way from that dangerous station; but his men with one voice resolutely opposed it, and even the too cautious Eurylochus himself withstood the proposal; so much did the temptation of a little ease and refreshment (ease tenfold sweet after such labours) prevail over the sagest counsels, and the apprehension of certain evil outweigh the prospect of contingent danger. They expostulated, that the nerves of Ulysses seemed to be made of steel, and his limbs not liable to lassitude like other men's; that waking or sleeping seemed indifferent to him; but that they were men, not gods, and felt the common appetites for food and sleep. That in the night-time all the winds most destructive to ships are generated. That black night still required to be served with meat, and sleep, and quiet havens and ease. That the best sacrifice to the sea was in the morning. With such sailor-like sayings and mutinous arguments, which the majority have always ready to justify disobedience to their betters, they forced Ulysses to comply with their requisition, and against his will to take up his night-quarters on shore. But he first exacted from them an oath that they would neither maim nor kill any of the cattle which they saw grazing, but content themselves with such food as Circe had stowed their vessel with when they parted from Æea. This they man by man severally promised, imprecating the heaviest curses on whoever should break it; and mooring their bark within a creek, they went to supper, contenting themselves that night with such food as Circe had given them, not without many sad thoughts of their friends whom Scylla had devoured, the grief of which kept them great part of the night waking.

In the morning Ulysses urged them again to a religious observance of the oath that they had sworn, not in any case to attempt the blood of those fair herds which they saw grazing, but to content themselves with the ship's food; for the god who owned those cattle sees and hears all.

They faithfully obeyed, and remained in that good mind for a month, during which they were confined to that station by contrary winds, till all the wine and the bread were gone, which they had brought with them. When their victuals were gone, necessity compelled them to stray in quest of whatever fish or fowl they could snare, which that coast did not yield in any great abundance. Then Ulysses prayed to all the gods that dwelt in bountiful heaven, that they would be pleased to yield them some means to stay their hunger without having recourse to profane and forbidden violations: but the ears of heaven seemed to be shut, or some god incensed plotted his ruin; for at mid-day, when he should chiefly have been vigilant and watchful to prevent mischief, a deep sleep fell upon the eyes of Ulysses, during which he lay totally insensible of all that passed in the world, and what his friends or what his enemies might do, for his welfare or destruction. Then Eurylochus took his advantage. He was the man of most authority with them after Ulysses. He represented to them all the misery of their condition; how that every death is hateful and grievous to mortality, but that of all deaths famine is attended with the most painful, loathsome, and humiliating circumstances; that the subsistence which they could hope to draw from fowling or fishing was too precarious to be depended upon; that there did not seem to be any chance of the winds changing to favour their escape, but that they must inevitably stay there and perish, if they let an irrational superstition deter them from the means which nature offered to their hands; that Ulysses might be deceived in his belief that these oxen had any sacred qualities above other oxen; and even admitting that they were the property of the god of the Sun, as he said they were, the Sun did neither eat nor drink, and the gods were best served not by a scrupulous conscience, but by a thankful heart, which took freely what they as freely offered: with these and such-like persuasions he prevailed on his half-famished and half-mutinous companions, to begin the impious violation of their oath by the slaughter of seven of the fairest of these oxen which were grazing. Part they roasted and eat, and part they offered in sacrifice to the gods, particularly to Apollo, god of the Sun, vowing to build a temple to his godhead, when they should arrive in Ithaca, and deck it with magnificent and numerous gifts: Vain men! and superstition worse than that which they so lately derided! to imagine that prospective penitence can excuse a present violation of duty, and that the pure natures of the heavenly powers will admit of compromise or dispensation for sin.

But to their feast they fell, dividing the roasted portions of the flesh, savoury and pleasant meat to them, but a sad sight to the eyes and a savour of death in the nostrils of the waking Ulysses; who just woke in time to witness, but not soon enough to prevent, their rash and sacrilegious banquet. He had scarce time to ask what great mischief was this which they had done unto him; when behold, a prodigy! the ox-hides which they had stripped began to creep, as if they had life; and the roasted flesh bellowed as the ox used to do when he was living. The hair of Ulysses stood up on end with affright at these omens; but his companions, like men whom the gods had infatuated to their destruction, persisted in their horrible banquet.

The Sun from its burning chariot saw how Ulysses' men had slain his oxen, and he cried to his father Jove: "Revenge me upon these impious men who have slain my oxen, which it did me good to look upon when I walked my heavenly round. In all my daily course I never saw such bright and beautiful creatures as those my oxen were." The father promised that ample retribution should be taken of those accursed men: which was fulfilled shortly after, when they took their leaves of the fatal island.

Six days they feasted in spite of the signs of heaven, and on the seventh, the wind changing, they set their sails and left the island; and their hearts were cheerful with the banquets they had held; all but the heart of Ulysses, which sank within him, as with wet eyes he beheld his friends, and gave them for lost, as men devoted to divine vengeance. Which soon overtook them: for they had not gone many leagues before a dreadful tempest arose, which burst their cables; down came their mast, crushing the scull of the pilot in its fall; off he fell from the stern into the water, and the bark wanting his management drove along at the wind's mercy: thunders roared, and terrible lightnings of Jove came down; first a bolt struck Eurylochus, then another, and then another, till all the crew were killed, and their bodies swam about like sea-mews; and the ship was split in pieces: only

Ulysses survived; and he had no hope of safety but in tying himself to the mast, where he sat riding upon the waves, like one that in no extremity would yield to fortune. Nine days was he floating about with all the motions of the sea, with no other support than the slender mast under him, till the tenth night cast him, all spent and weary with toil upon the friendly shores of the island Ogygia.

Chapter IV.

The Island of Calypso—Immortality refused.

HENCEFORTH the adventures of the single Ulysses must be pursued. Of all those faithful partakers of his toil, who with him left Asia, laden with the spoils of Troy, now not one remains, but all a prey to the remorseless waves, and food for some great fish; their gallant navy reduced to one ship, and that finally swallowed up and lost. Where now are all their anxious thoughts of home? that perseverance with which they went through the severest sufferings and the hardest labours to which poor seafarers were ever exposed, that their toils at last might be crowned with the sight of their native shores and wives at Ithaca!—Ulysses is now in the isle Ogygia; called the Delightful Island. The poor shipwrecked chief, the slave of all the elements, is once again raised by the caprice of fortune into a shadow of prosperity. He that was cast naked upon the shore, bereft of all his companions, has now a goddess to attend upon him, and his companions are the nymphs which never die.—Who has not heard of Calypso? her grove crowned with alders and poplars? her grotto, against which the luxuriant vine laid forth his purple grapes? her ever new delights, crystal fountains, running brooks, meadows flowering with sweet balm-gentle and with violet: blue violets which like veins enamelled the smooth breasts of each fragrant mead! It were useless to describe over again what has been so well told already: or to relate those soft arts of courtship which the goddess used to detain Ulysses; the same in kind which she afterwards practised upon his less wary son, whom Minerva, in the shape of Mentor, hardly preserved from her snares, when they came to the Delightful Island together in search of the scarce departed Ulysses.

A memorable example of married love, and a worthy instance how dear to every good man his country is, was exhibited by Ulysses. If Circe loved him sincerely, Calypso loves him with tenfold more warmth and passion: she can deny him nothing but his departure; she offers him everything, even to a participation of her immortality; if he will stay and share in her pleasures he shall never die. But death with glory has greater charms for a mind heroic than a life that shall never die with shame; and when he pledged his vows to his Penelope, he reserved no stipulation that he would forsake her whenever a goddess should think him worthy of her bed, but they had sworn to live and grow old together: and he would not survive her if he could, nor meanly share in immortality itself, from which she was excluded.

These thoughts kept him pensive and melancholy in the midst of pleasure. His heart was on the seas, making voyages to Ithaca. Twelve months had worn away, when Minerva from heaven saw her favourite, how he sat still pining on the sea shores (his daily custom), wishing for a ship to carry him home. She (who is wisdom herself) was indignant that so wise and brave a man as Ulysses should be held in effeminate bondage by an unworthy goddess: and at her request, her father Jove ordered Mercury to go down to the earth to command Calypso to dismiss her guest. The divine messenger tied fast to his feet his winged shoes, which bear him over land and seas, and took in his hand his golden rod, the ensign of his authority. Then wheeling in many an airy round, he stayed not till he alighted on the firm top of the mountain Pieria: thence he fetched a second circuit over the seas, kissing the waves in his flight with his feet, as light as any sea-mew fishing dips her wings, till he touched the isle Ogygia, and soared up from the blue sea to the grotto of the goddess, to whom his errand was ordained.

His message struck a horror, checked by love, through all the faculties of Calypso. She replied to it, incensed: "You gods are insatiate, past all that live, in all things which you affect; which makes you so envious and grudging. It afflicts you to the heart, when any goddess seeks the love of a mortal man in marriage, though you yourselves without scruple link yourselves to women of the earth. So it fared with you, when the delicious-fingered Morning shared Orion's bed; you could never satisfy your hate and your jealousy till you had incensed the chastity-loving dame, Diana, *who leads the precise life*, to come upon him by stealth in Ortygia, and pierce him through with her arrows. And when rich-haired Ceres gave the reins to her affections, and took Iasion (well worthy) to her arms, the secret was not so cunningly kept but Jove had soon notice of it, and the poor mortal paid for his felicity with death, struck through with lightnings. And now you envy me the possession of a wretched man, whom tempests have cast upon my shores, making him lawfully mine; whose ship Jove rent in pieces with his hot thunderbolts, killing all his friends. Him I have preserved, loved, nourished, made him mine by protection, my creature, by every tie of gratitude mine; have vowed to make him deathless like myself; him you will take from me. But I know your power, and that it is vain for me to resist. Tell your king that I obey his mandates."

With an ill grace Calypso promised to fulfil the commands of Jove; and, Mercury departing, she went to find Ulysses, where he sat outside the grotto, not knowing of the heavenly message, drowned in discontent, not seeing any human probability of his ever returning home.

She said to him: "Unhappy man, no longer afflict yourself with pining after your country, but build you a ship, with which you may return home; since it is the will of the gods: who, doubtless, as they are greater in power than I, are greater in skill, and best can tell what is fittest for man. But I call the gods and my inward conscience, to witness, that I had no thought but what stood with thy safety, nor would have done or counselled anything against thy good. I persuaded thee to nothing which I should not have followed myself in thy extremity: for my mind is innocent and simple. O, if thou knewest what dreadful sufferings thou must yet endure before ever thou reachest thy native land, thou wouldest not esteem so hardly of a goddess' offer to share her immortality with thee; nor, for a few years' enjoyment of a perishing Penelope, refuse an imperishable and never-dying life with Calypso."

He replied: "Ever-honoured, great Calypso, let it not displease thee, that I, a mortal man, desire to see and converse again with a wife that is mortal; human objects are best fitted to human infirmities. I well know how far in wisdom, in feature, in stature, proportion, beauty, in all the gifts of the mind, thou exceedest my Penelope: she a mortal, and subject to decay; thou immortal, ever growing, yet never old; yet in her sight all my desires terminate, all my wishes; in the sight of her, and of my country earth. If any god, envious of my return, shall lay his dreadful hand upon me as I pass the seas, I submit; for the same powers have given me a mind not to sink under oppression. In wars and waves my sufferings have not been small."

She heard his pleaded reasons, and of force she must assent; so to her nymphs she gave in charge from her sacred woods to cut down timber, to make Ulysses a ship. They obeyed, though in a work unsuitable to their soft fingers, yet to obedience no sacrifice is hard: and Ulysses busily bestirred himself, labouring far more hard than they, as was fitting, till twenty tall trees, driest and fittest for timber, were felled. Then like a skilful shipwright he fell to joining the planks, using the plane, the axe, and the augur, with such expedition, that in four days' time a ship was made, complete with all her decks, hatches, side-boards, yards. Calypso added linen for the sails, and tackling; and when she was finished, she was a goodly vessel for a man to sail in alone, or in company, over the wide seas. By the fifth morning she was launched; and Ulysses, furnished with store of provisions, rich garments, and gold and silver, given him by Calypso, took a last leave of her, and of her nymphs and of the isle Ogygia which had so befriended him.

Chapter V.

The tempest—The sea-bird's gift—The escape by swimming—The sleep in the woods.

At the stern of his solitary ship Ulysses sat and steered right artfully. No sleep could seize his eyelids. He beheld the Pleiads, the Bear which is by some called the Wain, that moves round about Orion, and keeps still above the ocean, and the slow-setting sign Bootes, which some name the Waggoner. Seventeen days he held his course, and on the eighteenth the coast of Phæacia was in sight. The figure of the land, as seen from the sea, was pretty and circular, and looked something like a shield.

Neptune returning from visiting his favourite Æthiopians, from the mountains of the Solymi, descried Ulysses ploughing the waves, his domain. The sight of the man he so much hated for Polyphemus' sake, his son, whose eye Ulysses had put out, set the god's heart on fire, and snatching into his hand his horrid sea-sceptre, the trident of his power, he smote the air and the sea, and conjured up all his black storms, calling down night from the cope of heaven and taking the earth into the sea, as it seemed, with clouds, through the darkness and indistinctness which prevailed, the billows rolling up before the fury of all the winds that contended together in their mighty sport.

Then the knees of Ulysses bent with fear, and then all his spirit was spent, and he wished that he had been among the number of his countrymen who fell before Troy, and had their funerals celebrated by all the Greeks, rather than to perish thus, where no man could mourn him or know him.

As he thought these melancholy thoughts, a huge wave took him and washed him overboard, ship and all upset amidst the billows, he struggling afar off, clinging to her stern broken off which he yet held, her mast cracking in two with the fury of that gust of mixed winds that struck it, sails and sail-yards fell into the deep, and he himself was long drowned under water, nor could get his head above, wave so met with wave, as if they strove which should depress him most, and the gorgeous garments given him by Calypso clung about him, and hindered his swimming; yet neither for this, nor for the overthrow of his ship, nor his own perilous condition, would he give up his drenched vessel, but, wrestling with Neptune, got at length hold of her again, and then sat in her bulk, insulting over death, which he had escaped, and the salt waves which he gave the sea again to give to other men: his ship, striving to live, floated at random, cuffed from wave to wave, hurled to and fro by all the winds; now Boreas tossed it to Notus, Notus passed it to Eurus, and Eurus to the west wind, who kept up the horrid tennis.

Them in their mad sport Ino Leucothea beheld; Ino Leucothea, now a sea-goddess, but once a mortal and the daughter of Cadmus; she with pity beheld Ulysses the mark of their fierce contention, and rising from the waves alighted on the ship, in shape like to the sea-bird which is called a cormorant, and in her beak she held a wonderful girdle made of sea-weeds which grow at the bottom of

K

the ocean, which she dropped at his feet, and the bird spake to Ulysses and counselled him not to trust any more to that fatal vessel against which god Neptune had levelled his furious wrath, nor to those ill-befriending garments which Calypso had given him, but to quit both it and them, and trust for his safety to swimming. "And here," said the seeming bird, "take this girdle and tie about your middle, which has virtue to protect the wearer at sea, and you shall safely reach the shore; but when you have landed cast it far from you back into the sea." He did as the sea-bird instructed him, he stripped himself naked, and fastening the wondrous girdle about his middle, cast himself into the seas to swim. The bird dived past his sight into the fathomless abyss of the ocean.

Two days and two nights he spent in struggling with the waves, though sore buffeted and almost spent, never giving up himself for lost, such confidence he had in that charm which he wore about his middle, and in the words of that divine bird. But the third morning the winds grew calm, and all the heavens were clear. Then he saw himself nigh land, which he knew to be the coast of the Phæacians, a people good to strangers, and abounding in ships, by whose favour he doubted not that he should soon obtain a passage to his own country. And such joy he conceived in his heart, as good sons have that esteem their father's life dear, when long sickness has held him down to his bed, and wasted his body, and they see at length health return to the old man, with restored strength and spirits, in reward of their many prayers to the gods for his safety: so precious was the prospect of home-return to Ulysses, that he might restore health to his country (his better parent), that had long languished as full of distempers in his absence. And then for his own safety's sake he had joy to see the shores, the woods, so nigh and within his grasp as they seemed, and he laboured with all the might of hands and feet to reach with swimming that nigh-seeming land.

But when he approached near, a horrid sound of a huge sea beating against rocks informed him that here was no place for landing, nor any harbour for man's resort, but through the weeds and the foam which the sea belched up against the land he could dimly discover the rugged shore all bristled with flints, and all that part of the coast one impending rock that seemed impossible to climb, and the water all about so deep, that not a sand was there for any tired foot to rest upon, and every moment he feared lest some wave more cruel than the rest should crush him against a cliff, rendering worse than vain all his landing: and should he swim to seek a more commodious haven farther on, he was fearful lest, weak and spent as he was, the winds would force him back a long way off into the main, where the terrible god Neptune, for wrath that he had so nearly escaped his power, having gotten him again into his domain, would send out some great whale (of which those seas breed a horrid number) to swallow him up alive; with such malignity he still pursued him.

While these thoughts distracted him with diversity of dangers, one bigger wave drove against a sharp rock his naked body, which it gashed and tore, and wanted little of breaking all his bones, so rude was the shock. But in this extremity she prompted him that never failed him at need. Minerva (who is wisdom itself) put it into his thoughts no longer to keep swimming off and on, as one dallying with danger, but boldly to force the shore that threatened him, and to hug the rock that had torn him so rudely; which with both hands he clasped, wrestling with extremity, till the rage of that billow which had driven him upon it was past; but then again the rock drove back that wave so furiously, that it reft him of his hold, sucking him with it in his return, and the sharp rock (his cruel friend) to which he clinged for succour, rent the flesh so sore from his hands in parting, that he fell off, and could sustain no longer: quite under water he fell, and past the help of fate, there had the hapless

Ulysses lost all portion that he had in this life, if Minerva had not prompted his wisdom in that peril to essay another course, and to explore some other shelter, ceasing to attempt that landing-place.

She guided his wearied and nigh-exhausted limbs to the mouth of the fair river Calliroe, which not far from thence disbursed its watery tribute to the ocean. Here the shores were easy and accessible, and the rocks, which rather adorned than defended its banks, so smooth, that they seemed polished of purpose to invite the landing of our sea-wanderer, and to atone for the uncourteous treatment which those less hospitable cliffs had afforded him. And the god of the river, as if in pity, stayed his current and smoothed his waters, to make his landing more easy; for sacred to the ever-living deities of the fresh waters, be they mountain-stream, river, or lake, is the cry of erring mortals that seek their aid, by reason that being inland-bred they partake more of the gentle humanities of our nature than those marine deities, whom Neptune trains up in tempests in the unpitying recesses of his salt abyss.

So by the favour of the river's god Ulysses crept to land half-drowned; both his knees faltering, his strong hands falling down through weakness from the excessive toils he had endured, his cheek and nostrils flowing with froth of the sea-brine, much of which he had swallowed in that conflict, voice and breath spent, down he sank as in death. Dead weary he was. It seemed that the sea had soaked through his heart, and the pains he felt in all his veins were little less than those which one feels that has endured the torture of the rack. But when his spirits came a little to themselves, and his recollection by degrees began to return, he rose up, and unloosing from his waist the girdle or charm which that divine bird had given him, and remembering the charge which he had received with it, he flung it far from him into the river. Back it swam with the course of the ebbing stream till it reached the sea, where the fair hands of Ino Leucothea received it to keep it as a pledge of safety to any future shipwrecked mariner that like Ulysses should wander in those perilous waves.

Then he kissed the humble earth in token of safety, and on he went by the side of that pleasant river till he came where a thicker shade of rushes that grew on its banks seemed to point out the place where he might rest his sea-wearied limbs. And here a fresh perplexity divided his mind, whether he should pass the night, which was coming on, in that place, where, though he feared no other enemies, the damps and frosts of the chill sea-air in that exposed situation might be death to him in his weak state; or whether he had better climb the next hill, and pierce the depth of some shady wood, in which he might find a warm and sheltered though insecure repose, subject to the approach of any wild beast that roamed that way. Best did this last course appear to him, though with some danger, as that which was more honourable and savoured more of strife and self-exertion, than to perish without a struggle the passive victim of cold and the elements.

So he bent his course to the nearest woods, where, entering in, he found a thicket, mostly of wild olives and such low trees, yet growing so intertwined and knit together that the moist wind had not leave to play through their branches, nor the sun's scorching beams to pierce their recesses, nor any shower to beat through, they grew so thick and as it were folded each in the other; here creeping in, he made his bed of the leaves which were beginning to fall, of which was such abundance that two or three men might have spread them ample coverings, such as might shield them from the winter's rage, though the air breathed steel and blew as it would burst. Here creeping in, he heaped up store of leaves all about him, as a man would billets upon a winter fire, and lay down in the midst. Rich seed of virtue lying hid in poor leaves! Here Minerva soon gave him sound sleep; and here all his long toils past seemed to be concluded and shut up within the little sphere of his refreshed and closed eyelids.

Chapter VI.

The princess Nausicaa—The washing—The game with the ball—The Court of Phæacia and king Alcinous.

MEANTIME Minerva, designing an interview between the king's daughter of that country and Ulysses when he should awake, went by night to the palace of king Alcinous, and stood at the bedside of the princess Nausicaa in the shape of one of her favourite attendants, and thus addressed the sleeping princess.

"Nausicaa, why do you lie sleeping here, and never bestow a thought upon your bridal ornaments, of which you have many and beautiful, laid up in your wardrobe against the day of your marriage, which cannot be far distant; when you shall have need of all, not only to deck your own person, but to give away in presents to the virgins that honouring you shall attend you to the temple? Your reputation stands much upon the timely care of these things; these things are they which fill father and reverend mother with delight. Let us arise betimes to wash your fair vestments of linen and silks in the river; and request your sire to lend you mules and a coach, for your wardrobe is heavy, and the place where we must wash is distant, and besides it fits not a great princess like you to go so far on foot."

So saying she went away, and Nausicaa awoke, full of pleasing thoughts of her marriage, which the dream had told her was not far distant: and as soon as it was dawn, she arose and dressed herself and went to find her parents.

The queen her mother was already up, and seated among her maids, spinning at her wheel, as the fashion was in those primitive times, when great ladies did not disdain housewifery; and the king her father was preparing to go abroad at that early hour to council with his grave senate.

"My father," she said, "will you not order mules and a coach to be got ready, that I may go and wash, I and my maids, at the cisterns that stand without the city?"

"What washing does my daughter speak of?" said Alcinous.

"Mine and my brothers' garments," she replied, "that have contracted soil by this time with lying by so long in the wardrobe. Five sons have you, that are my brothers; two of them are married, and three are bachelors; these last it concerns to have their garments neat and unsoiled; it may advance their fortunes in marriage: and who but I their sister should have a care of these things? You yourself, my father, have need of the whitest apparel, when you go, as now, to the council."

She used this plea, modestly dissembling her care of her own nuptials to her father; who was not displeased at this instance of his daughter's discretion: for a seasonable care about marriage may be permitted to a young maiden, provided it to be accompanied with modesty and dutiful submission to her parents in the choice of her future husband: and there was no fear of Nausicaa choosing wrongly or improperly, for she was as wise as she was beautiful, and the best in all Phæacia were suitors to her for her love. So Alcinous readily gave consent that she should go, ordering mules and a coach to be prepared. And Nausicaa brought from her chamber all her vestments, and laid them up in the coach, and her mother placed bread and wine in the coach, and oil in a golden cruse, to soften the bright skins of Nausicaa and her maids when they came out of the river.

Nausicaa making her maids get up into the coach with her, lashed the mules, till they brought her to the cisterns which stood a little on the outside of the town, and were supplied with water from the river Calliroe.

There her attendants unyoked the mules, took out the clothes, and steeped them in the cisterns, washing them in several waters, and afterwards treading them clean with their feet, venturing wagers who should have done soonest and cleanest, and using many pretty pastimes to beguile their labour as young maids use, while the princess looked on. When they had laid their clothes to dry, they fell to playing again, and Nausicaa joined them in a game with the ball, which is used in that country, which is performed by tossing the ball from hand to hand with great expedition, she who begins the pastime singing a song. It chanced that the princess, whose turn it became to toss the ball, sent it so far from its mark, that it fell beyond into one of the cisterns of the river: at which the whole company, in merry consternation, set up a shriek so loud as waked the sleeping Ulysses, who was taking his rest, after his long toils, in the woods not far distant from the place where these young maids had come to wash.

At the sound of female voices Ulysses crept forth from his retirement, making himself a covering with boughs and leaves as well as he could to shroud his nakedness. The sudden appearance of his weather-beaten and almost naked form so frighted the maidens that they scudded away into the woods and all about to hide themselves, only Minerva (who had brought about this interview to admirable purposes, by seemingly accidental means) put courage into the breast of Nausicaa, and she stayed where she was, and resolved to know what manner of man he was, and what was the occasion of his strange coming to them.

He not venturing (for delicacy) to approach and clasp her knees, as suppliants should, but standing far off, addressed this speech to the young princess.

"Before I presume rudely to press my petitions, I should first ask whether I am addressing a mortal woman, or one of the goddesses. If a goddess, you seem to me to be likest to Diana, the chaste huntress, the daughter of Jove. Like hers are your lineaments, your stature, your features, and air divine."

She making answer that she was no goddess, but a mortal maid, he continued :

"If a woman, thrice blessed are both the authors of your birth, thrice blessed are your brothers, who even to rapture must have joy in your perfections, to see you grown so like a young tree, and so graceful. But most blessed of all that breathe is he that has the gift to engage your young neck in the yoke of marriage. I never saw that man that was worthy of you. I never saw man or woman that at all parts equalled you. Lately at Delos (where I touched) I saw a young palm which grew beside Apollo's temple ; it exceeded all the trees which ever I beheld for straightness and beauty : I can compare you only to that. A stupor past admiration strikes me, joined with fear, which keeps me back from approaching you, to embrace your knees. Nor is it strange ; for one of freshest and firmest spirit would falter, approaching near to so bright an object : but I am one whom a cruel habit of calamity has prepared to receive strong impressions. Twenty days the unrelenting seas have tossed me up and down coming from Ogygia, and at length cast me shipwrecked last night upon your coast. I have seen no man or woman since I landed but yourself. All that I crave is clothes, which you may spare me, and to be shown the way to some neighbouring town. The gods who have care of strangers, will requite you for these courtesies."

She, admiring to hear such complimentary words proceed out of the mouth of one whose outside looked so rough and unpromising, made answer : "Stranger, I discern neither sloth nor folly in you, and yet I see that you are poor and wretched ; from which I gather that neither wisdom nor industry can secure felicity ; only Jove bestows it upon whomsoever he pleases. He perhaps has reduced you to this plight. However, since your wanderings have brought you so near to our city, it lies in our duty to supply your wants. Clothes and what else a human hand should give to one so suppliant, and so tamed with calamity, you shall not want. We will show you our city and tell you the name of our people. This is the land of the Phæacians, of which my father Alcinous is king."

Then calling her attendants, who had dispersed on the first sight of Ulysses, she rebuked them for their fear, and said: "This man is no Cyclop, nor monster of sea or land, that you should fear him; but he seems manly, staid, and discreet, and though decayed in his outward appearance, yet he has the mind's riches,—wit and fortitude, in abundance. Show him the cisterns where he may wash him from the sea-weeds and foam that hang about him, and let him have garments that fit him out of those which we have brought with us to the cisterns."

Ulysses, retiring a little out of sight, cleansed him in the cisterns from the soil and impurities with which the rocks and waves had covered all his body, and clothing himself with befitting raiment, which the princess' attendants had given him, he presented himself in more worthy shape to Nausicaa. She admired to see what a comely personage he was, now he was dressed in all parts; she thought him some king or hero: and secretly wished that the gods would be pleased to give her such a husband.

Then causing her attendants to yoke her mules, and lay up the vestments, which the sun's heat had sufficiently dried, in the coach, she ascended with her maids, and drove off to the palace; bidding Ulysses, as she departed, keep an eye upon the coach, and to follow it on foot at some distance: which she did, because if she had suffered him to have rode in the coach with her, it might have subjected her to some misconstructions of the common people, who are always ready to vilify and censure their betters, and to suspect that charity is not always pure charity, but that love or some sinister intention lies hid under its disguise. So discreet and attentive to appearance in all her actions was this admirable princess.

Ulysses, as he entered the city, wondered to see its magnificence, its markets, buildings, temples; its walls and rampires; its trade and resort of men; its harbours for shipping, which is the strength of the Phæacian state. But when he approached the palace, and beheld its riches, the proportion of its architecture, its avenues, gardens, statues, fountains, he stood rapt in admiration, and almost forgot his own condition in surveying the flourishing estate of others: but recollecting himself, he passed on boldly into the inner apartment, where the king and queen were sitting at dinner with their peers; Nausicaa having prepared them for his approach.

To them, humbly kneeling, he made it his request, that since fortune had cast him naked upon their shores, they would take him into their protection, and grant him a conveyance by one of the ships, of which their great Phæacian state had such good store, to carry him to his own country. Having delivered his request, to grace it with more humility, he went and sat himself down upon the hearth among the ashes, as the custom was in those days when any would make a petition to the throne.

He seemed a petitioner of so great state and of so superior a deportment, that Alcinous himself arose to do him honour, and causing him to leave that abject station which he had assumed, placed him next to his throne, upon a chair of state, and thus he spake to his peers:

"Lords and counsellors of Phæacia, ye see this man, who he is we know not, that is come to us in the guise of a petitioner: he seems no mean one; but whoever he is, it is fit, since the gods have cast him upon our protection, that we grant him the rites of hospitality while he stays with us, and at his departure a ship well manned to convey so worthy a personage as he seems to be in a manner suitable to his rank, to his own country."

This counsel the peers with one consent approved; and wine and meat being set before Ulysses, he ate and drank, and gave the gods thanks who had stirred up the royal bounty of Alcinous to aid him in that extremity.

But not as yet did he reveal to the king and queen who he was, or whence he had come; only in brief terms he related his being cast upon their shores, his sleep in the woods, and his meeting with the princess Nausicaa: whose generosity, mingled with discretion, filled her parents with delight, as Ulysses in eloquent phrases adorned and commended her virtues. But Alcinous, humanely considering that the troubles which his guest had undergone required rest, as well as refreshment by food, dismissed him early in the evening to his chamber; where in a magnificent apartment Ulysses found a smoother bed, but not a sounder repose, than he had enjoyed the night before, sleeping upon leaves which he had scraped together in his necessity.

Chapter VII.

The songs of Demodocus—The convoy home—The mariners transformed to stone—The young shepherd.

WHEN it was day-light, Alcinous caused it to be proclaimed by the heralds about the town that there was come to the palace a stranger, shipwrecked on their coast, that in mien and person resembled a god; and inviting all the chief people of the city to come and do honour to the stranger.

The palace was quickly filled with guests, old and young, for whose cheer, and to grace Ulysses more, Alcinous made a kingly feast, with banquetings and music. Then Ulysses being seated at a table next the king and queen, in all men's view; after they had feasted, Alcinous ordered Demodocus, the court-singer, to be called to sing some song of the deeds of heroes, to charm the ear of his guest. Demodocus came and reached his harp, where it hung between two pillars of silver; and then the blind singer, to whom, in recompense of his lost sight, the muses had given an inward discernment, a soul and a voice to excite the hearts of men and gods to delight, began in grave and solemn strains to sing the glories of men highliest famed. He chose a poem, whose subject was the stern strife stirred up between Ulysses and great Achilles, as at a banquet sacred to the gods in dreadful language they expressed their difference; while Agamemnon sat rejoiced in soul to hear those Grecians jar: for the oracle in Pytho had told him that the period of their wars in Troy should then be, when the kings of Greece, anxious to arrive at the wished conclusion, should fall to strife, and contend which must end the war, force or stratagem.

This brave contention he expressed so to the life, in the very words which they both used in the quarrel, as brought tears into the eyes of Ulysses at the remembrance of past passages of his life, and he held his large purple weed before his face to conceal it. Then craving a cup of wine, he poured it out in secret libation to the gods, who had put into the mind of Demodocus unknowingly to do him so much honour. But when the moving poet began to tell of other occurrences where Ulysses had been present, the memory of his brave followers who had been with him in all difficulties, now swallowed up and lost in the ocean, and of those kings that had fought with him at Troy, some of whom were dead, some exiles like himself, forced itself so strongly upon his mind, that forgetful where he was, he sobbed outright with passion; which yet he restrained, but not so cunningly but Alcinous perceived it, and without taking notice of it to Ulysses, privately gave signs that Demodocus should cease from his singing.

Next followed dancing in the Phæacian fashion, when they would show respect to their guests; which was succeeded by trials of skill, games of strength, running, racing, hurling of the quoit, mock fights, hurling of the javelin, shooting with the bow; in some of which Ulysses modestly challenging his entertainers, performed such feats of strength and prowess as gave the admiring

Phæacians fresh reason to imagine that he was either some god or hero of the race of the gods.

These solemn shows and pageants in honour of his guest, king Alcinous continued for the space of many days, as if he could never be weary of showing courtesies to so worthy a stranger. In all this time he never asked him his name, nor sought to know more of him than he of his own accord disclosed: till on a day as they were seated feasting, after the feast was ended, Demodocus being called, as was the custom, to sing some grave matter, sang how Ulysses, on that night when Troy was fired, made dreadful proof of his valour, maintaining singly a combat against the whole household of Deiphobus, to which the divine expresser gave both act and passion, and breathed such a fire into Ulysses' deeds, that it inspired old death with life in the lively expressing of slaughters, and rendered life so sweet and passionate in the hearers, that all who heard felt it fleet from them in the narration: which made Ulysses even pity his own slaughterous deeds, and feel touches of remorse, to see how song can revive a dead man from the grave, yet no way can it defend a living man from death: and in imagination he underwent some part of death's horrors, and felt in his living body a taste of those dying pangs which he had dealt to others; that with the strong conceit, tears (the true interpreters of unutterable emotion) stood in his eyes.

Which, king Alcinous noting, and that this was now the second time that he had perceived him to be moved at the mention of events touching the Trojan wars, he took occasion to ask whether his guest had lost any friend or kinsman at Troy, that Demodocus' singing had brought into his mind. Then Ulysses, drying the tears with his cloak, and observing that the eyes of all the company were upon him, desirous to give them satisfaction in what he could, and thinking this a fit time to reveal his true name and destination, spake as follows:

"The courtesies which ye all have shown me, and in

particular yourself and princely daughter, O king Alcinous, demand from me that I should no longer keep you in ignorance of what or who I am; for to reserve any secret from you, who have with such openness of friendship embraced my love, would argue either a pusillanimous or an ungrateful mind in me. Know then that I am that *Ulysses*, of whom I perceive ye have heard something; who heretofore have filled the world with the renown of my policies. I am he by whose counsels, if Fame is to be believed at all, more than by the united valour of all the Grecians, Troy fell. I am that unhappy man whom the heavens and angry gods have conspired to keep an exile on the seas, wandering to seek my home which still flies from me. The land which I am in quest of is Ithaca; in whose ports some ship belonging to your navigation-famed Phæacian state may haply at some time have found a refuge from tempests. If ever you have experienced such kindness, requite it now, by granting to me, who am the king of that land, a passport to that land.

Admiration seized all the court of Alcinous to behold in their presence one of the number of those heroes who fought at Troy, whose divine story had been made known to them by songs and poems, but of the truth they had little known, or rather they had hitherto accounted those heroic exploits as fictions and exaggerations of poets; but having seen and made proof of the real Ulysses, they began to take those supposed inventions to be real verities, and the tale of Troy to be as true as it was delightful.

Then king Alcinous made answer: "Thrice fortunate ought we to esteem our lot, in having seen and conversed with a man of whom report hath spoken so loudly, but, as it seems, nothing beyond the truth. Though we could desire no felicity greater than to have you always among us, renowned Ulysses, yet your desire having been expressed so often and so deeply to return home, we can deny you nothing, though to our own loss. Our kingdom of Phæacia, as you know, is chiefly rich in shipping. In all parts of the world, where there are navigable seas, or ships can pass, our vessels will be found. You cannot name a coast to which they do not resort. Every rock and deep quicksand is known to them that lurks in the vast deep. They pass a bird in flight; and with such unerring certainty they make to their destination, that some have said they have no need of pilot or rudder, but that they move instinctively, self-directed, and know the minds of their voyagers. Thus much, that you may not fear to trust yourself in one of our Phæacian ships. To-morrow if you please you shall launch forth. To-day spend with us in feasting: who never can do enough when the gods send such visitors."

Ulysses acknowledged king Alcinous' bounty; and while these two royal personages stood interchanging courteous expressions, the heart of the princess Nausicaa was overcome; she had been gazing attentively upon her father's guest as he delivered his speech, but when he came to that part where he declared himself to be Ulysses, she blessed herself and her fortune that in relieving a poor shipwrecked mariner, as he seemed no better, she had conferred a kindness on so divine a hero as he proved: and scarce waiting till her father had done speaking, with a cheerful countenance she addressed Ulysses, bidding him be cheerful, and when he returned home, as by her father's means she trusted he would shortly, sometimes to remember to whom he owed his life, and who met him in the woods by the river Calliroe.

"Fair flower of Phæacia," he replied, "so may all the gods bless me with the strife of joys in that desired day, whenever I shall see it, as I shall always acknowledge to be indebted to your fair hand for the gift of life which I enjoy, and all the blessings which shall follow upon my home return. The gods give thee, Nausicaa, a princely husband; and from you two spring blessings to this state." So prayed Ulysses, his heart overflowing with admiration and grateful recollections of king Alcinous' daughter.

Then at the king's request he gave them a brief relation of all the adventures that had befallen him since he launched forth from Troy, during which the princess Nausicaa took great delight (as ladies are commonly taken with these kind of travellers' stories) to hear of the monster Polyphemus, of the men that devour each other in Læstrygonia, of the enchantress Circe, of Scylla, and the rest;.. to which she listened with a breathless attention, letting fall a shower of tears from her fair eyes every now and then, when Ulysses told of some more than usual distressful passage in his travels: and all the rest of his auditors, if they had before entertained a high respect for their guest, now felt their veneration increased tenfold, when they learnt from his own mouth what perils, what sufferings, what endurance, of evils beyond man's strength to support, this much-sustaining, almost heavenly man, by the greatness of his mind, and by his invincible courage, had struggled through.

The night was far spent before Ulysses had ended his narrative, and with wishful glances he cast his eyes towards the eastern parts, which the sun had begun to flecker with his first red: for on the morrow Alcinous had promised that a bark should be in readiness to convoy him to Ithaca.

In the morning a vessel well manned and appointed was waiting for him; into which the king and queen heaped presents of gold and silver, massy plate, apparel, armour, and whatsoever things of cost or rarity they judged would be most acceptable to their guest: and the sails being set, Ulysses embarking with expressions of regret took his leave of his royal entertainers, of the fair princess (who had been his first friend), and of the peers of Phæacia; who crowding down to the beach to have the last sight of their illustrious visitant, beheld the gallant ship with all her canvas spread, bounding and curveting over the waves, like a horse proud of his rider; or as if she knew that in her capacious womb's rich freightage she bore Ulysses.

L

He whose life past had been a series of disquiets, in seas among rude waves, in battles amongst ruder foes, now slept securely, forgetting all; his eyelids bound in such deep sleep, as only yielded to death; and when they reached the nearest Ithacan port by the next morning, he was still asleep. The mariners not willing to awake him, landed him softly, and laid him in a cave at the foot of an olive-tree, which made a shady recess in that narrow harbour, the haunt of almost none but the sea-nymphs, which are called Naiads; few ships before this Phæacian vessel having put into that haven, by reason of the difficulty and narrowness of the entrance. Here leaving him asleep, and disposing in safe places near him the presents with which king Alcinous had dismissed him, they departed for Phæacia; where these wretched mariners never again set foot; but just as they arrived, and thought to salute their country earth; in sight of their city's turrets, and in open view of their friends who from the harbour with shouts greeted their return; their vessel and all the mariners which were in her were turned to stone, and stood transformed and fixed in sight of the whole Phæacian city, where it yet stands, by Neptune's vindictive wrath; who resented thus highly the contempt which those Phæacians had shown in convoying home a man whom the god had destined to destruction. Whence it comes to pass that the Phæacians at this day will at no price be induced to lend their ships to strangers, or to become the carriers for other nations, so highly do they still dread the displeasure of the sea-god, while they see that terrible monument ever in sight.

When Ulysses awoke, which was not till some time after the mariners had departed, he did not at first know his country again, either that long absence had made it strange, or that Minerva (which was more likely) had cast a cloud about his eyes, that he should have greater pleasure hereafter in discovering his mistake: but like a man suddenly awaking in some desert isle, to which his sea-mates have transported him in his sleep, he looked around, and discerning no known objects, he cast his hands to heaven for pity, and complained on those ruthless men who had beguiled him with a promise of conveying him home to his country, and perfidiously left him to perish in an unknown land. But then the rich presents of gold and silver given him by Alcinous, which he saw carefully laid up in secure places near him, staggered him: which seemed not like the act of wrongful or unjust men, such as turn pirates for gain, or land helpless passengers in remote coasts to possess themselves of their goods.

While he remained in this suspense, there came up to him a young shepherd, clad in the finer sort of apparel, such as kings' sons wore in those days when princes did not disdain to tend sheep, who accosting him, was saluted again by Ulysses, who asked him what country that was, on which he had been just landed, and whether it were a part of a continent or an island. The young shepherd made show of wonder, to hear any one ask the name of that land; as country people are apt to esteem those for mainly ignorant and barbarous who do not know the names of places which are familiar to *them*, though perhaps they who ask have had no opportunities of knowing, and may have come from far countries.

"I had thought," said he, "that all people knew our land. It is rocky and barren, to be sure; but well enough: it feeds a goat or an ox well; it is not wanting neither in wine nor in wheat; it has good springs of water, some fair rivers; and wood enough, as you may see: it is called Ithaca."

Ulysses was joyed enough to find himself in his own country; but so prudently he carried his joy, that dissembling his true name and quality, he pretended to the shepherd that he was only some foreigner who by stress of weather had put into that port; and framed on the sudden a story to make it plausible, how he had come from Crete in a ship of Phæacia; when the young shepherd laughing, and taking Ulysses' hand in both his, said to him: "He must be cunning, I find, who thinks to overreach you. What, cannot you quit your wiles and your subtleties, now that you are in a state of security? must the first word with which you salute your native earth be an untruth? and think you that you are unknown?"

Ulysses looked again; and he saw, not a shepherd, but a beautiful woman, whom he immediately knew to be the goddess Minerva, that in the wars of Troy had frequently vouchsafed her sight to him; and had been with him since in perils, saving him unseen.

"Let not my ignorance offend thee, great Minerva," he cried, "or move thy displeasure, that in that shape I knew thee not; since the skill of discerning the deities is not attainable by wit or study, but hard to be hit by the wisest of mortals. To know thee truly through all thy changes is only given to those whom thou art pleased to grace. To all men thou takest all likenesses. All men in their wits think that they know thee, and that they have thee. Thou art wisdom itself. But a semblance of thee, which is false wisdom, often is taken for thee: so thy counterfeit view appears to many, but thy true presence to few: those are they which, loving thee above all, are inspired with light from thee to know thee. But this I surely know, that all the time the sons of Greece waged war against Troy, I was sundry times graced with thy appearance; but since, I have never been able to set eyes upon thee till now; but have wandered at my own discretion, to myself a blind guide, erring up and down the world, wanting thee."

Then Minerva cleared his eyes, and he knew the ground on which he stood to be Ithaca, and that cave to be the same which the people of Ithaca had in former times made sacred to the sea-nymphs, and where he himself had done sacrifices to them a thousand times; and full in his view stood Mount Nerytus with all its woods: so that now he knew for a certainty that he was arrived in his own country, and with the delight which he felt he could not forbear stooping down and kissing the soil.

Chapter VIII.

The change from a king to a beggar—Eumæus and the herdsmen—Telemachus.

NOT long did Minerva suffer him to indulge vain transports, but briefly recounting to him the events which had taken place in Ithaca during his absence, she showed him that his way to his wife and throne did not lie so open, but that before he was reinstated in the secure possession of them, he must encounter many difficulties. His palace, wanting its king, was become a resort of insolent and imperious men, the chief nobility of Ithaca and of the neighbouring isles, who, in the confidence of Ulysses being dead, came as suitors to Penelope. The queen (it was true) continued single, but was little better than a state-prisoner in the power of these men, who under a pretence of waiting her decision, occupied the king's house, rather as owners than guests, lording and domineering at their pleasure, profaning the palace, and wasting the royal substance, with their feasts and mad riots. Moreover the goddess told him how, fearing the attempts of these lawless men upon the person of his young son Telemachus, she herself had put it into the heart of the prince to go and seek his father in far countries; how in the shape of Mentor she had borne him company in his long search; which, though failing, as she meant it should fail, in its first object, had yet had this effect, that through hardships he had learned endurance, through experience he had gathered wisdom, and wherever his footsteps had been he had left such memorials of his worth, as the fame of Ulysses' son was already blown throughout the world. That it was now not many days since Telemachus had arrived in the island, to the great joy of the queen his mother, who had thought him dead, by reason of his long absence, and had begun to mourn for him with a grief equal to that which she endured for Ulysses; the goddess herself having so ordered the course of his adventures, that the time of his return should correspond with the return of Ulysses, that they might together concert measures how to repress the power and insolence of those wicked suitors. This the goddess told him; but of the particulars of his son's adventures, of his having been detained in the Delightful Island, which his father had so lately left, of Calypso, and her nymphs, and the many strange occurrences which may be read with profit and delight in the history of the prince's adventures, she forbore to tell him as yet, as judging that he would hear them with greater pleasure from the lips of his son, when he should have him in an hour of stillness and safety, when their work should be done, and none of their enemies left alive to trouble them.

Then they sat down, the goddess and Ulysses, at the foot of a wild olive-tree, consulting how they might with safety bring about his restoration. And when Ulysses revolved in his mind how that his enemies were a multitude, and he single, he began to despond, and he said, "I shall die an ill death like Agamemnon; in the threshold of my own house I shall perish, like that unfortunate monarch, slain by some one of my wife's suitors." But then again calling to mind his ancient courage, he secretly wished that Minerva would but breathe such a spirit into his bosom as she enflamed him with in the day of Troy's destruction, that he might encounter with three hundred of those impudent suitors at once, and strew the pavements of his beautiful palace with their bloods and brains.

And Minerva knew his thoughts, and she said, "I will be strongly with thee, if thou fail not to do thy part. And for a sign between us that I will perform my promise, and for a token on thy part of obedience, I must change thee, that thy person may not be known of men."

Then Ulysses bowed his head to receive the divine impression, and Minerva by her great power changed his person so that it might not be known. She changed him to appearance into a very old man, yet such a one as by his limbs and gait seemed to have been some considerable person in his time, and to retain yet some remains of his once prodigious strength. Also, instead of those rich robes in which king Alcinous had clothed him, she threw over his limbs such old and tattered rags as wandering beggars usually wear. A staff supported his steps, and a scrip hung to his back, such as travelling mendicants use, to hold the scraps which are given to them at rich men's doors. So from a king he became a beggar, as wise Tiresias had predicted to him in the shades.

To complete his humiliation, and to prove his obedience by suffering, she next directed him in this beggarly attire to go and present himself to his old herdsman Eumæus, who had the care of his swine and his cattle, and had been a faithful steward to him all the time of his absence. Then strictly charging Ulysses that he should reveal himself to no man but to his own son, whom she would send to him when she saw occasion, the goddess went her way.

The transformed Ulysses bent his course to the cottage of the herdsman, and entering in at the front court, the dogs, of which Eumæus kept many fierce ones for the protection of the cattle, flew with open mouths upon him, as those ignoble animals have oftentimes an antipathy to the sight of anything like a beggar, and would have rent him in pieces with their teeth, if Ulysses had not had the prudence to let fall his staff, which had chiefly provoked their fury, and sat himself down in a careless fashion upon the ground; but for all that some serious hurt had certainly been done to him, so raging the dogs were, had not the herdsman, whom the barking of the dogs had fetched out of the house, with shouting and with throwing of stones repressed them.

He said, when he saw Ulysses, "Old father, how near

you were to being torn in pieces by these rude dogs! I should never have forgiven myself, if through neglect of mine any hurt had happened to you. But heaven has given me so many cares to my portion, that I might well be excused for not attending to everything: while here I lie grieving and mourning for the absence of that majesty which once ruled here, and am forced to fatten his swine and his cattle for evil men, who hate him, and who wish his death; when he perhaps strays up and down the world, and has not wherewith to appease hunger, if indeed he yet lives (which is a question) and enjoys the cheerful light of the sun." This he said, little thinking that he of whom he spoke now stood before him, and that in that uncouth disguise and beggarly obscurity was present the hidden majesty of Ulysses.

Then he had his guest into the house, and set meat and drink before him; and Ulysses said, "May Jove and all the other gods requite you for the kind speeches and hospitable usage which you have shown me!"

Eumæus made answer, "My poor guest, if one in much worse plight than yourself had arrived here, it were a shame to such scanty means as I have, if I had let him depart without entertaining him to the best of my ability. Poor men, and such as have no houses of their own, are by Jove himself recommended to our care. But the cheer which we that are servants to other men have to bestow, is but sorry at most, yet freely and lovingly I give it you. Indeed there once ruled here a man, whose return the gods have set their faces against, who, if he had been suffered to reign in peace and grow old among us, would have been kind to me and mine. But he is gone; and for his sake would to God that the whole posterity of Helen might perish with her, since in her quarrel so many worthies have perished. But such as your fare is, eat it, and be welcome; such lean beasts as are food for poor herdsmen. The fattest go to feed the voracious stomachs of the queen's suitors. Shame on their unworthiness there is no day in which two or three of the noblest of the herd are not slain to support their feasts and their surfeits."

Ulysses gave good ear to his words, and as he ate his meat, he even tore it and rent it with his teeth, for mere vexation that his fat cattle should be slain to glut the appetites of those godless suitors. And he said, "What chief or what ruler is this, that thou commendest so highly, and sayest that he perished at Troy? I am but a stranger in these parts. It may be I have heard of some such in my long travels."

Eumæus answered, "Old father, never one of all the strangers that have come to our coast with news of Ulysses being alive, could gain credit with the queen or her son yet. These travellers, to get raiment or a meal, will not stick to invent any lie. Truth is not the commodity they deal in. Never did the queen get anything of them but lies. She receives all that come graciously, hears their stories, inquires all she can, but all ends in tears and dissatisfaction. But in God's name, old father, if you have got a tale, make the most on't, it may gain you a cloak or a coat from somebody to keep you warm: but for him who is the subject of it, dogs and vultures long since have torn him limb from limb, or some great fish at sea has devoured him, or he lieth with no better monument upon his bones than the sea-sand. But for me, past all the race of men, were tears created: for I never shall find so kind a royal master more; not if my father or my mother could come again and visit me from the tomb, would my eyes be so blessed, as they should be with the sight of him again, coming as from the dead. In his last rest my soul shall love him. He is not here, nor do I name him as a flatterer, but because I am thankful for his love and care which he had to me a poor man; and if I knew surely that he were past all shores that the sun shines upon, I would invoke him as a deified thing."

For this saying of Eumæus the waters stood in Ulysses' eyes, and he said, "My friend, to say and to affirm positively that he cannot be alive, is to give too much license to incredulity. For, not to speak at random, but with as much solemnity as an oath comes to, I say to you that Ulysses shall return, and whenever that day shall be, then shall you give to me a cloak and a coat; but till then, I will not receive so much as a thread of a garment, but rather go naked; for no less than the gates of hell do I hate that man, whom poverty can force to tell an untruth. Be Jove then witness to my words, that this very year, nay ere this month be fully ended, your eyes shall behold Ulysses, dealing vengeance in his own palace upon the wrongers of his wife and his son."

To give the better credence to his words, he amused Eumæus with a forged story of his life, feigning of himself that he was a Cretan born, and one that went with Idomeneus to the wars of Troy. Also he said that he knew Ulysses, and related various passages which he alleged to have happened betwixt Ulysses and himself, which were either true in the main, as having really happened between Ulysses and some other person, or were so like to truth, as corresponding with the known character and actions of Ulysses that Eumæus' incredulity was not a little shaken. Among other things he asserted that he had lately been entertained in the court of Thesprotia, where the king's son of the country had told him, that Ulysses had been there but just before him, and was gone upon a voyage to the oracle of Jove in Dodona, whence he should shortly return, and a ship would be ready by the bounty of the Thesprotians to convoy him straight to Ithaca. "And in token that what I tell you is true," said Ulysses, "if your king come not within the period which I have named, you shall have leave to give your servants commandment to take my old carcass, and throw it headlong from some steep rock into the sea, that poor men, taking example by me, may fear to lie." But Eumæus made answer that that should be small satisfaction or pleasure to him.

So while they sat discoursing in this manner, supper

was served in, and the servants of the herdsman, who had been out all day in the fields, came in to supper, and took their seats at the fire, for the night was bitter and frosty. After supper, Ulysses, who had well eaten and drunken, and was refreshed with the herdsman's good cheer, was resolved to try whether his host's hospitality would extend to the lending him a good warm mantle or rug to cover him in the night-season; and framing an artful tale for the purpose, in a merry mood, filling a cup of Greek wine, he thus began:

"I will you a story of your king Ulysses and myself. If there is ever a time when a man may have leave to tell his own stories, it is when he has drunken a little too much. Strong liquor driveth the fool, and moves even the heart of the wise, moves and impels him to sing and to dance, and break forth in pleasant laughters, and perchance to prefer a speech too which were better kept in. When the heart is open, the tongue will be stirring. But you shall hear. We led our powers to ambush once under the walls of Troy."

The herdsmen crowded about him eager to hear anything which related to their king Ulysses and the wars of Troy, and thus he went on:

"I remember Ulysses and Menelaus had the direction of that enterprise, and they were pleased to join me with them in the command. I was at that time in some repute among men, though fortune has played me a trick since, as you may perceive. But I was somebody in those times, and could do something. Be that as it may, a bitter freezing night it was, such a night as this, the air cut like steel, and the sleet gathered on our shields like crystal. There was some twenty of us that lay close crouched down among the reeds and bulrushes that grew in the moat that goes round the city. The rest of us made tolerable shift, for every man had been careful to bring with him a good cloak or mantle to wrap over his armour and keep himself warm; but I, as it chanced, had left my cloak behind me, as not expecting that the night would prove so cool, or rather I believe because I had at that time a brave suit of new armour on, which being a soldier, and having some of the soldier's vice about me, *vanity*, I was not willing should be hidden under a cloak; but I paid for my indiscretion with my sufferings, for the inclement night, and the wet of the ditch in which we lay, I was well-nigh frozen to death; and when I could endure no longer, I jogged Ulysses, who was next to me, and had a nimble ear, and make known my case to him, assuring him that I must inevitably perish. He answered in a low whisper, 'Hush, lest any Greek should hear you, and take notice of your softness.' Not a word more he said, but showed as if he had no pity for the plight I was in. But he was as considerate as he was brave, and even then, as he lay with his head reposing upon his hand, he was meditating how to relieve me, without exposing my weakness to the soldiers. At last raising up his head, he made as if he had been asleep, and said, 'Friends, I have been warned in a dream to send to the fleet to king Agamemnon for a supply, to recruit our numbers, for we are not sufficient for this enterprise;' and they believing him, one Thoas was despatched on that errand, who departing, for more speed, as Ulysses had foreseen, left his upper garment behind him, a good warm mantle, to which I succeeded, and by the help of it got through the night with credit. This shift Ulysses made for one in need, and would to heaven that I had now that strength in my limbs, which made me in those days to be accounted fit to be a leader under Ulysses! I should not then want the loan of a cloak or mantle, to wrap about me and shield my old limbs from the night-air."

The tale pleased the herdsmen; and Eumæus, who more than all the rest was gratified to hear tales of Ulysses, true or false, said, that for his story he deserved a mantle and a night's lodging, which he should have; and he spread for him a bed of goat and sheep skins by the fire; and the seeming beggar, who was indeed the true Ulysses, lay down and slept under that poor roof, in that abject disguise to which the will of Minerva had subjected him.

When morning was come, Ulysses made offer to depart, as if he were not willing to burthen his host's hospitality any longer, but said that he would go and try the humanity of the town's folk, if any there would bestow upon him a bit of bread or a cup of drink. Perhaps the queen's suitors (he said) out of their full feasts would bestow a scrap on him: for he could wait at table, if need were, and play the nimble serving-man, he could fetch wood (he said) or build a fire, prepare roast meat or boiled, mix the wine with water, or do any of those offices which recommended poor men like him to services in great men's houses.

"Alas! poor guest," said Eumæus, "you know not what you speak. What should so poor and old a man as you do at the suitors' tables? Their light minds are not given to such grave servitors. They must have youths, richly tricked out in flowing vests, with curled hair, like so many of Jove's cup-bearers, to fill out the wine to them as they sit at table, and to shift their trenchers. Their gorged insolence would but despise and make a mock at thy age. Stay here. Perhaps the queen, or Telemachus, hearing of thy arrival, may send to thee of their bounty."

As he spake these words, the steps of one crossing the front court were heard, and a noise of the dogs fawning and leaping about as for joy; by which token Eumæus guessed that it was the prince, who hearing of a traveller being arrived at Eumæus' cottage that brought tidings of his father, was come to search the truth, and Eumæus said: "It is the tread of Telemachus, the son of king Ulysses." Before he could well speak the words, the prince was at the door, whom Ulysses rising to receive, Telemachus would not suffer that so aged a man, as he appeared, should rise to do respect to him, but he courteously and reverently took him by the hand, and inclined his head to him, as if he had surely known that it was his father indeed: but Ulysses covered his eyes with his hands, that he might not show the waters which stood in them. And Telemachus said, "Is this the man who can tell us tidings of the king my father?"

"He brags himself to be a Cretan born," said Eumæus, "and that he has been a soldier and a traveller, but whether he speak the truth or not, he alone can tell. But whatsoever he has been, what he is now is apparent. Such as he appears, I give him to you; do what you will with him; his boast at present is that he is at the very best a supplicant."

"Be he what he may," said Telemachus, "I accept him at your hands. But where I should bestow him I know not, seeing that in the palace his age would not exempt him from the scorn and contempt which my mother's suitors in their light minds would be sure to fling upon him. A mercy if he escaped without blows: for they are a company of evil men, whose profession is wrongs and violence."

Ulysses answered: "Since it is free for any man to speak in presence of your greatness, I must say that my heart puts on a wolfish inclination to tear and to devour, hearing your speech, that these suitors should with such injustice rage, where you should have the rule solely. What should the cause be? do you wilfully give way to their ill manners? or has your government been such as has procured ill-will towards you from your people? or do you mistrust your kinsfolk and friends in such sort, as without trial to decline their aid? a man's kindred are they that he might trust to when extremities ran high."

Telemachus replied: "The kindred of Ulysses are few. I have no brothers to assist me in the strife. But the suitors are powerful in kindred and friends. The house of old Arcesius has had this fate from the heavens, that from old it still has been supplied with single heirs. To Arcesius Laertes only was born, from Laertes descended only Ulysses, from Ulysses I alone have sprung, whom he left so young, that from me never comfort arose to him. But the end of all rests in the hands of the gods."

Then Eumæus departing to see to some necessary business of his herds, Minerva took a woman's shape, and stood in the entry of the door, and was seen to Ulysses, but by his son she was not seen, for the presences of the gods are invisible save to those to whom they will to reveal themselves. Nevertheless the dogs which were about the door saw the goddess, and durst not bark, but went crouching and licking of the dust for fear. And giving signs to Ulysses that the time was now come in which he should make himself known to his son, by her great power she changed back his shape into the same which it was before she transformed him; and Telemachus, who saw the change, but nothing of the manner by which it was effected, only he saw the appearance of a king in the vigour of his age where but just now he had seen a worn and decrepit beggar, was struck with fear, and said, "Some god has done this house this honour," and he turned away his eyes, and would have worshipped. But his father permitted not, but said, "Look better at me; I am no deity, why put you upon me the reputation of godhead? I am no more but thy father: I am even he; I am that Ulysses, by reason of whose absence thy youth has been exposed to such wrongs from injurious men." Then kissed he his son, nor could any longer refrain those tears which he had held under such mighty restraint before, though they would ever be forcing themselves out in spite of him; but now, as if their sluices had burst, they came out like rivers, pouring upon the warm cheeks of his son. Nor yet by all these violent arguments could Telemachus be persuaded to believe that it was his father, but he said, some deity had taken that shape to mock him; for he affirmed, that it was not in the power of any man, who is sustained by mortal food, to change his shape so in a moment from age to youth: for "but now," said he, "you were all wrinkles, and were old, and now you look as the gods are pictured."

His father replied: "Admire, but fear not, and know me to be at all parts substantially thy father, who in the inner powers of his mind, and the unseen workings of a father's love to thee, answers to his outward shape and pretence! There shall no more Ulysseses come here. I am he that after twenty years' absence, and suffering a world of ill, have recovered at last the sight of my country earth. It was the will of Minerva that I should be changed as you saw me. She put me thus together; she puts together or takes to pieces whom she pleases. It is in the law of her free power to do it: sometimes to show her favourites under a cloud, and poor, and again to restore to them their ornaments. The gods raise and throw down men with ease."

Then Telemachus could hold out no longer, but he gave way now to a full belief and persuasion, of that which for joy at first he could not credit, that it was indeed his true and very father, that stood before him; and they embraced, and mingled their tears.

Then said Ulysses, "Tell me who these suitors are, what are their numbers, and how stands the queen thy mother affected to them?"

"She bears them still in expectation," said Telemachus, "which she never means to fulfil, that she will accept the hand of some one of them in second nuptials. For she fears to displease them by an absolute refusal. So from day to day she lingers them on with hope, which they are content to bear the deferring of, while they have entertainment at free cost in our palace."

Then said Ulysses, "Reckon up their numbers that we may know their strength and ours, if we having none but ourselves may hope to prevail against them."

"O father," he replied, "I have ofttimes heard of your fame for wisdom, and of the great strength of your arm, but the venturous mind which your speeches now indicate moves me even to amazement: for in no wise can it consist with wisdom or a sound mind, that two should try their strengths against a host. Nor five, or ten, or twice ten strong are these suitors, but many more by much: from Dulichium came there fifty and two, they and their servants; twice twelve crossed the seas hither from Samos; from Zacynthus twice ten; of our native Ithacans, men of chief note, are twelve who aspire to the bed and crown of Penelope; and all these under one strong roof, a fearful odds against two! My father, there is need of caution, lest the cup which your great mind so thirsts to taste of vengeance prove bitter to yourself in the drinking. And therefore it were well that we would bethink us of some one who might assist us in this undertaking."

"Thinkest thou," said his father, "if we had Minerva and the king of skies to be our friends, would their sufficiencies make strong our part; or must we look out for some further aid yet?"

"They you speak of are above the clouds," said Telemachus, "and are sound aids indeed; as powers that not only exceed human, but bear the chiefest sway among the gods themselves."

Then Ulysses gave directions to his son to go and mingle with the suitors, and in no wise to impart his secret to any, not even to the queen his mother, but to hold himself in readiness, and to have his weapons and his good armour in preparation. And he charged him, that when he himself should come to the palace, as he meant to follow shortly after and present himself in his beggar's likeness to the suitors, that whatever he should see which might grieve his heart, with what foul usage and contumelious language soever the suitors should receive his father, coming in that shape, though they should strike and drag him by the heels along the floors, that he should not stir nor make offer to oppose them, further than by mild words to expostulate with them, until Minerva from heaven should give the sign which should be the prelude to their destruction. And Telemachus promising to obey his instructions departed; and the shape of Ulysses fell to what it had been before, and he became to all outward appearance a beggar, in base and beggarly attire.

Chapter IX.

The queen's suitors—The battle of the beggars—The armour taken down—The meeting with Penelope

From the house of Eumæus the seeming beggar took his way, leaning on his staff, till he reached the palace, entering in at the hall where the suitors sat at meat. They in the pride of their feasting began to break their jests in mirthful manner, when they saw one looking so poor and so aged approach. He who expected no better entertainment was nothing moved at their behaviour, but, as became the character which he had assumed, in a suppliant posture crept by turns to every suitor, and held out his hands for some charity, with such a natural and beggar-resembling grace, that he might seem to have practised begging all his life; yet there was a sort of dignity in his most abject stoopings, that whoever had seen him, would have said, If it had pleased heaven that this poor man had been born a king, he would gracefully have filled a throne. And some pitied him, and some gave him alms, as their present humours inclined them, but the greater part reviled him, and bid him begone, as one that spoiled their feast; for the presence of misery has this power with it, that while it stays, it can dash and overturn the mirth even of those who feel no pity or wish to relieve it; nature bearing this witness of herself in the hearts of the most obdurate.

Now Telemachus sat at meat with the suitors, and knew that it was the king his father, who in that shape begged an alms; and when his father came and presented himself before him in turn, as he had done to the suitors one by one, he gave him of his own meat which he had in his dish, and of his own cup to drink. And the suitors were past measure offended to see a pitiful beggar, as they esteemed him, to be so choicely regarded by the prince.

Then Antinous, who was a great lord, and of chief note among the suitors, said, "Prince Telemachus does ill to encourage these wandering beggars, who go from place to place, affirming that they have been some considerable persons in their time, filling the ears of such as hearken to them with lies, and pressing with their bold feet into kings' palaces. This is some saucy vagabond, some travelling Egyptian."

"I see," said Ulysses, "that a poor man should get but little at your board, scarce should he get salt from your hands if he brought his own meat."

Lord Antinous, indignant to be answered with such sharpness by a supposed beggar, snatched up a stool, with which he smote Ulysses where the neck and shoulders join. This usage moved not Ulysses; but in his great heart he meditated deep evils to come upon them all, which for a time must be kept close, and he went and sat himself down in the doorway to eat of that which was given him, and he said, "For life or possessions a man will fight, but for his belly this man smites. If a poor man has any god to take his part, my lord Antinous shall not live to be the queen's husband."

Then Antinous raged highly, and threatened to drag him by the heels, and to rend his rags about his ears, if he spoke another word.

But the other suitors did in no wise approve of the harsh language, nor of the blow which Antinous had dealt; and some of them said, "Who knows but one of the deities goes about, hid under that poor disguise? for in the likeness of poor pilgrims the gods have many times descended to try the dispositions of men, whether they be humane or impious." While these things passed, Telemachus sat and observed all, but held his peace, remembering the instructions of his father. But secretly he waited for the sign which Minerva was to send from heaven.

That day there followed Ulysses to the court one of the common sort of beggars, Irus by name, one that had received alms beforetime of the suitors, and was their ordinary sport, when they were inclined (as that day) to give way to mirth, to see him eat and drink; for he had the appetite of six men; and was of huge stature and proportions of body; yet had in him no spirit nor courage of a man. This man, thinking to curry favour with the suitors, and recommend himself especially to such a great lord as Antinous was, began to revile and scorn Ulysses, putting foul language upon him, and fairly challenging him to fight with the fist. But Ulysses, deeming his railings to be nothing more than jealousy and that envious disposition which beggars commonly manifest to brothers in their trade, mildly besought him not to trouble him, but to enjoy that portion which the liberality of their entertainers gave him, as he did, quietly; seeing that of their bounty there was sufficient for all.

But Irus, thinking that this forbearance in Ulysses was nothing more than a sign of fear, so much the more highly stormed, and bellowed, and provoked him to fight; and by this time the quarrel had attracted the notice of the suitors, who with loud laughters and shouting egged on the dispute, and lord Antinous swore by all the gods it should be a battle, and that in that hall the strife should be determined. To this the rest of the suitors with violent clamours acceded, and a circle was made for the combatants, and a fat goat was proposed as the victor's prize, as at the Olympic or the Pythian games. Then Ulysses, seeing no remedy, or being not unwilling that the suitors should behold some proof of that strength which ere long in their own persons they were to taste of, stripped himself, and prepared for the combat. But first he demanded that he should have fair play shown him, that none in that assembly should aid his opponent, or take part against him, for, being an old man, they might easily crush him with their strengths. And Telemachus passed his word that no foul play should be shown him, but that each party should be left to their own unassisted strengths, and to this he made Antinous and the rest of the suitors swear.

But when Ulysses had laid aside his garments, and was bare to the waist, all the beholders admired at the goodly sight of his large shoulders being of such exquisite shape and whiteness, and at his great and brawny bosom, and the youthful strength which seemed to remain in a man thought so old; and they said, "What limbs and what sinews he has!" and coward fear seized on the mind of that great vast beggar, and he dropped his threats and big words, and would have fled, but lord Antinous stayed him, and threatened him that if he declined the combat, he would put him a ship, and land him on the shores where king Echetus reigned, the roughest tyrant which at that time the world contained, and who had that antipathy to rascal beggars, such as he, that when any landed on his coast, he would crop their ears and noses and give them to the dogs to tear. So Irus, in whom fear of king Echetus prevailed above the fear of Ulysses, addressed himself to fight. But Ulysses, provoked to be engaged in so odious a strife with a fellow of his base conditions, and loathing longer to be made a spectacle to entertain the eyes of his foes, with one blow which he struck him beneath the ear, so shattered the teeth and jawbone of this soon baffled coward, that he laid him sprawling in the dust, with small stomach or ability to renew the contest. Then raising him on his feet, he led him bleeding and sputtering to the door, and put his staff into his hand, and bid him go use his command upon dogs and swine, but not presume himself to be lord of the guests another time, nor of the beggary!

The suitors applauded in their vain minds the issue of the contest, and rioted in mirth at the expense of poor Irus, who they vowed should be forthwith embarked and sent to king Echetus; and they bestowed thanks on

Ulysses for ridding the court of that unsavoury morsel, as they called him; but in their inward souls they would not have cared if Irus had been victor, and Ulysses had taken the foil, but it was mirth to them to see the beggars fight. In such pastimes and light entertainments the day wore away.

When evening was come the suitors betook themselves to music and dancing. And Ulysses leaned his back against a pillar from which certain lamps hung which gave light to the dancers, and he made show of watching the dancers, but very different thoughts were in his head. And as he stood near the lamps, the light fell upon his head, which was thin of hair and bald, as an old man's. And Eurymachus, a suitor, taking occasion from some words which were spoken before, scoffed and said, "Now I know for a certainty that some god lurks under the poor and beggarly appearance of this man, for as he stands by the lamps, his sleek head throws beams around it, like as it were a glory." And another said, "He passes his time too not much unlike the gods, lazily living exempt from labour, taking offerings of men." "I warrant," said Eurymachus again, "he could not raise a fence or dig a ditch for his livelihood, if a man would hire him to work in a garden."

"I wish," said Ulysses, "that you who speak this and myself were to be tried at any task-work, that I had a good crooked scythe put in my hand, that was sharp and strong, and you such another, where the grass grew longest, to be up by daybreak, mowing the meadows till the sun went down, not tasting of food till we had finished, or that we were set to plough four acres in one day of good glebe land, to see whose furrows were evenest and cleanest, or that we might have one wrestling-bout together, or that in our right hands a good steel-headed lance were placed, to try whose blows fell heaviest and thickest upon the adversary's headpiece. I would cause you such work, as you should have small reason to reproach me with being slack at work. But you would do well to spare me this reproach, and to save your strength, till the owner of this house shall return, till the day when Ulysses shall return, when returning he shall enter upon his birthright."

This was a galling speech to those suitors, to whom Ulysses' return was indeed the thing which they most dreaded; and a sudden fear fell upon their souls, as if they were sensible of the real presence of that man who did indeed stand amongst them, but not in that form as they might know him; and Eurymachus, incensed, snatched a massy cup which stood on a table near, and hurled it at the head of the supposed beggar, and but narrowly missed the hitting of him; and all the suitors rose, as at once, to thrust him out of the hall, which they said his beggarly presence and his rude speeches had profaned. But Telemachus cried to them to forbear, and not to presume to lay hands upon a wretched man to whom he had promised protection. He asked if they were mad, to mix such abhorred uproar with his feasts. He bade them take their food and their wine, to sit up or go to bed at their free pleasures, so long as he should give licence to that freedom; but why should they abuse his banquet, or let the words which a poor beggar spake have power to move their spleens so fiercely?

They bit their lips and frowned for anger, to be checked so by a youth; nevertheless for that time they had the grace to abstain, either for shame, or that Minerva had infused into them a terror of Ulysses' son.

So that day's feast was concluded without bloodshed, and the suitors, tired with their sports, departed severally each man to his apartment. Only Ulysses and Telemachus remained. And now Telemachus, by his father's direction, went and brought down into the hall armour and lances from the armoury: for Ulysses said, "On the morrow we shall have need of them." And moreover he said, "If any one shall ask why you have taken them down, say, it is to clean them and scour them from the rust which they have gathered since the owner of this house went for Troy." And as Telemachus stood by the armour, the lights were all gone out, and it was pitch-dark, and the armour gave out glistening beams as of fire, and he said to his father, "The pillars of the house are on fire." And his father said, "It is the gods who sit above the stars and have power to make the night as light as the day." And he took it for a good omen. And Telemachus fell to cleaning and sharpening of the lances.

Now Ulysses had not seen his wife Penelope in all the time since his return; for the queen did not care to mingle with the suitors at their banquets, but, as became one that had been Ulysses' wife, kept much in private, spinning and doing her excellent housewiferies among her maids in the remote apartments of the palace. Only upon solemn days she would come down and show herself to the suitors. And Ulysses was filled with a longing desire to see his wife again, whom for twenty years he had not beheld, and he softly stole through the known passages of his beautiful house, till he came where the maids were lighting the queen through a stately gallery that led to the chamber where she slept. And when the maids saw Ulysses, they said, "It is the beggar who came to the court to-day, about whom all that uproar was stirred up in the hall: what does he here?" But Penelope gave commandment that he should be brought before her, for she said, "It may be that he has travelled, and has heard something concerning Ulysses."

Then was Ulysses right glad to hear himself named by his queen, to find himself in nowise forgotten, nor her great love towards him decayed in all that time that he had been away. And he stood before his queen, and she knew him not to be Ulysses, but supposed that he had been some poor traveller. And she asked him of what country he was.

He told her (as he had before told to Eumæus) that he was a Cretan born, and however poor and cast down he now seemed, no less a man than brother to Idomeneus, who was grandson to king Minos, and though he now wanted bread, he had once had it in his power to feast Ulysses. Then he feigned how Ulysses, sailing for Troy, was forced by stress of weather to put his fleet in at a port of Crete, where for twelve days he was his guest, and entertained by him with all befitting guest-rites. And he described the very garments which Ulysses had on, by which Penelope knew that he had seen her lord.

In this manner Ulysses told his wife many tales of himself, at most but painting, but painting so near to the life, that the feeling of that which she took at her ears became so strong, that the kindly tears ran down her fair cheeks, while she thought upon her lord, dead she thought him, and heavily mourned the loss of him, whom she missed, whom she could not find, though in very deed he stood so near her.

Ulysses was moved to see her weep, but he kept his own eyes as dry as iron or horn in their lids, putting a bridle upon his strong passion, that it should not issue to sight.

Then he told her how he had lately been at the court of Thesprotia, and what he had learned concerning Ulysses there, in order as he had delivered to Eumæus: and Penelope was won to believe that there might be a possibility of Ulysses being alive, and she said, "I dreamed a dream this morning. Methought I had twenty household fowl which did eat wheat steeped in water from my hand, and there came suddenly from the clouds a crook-beaked hawk who soused on them and killed them all, trussing their necks, then took his flight back up to the clouds. And in my dream methought that I wept and made great moan for my fowls, and for the destruction which the hawk had made; and my maids came about me to comfort me. And in the height of my griefs the hawk came back, and lighting upon the beam of my chamber, he said to me in a man's voice, which sounded strangely even in my dream, to hear a hawk to speak: 'Be of good cheer,' he said, 'O daughter of Icarius; for this is no dream which thou hast seen, but that which shall happen to thee indeed. Those household fowl which thou lamentest so without reason, are the suitors who devour thy substance, even as thou sawest the fowl eat from thy hand, and the hawk is thy husband, who is coming to give death to the suitors.' And I awoke, and went to see to my fowls if they were alive, whom I found eating wheat from their troughs, all well and safe as before my dream."

Then said Ulysses, "This dream can endure no other interpretation than that which the hawk gave to it, who is your lord, and who is coming quickly to effect all that his words told you."

"Your words," she said, "my old guest, are so sweet, that would you sit and please me with your speech, my ears would never let my eyes close their spheres for very joy of your discourse; but none that is merely mortal can live without the death of sleep, so the gods who are without death themselves have ordained it, to keep the memory of our mortality in our minds, while we experience that as much as we live we die every day: in which consideration I will ascend my bed, which I have nightly watered with my tears since he that was the joy of it departed for that bad city;" she so speaking, because she could not bring her lips to name the name of Troy so much hated. So for that night they parted, Penelope to her bed, and Ulysses to his son, and to the armour and the lances in the hall, where they sat up all night cleaning and watching by the armour.

Chapter X.

The madness from above—The bow of Ulysses—The slaughter—The conclusion.

When daylight appeared, a tumultuous concourse of suitors again filled the hall; and some wondered, and some inquired what meant that glittering store of armour and lances which lay on heaps by the entry of the door; and to all that asked Telemachus made reply, that he had caused them to be taken down to cleanse them of the rust and of the stain which they had contracted by lying so long unused, even ever since his father went for Troy; and with that answer their minds were easily satisfied. So to their feasting and vain rioting again they fell. Ulysses by Telemachus' order had a seat and a mess assigned to him in the doorway, and he had his eye ever on the lances. And it moved gall in some of the great ones there present, to have their feast still dulled with the society of that wretched beggar as they deemed him, and they reviled and spurned at him with their feet. Only there was one Philœtius, who had something a better nature than the rest, that spake kindly to him, and had his age in respect. He coming up to Ulysses, took him by the hand with a kind of fear, as if touched exceedingly with imagination of his great worth, and said thus to him, "Hail! father stranger! my brows have sweat to see the injuries which you have received, and my eyes have broke forth in tears, when I have only thought that such being oftentimes the lot of worthiest men, to this plight Ulysses may be reduced, and that he now may wander from place to place as you do; for such who are compelled by need to range here and there, and have no firm home to fix their feet upon, God keeps them in this earth, as under water; so are they kept down and depressed. And a dark thread is sometimes spun in the fates of kings."

At this bare likening of the beggar to Ulysses, Minerva from heaven made the suitors for foolish joy to go mad, and roused them to such a laughter as would never stop, they laughed without power of ceasing, their eyes stood full of tears for violent joys; but fears and horrible misgivings succeeded: and one among them stood up and prophesied: "Ah, wretches!" he said, "what madness from heaven has seized you, that you can laugh? see you not that your meat drops blood? a night, like the night of death, wraps you about, you shriek without knowing it; your eyes thrust forth tears; the fixed walls, and the beam that bears the whole house up, fall blood; ghosts choke up the entry; full is the hall with apparitions of murdered men; under your feet is hell; the sun falls from heaven, and it is midnight at noon." But like men whom the gods had infatuated to their destruction, they mocked at his fears, and Eurymachus said, "This man is surely mad, conduct him forth into the marketplace, set him in the light, for he dreams that 'tis night within the house."

But Theoclymenus (for that was the prophet's name), whom Minerva had graced with a prophetic spirit, that he foreseeing might avoid the destruction which awaited them, answered and said: "Eurymachus, I will not require a guide of thee, for I have eyes and ears, the use of both my feet, and a sane mind within me, and with these I will go forth of the doors, because I know the imminent evils which await all you that stay, by reason of this poor guest who is a favourite with all the gods." So saying he turned his back upon those inhospitable men, and went away home, and never returned to the palace.

These words which he spoke were not unheard by Telemachus, who kept still his eye upon his father, expecting fervently when he would give the sign, which was to precede the slaughter of the suitors.

They dreaming of no such thing, fell sweetly to their dinner, as joying in the great store of banquet which was heaped in full tables about them; but there reigned not a bitterer banquet planet in all heaven, than that which hung over them this day by secret destination of Minerva.

There was a bow which Ulysses left when he went for Troy. It had lain by since that time, out of use and unstrung, for no man had strength to draw that bow, save Ulysses. So it had remained as a monument of the great strength of its master. This bow, with the quiver of arrows belonging thereto, Telemachus had brought down from the armoury on the last night along with the lances; and now Minerva, intending to do Ulysses an honour, put it into the mind of Telemachus to propose to the suitors to try who was strongest to draw that bow; and he promised that to the man who should be able to draw that bow, his mother should be given in marriage; Ulysses' wife, the prize to him who should bend the bow of Ulysses.

There was great strife and emulation stirred up among the suitors at those words of the prince Telemachus. And to grace her son's words, and to confirm the promise which he had made, Penelope came and showed herself that day to the suitors; and Minerva made her that she appeared never so comely in their sight as that day, and they were inflamed with the beholding of so much beauty, proposed as the price of so great manhood; and they cried out, that if all those heroes who sailed to Colchos for the rich purchase of the golden-fleeced ram, had seen earth's richer prize, Penelope, they would not have made their voyage, but would have vowed their valours and their lives to her, for she was at all parts faultless.

And she said, "The gods have taken my beauty from me, since my lord went for Troy." But Telemachus willed his mother to depart and not be present at that contest, for he said, "It may be, some rougher strife shall chance of this, than may be expedient for a woman to witness." And she retired, she and her maids, and left the hall.

Then the bow was brought into the midst, and a mark was set up by prince Telemachus: and lord Antinous as the chief among the suitors had the first offer, and he took the bow and fitting an arrow to the string, he strove to bend it, but not with all his might and main could he once draw together the ends of that tough bow; and when he found how vain a thing it was to endeavour to draw Ulysses' bow, he desisted, blushing for shame and for mere anger. Then Eurymachus adventured, but with no better success; but as it had torn the hands of Antinous, so did the bow tear and strain his hands, and marred his delicate fingers, yet could he not once stir the string. Then called he to the attendants to bring fat and unctuous matter, which melting at the fire, he dipped the bow therein, thinking to supple it and make it more pliable, but not with all the helps of art could he succeed in making it to move. After him Liodes, and Amphinomus, and Polybus, and Eurynomus, and Polyctorides, assayed their strength, but not any one of them, or of the rest of those aspiring suitors, had any better luck : yet not the meanest of them there but thought himself well worthy of Ulysses' wife, though to shoot with Ulysses' bow the completest champion among them was by proof found too feeble.

Then Ulysses prayed them that he might have leave to try; and immediately a clamour was raised among the suitors, because of his petition, and they scorned and swelled with rage at his presumption, and that a beggar should seek to contend in a game of such noble mastery. But Telemachus ordered that the bow should be given him, and that he should have leave to try, since they had failed; "for," he said, "the bow is mine, to give or to withhold:" and none durst gainsay the prince.

Then Ulysses gave a sign to his son, and he commanded the doors of the hall to be made fast, and all wondered at his words, but none could divine the cause. And Ulysses took the bow into his hands, and before he essayed to bend it, he surveyed it at all parts to see whether, by long lying by, it had contracted any stiffness which hindered the drawing; and as he was busied in the curious surveying of his bow, some of the suitors mocked him and said, "Past doubt this man is a right cunning archer, and knows his craft well. See how he turns it over and over, and looks into it as if he could see through the wood." And others said, "We wish some one would tell out gold into our laps but for so long a time as he shall be in drawing of that string." But when he had spent some little time in making proof of the bow, and had found it to be in good plight, like as a harper in tuning of his harp draws out a string, with such ease or much more did Ulysses draw to the head the string of his own tough bow, and in letting of it go, it twanged with such a shrill noise as a swallow makes when it sings through the air; which so much amazed the suitors, that their colours came and went, and the skies gave out a noise of thunder, which at heart cheered Ulysses, for he knew that now his long labours by the disposal of the fates drew to an end. Then fitted he an arrow to the bow, and drawing it to the head, he sent it right to the mark which the prince had set up. Which done, he said to Telemachus, "You have got no disgrace yet by your guest, for I have struck the mark I shot at, and gave myself no such trouble in teasing the bow with fat and fire, as these men did, but have made proof that my strength is not impaired, nor my age so weak and contemptible as these were pleased to think it. But come, the day going down calls us to supper, after which succeed poem and harp, and all delights which use to crown princely banquetings."

So saying, he beckoned to his son, who straight girt his sword to his side, and took one of the lances (of which there lay great store from the armoury) in his hand, and armed at all points, advanced towards his father.

The upper rags which Ulysses wore fell from his shoulder, and his own kingly likeness returned, when he rushed to the great hall door with bow and quiver full of shafts, which down at his feet he poured, and in bitter words presignified his deadly intent to the suitors. "Thus far," he said, "this contest has been decided harmless: now for us there rests another mark, harder to hit, but which my hands shall essay notwithstanding, if Phœbus, god of archers, be pleased to give me mastery." With that he let fly a deadly arrow at Antinous, which pierced him in the throat as he was in the act of lifting a cup of wine to his mouth. Amazement seized the suitors, as their great champion fell dead, and they raged highly against Ulysses, and said that it should prove the dearest shaft which he ever let fly, for he had slain a man, whose like breathed not in any part of the kingdom: and they flew to their arms, and would have seized the lances, but Minerva struck them with dimness of sight that they went erring up and down the hall, not knowing where to find them. Yet so infatuated were they by the displeasure of heaven, that they did not see the imminent peril which impended over them, but every man believed that this accident had happened beside the intention of the doer. Fools! to think by shutting their eyes to evade destiny, or that any other cup remained for them, but that which their great Antinous had tasted!

Then Ulysses revealed himself to all in that presence, and that he was the man whom they held to be dead at Troy, whose palace they had usurped, whose wife in his lifetime they had sought in impious marriage, and that for this reason destruction was come upon them. And he dealt his deadly arrows among them, and there was no avoiding him, nor escaping from his horrid person, and Telemachus by his side plied them thick with those murderous lances from which there was no retreat, till fear itself made them valiant, and danger gave them eyes to understand the peril; then they which had swords drew them, and some with shields, that could find them, and some with tables and benches snatched up in haste, rose in a mass to overwhelm and crush those two; yet they singly bestirred themselves like men, and defended themselves against that great host, and through tables, shields and all, right through the arrows of Ulysses clove, and the irresistible lances of Telemachus; and many lay dead, and all had wounds, and Minerva in the likeness of a bird sate upon the beam which went across the hall, clapping her wings with a fearful noise, and sometimes the great bird would fly among them, cuffing at the swords and at the lances, and up and down the hall would go, beating her wings, and troubling everything, that it was frightful to behold, and it frayed the blood from the cheeks of those heaven-hated suitors: but to

Ulysses and his son she appeared in her own divine similitude, with her snake-fringed shield, a goddess armed, fighting their battles. Nor did that dreadful pair desist till they had laid all their foes at their feet. At their feet they lay in shoals; like fishes, when the fishermen break up their nets, so they lay gasping and sprawling at the feet of Ulysses and his son. And Ulysses remembered the prediction of Tiresias, which said that he was to perish by his own guests, unless he slew those who knew him not.

Then certain of the queen's household went up and told Penelope what had happened, and how her lord Ulysses had come home, and had slain the suitors. But she gave no heed to their words, but thought that some frenzy possessed them, or that they mocked her: for it is the property of such extremes of sorrow as she had felt, not to believe when any great joy cometh. And she rated and chid them exceedingly for troubling her. But they the more persisted in their asseverations of the truth of what they had affirmed; and some of them had seen the slaughtered bodies of the suitors dragged forth of the hall. And they said, "That poor guest whom you talked with last night was Ulysses." Then she was yet more fully persuaded that they mocked her, and she wept. But they said, "This thing is true which we have told. We sat within, in an inner room in the palace, and the doors of the hall were shut on us, but we heard the cries and the groans of the men that were killed, but saw nothing, till at length your son called to us to come in, and entering we saw Ulysses standing in the midst of the slaughtered." But she persisting in her unbelief, said, that it was some god which had deceived them to think it was the person of Ulysses.

By this time Telemachus and his father had cleansed their hands from the slaughter, and were come to where the queen was talking with those of her household; and when she saw Ulysses, she stood motionless, and had no power to speak, sudden surprise and joy and fear and many passions so strove within her. Sometimes she was clear that it was her husband that she saw, and sometimes the alterations which twenty years had made in his person (yet that was not much) perplexed her that she knew not what to think, and for joy she could not believe; and yet for joy she would not but believe; and, above all, that sudden change from a beggar to a king troubled her, and wrought uneasy scruples in her mind. But Telemachus seeing her strangeness, blamed her, and called her an ungentle and tyrannous mother! and said that she showed a too great curiousness of modesty, to abstain from embracing his father, and to have doubts of his person, when to all present it was evident that he was the very real and true Ulysses.

Then she mistrusted no longer, but ran and fell upon Ulysses' neck, and said, "Let not my husband be angry, that I held off so long with strange delays; it is the gods, who severing us for so long time, have caused this unseemly distance in me. If Menelaus' wife had used half my caution, she would never have taken so freely to a stranger's bed; and she might have spared us all these plagues which have come upon us through her shameless deed."

These words with which Penelope excused herself, wrought more affection in Ulysses than if upon a first sight she had given up herself implicitly to his embraces; and he wept for joy to possess a wife so discreet, so answering to his own staid mind, that had a depth of wit proportioned to his own, and one that held chaste virtue at so high a price, and he thought the possession of such a one cheaply purchased with the loss of all Circe's delights, and Calypso's immortality of joys; and his long labours and his severe sufferings past seemed as nothing, now they were crowned with the enjoyment of his virtuous and true wife Penelope. And as sad men at sea whose ship has gone to pieces nigh shore, swimming for their lives, all drenched in foam and brine, crawl up to some poor patch of land, which they take possession of with as great a joy as if they had the world given them in fee, with such delight did this chaste wife cling to her lord restored, till the dark night fast coming on reminded her of that more intimate and happy union when in her long-widowed bed she should once again clasp a living Ulysses.

So from that time the land had rest from the suitors. And the happy Ithacans with songs and solemn sacrifices of praise to the gods celebrated the return of Ulysses: for he that had been so long absent was returned to wreak the evil upon the heads of the doers; in the place where they had done the evil, there wreaked he his vengeance upon them.

GUY FAUX.

A VERY ingenious and subtle writer, whom there is good reason for suspecting to be an ex-Jesuit, not unknown at Douay some five-and-twenty years since (he will not obtrude himself at M——th again in a hurry), about a twelvemonth back set himself to prove the character of the Powder Plot Conspirators to have been that of heroic self-devotedness and true Christian martyrdom. Under the mask of Protestant candour, he actually gained admission for his treatise into a London weekly paper not particularly distinguished for its zeal towards either religion. But, admitting Catholic principles, his arguments are shrewd and incontrovertible. He says:—

"Guy Faux was a fanatic; but he was no hypocrite. He ranks among *good haters*. He was cruel, bloody-minded, reckless of all considerations but those of an infuriated and bigoted faith; but he was a true son of the Catholic Church, a martyr, and a confessor, for all that. He who can prevail upon himself to devote his life to a cause, however we may condemn his opinions or abhor his actions, vouches at least for the honesty of his principles and the disinterestedness of his motives. He may be guilty of the worst practices; but he is capable of the greatest. He is no longer a slave, but free. The contempt of death is the beginning of virtue. The hero of the Gunpowder Plot was, if you will, a fool, a madman, an assassin; call him what names you please: still he was neither knave nor coward. He did not propose

to blow up the Parliament, and come off scot-free himself;
he showed that he valued his own life no more than
theirs in such a cause, where the integrity of the Catholic
faith and the salvation of perhaps millions of souls was
at stake. He did not call it a murder, but a sacrifice,
which he was about to achieve; he was armed with the
Holy Spirit and with fire; he was the Church's chosen
servant, and her blessed martyr. He comforted himself
as 'the best of cut-throats.' How many wretches are
there who would have undertaken to do what he intended
for a sum of money, if they could have got off with im-
punity! How few are there who would have put themselves in Guy Faux's situation to save the universe! Yet,
in the latter case, we affect to be thrown into greater
consternation than at the most unredeemed acts of villainy;
as if the absolute disinterestedness of the motive doubled
the horror of the deed! The cowardice and selfishness
of mankind are in fact shocked at the consequences to
themselves (if such examples are held up for imitation);
and they make a fearful outcry against the violation of
every principle of morality, lest they, too, should be called
on for any such tremendous sacrifices; lest they in their
turn, should have to go on the forlorn hope of extra-official
duty. *Charity begins at home*, is a maxim that prevails
as well in the courts of consciousness as in those of
prudence. We would be thought to shudder at the consequences of crime to others, while we tremble for them
to ourselves. We talk of the dark and cowardly assassin;
and this is well, when an individual shrinks from the face
of an enemy, and purchases his own safety by striking a
blow in the dark; but how the charge of cowardly can
be applied to the public assassin, who, in the very act of
destroying another, lays down his life as the pledge and
forfeit of his sincerity and boldness, I am at a loss to
devise. There may be barbarous prejudice, rooted hatred,
unprincipled treachery in such an act; but he who
resolves to take all the danger and odium upon himself
can no more be branded with cowardice than Regulus

devoting himself for his country, or Codrus leaping into the fiery gulf. A wily Father Inquisitor, coolly and with plenary authority condemning hundreds of helpless, unoffending victims to the flames, or the horrors of a living tomb, while he himself would not suffer a hair of his head to be hurt, is, to me, a character without any qualifying trait in it. Again: The Spanish conqueror and hero, the favourite of his monarch, who enticed thirty thousand poor Mexicans into a large open building under promise of strict faith and cordial good-will, and then set fire to it, making sport of the cries and agonies of these deluded creatures, is an instance of uniting the most hardened cruelty with the most heartless selfishness. His plea was, keeping no faith with heretics; this was Guy Faux's too: but I am sure at least that the latter kept faith with himself; he was in earnest in his professions. *His* was not gay, wanton, unfeeling depravity; he did not murder in sport: it was serious work that he had taken in hand. To see this arch-bigot, this heart-whole traitor, this pale miner in the infernal regions, skulking in his retreat with his cloak and dark lantern, moving cautiously about among his barrels of gunpowder loaded with death, but not yet ripe for destruction, regardless of the lives of others, and more than indifferent to his own, presents a picture of the strange infatuation of the human understanding, but not of the depravity of the human will, without an equal. There were thousands of pious Papists privy to and ready to applaud the deed when done; there was no one but our old fifth-of-November friend, who still flutters in rags and straw on the occasion, that had the courage to attempt it. In him stern duty and unshaken faith prevailed over natural frailty."

It is impossible, upon Catholic principles, not to admit the force of this reasoning: we can only not help smiling (with the writer) at the simplicity of the gulled editor, swallowing the dregs of Loyola for the very quintessence of sublimated reason in England at the commencement of the nineteenth century. We will just, as a contrast, show what we Protestants (who are a party concerned) thought upon the same subject at a period rather nearer to the heroic project in question.

The Gunpowder Treason was the subject which called forth the earliest specimen which is left us of the pulpit eloquence of Jeremy Taylor. When he preached the sermon on that anniversary, which is printed at the end of the folio edition of his Sermons, he was a young man, just commencing his ministry under the auspices of Archbishop Laud. From the learning and maturest oratory which it manifests, one should rather have conjectured it to have proceeded from the same person after he was ripened by time into a Bishop and Father of the Church. "And, really, these *Romano-barbari* could never pretend to any precedent for an act so barbarous as theirs. Adramelech, indeed, killed a king; but he spared the people. Haman would have killed the people, but spared the king; but that both king and people, princes and judges, branch and rush and root, should die at once (as if Caligula's wish were actuated, and all England upon one head), was never known till now, that all the malice of the world met in this as in a centre. The Sicilian even-song, the matins of St. Bartholomew, known for the pitiless and damned massacres, were but κάπνου σκίας ὄναρ, the dream of the shadow of smoke, if compared with this great fire. *In tam occupato sæculo fabulas vulgares nequitia non invenit.* This was a busy age. Herostratus must have invented a more sublimed malice than the burning of one temple, or not have been so much as spoke of since the discovery of the powder treason. But I must make more haste; I shall not else climb the sublimity of this impiety. Nero was sometimes the *populare odium*, was popularly hated, and deserved it too: for he slew his master, and his wife, and all his family, once or twice over; opened his mother's womb; fired the city, laughed at it, slandered the Christians for it: but yet all these were but *principia malorum,* the very first rudiments of evil. Add, then, to these, Herod's masterpiece at Ramah, as it was deciphered by the tears and sad threnes of the matrons in a universal mourning for the loss of their pretty infants; yet this of Herod will prove but an infant wickedness, and that of Nero the evil but of one city. I would willingly have found out an example, but see I cannot. Should I put into the scale the extract of the old tyrants famous in antique stories :—

> 'Bistonii stabulum regis, Busiridis aras,
> Antiphatæ mensas, et Taurica regna Thoantis;'—

should I take for true story the highest cruelty as it was fancied by the most hieroglyphical Egyptian,—this alone would weigh them down, as if the Alps were put in scale against the dust of a balance. For, had this accursed treason prospered, we should have had the whole kingdom mourn for the inestimable loss of its chiefest glory, its life, its present joy, and all its very hopes for the future. For such was their destined malice, that they would not only have inflicted so cruel a blow, but have made it incurable, by cutting off our supplies of joy, the whole succession of the Line Royal. Not only the vine itself, but all the *gemmulæ,* and the tender olive branches, should either have been bent to their intentions, and made to grow crooked, or else been broken.

"And now, after such a sublimity of malice, I will not instance in the sacrilegious ruin of the neighbouring temples, which needs must have perished in the flame; nor in the disturbing the ashes of our entombed kings, devouring their dead ruins like sepulchral dogs: these are but minutes in respect of the ruin prepared for the living temples :—

> 'Stragem sed istam non tulit
> Christus cadentum Principum
> Impune, ne forsan sui
> Patris periret fabrica.
> Ergo quæ poterit lingua retexere
> Laudes, Christe, tuas, qui domitum struis
> Infidum populum cum Duce perfido!'"

In such strains of eloquent indignation did Jeremy Taylor's young oratory inveigh against that stupendous attempt which he truly says had no parallel in ancient or modern times. A century and a half of European crimes has elapsed since he made the assertion, and his position remains in its strength. He wrote near the time in which the nefarious project had like to have been completed. Men's minds still were shuddering from the recentness of the escape. It must have been within his memory, or have been sounded in his ears so young by his parents, that he would seem, in his maturer years, to have remembered it. No wonder, then, that he describes it in words that burn. But to us, to whom the tradition has come slowly down, and has had time to cool, the story of Guido Vaux sounds rather like a tale, a fable, and an invention, than true history. It supposes such gigantic audacity of daring, combined with such more than infantile stupidity in the motive,—such a combination of the fiend and the monkey, that credulity is almost swallowed up in contemplating the singularity of the attempt. It has accordingly, in some degree, shared the fate of fiction. It is familiarised to us in a kind of serio-ludicrous way, like the story of *Guy of Warwick* or *Valentine and Orson*. The way which we take to perpetuate the memory of this deliverance is well adapted to keep up this fabular notion. Boys go about the streets annually with a beggarly scarecrow dressed up, which is to be burnt indeed, at night, with holy zeal; but, meantime, they beg a penny for *poor Guy:* this periodical petition, which we have heard from our infancy, combined with the dress and appearance of the effigy, so well calculated to move compassion, has the effect of quite removing from our fancy the horrid circumstances of the story which is thus commemorated; and in *poor Guy* vainly should we try to recognise any of the features of that tremendous madman in iniquity, Guido Vaux, with his horrid crew of accomplices, that sought to emulate earthquakes and bursting volcanoes in their more than mortal mischief.

Indeed, the whole ceremony of burning Guy Faux, or *the Pope*, as he is indifferently called, is a sort of *Treason Travestie*, and admirably adapted to lower our feelings upon this memorable subject. The printers of the little duodecimo *Prayer Book*, printed by T. Baskett,[1] in 1749, which has the effigy of his sacred majesty George II. piously prefixed, have illustrated the service (a very fine one in itself) which is appointed for the anniversary of this day with a print which it is not very easy to describe; but the contents appear to be these: The scene is a room, I conjecture in the king's palace. Two persons —one of whom I take to be James himself, from his wearing his hat, while the other stands bareheaded—are intently surveying a sort of speculum, or magic mirror, which stands upon a pedestal in the midst of the room, in which a little figure of Guy Faux with his dark lantern, approaching the door of the Parliament House, is made discernible by the light proceeding from a *great eye* which shines in from the topmost corner of the apartment; by which eye the pious artist no doubt meant to designate Providence. On the other side of the mirror is a figure doing something, which puzzled me when a child, and continues to puzzle me now. The best I can make of it is, that it is a conspirator busy laying the train; but then, why is he represented in the king's chamber? Conjecture upon so fantastical a design is vain; and I only notice the print as being one of the earliest graphic representations which woke my childhood into wonder, and doubtless combined, with the mummery before mentioned, to take off the edge of that horror which the naked historical mention of Guido's conspiracy could not have failed of exciting.

---

[1] The same, I presume, upon whom the clergyman in the song of the "Vicar and Moses," not without judgment, passes this memorable censure:

"Here, Moses the king:
'Tis a scandalous thing
That this Baskett should print for the Crown."

Now that so many years are past since that abominable machination was happily frustrated, it will not, I hope, be considered a profane sporting with the subject if we take no very serious survey of the consequences that would have flowed from this plot if it had had a successful issue. The first thing that strikes us, in a selfish point of view, is the material change which it must have produced in the course of the nobility. All the ancient peerage being extinguished, as it was intended, at one blow, the *Red Book* must have been closed for ever, or a new race of peers must have been created to supply the deficiency. As the first part of this dilemma is a deal too shocking to think of, what a fund of mouth-watering reflections does this give rise to in the breast of us plebeians of A.D. 1823! Why, you or I, reader, might have been Duke of ——, or Earl of ——. I particularise no titles, to avoid the least suspicion of intention to usurp the dignities of the two noblemen whom I have in my eye; but a feeling more dignified than envy sometimes excites a sigh, when I think how the posterity of Guido's Legion of Honour (among whom you or I might have been) might have rolled down "dulcified," as Burke expresses it, "by an exposure to the influence of heaven in a long flow of generations, from the hard, acidulous, metallic tincture of the spring."[1] What new orders of merit, think you, this English Napoleon would have chosen? Knights of the Barrel, or Lords of the Tub, Grand Almoners of the Cellar, or Ministers of Explosion? We should have given the train *couchant*, and the fire *rampant*, in our arms; we should have quartered the dozen white matches in our coats: the Shallows would have been nothing to us.

Turning away from these mortifying reflections, let us contemplate its effects upon the *other house;* for they were all to have gone together,—king, lords, commons.

To assist our imagination, let us take leave to suppose (and we do it in the harmless wantonness of fancy) that the tremendous explosion had taken place in our days.

[1] Letter to a Noble Lord.

We better know what a House of Commons is in our days, and can better estimate our loss. Let us imagine, then, to ourselves, the united members sitting in full conclave above; Faux just ready with his train and matches below,—in his hand a "reed tipt with fire." He applies the fatal engine——.

To assist our notions still further, let us suppose some lucky dog of a reporter, who had escaped by miracle upon some plank of St. Stephen's benches, and came plump upon the roof of the adjacent Abbey, from whence descending, at some neighbouring coffee-house, first wiping his clothes and calling for a glass of lemonade, he sits down and reports what he had heard and seen (*quorum pars magna fuit*), for the *Morning Post* or the *Courier*. We can scarcely imagine him describing the event in any other words but some such as these :—

"A *Motion* was put and carried, that this House do *adjourn;* that the Speaker do *quit the chair.* The House ROSE amid clamours for Order."

In some such way the event might most technically have been conveyed to the public. But a poetical mind, not content with this dry method of narration, cannot help pursuing the effects of this tremendous blowing up, this adjournment in the air, *sine die.* It sees the benches mount,—the Chair first, and then the benches; and first the Treasury Bench, hurried up in this nitrous explosion,—the Members, as it were, pairing off; Whigs and Tories taking their friendly apotheosis together (as they did their sandwiches below in Bellamy's room). Fancy, in her flight, keeps pace with the aspiring legislators: she sees the awful seat of order mounting, till it becomes finally fixed, a constellation, next to Cassiopeia's chair,—the wig of him that sat in it taking its place near Berenice's curls. St. Peter, at heaven's wicket,—no, not St. Peter,—St. Stephen, with open arms, receives his own——.

While Fancy beholds these Celestial appropriations, Reason, no less pleased, discerns the mighty benefit which so complete a renovation must produce below. Let the most determined foe to corruption, the most thorough-paced redresser of abuses, try to conceive a more absolute purification of the House than this was calculated to produce. Why, Pride's Purge was nothing to it. The whole borough-mongering system would have been got rid of, fairly *exploded;* with it the senseless distinctions of party must have disappeared, faction must have vanished, corruption have expired in the air. From Hundred, Tything, and Wapentake, some new Alfred would have convened, in all its purity, the primitive Witenagemote,—fixed upon a basis of property or population permanent as the poles———.

From this dream of universal restitution, Reason and Fancy with difficulty awake to view the real state of things. But, blessed be Heaven! St. Stephen's walls are standing, all her seats firmly secured; nay, some have doubted (since the Septennial Act) whether gunpowder itself, or anything short of a *committee above stairs,* would be able to shake any one member from his seat;—that great and final improvement to the Abbey, which is all that seems wanting,—the removing Westminster Hall and its appendages, and letting in the view of the Thames,—must not be expected in our days. Dismissing, therefore, all such speculations as mere tales of a tub, it is the duty of every honest Englishman to endeavour, by means less wholesale than Guido's, to ameliorate, without extinguishing parliaments; to hold the *lantern* to the dark places of corruption; to apply the *match* to the rotten parts of the system only; and to wrap himself up, not in the muffling mantle of conspiracy, but in the warm honest *cloak* of integrity and patriotic intention.

ON THE AMBIGUITIES ARISING FROM PROPER NAMES.

How oddly it happens that the same sound shall suggest to the minds of two persons hearing it ideas the most opposite! I was conversing, a few years since, with a young friend upon the subject of poetry, and particularly that species of it which is known by the name of the Epithalamium. I ventured to assert that the most perfect specimen of it in our language was the Epithalamium of Spenser upon his own marriage.

My young gentleman, who has a smattering of taste, and would not willingly be thought ignorant of anything remotely connected with the *belles-lettres*, expressed a degree of surprise, mixed with mortification, that he should never have heard of this poem; Spenser being an author with whose writings he thought himself peculiarly conversant.

I offered to show him the poem in the fine folio copy of the poet's works which I have at home. He seemed pleased with the offer, though the mention of the folio seemed again to puzzle him. But, presently after, assuming a grave look, he compassionately muttered to himself, "Poor Spencer!"

There was something in the tone with which he spoke these words that struck me not a little. It was more like the accent with which a man bemoans some recent calamity that has happened to a friend than that tone of sober grief with which we lament the sorrows of a person, however excellent and however grievous his afflictions may have been, who has been dead more than two centuries. I had the curiosity to inquire into the reasons of so uncommon an ejaculation. My young gentleman, with a more solemn tone of pathos than before, repeated, "Poor Spencer!" and added, "He has lost his wife!"

My astonishment at this assertion rose to such a height, that I began to think the brain of my young friend must be cracked, or some unaccountable reverie had gotten possession of it. But, upon further explanation, it appeared that the word "Spenser"—which to you or me, reader, in a conversation upon poetry too, would naturally have called up the idea of an old poet in a ruff, one Edmund Spenser, that flourished in the days of Queen Elizabeth, and wrote a poem called "The Faëry Queene," with "The Shepherd's Calendar," and many more verses besides—did, in the mind of my young friend, excite a very different and quite modern idea; namely, that of the Honourable William Spencer, one of the living ornaments, if I am not misinformed, of this present poetical era, A.D. 1811.

ON THE CUSTOM OF HISSING AT THE THEATRES.

WITH SOME ACCOUNT OF A CLUB OF DAMNED AUTHORS.

MR. REFLECTOR—I am one of those persons whom the world has thought proper to designate by the title of Damned Authors. In that memorable season of dramatic failures, 1806-7,—in which no fewer, I think, than two tragedies, four comedies, one opera, and three farces suffered at Drury Lane Theatre,—I was found guilty of constructing an afterpiece, and was *damned.*

Against the decision of the public in such instances there can be no appeal. The Clerk of Chatham might as well have protested against the decision of Cade and his followers who were then *the public.* Like him, I was condemned because I could write.

Not but it did appear to some of us that the measures of the popular tribunal at that period savoured a little of harshness and of the *summum jus.* The public mouth was early in the season fleshed upon the "Vindictive Man," and some pieces of that nature; and it retained, through the remainder of it, a relish of blood. As Dr. Johnson would have said, "Sir, there was a habit of sibilation in the house."

Still less am I disposed to inquire into the reason of the comparative lenity, on the other hand, with which some pieces were treated, which, to indifferent judges, seemed at least as much deserving of condemnation as some of those which met with it. I am willing to put a favourable construction upon the votes that were given against us; I believe that there was no bribery or designed partiality in the case; only "our nonsense did not happen to suit their nonsense;" that was all.

But against the *manner* in which the public, on these occasions, think fit to deliver their disapprobation, I must and ever will protest.

Sir, imagine—but you have been present at the damning of a piece—those who never had that felicity, I beg them to imagine—a vast theatre, like that which Drury Lane was before it was a heap of dust and ashes (I insult not over its fallen greatness; let it recover itself when it can for me, let it lift up its towering head once more, and take in poor authors to write for it; *hic cæstus artemque repono*),—a theatre like that, filled with all sorts of disgusting sounds,—shrieks, groans, hisses, but chiefly the last, like the noise of many waters, or that which Don Quixote heard from the fulling-mills, or that wilder combination of devilish sounds which St. Anthony listened to in the wilderness.

Oh! Mr. Reflector, is it not a pity that the sweet human voice, which was given man to speak with, to sing with, to whisper tones of love in, to express compliance, to convey a favour, or to grant a suit,—that voice, which in a Siddons or a Braham rouses us, in a Siren Catalani charms and captivates us,—that the musical, expressive human voice should be converted into a rival of the noises of silly geese, and irrational, venomous snakes?

I never shall forget the sounds on *my night*. I never before that time fully felt the reception which the Author of All Ill, in the "Paradise Lost," meets with from the critics in the *pit*, at the final close of his Tragedy upon the Human Race,—though that, alas! met with too much success:—

"From innumerable tongues
A dismal universal *hiss*, the sound

> Of public scorn. Dreadful was the din
> Of *hissing* through the hall, thick swarming now
> With complicated monsters, head and tail,
> Scorpion and asp, and Amphisbæna dire,
> Cerastes horn'd, Hydrus, and Elops drear,
> And Dipsas."

For *hall* substitute *theatre*, and you have the very image of what takes place at what is called the *damnation* of a piece,—and properly so called; for here you see its origin plainly, whence the custom was derived, and what the first piece was that so suffered. After this, none can doubt the propriety of the appellation.

But, sir, as to the justice of bestowing such appalling, heart-withering denunciations of the popular obloquy upon the venial mistake of a poor author, who thought to please us in the act of filling his pockets,—for the sum of his demerits amounts to no more than that,—it does, I own, seem to me a species of retributive justice far too severe for the offence. A culprit in the pillory (bate the eggs) meets with no severer exprobration.

Indeed, I have often wondered that some modest critic has not proposed that there should be a wooden machine to that effect erected in some convenient part of the proscenium, which an unsuccessful author should be required to mount, and stand his hour, exposed to the apples and oranges of the pit. This *amende honorable* would well suit with the meanness of some authors, who, in their prologues fairly prostrate their skulls to the audience, and seem to invite a pelting.

Or why should they not have their pens publicly broke over their heads, as the swords of recreant knights in old times were, and an oath administered to them that they should never write again?

Seriously, *Messieurs the Public*, this outrageous way which you have got of expressing your displeasures is too much for the occasion. When I was deafening under the effects of it, I could not help asking what crime of great moral turpitude I had committed: for every man about me seemed to feel the offence as personal to himself: as something which public interest and private feelings alike called upon him in the strongest possible manner, to stigmatise with infamy.

The Romans, it is well-known to you, Mr. Reflector, took a gentler method of marking their disapprobation of an author's work. They were a humane and equitable nation. They left the *furca* and the *patibulum*, the axe and the rods, to great offenders: for these minor and (if I may so term them) extra-moral offences, *the bent thumb* was considered as a sufficient sign of disapprobation,— *vertere pollicem;* as *the pressed thumb, premere pollicem*, was a mark of approving.

And really there seems to have been a sort of fitness in this method, a correspondency of sign in the punishment to the offence. For, as the action of *writing* is performed by bending the thumb forward, the retroversion or bending back of that joint did not unaptly point to the *opposite of that action;* implying that it was the will of the audience that the author should *write no more:* a much more significant as well as more humane way of expressing that desire than our custom of hissing, which is altogether senseless and indefensible. Nor do we find that the Roman audiences deprived themselves, by this lenity, of any tittle of that supremacy which audiences in all ages have thought themselves bound to maintain over such as have been candidates for their applause. On the contrary, by this method they seem to have had the author, as we should express it, completely *under finger and thumb*.

The provocations to which a dramatic genius is exposed from the public are so much the more vexatious as they are removed from any possibility of retaliation, which sweetens most other injuries; for the public *never writes itself*. Not but something very like it took place at the time of the O.P. differences. The placards which were nightly exhibited were, properly speaking, the composition of the public. The public wrote them, the public applauded them; and precious morceaux of wit and eloquence they were,—except some few of a better quality, which it is well known were furnished by professed dramatic writers. After this specimen of what the public can do for itself, it should be a little slow in condemning what others do for it.

As the degrees of malignancy vary in people according as they have more or less of the Old Serpent (the father of hisses) in their composition, I have sometimes amused myself with analysing this many-headed hydra, which calls itself the public, into the component parts of which it is "complicated, head and tail," and seeing how many varieties of the snake kind it can afford.

First, there is the Common English Snake.—This is that part of the auditory who are always the majority at damnations; but who, having no critical venom in themselves to sting them on, stay till they hear others hiss, and then join in for company.

The Blind Worm is a species very nearly allied to the foregoing. Some naturalists have doubted whether they are not the same.

The Rattlesnake.—These are your obstreperous talking critics,—the impertinent guides of the pit,—who will not give a plain man leave to enjoy an evening's entertainment; but with their frothy jargon and incessant finding of faults, either drown his pleasure quite, or force him, in his own defence, to join in their clamorous censure. The hiss always originates with these. When this creature springs his *rattle*, you would think, from the noise it makes, there was something in it; but you have only to examine the instrument from which the noise proceeds, and you will find it typical of a critic's tongue,—a shallow membrane, empty, voluble, and seated in the most contemptible part of the creature's body.

The Whipsnake.—This is he that lashes the poor author the next day in the newspapers.

The Deaf Adder, or *Surda Echidna* of Linnæus.— Under this head may be classed all that portion of the spectators (for audience they properly are not), who, not finding the first act of a piece answer to their preconceived notions of what a first act should be, like Obstinate in John Bunyan, positively thrust their fingers in their ears, that they may not hear a word of what is coming, though perhaps the very next act may be composed in a style as different as possible, and be written quite to their own tastes. These adders refuse to hear the voice of the charmer, because the tuning of his instrument gave them offence.

I should weary you and myself too, if I were to go through all the classes of the serpent kind. Two qualities are common to them all. They are creatures of remarkably cold digestions, and chiefly haunt *pits* and low grounds.

I proceed with more pleasure to give you an account of a club to which I have the honour to belong. There are fourteen of us, who are all authors that have been once in our lives what is called *damned*. We meet on the anniversary of our respective nights, and make ourselves merry at the expense of the public. The chief tenets which distinguish our society, and which every man among us is bound to hold for gospel, are—

That the public, or mob, in all ages have been a set of blind, deaf, obstinate, senseless, illiterate savages. That no man of genius, in his senses, would be ambitious of pleasing such a capricious, ungrateful rabble. That the only legitimate end of writing for them is to pick their pockets; and, that failing, we are at full liberty to vilify and abuse them as much as ever we think fit.

That authors, by their affected pretences to humility, which they made use of as a cloak to insinuate their writings into the callous senses of the multitude, obtuse to everything but the grossest flattery, have by degrees made that great beast their master; as we may act submission to children till we are obliged to practise it in earnest. That authors are and ought to be considered the masters and preceptors of the public, and not *vice versâ.* That it was so in the days of Orpheus, Linus, and Musæus; and would be so again, if it were not that writers prove traitors to themselves. That, in particular, in the days of the first of those three great authors just mentioned, audiences appear to have been perfect models of what audiences should be; for though, along with the trees and the rocks and the wild creatures which he drew after him to listen to his strains, some serpents doubtless came to hear his music, it does not appear that any one among them ever lifted up *a dissentient voice.* They knew what was due to authors in those days. Now every stock and stone turns into a serpent, and has a voice.

That the terms "Courteous Reader" and "Candid Auditors," as having given rise to a false notion in those to whom they were applied, as if they conferred upon them some right, *which they cannot have,* of exercising their judgments, ought to be utterly banished and exploded.

These are our distinguishing tenets. To keep up the memory of the cause in which we suffered, as the ancients sacrificed a goat, a supposed unhealthy animal, to Æsculapius, on our feast-nights we cut up a goose, an animal typical of *the popular voice,* to the deities of Candour and Patient Hearing. A zealous member of the society once proposed that we should revive the obsolete luxury of viper-broth; but the stomachs of some of the company rising at the proposition, we lost the benefit of that highly salutary and *antidotal dish.*

The privilege of admission to our club is strictly limited to such as have been fairly *damned.* A piece that has met with ever so little applause, that has but languished its night or two, and then gone out, will never entitle its author to a seat among us. An exception to our usual readiness in conferring this privilege is in the case of a writer, who, having been once condemned, writes again, and becomes candidate for a second martyrdom. Simple damnation we hold to be a merit; but to be twice-damned we adjudge infamous. Such a one we utterly reject, and blackball without a hearing :—

"*The common damned shun his society.*"

Hoping that your publication of our Regulations may be a means of inviting some more members into our society, I conclude this long letter.

I am, Sir, yours,

SEMEL-DAMNATUS.

THE GOOD CLERK, A CHARACTER;

WITH SOME ACCOUNT OF "THE COMPLETE ENGLISH TRADESMAN."

THE Good Clerk.—He writeth a fair and swift hand, and is competently versed in the four first rules of arithmetic, in the Rule of Three (which is sometimes called the Golden Rule), and in Practice. We mention these things that we may leave no room for cavillers to say that anything essential hath been omitted in our definition; else, to speak the truth, these are but ordinary accomplishments, and such as every understrapper at a desk is commonly furnished with. The character we treat of soareth higher.

He is clean and neat in his person; not from a vainglorious desire of setting himself forth to advantage in the eyes of the other sex (with which vanity too many of our young sparks nowadays are infected), but to do credit, as we say, to the office. For this reason, he evermore taketh care that his desk or his books receive no soil; the which things he is commonly as solicitous to have fair and unblemished, as the owner of a fine horse is to have him appear in good keep.

He riseth early in the morning; not because early rising conduceth to health (though he doth not altogether despise that consideration), but chiefly to the intent that he may be first at the desk. There is his post,—there he delighteth to be, unless when his meals or necessity calleth him away; which time he alway esteemeth as loss, and maketh as short as possible.

He is temperate in eating and drinking, that he may preserve a clear head and steady hand for his master's service. He is also partly induced to this observation to the rules of temperance by his respect for religion and the laws of his country; which things, it may once for all be noted, do add special assistances to his actions, but do not and cannot furnish the mainspring or motive thereto. His first ambition, as appeareth all along, is to be a good Clerk; his next, a good Christian, a good Patriot, etc.

Correspondent to this, he keepeth himself honest, not for fear of the laws, but because he hath observed how unseemly an article it maketh in the Day-Book or Ledger when a sum is set down lost or missing; it being his pride to make these books to agree and to tally, the one side with the other, with a sort of architectural symmetry and correspondence.

He marrieth, or marrieth not, as best suiteth with his employer's views. Some merchants do the rather desire to have married men in their Counting-houses, because they think the married state a pledge for their servants' integrity, and an incitement to them to be industrious; and it was an observation of a late Lord Mayor of London, that the sons of clerks do generally prove clerks themselves, and that merchants encouraging persons in their employ to marry, and to have families, was the best method of securing a breed of sober, industrious young men attached to the mercantile interest. Be this as it may, such a character as we have been describing will wait till the pleasure of his employer is known on this point; and regulateth his desires by the custom of the house or firm to which he belongeth.

He avoideth profane oaths and jesting, as so much time lost from his employ; what spare time he hath for conversation, which, in a counting-house such as we have been supposing, can be but small, he spendeth in putting seasonable questions to such of his fellows (and sometimes *respectfully* to the master himself) who can give him information respecting the price and quality of goods, the state of exchange, or the latest improvements in book-keeping; thus making the motion of his lips, as well as of his fingers, subservient to his master's interest. Not that he refuseth a brisk saying, or a cheerful sally of wit, when it comes unforced, is free of offence, and hath a convenient brevity. For this reason, he hath commonly some such phrase as this in his mouth:—

> It's a slovenly look
> To blot your book.

Or,

> Red ink for ornament, black for use:
> The best of things are open to abuse.

So upon the eve of any great holy-day, of which he keepeth one or two at least every year, he will merrily say, in the hearing of a confidential friend, but to none other,—

> All work and no play
> Makes Jack a dull boy.

Or,

> A bow always bent must crack at last.

But then this must always be understood to be spoken confidentially, and, as we say, *under the rose*.

Lastly, his dress is plain, without singularity; with no other ornament than the quill, which is the badge of his function, stuck behind the dexter ear, and this rather for convenience of having it at hand, when he hath been called away from his desk, and expecteth to resume his seat there again shortly, than from any delight which he taketh in foppery or ostentation. The colour of his clothes is generally noted to be black rather than brown, brown rather than blue or green. His whole deportment is staid, modest, and civil. His motto is Regularity——.

This Character was sketched in an interval of business, to divert some of the melancholy hours of a Counting-house. It is so little a creature of fancy, that it is scarce anything more than a recollection of some of those frugal and economical maxims which, about the beginning of the last century (England's meanest period), were endeavoured to be inculcated and instilled into the breasts of the London Apprentices[1] by a class of instructors who might not inaptly be termed *The Masters of Mean Morals.* The astonishing narrowness and illiberality of the lessons contained in some of those books is inconceivable by those whose studies have not led them that way, and would almost induce one to subscribe to the hard censure which Drayton has passed upon the mercantile spirit :—

> The gripple merchant, born to be the curse
> Of this brave isle.

I have now lying before me that curious book by Daniel Defoe, *The Complete English Tradesman.* The pompous detail, the studied analysis of every little mean art, every sneaking address, every trick and subterfuge short of larceny that is necessary to the tradesman's occupation, with the hundreds of anecdotes, dialogues (in Defoe's liveliest manner) interspersed, all tending to the same amiable purpose,—namely, the sacrificing of every honest emotion of the soul to what he calls the main chance,—if you read it in an *ironical sense,* and as a piece of *covered satire,* make it one of the most amusing books which Defoe ever writ, as much so as any of his best novels. It is difficult to say what his intention was in writing it. It is almost impossible to suppose him in earnest. Yet such is the bent of the book to narrow and to degrade the heart, that if such maxims were as catching and infectious as those of a licentious cast, which happily is not the case, had I been living at that time, I certainly should have recommended to the Grand Jury of Middlesex, who presented *The Fable of the Bees,* to have presented this book of Defoe's in preference, as of a far more vile

[1] This term designated a larger class of young men than that to which it is now confined. It took in the articled clerks of merchants and bankers, the George Barnwells of the day.

and debasing tendency. I will give one specimen of his advice to the young tradesman on the *Government of his Temper:* "The retail tradesman in especial, and even every tradesman in his station, must furnish himself with a competent stock of patience. I mean that sort of patience which is needful to bear with all sorts of impertinence, and the most provoking curiosity that it is possible to imagine the buyers, even the worst of them, are, or can be, guilty of. *A tradesman behind his counter must have no flesh and blood about him, no passions, no resentment;* he must never be angry,—no, not so much as seem to be so, if a customer tumbles him five hundred pounds' worth of goods, and scarce bids money for anything; nay, though they really come to his shop with no intent to buy, as many do, only to see what is to be sold, and though he knows they cannot be better pleased than they are at some other shop where they intend to buy, 'tis all one; the tradesman must take it; he must place it to the account of his calling, that *'tis his business to be ill used and resent nothing;* and so must answer as obligingly to those that give him an hour or two's trouble and buy nothing, as he does to those who, in half the time, lay out ten or twenty pounds. The case is plain; and if some do give him trouble, and do not buy, others make amends, and do buy; and as for the trouble, 'tis the business of the shop."

Here follows a most admirable story of a mercer who, by his indefatigable meanness and more than Socratic patience under affronts, overcame and reconciled a lady, who, upon the report of another lady that he had behaved saucily to some third lady, had determined to shun his shop, but, by the over-persuasions of a fourth lady, was induced to go to it; which she does, declaring beforehand that she will buy nothing, but give him all the trouble she can. Her attack and his defence, her insolence and his persevering patience, are described in colours worthy of a Mandeville; but it is too long to recite. "The short inference from this long discourse," says he, "is this,—that here you see, and I could give you many examples like this, how and in what manner a shopkeeper is to behave himself in the way of his business; what impertinences, what taunts, flouts, and ridiculous things he must bear in his trade, and must not show the least return, or the least signal of disgust: he must have no passions, no fire in his temper; he must be all soft and smooth; nay, if his real temper be naturally fiery and hot, he must show none of it in his shop; he must be a perfect *complete hypocrite*, if he will be a *complete tradesman*.[1]" It is true, natural tempers are not to be always counterfeited: the man cannot easily be a lamb in his shop and a lion in himself; but, let it be easy or hard, it must be done, and is done. There are men who have by custom and usage brought themselves to it, that nothing could be meeker and milder than they when behind the counter, and yet nothing be more furious and raging in every other part of life: nay, the provocations they have met with in their shops have so irritated their rage, that they would go upstairs from their shop, and fall into frenzies, and a kind of madness, and beat their heads against the wall, and perhaps mischief themselves, if not prevented, till the violence of it had gotten vent, and the passions abate and cool. I heard once of a shopkeeper that behaved himself thus to such an extreme, that when he was provoked by the impertinence of the customers beyond what his temper could bear, he would go upstairs and beat his wife, kick his children about like dogs, and be as furious for two or three minutes as a man chained down in Bedlam; and again, when that heat was over, would sit down and cry faster than the children he had abused; and, after the fit, he would go down into the shop again, and be as humble, courteous, and as calm as any man whatever; so absolute a government of his passions had he in the shop, and so little out of it: in the shop, a soulless animal that would resent nothing;

---

[1] As no qualification accompanies this maxim, it must be understood as the genuine sentiment of the author!

and in the family, a madman: in the shop, meek like a lamb; but in the family outrageous, like a Libyan lion. The sum of the matter is, it is necessary for a tradesman to subject himself, by all the ways possible, to his business; *his customers are to be his idols; so far as he may worship idols, by allowance, he is to bow down to them, and worship them;* at least he is not in any way to displease them, or show any disgust or distaste whatsoever they may say or do. The bottom of all is that he is intending to get money by them; and it is not for him that gets money to offer the least inconvenience to them by whom he gets it: he is to consider that, as Solomon says, "the borrower is servant to the lender; so the seller is servant to the buyer." What he says on the head of "Pleasures and Recreations" is not less amusing: "The tradesman's pleasure should be in his business: his companions should be in his books" (he means his Ledger, Waste-book, etc), "and if he has a family he makes his excursions upstairs and no further. None of my cautions aim at restraining a tradesman from diverting himself, as we call it, with his fireside, or keeping company with his wife and children." Liberal allowance! nay, almost licentious and criminal indulgence! But it is time to dismiss this *Philosopher of Meanness.* More of this stuff would illiberalise the pages of the *Reflector.* Was the man in earnest, when he could bring such powers of description, and all the charms of natural eloquence, in commendation of the meanest, vilest, wretchedest degradations of the human character? or did he not rather laugh in his sleeve at the doctrines which he inculcated; and, retorting upon the grave citizens of London their own arts, palm upon them a sample of disguised satire under the name of wholesome Instruction?

THE REYNOLDS GALLERY.

The Reynolds Gallery has, upon the whole, disappointed me. Some of the portraits are interesting. They are faces of characters whom we (middle-aged gentlemen) were born a little too late to remember, but about whom we have heard our fathers tell stories till we almost fancy to have seen them. There is a charm in the portrait of a Rodney or a Keppel, which even a picture of Nelson must want for me. I should turn away after a slight inspection from the best likeness that could be made of Mrs. Anne Clarke; but Kitty Fisher is a considerable personage. Then the dresses of some of the women so exactly remind us of modes which we can just recall; of the forms under which the venerable relationship of aunt or mother first presented themselves to our young eyes; the aprons, the coifs, the lappets, the hoods. Mercy on us! what a load of head ornaments seem to have conspired to bury a pretty face in the picture of Mrs. Long, *yet could not!* Beauty must have some "charmed life" to have been able to surmount the conspiracy of fashion in those days to destroy it.

The portraits which least pleased me were those of boys as infant Bacchuses, Jupiters, etc. But the artist is not to be blamed for the disguise. No doubt the parents wished to see their children deified in their lifetime. It was but putting a thunderbolt (instead of a squib) into young master's hands; and a whey-faced chit was transformed into the infant ruler of Olympus,—him who was afterward to shake heaven and earth with his black brow. Another good boy pleased his grandmamma so well, and the blameless dotage of the good old woman imagined in him an adequate representative of the awful Prophet Samuel. *But the great historical compositions, where the artist was at liberty* to paint from *his own idea,—the Beaufort and the Ugolino:* why then, I must confess, pleading the liberty of table-talk for my presumption, that they have not left any very elevating impression on my mind. Pardon a ludicrous comparison. I know, madam, you admire them both; but placed opposite to each other as they are at the gallery, as if to set the one work in competition with the other, they did remind me of the famous contention for the prize of deformity, mentioned in the 173d Number of the *Spectator.* The one stares, and the other grins; but is there common dignity in their countenances? Does anything of the history of their life gone by peep through the ruins of the mind in the face, like the unconquerable grandeur that surmounts the distortions of the Laocoön? The figures which stand by the bed of Beaufort are indeed happy representations of the plain unmannered old nobility of the English historical plays of Shakspere; but, for anything else;—Give me leave to recommend those macaroons.

After leaving the Reynolds Gallery (where, upon the whole, I received a good deal of pleasure), and feeling that I had quite had my fill of paintings, I stumbled upon a picture in Piccadilly (No. 22, I think), which purports to be a portrait of Francis the First, by Leonardo da Vinci. Heavens, what a difference! It is but a portrait, as most of those I had been seeing; but, placed by them, it would kill them, swallow them up as Moses' rod the other rods. Where did these old painters get their models? I see no such figures, not in my dreams, as this Francis, in the character, or rather with the attributes, of John the Baptist. A more than martial majesty in the brow and upon the eyelid; an arm, muscular, beautifully formed; the long, graceful, massy fingers compressing, yet so as not to hurt, a lamb more lovely, more sweetly shrinking, than we can conceive that milk-white one which followed Una; the picture altogether looking as if it were eternal,—combining the truth of flesh with a promise of permanence like marble.

Leonardo, from the one or two specimens we have of him in England, must havè been a stupendous genius. I can scarce think he has had his full fame—he who could paint that wonderful personification of the Logos, or second person of the Trinity, grasping a globe, late in the possession of Mr. Troward of Pall Mall, where the hand was, by the boldest licence, twice as big as the truth of drawing warranted; yet the effect, to every one that saw it, by some magic of genius was confessed to be not *monstrous*, but *miraculous* and *silencing*. It could not be gainsaid.

WORDSWORTH'S "EXCURSION."

The *Quarterly Review*, October, 1814.

THE volume before us, as we learn from the Preface, is "a detached portion of an unfinished poem, containing views of man, nature, and society;" to be called the Recluse, as having for its principal subject the "sensations and opinions of a poet living in retirement;" and to be preceded by a "record in verse of the origin and progress of the author's own powers, with reference to the fitness which they may be supposed to have conferred for the task." To the completion of this plan we look forward with a confidence which the execution of the finished part is well calculated to inspire.—Meanwhile, in what is before us there is ample matter for entertainment: for the "Excursion" is not a branch (as might have been suspected) prematurely plucked from the parent tree to gratify an overhasty appetite for applause; but is, in itself, a complete and legitimate production.

It opens with the meeting of the poet with an aged man whom he had known from his schooldays; in plain words, a Scottish pedlar; a man who, though of low origin, had received good learning and impressions of the strictest piety from his stepfather, a minister and village schoolmaster. Among the hills of Athol, the child is described to have become familiar with the appearances of nature in his occupation as a feeder of sheep; and from her silent influences to have derived a character, meditative, tender, and poetical. With an imagination and feelings thus nourished—his intellect not unaided by books, but those, few, and chiefly of a religious cast—the necessity of seeking a maintenance in riper years had induced him to make choice of a profession, the *appellation* for which has been gradually declining into contempt, but which formerly designated a class of men, who, journeying in country places, when roads presented less facilities for travelling, and the intercourse between towns and villages was unfrequent and hazardous, became a sort of link of neighbourhood to distant habitations; resembling, in some small measure, in the effects of their periodical returns, the caravan which Thomson so feelingly describes as blessing the cheerless Siberian in its annual visitation, with "news of human kind."

In the solitude incident to this rambling life, power had been given him to keep alive that devotedness to nature which he had imbibed in his childhood, together with the opportunity of gaining such notices of persons and things from his intercourse with society, as qualified him to become a "teacher of moral wisdom." With this man, then, in a hale old age, released from the burthen of his occupation, yet retaining much of its active habits, the poet meets, and is by him introduced to a second character—a sceptic—one who had been partially roused from an overwhelming desolation, brought upon him by the loss of wife and children, by the powerful incitement of hope which the French Revolution in its commencement put forth, but who, disgusted with the failure of all its promises, had fallen back into a laxity of faith and conduct which induced at length a total despondence as to the dignity and final destination of his species. In the language of the poet, he

> . . . broke faith with those whom he had laid
> In earth's dark chambers.

Yet he describes himself as subject to compunctious visitations from that silent quarter.

> . . . Feebly must they have felt,
> Who, in old time, attired with snakes and whips

> The vengeful Furies. Beautiful regards
> Were turned on me—the face of her I loved;
> The wife and mother; pitifully fixing
> Tender reproaches, insupportable!—p. 133.

The conversations with this person, in which the Wanderer asserts the consolatory side of the question against the darker views of human life maintained by his friend, and finally calls to his assistance the experience of a village priest, the third, or rather fourth interlocutor, (for the poet himself is one), form the groundwork of the "Excursion."

It will be seen by this sketch that the poem is of a didactic nature, and not a fable or story; yet it is not wanting in stories of the most interesting kind,—such as the lovers of Cowper and Goldsmith will recognise as something familiar and congenial to them. We might instance the "Ruined Cottage," and the Solitary's own story, in the first half of the work; and the second half, as being almost a continued cluster of narration. But the prevailing charm of the poem is, perhaps, that, conversational as it is in its plan, the dialogue throughout is carried on in the very heart of the most romantic scenery which the poet's native hills could supply; and which, by the perpetual references made to it either in the way of illustration or for variety and pleasurable description's sake, is brought before us as we read. We breathe in the fresh air, as we do while reading Walton's "Complete Angler;" only the country about us is as much bolder than Walton's, as the thoughts and speculations, which form the matter of the poem, exceed the trifling pastime and low-pitched conversation of his humble fishermen. We give the description of the "two huge peaks," which from some other vale peered into that in which the Solitary is entertaining the poet and companion. "Those," says their host,

> . . . . . . if here you dwelt, would be
> Your prized companions. Many are the notes
> Which in his tuneful course the wind draws forth

> From rocks, woods, caverns, heaths, and dashing shores;
> And well those lofty brethren bear their part
> In the wild concert: chiefly when the storm
> Rides high; then all the upper air they fill
> With roaring sound, that ceases not to flow,
> Like smoke, along the level of the blast
> In mighty current; theirs, too, is the song
> Of stream and headlong flood that seldom fails;
> And in the grim and breathless hour of noon,
> Methinks that I have heard them echo back
> The thunder's greeting: nor have Nature's laws
> Left them ungifted with a power to yield
> Music of finer frame; a harmony,
> So do I call it, though it be the hand
> Of silence, though there be no voice; the clouds,
> The mist, the shadows, light of golden suns,
> Motions of moonlight, all come thither—touch,
> And have an answer—thither come, and shape
> A language not unwelcome to sick hearts,
> And idle spirits: there the sun himself
> At the calm close of summer's longest day
> Rests his substantial orb;—between those heights,
> And on the top of either pinnacle,
> More keenly than elsewhere in night's blue vault,
> Sparkle the stars as of their station proud.
> Thoughts are not busier in the mind of man,
> Than the mute agents stirring there:—alone
> Here do I sit and watch.—p. 84.

To a mind constituted like that of Mr. Wordsworth, the stream, the torrent, and the stirring leaf—seem not merely to suggest associations of deity, but to be a kind of speaking communication with it. He walks through every forest, as through some Dodona; and every bird that flits among the leaves, like that miraculous one[1] in Tasso, but in language more intelligent, reveals to him far higher love-lays. In his poetry nothing in Nature is

---

[1] With party-coloured plumes, and purple bill,
A wondrous bird among the rest there flew,
That in plain speech sung love-lays loud and shrill;
Her leden was like human language true;
So much she talk'd, and with such wit and skill,
That strange it seemed how much good she knew.
Fairfax's Translation.

dead. Motion is synonymous with life. "Beside yon spring," says the Wanderer, speaking of a deserted well, from which, in former times, a poor woman, who died heart-broken, had been used to dispense refreshment to the thirsty traveller,

> . . . . . beside yon spring I stood,
> And eyed its waters, till we seem'd to feel
> One sadness, they and I. For them a bond
> Of brotherhood is broken : time has been
> When every day the touch of human hand
> Dislodged the natural sleep that binds them up
> In mortal stillness.—p. 27.

To such a mind, we say—call it strength or weakness —if weakness, assuredly a fortunate one—the visible and audible things of creation present, not dim symbols, or curious emblems, which they have done at all times to those who have been gifted with the poetical faculty, but revelations and quick insights into the life within us, the pledge of immortality :—

> . . . . . the whispering air
> Sends inspiration from her shadowy heights,
> And blind recesses of the cavern'd rocks :
> The little rills, and waters numberless,
> Inaudible by day-light.

"I have seen," the poet says, and the illustration is a happy one—

> . . . . . I have seen
> A curious child, applying to his ear
> The convolutions of a smooth-lipp'd shell
> To which, in silence hush'd, his very soul
> Listen'd intensely, and his countenance soon
> Brighten'd with joy ; for murmurings from within
> Were heard—sonorous cadences ! whereby,
> To his belief, the monitor express'd
> Mysterious union with its native sea.
> Even such a shell the universe itself
> Is to the ear of faith ; and doth impart
> Authentic tidings of invisible things :
> Of ebb and flow, and ever during power ;
> And central peace subsisting at the heart
> Of endless agitation.—p. 191.

Sometimes this harmony is imaged to us by an echo; and in one instance, it is with such transcendent beauty set forth by a shadow and its corresponding substance, that it would be a sin to cheat our readers at once of so happy an illustration of the poet's system, and so fair a proof of his descriptive powers.

> Thus having reached a bridge, that over-arch'd
> The hasty rivulet where it lay becalm'd
> In a deep pool, by happy chance we saw
> A twofold image; on a grassy bank
> A snow-white ram, and in the crystal flood
> Another and the same! Most beautiful,
> On the green turf, with his imperial front,
> Shaggy and bold, and wreathèd horns superb,
> The breathing creature stood; as beautiful,
> Beneath him, show'd his shadowy counterpart.
> Each had his glowing mountains, each his sky,
> And each seem'd centre of his own fair world:
> Antipodes unconscious of each other,
> Yet, in partition, with their several spheres,
> Blended in perfect stillness, to our sight!—p. 407.

Combinations, it is confessed, "like those reflected in that quiet pool," cannot be lasting: it is enough for the purpose of the poet, if they are felt.—They are at least his system; and his readers, if they reject them for their creed, may receive them merely as poetry. In him, *faith*, in friendly alliance and conjunction with the religion of his country, appears to have grown up, fostered by meditation and lonely communions with Nature—an internal principle of lofty consciousness, which stamps upon his opinions and sentiments (we were almost going to say) the character of an expanded and generous Quakerism.

From such a creed we should expect unusual results; and, when applied to the purposes of consolation, more touching considerations than from the mouth of common teachers. The finest speculation of this sort perhaps in the poem before us, is the notion of the thoughts which may sustain the spirit, while they crush the frame of the sufferer, who from loss of objects of love by death, is commonly supposed to pine away under a broken heart.

> . . . If there be, whose tender frames have drooped
> Even to the dust, apparently, through weight
> Of anguish unrelieved, and lack of power
> An agonising spirit to transmute,
> Infer not hence a hope from those withheld
> When wanted most; a confidence impaired
> So pitiably, that, having ceased to see
> With bodily eyes, they are borne down by love
> Of what is lost, and perish through regret,
> Oh no! full oft the *innocent sufferer sees*
> *Too clearly; feels too vividly; and longs*
> *To realise the vision with intense*
> *And over constant yearning;*—there, there lies
> The excess, by which the balance is destroyed.
> Too, too contracted are these walls of flesh,
> This vital warmth too cold, these visual orbs,
> Though inconceivably endowed, too dim
> For any passion of the soul that leads
> To extasy; and, all the crooked paths
> Of time and change disdaining, takes its course
> Along the line of limitless desires.—p. 148.

With the same modifying and incorporating power, he tells us,—

> Within the soul a faculty abides
> That with interpositions, which would hide
> And darken, so can deal, that they become
> Contingencies of pomp; and serve to exalt
> Her native brightness. As the ample moon,
> In the deep stillness of a summer eve,
> Rising behind a thick and lofty grove,
> Burns like an unconsuming fire of light
> In the green trees; and, kindling on all sides
> Their leafy umbrage, turns the dusky veil
> Into a substance glorious as her own,
> Yea, with her own incorporate, by power
> Capacious and serene. Like power abides
> In man's celestial spirit; Virtue thus
> Sets forth and magnifies herself; thus feeds
> A calm, a beautiful, and silent fire,
> From the incumbrances of mortal life,
> From error, disappointment, nay, from guilt;
> And sometimes, so relenting justice wills,
> From palpable oppressions of despair.—p. 188.

This is high poetry; though (as we have ventured

to lay the basis of the author's sentiments in a sort of liberal Quakerism) from some parts of it, others may, with more plausibility, object to the appearance of a kind of Natural Methodism: we could have wished therefore that the tale of Margaret had been postponed, till the reader had been strengthened by some previous acquaintance with the author's theory; and not placed in the front of the poem, with a kind of ominous aspect, beautifully tender as it is. It is a tale of a cottage, and its female tenant, gradually decaying together, while she expected the return of one whom poverty and not unkindness had driven from her arms. We trust ourselves only with the conclusion—

> . . . . nine tedious years
> From their first separation, nine long years,
> She lingered in unquiet widowhood,
> A wife and widow. I have heard, my friend,
> That in yon arbour oftentimes she sate
> Alone, through half the vacant Sabbath day;
> And, if a dog passed by, she still would quit
> The shade, and look abroad. On this old bench
> For hours she sate; and evermore her eye
> Was busy in the distance, shaping things
> That made her heart beat quick. You see that path;
> There to and fro she paced through many a day
> Of the warm summer, from a belt of hemp
> That girt her waist, spinning the long-drawn thread
> With backward steps. Yet ever as there pass'd
> A man whose garments showed the soldier's[1] red,
> The little child who sate to turn the wheel
> Ceased from his task; and she with faultering voice
> Made many a fond inquiry; and when they,
> Whose presence gave no comfort, were gone by,
> Her heart was still more sad. And by yon gate,
> That bars the traveller's road, she often stood,
> And, when a stranger horseman came, the latch
> Would lift, and in his face look wistfully;
> Most happy, if from aught discovered there
> Of tender feeling, she might dare repeat
> The same sad question. Meanwhile her poor hut
> Sank to decay: for *he* was gone, whose hand,

---

[1] Her husband had enlisted for a soldier.

> At the first nipping of October frost,
> Closed up each chink, and with fresh bands of straw
> Chequered the green grown thatch. And so she lived
> Through the long winter, reckless and alone;
> Until her house by frost, and thaw, and rain
> Was sapped; and, while she slept, the nightly damps
> Did chill her breast; and in the stormy day
> Her tattered clothes were ruffled by the wind,
> Even at the side of her own fire. Yet still
> She loved this wretched spot, nor would for worlds
> Have parted hence : and still that length of road,
> And this rude bench, one torturing hope endeared,
> Fast rooted at her heart : and here, my friend,
> In sickness she remained ; and here she died,
> Last human tenant of these ruined walls !—p. 46.

The fourth book, entitled "Despondency Corrected," we consider as the most valuable portion of the poem. For moral grandeur; for wide scope of thought and a long train of lofty imagery; for tender personal appeals; and a *versification* which we feel we ought to notice, but feel it also so involved in the poetry, that we can hardly mention it as a distinct excellence; it stands without competition among our didactic and descriptive verse. The general tendency of the argument (which we might almost affirm to be the leading moral of the poem) is to abate the pride of the calculating *understanding*, and to reinstate the *imagination* and the *affections* in those seats from which modern philosophy has laboured but too successfully to expel them.

"Life's autumn past," says the gray-haired Wanderer,

> . . . I stand on winter's verge,
> And daily lose what I desire to keep;
> Yet rather would I instantly decline
> To the traditionary sympathies
> Of a most rustic ignorance, and take
> A fearful apprehension from the owl
> Or death-watch—and as readily rejoice
> If two auspicious magpies crossed my way—
> This rather would I do than see and hear
> The repetitions wearisome of sense,
> Where soul is dead and feeling hath no place.—p. 168.

In the same spirit, those illusions of the imaginative faculty to which the peasantry in solitary districts are peculiarly subject, are represented as the kindly ministers of *conscience:*

> . . . with whose service charged
> They come and go, appear and disappear;
> Diverting evil purposes, remorse
> Awakening, chastening an intemperate grief,
> Or pride of heart abating.

Reverting to more distant ages of the world, the operation of that same faculty in producing the several fictions of Chaldean, Persian, and Grecian idolatry, is described with such seductive power, that the Solitary, in good earnest, seems alarmed at the tendency of his own argument. Notwithstanding his fears, however, there is one thought so uncommonly fine, relative to the spirituality which lay hid beneath the gross material forms of Greek worship, in metal or stone, that we cannot resist the allurement of transcribing it—

> . . . Triumphant o'er his pompous show
> Of art, this palpable array of sense,
> On every side encountered; in despite
> Of the gross fictions chanted in the streets
> By wandering rhapsodists; and in contempt
> Of doubt and bold denials hourly urged
> Amid the wrangling schools—a SPIRIT hung,
> Beautiful Region! o'er thy towns and farms,
> Statues and temples, and memorial tombs;
> And emanations were perceived; and acts
> Of immortality, in Nature's course,
> Exemplified by mysteries, that were felt
> As bonds, on grave Philosopher imposed
> And armed Warrior; and in every grove
> A gay or pensive tenderness prevailed,
> When piety more awful had relaxed.
> "*Take, running river, take these locks of mine*"—
> Thus would the votary say—"*this severed hair,*
> *My vow fulfilling, do I here present,*
> *Thankful for my beloved child's return.*
> *Thy banks, Cephisus, he again hath trod,*
> *Thy murmurs heard, and drunk the crystal lymph*
> *With which thou dost refresh the thirsty lip,*

> *And moisten all day long these flowery fields."*
> And doubtless, sometimes, when the hair was shed
> Upon the flowing stream, a thought arose
> Of Life continuous, Being unimpaired;
> That hath been, is, and where it was and is
> There shall be; seen, and heard, and felt, and known,
> And recognised—existence unexposed
> To the blind walk of mortal accident;
> From diminution safe and weakening age;
> While man grows old, and dwindles and decays;
> And countless generations of mankind
> Depart, and leave no vestige where they trod.—p. 174.

In discourse like this the first day passes away. The second (for this almost dramatic poem takes up the action of two summer days) is varied by the introduction of the village priest; to whom the Wanderer resigns the office of chief speaker, which had been yielded to his age and experience on the first. The conference is begun at the gate of the churchyard; and after some natural speculations concerning death and immortality—and the custom of funereal and sepulchral observances, as deduced from a feeling of immortality—certain doubts are proposed respecting the quantity of moral worth existing in the world, and in that mountainous district in particular. In the resolution of these doubts, the priest enters upon a most affecting and singular strain of narration, derived from the graves around him. Pointing to hillock after hillock, he gives short histories of their tenants, disclosing their humble virtues, and touching with tender hand upon their frailties.

Nothing can be conceived finer than the manner of introducing these tales. With heaven above his head, and the mouldering turf at his feet—standing betwixt life and death—he seems to maintain that spiritual relation which he bore to his living flock in its undiminished strength, even with their ashes; and to be in his proper cure, or diocese, among the dead.

We might extract powerful instances of pathos from these tales—the story of Ellen in particular—but their force is in combination, and in the circumstances under which they are introduced. The traditionary anecdote of the Jacobite and Hanoverian, as less liable to suffer by transplanting, and as affording an instance of that finer species of humour, that thoughtful playfulness in which the author more nearly perhaps than in any other quality resembles Cowper, we shall lay (at least a part of it) before our readers. It is the story of a whig who, having wasted a large estate in election contests, retired "beneath a borrowed name" to a small town among these northern mountains, where a Caledonian laird, a follower of the house of Stuart, who had fled his country after the overthrow at Culloden, returning with the return of lenient times, had also fixed his residence.

> . . . . . . Here, then, they met,
> Two doughty champions ; flaming Jacobite,
> And sullen Hanoverian ! you might think
> That losses and vexations, less severe
> Than those which they had severally sustained,
> Would have inclined each to abate his zeal
> For his ungrateful cause ; no,—I have heard
> My reverend father tell that, mid the calm
> Of that small town encountering thus, they filled
> Daily its bowling-green with harmless strife,
> Plagued with uncharitable thoughts the church,
> And vex'd the market-place ! But in the breasts
> Of these opponents gradually was wrought,
> With little change of general sentiment,
> Such change towards each other, that their days
> By choice were spent in constant fellowship ;
> And, if at times they fretted with the yoke,
> Those very bickerings made them love it more.
>   A favourite boundary to their lengthened walks
> This churchyard was. And, whether they had come
> Treading their path in sympathy, and linked
> In social converse, or by some short space
> Discreetly parted to preserve the peace,
> One spirit seldom failed to extend its sway
> Over both minds, when they awhile had marked
> The visible quiet of this holy ground
> And breathed its soothing air——
>   There live who yet remember to have seen
> Their courtly figures—seated on a stump
> Of an old yew, their favourite resting place.

> But, as the remnant of the long-lived tree
> Was disappearing by a swift decay,
> They with joint care determined to erect,
> Upon its site, a dial, which should stand
> For public use ; and also might survive
> As their own private monument ; for this
> Was the particular spot, in which they wished
> (And heaven was pleased to accomplish their desire)
> That, undivided, their remains should lie.
> So, where the mouldered tree had stood, was raised
> Yon structure, framing, with the ascent of steps
> That to the decorated pillar lead,
> A work of art, more sumptuous, as might seem,
> Than suits this place ; yet built in no proud scorn
> Of rustic homeliness ; they only aimed
> To ensure for it respectful guardianship.
> Around the margin of the plate, whereon
> The shadow falls, to note the stealthy hours,
> Winds an inscriptive legend——
>   At these words
> Thither we turned ; and gathered, as we read,
> The appropriate sense, in Latin numbers couched.
> " Time flies ; it is his melancholy task
> To bring, and bear away, delusive hopes,
> And reproduce the troubles he destroys.
> But, while his business thus is occupied,
> Discerning mortal ! do thou serve the will
> Of Time's eternal Master, and that peace,
> Which the world wants, shall be for thee confirmed."—
>   pp. 270-273.

The causes which have prevented the poetry of Mr. Wordsworth from attaining its full share of popularity are to be found in the boldness and originality of his genius. The times are past when a poet could securely follow the direction of his own mind into whatever tracts it might lead. A writer, who would be popular, must timidly coast the shore of prescribed sentiment and sympathy. He must have just as much more of the imaginative faculty than his readers as will serve to keep their apprehensions from stagnating, but not so much as to alarm their jealousy. He must not think or feel too deeply.

If he has had the fortune to be bred in the midst of

the most magnificent objects of creation, he must not have given away his heart to them; or if he have, he must conceal his love, or not carry his expressions of it beyond that point of rapture which the occasional tourist thinks it not overstepping decorum to betray, or the limit which that gentlemanly spy upon Nature, the picturesque traveller, has vouchsafed to countenance. He must do this, or be content to be thought an enthusiast.

If from living among simple mountaineers, from a daily intercourse with them, not upon the footing of a patron, but in the character of an equal, he has detected, or imagines that he has detected, through the cloudy medium of their unlettered discourse, thoughts and apprehensions not vulgar; traits of patience and constancy, love unwearied, and heroic endurance, not unfit (as he may judge) to be made the subject of verse, he will be deemed a man of perverted genius by the philanthropist who, conceiving of the peasantry of his country only as objects of a pecuniary sympathy, starts at finding them elevated to a level of humanity with himself, having their own loves, enmities, cravings, aspirations, etc., as much beyond his faculty to believe, as his beneficence to supply.

If from a familiar observation of the ways of children, and much more from a retrospect of his own mind when a child, he has gathered more reverential notions of that state than fall to the lot of ordinary observers, and, escaping from the dissonant wranglings of men, has tuned his lyre, though but for occasional harmonies, to the milder utterance of that soft age,—his verses shall be censured as infantile by critics who confound poetry "having children for its subject" with poetry that is "childish," and who, having themselves perhaps never been *children*, never having possessed the tenderness and docility of that age, know not what the soul of a child is—how apprehensive! how imaginative! how religious!

We have touched upon some of the causes which we

conceive to have been unfriendly to the author's former poems. We think they do not apply in the same force to the one before us. There is in it more of uniform elevation, a wider scope of subject, less of manner, and it contains none of those starts and imperfect shapings which in some of this author's smaller pieces offended the weak, and gave scandal to the perverse. It must indeed be approached with seriousness. It has in it much of that quality which "draws the devout, deterring the profane." Those who hate the "Paradise Lost" will not love this poem. The steps of the great master are discernible in it; not in direct imitation or injurious parody, but in the following of the spirit, in free homage and generous subjection.

One objection it is impossible not to foresee. It will be asked, why put such eloquent discourse in the mouth of a pedlar? It might be answered that Mr. Wordsworth's plan required a character in humble life to be the organ of his philosophy. It was in harmony with the system and scenery of his poem. We read "Piers Plowman's Creed," and the lowness of the teacher seems to add a simple dignity to the doctrine. Besides, the poet has bestowed an unusual share of education upon him. Is it too much to suppose that the author, at some early period of his life, may himself have known such a person, a man endowed with sentiments above his situation, another Burns; and that the dignified strains which he has attributed to the Wanderer may be no more than recollections of his conversation, heightened only by the amplification natural to poetry, or the lustre which imagination flings back upon the objects and companions of our youth? After all, if there should be found readers willing to admire the poem, who yet feel scandalised at a *name*, we would advise them, wherever it occurs, to substitute silently the word *Palmer*, or *Pilgrim*, or any less offensive designation, which shall connect the notion of sobriety in heart and manners with the experience and privileges which a wayfaring life confers.

THEATRICAL NOTICES.

RICHARD BROME'S *JOVIAL CREW*.

THE *Jovial Crew*, or the *Merry Beggars*, has been revived here [at the English Opera] after an interval, as the bills tell us, of seven years. Can it be so long (it seems but yesterday) since we saw poor Lovegrove in Justice Clack? His childish treble still pipes in our ears; "Whip 'em, whip 'em, whip 'em." Dowton was the representative of the Justice the other night, and shook our ribs most incontinently. He was in "excellent foolery," and our lungs crowed chanticleer. Yet it appears to us that there was a still higher strain of fatuity in his predecessor—that his eyes distilled a richer dotage. Perhaps, after all, it was an error of the memory. Defunct merit comes out upon us strangely.

Easy natural Wrench was the Springlove; too comfortable a personage perhaps to personify Springlove, in whom the voice of the bird awakens a restless instinct of roaming that had slept during the winter. Miss Stevenson certainly leaves us nothing to regret for the absence of the lady, however agreeable, who formerly performed the part of Meriel. Miss Stevenson is a fine open-countenanced lass, with glorious girlish manners. But the Princess of Mumpers, and Lady Paramount of beggarly counterfeit accents, was *she* that played Rachel. Her gabbling lachrymose petitions; her tones, such as we have heard by the side of old woods, when an irresistible face has come peeping on one on a sudden; with her full black locks, and a *voice*—how shall we describe it?—a voice that was by nature meant to convey nothing but truth and goodness, but warped by circumstance into an assurance that she is telling us a lie—that catching twitch of the thievish irreprovable finger—those ballad-singers' notes, so vulgar, yet so unvulgar—that assurance so like impudence and yet so many countless leagues removed from it—her jeers, which we had rather stand, than be caressed with other ladies' compliments, a summer's day long—her face with a wild out-of-doors grace upon it——

Altogether, a brace of more romantic she-beggars it was never our fortune to meet in this supplicatory world. The youngest might have sat for "pretty Bessy," whose father was an Earl, and whose legend still adorns the front of mine hostess's doors at Bethnal Green; and the other could be no less than the "Beggar Maid" whom "King Cophetua wooed." "What a lass that were," said a stranger who sate beside us, speaking of Miss Kelly in Rachel, "to go a-gypsying through the world with." We confess we longed to drop a tester in her lap, she begged so masterly.

By-the-way, this is the true *Beggar's Opera*. The other should have been called the *Mirror for Highwaymen*. We wonder the Societies for the Suppression of Mendicity (and other good things) do not club for the putting down of this infamous protest in favour of air, and clear liberty, and honest license, and blameless assertion of man's original blest charter of blue skies, and vagrancy, and nothing-to-do.

July 4, 1819.

ISAAC BICKERSTAFF'S *HYPOCRITE*.

BY one of those perversions which actuate poor mortals in the place of motives (to persuade us into the notion that we are free agents, we presume), we had never till the other evening seen Dowton [at the English Opera] in Dr. Cantwell. By a pious fraud of Mr. Arnold's, who by a process as simple as some of those by which Mathews metamorphoses his person, has converted the play into an opera,—a conversion, by-the-way, for which we are deeply indebted to him,—we have been favoured with this rich novelty at our favourite theatre. It seems a little unreasonable to come lagging in with a posthumous testimony to the merits of a performance of which the town has long rung, but we cannot help remarking in Mr. Dowton's acting, the subtle *gradations* of the hypocrisy; the length to which it runs in proportion as the recipient is capable of taking it in; the gross palpable way in which he administers the dose in wholesale to old Lady Lambert, that rich fanatic; the somewhat more guarded manner in which he retails it out, only so much a time as he can bear, to the somewhat less bitten fool her son; and the almost absence of it before the younger members of the family, when nobody else is by; how the cloven foot peeps out a little and a little more, till the diabolical nature is stung out at last into full manifestation of its horrid self. What a grand insolence in the tone which he assumes, when he commands Sir John to quit *his* house; and then the tortures and agonies when he is finally baffled! It is in these last perhaps that he is greatest, and we should be doing injustice not to compare this part of the performance with, and in some respects to give it the preference above, the acting of Mr. Kean, in a situation nearly analogous, at the conclusion of the *City Madam*. Cantwell reveals his pangs with quite as much force, and without the assistance of those contortions which transform the detected Luke into the similitude of a mad tiger, or a foaming demon. Dowton plays it neither like beast nor demon, but simply as it should be, a bold bad man pushed to extremity. Humanity is never once overstepped. Has it ever been noticed, the exquisite modulation with which he drawls out the word "Charles," when he calls his secretary, so humble, so seraphic, so resigned. The most diabolical of her sex that we ever knew accented her honey devil words in just such a hymn-like smoothness. The spirit of Whitfield seems hovering in the air, to suck the blessed tones so much like his own upon earth: Lady Huntingdon claps her neat white wings, and gives it out again in heaven to the sainted ones, in approbation.

Miss Kelly is not quite at home in Charlotte; she is too good for such parts. Her cue is to be natural; she cannot put on the modes of artificial life, and play the coquette as it is expected to be played. There is a frankness in her tones which defeats her purposes; we could not help wondering why her lover (Mr. Pearman) looked so rueful; we forgot that she was acting airs and graces, as she seemed to forget it herself, turning them into a playfulness which could breed no doubt for a moment which way her inclinations ran. She is in truth not framed to tease or torment even in jest, but to utter a hearty *Yes* or *No;* to yield or refuse assent with a noble sincerity. We have not the pleasure of being acquainted with her, but we have been told that she carries the same cordial manners into private life. We have heard, too, of some virtues which she is in the practice of; but they are of a description which repay themselves, and with them neither we nor the public have anything to do.

One word about Wrench who played the Colonel:— Was this man never unhappy? It seems as if care never came near him, as if the black ox could never tread upon his foot; we want something calamitous to befall him, to bring him down to us. It is a shame he should be suffered to go about with his well-looking happy face and tones insulting us thin race of irritable and irritable-making critics.

August 2, 1819.

NEW PIECES AT THE LYCEUM.

A PLOT has broke out at this theatre. Some quarrel has been breeding between the male and female performers, and the women have determined to set up for themselves. Seven of them, *Belles without Beaux* they call themselves, have undertaken to get up a piece without any assistance from the men, and in our opinion have established their point most successfully. There is Miss Carew with her silvery tones, and Miss Stevenson with her delicious mixture of the school-girl and the waiting-maid, and Miss Kelly, sure to be first in any mischief, and Mrs. Chatterly, with some of the best acting we have ever witnessed, and Miss Love, worthy of the *name*, and Mrs. Grove that rhymes to her, and Mrs. Richardson who might in charity have been allowed somewhat a larger portion of the dialogue. The effect was enchanting. We mean for once. We do not want to encourage these Amazonian vanities. Once or twice we longed to have Wrench bustling among them. A lady who sate near us was observed to gape for want of variety. To us it was delicate quintessence, an apple-pie made all of quinces. We remember poor Holcroft's last comedy, which positively died from the opposite excess; it was choked up with men, and perished from a redundancy of male population. It had nine principal men characters in it, and but one woman, and she of no very ambiguous character. Mrs. Harlow, to do the part justice, chose to play it in scarlet.

We did not know Mrs. Chatterly's merits before; she plays, with downright sterling good acting, a prude who is to be convinced out of her prudery by Miss Kelly's (we did not catch her stage name) assumption of the dress and character of a brother of seventeen, who makes the prettiest unalarming platonic approaches; and in the shyest mark of moral battery, no one step of which you can detect, or say *this* is decidedly going too far, vanquishes at last the ice of her scruples, brings her into an infinite scrape, and then with her own infinite good humour sets all to right, and brings her safe out of it again with an explanation. Mrs. Chatterly's embarrassments were masterly. Miss Stevenson, her maid's, start at surprising a youth in her mistress's closet at midnight, was quite as good. Miss Kelly we do not care to say anything about, because we have been accused of flattering her. The truth is, this lady puts so much intelligence and good sense into every part which she plays, that there is no expressing an honest sense of her merits, without incurring a suspicion of that sort. But what have we to gain by praising Miss Kelly?

Altogether, this little feminine republic, this provoking experiment, went off most smoothly. What a nice world it would be, we sometimes think, *all women!* but then we are afraid, we slip in a fallacy unawares into the hypothesis; we somehow edge in the idea of ourselves as spectators or something among them.

We saw Wilkinson after it in *Walk for a Wager*. What a picture of forlorn hope! of abject orphan destitution! he seems to have no friends in the world but his legs, and he plies them accordingly. He goes walking on like a perpetual motion. His continual ambulatory presence performs the part of a Greek chorus. He is the walking gentleman of the piece; a peripatetic that would make a stoic laugh. He made us cry. His Muffincap in *Amateurs and Actors* is just such another piece of acting. We have seen charity boys, both of St. Clement's and Farringdon Without, looking just as old, ground down out of all semblance of youth, by abject and hopeless neglect—you cannot guess their age between fifteen and fifty. If Mr. Peake is the author of these pieces he has no reason to be piqued at their reception.

We must apologise for an oversight in our last week's article. The allusion made to Mr. Kean's acting of Luke in the *City Madam* was totally inapplicable to the part and to the play. We were thinking of his performance of the concluding scenes of *The New Way to Pay Old*

Debts. We confounded one of Massinger's strange heroes with the other. It was Sir Giles Overreach we meant; nor are we sure that our remark was just, even with this explanation. When we consider the intense tone in which Mr. Kean thinks it proper (and he is quite as likely to be in the right as his blundering critic) to pitch the temperament of that monstrous character from the beginning, it follows but logically and naturally that where the wild uncontrollable man comes to be baffled of his purpose, his passion should assume a frenzied manner, which it was altogether absurd to expect should be the same with the manner of the cautious and self-restraining Cantwell, even when he breaks loose from all bonds in the agony of his final exposure. We never felt more strongly the good sense of the saying—comparisons are odious. They betray us not seldom into bitter errors of judgment; and sometimes, as in the present instance, into absolute matter-of-fact blunders. But we have recanted.

August 1819.

MISS KELLY AT BATH.

DEAR G——,—I was thinking yesterday of our old play-going days, of your and my partiality to Mrs. Jordan, of our disputes as to the relative merits of Dodd and Parsons, and whether Smith or Jack Palmer were the most of a gentleman. The occasion of my falling into this train of thinking, was my learning from the newspapers that Miss Kelly is paying the Bath Theatre a visit (your own theatre, I am sorry to find, is shut up, either from parsimonious feelings, or through the influence of ——— principles).[1] This lady has long ranked among the most considerable of our London performers. If there are one or two of greater name, I must impute

---

[1] The word here omitted by the Bristol Editor, we suppose, is Methodistical.

it to the circumstance that she has never burst upon the town at once in the maturity of her powers, which is a great advantage to *débutantes* who have passed their probationary years in Provincial Theatres. We do not hear them tuning their instruments. But she has been winning her patient way from the humblest degradations to the eminence which she has now attained, on the self-same boards which supported her first in the slender pretensions of chorus singer. I very much wish you would go and see her. You will not see Mrs. Jordan, but something else; something on the whole very little, if at all, inferior to that lady in her best days. I cannot hope that you will think so, I do not even wish that you should. Our longest remembrances are the most sacred, and I shall revere the prejudice that shall prevent you from thinking quite so favourably of her as I do. I do not well know how to draw a parallel between their distinct manners of acting. I seem to recognise the same pleasantness and nature in both. But Mrs. Jordan's was the carelessness of a child; her childlike spirit shook off the load of years from her spectators; she seemed one whom care could not come near; a privileged being sent to teach mankind what he most wants—joyousness. Hence, if we had more unmixed pleasure from her performances, we had perhaps less sympathy with them than with those of her successor. This latter lady's is the joy of a freed spirit escaping from care, as a bird that had been limed; her smiles, if I may use the expression, seemed saved out of the fire, relics which a good spirit had snatched up as most portable; her discontents are visitors and not inmates: she can lay them by altogether, and when she does so, I am not sure that she is not greatest. She is in truth no ordinary tragedian. Her Yarico is the most intense piece of acting which I ever witnessed, the most heart-rending spectacle. To see her leaning upon that wretched reed, her lover—the very exhibition of whose character would be a moral offence, but for her clinging and noble credulity—to see her lean upon that flint, and by the strong workings of passion, imagine it a god, is one of the most afflicting lessons of the yearnings of the human heart, and its mistakes, that was ever read upon a stage. The whole performance is everywhere African, fervid, glowing. Nor is this anything more than the wonderful forcè of imagination in this performer; for turn but the scene, and you shall have her come forward in some kindly home-drawn character of an English rustic, a Phœbe, or a Dinah Cropley where you would swear that her thoughts had never strayed beyond the precincts of the dairy or the farm, or her mind known less tranquil passions than she might have learned among the flock, her out-of-door companions. See her again in parts of pure fun, such as the Housemaid in the Merry Mourners, where the suspension of the broom in her hand, which she has been delightfully twirling, on unexpectedly encountering her sweetheart in the character of her fellow-servant, is quite equal to Mrs. Jordan's cordial inebriation in Nell. I do not know whether I am not speaking it to her honour, that she does not succeed in what are called fine lady parts. Our friend C―― once observed that no man of genius ever figured as a gentleman. Neither did any woman gifted with Mrs. Jordan's or Miss Kelly's sensibilities ever take upon herself to shine as a fine lady; the very essence of this character consisting in the entire repression of all genius and all feeling. To sustain a part of this kind to the life, a performer must be haunted by a perpetual self-reference, she must be always thinking of herself, and how she looks, and how she deports herself in the eyes of the spectators; whereas the delight of actresses of true feeling and their chief power, is to elude the personal notice of an audience, to escape into their parts and hide themselves under the hood of their assumed character. Their most self-possession is in fact a self-forgetfulness; an oblivion alike of self and spectators. For this reason your most approved epilogue-speakers have been always ladies who have possessed least of this self-forgetting quality; and I think I have seen the amiable actress in question suffering some embarrassment, when she has had an address of the sort to deliver; when she found the modest veil of personation, which had half hid her from the audience, suddenly withdrawn, and herself brought without any such gratifying intervention before the public.

I would apologise for the length of this letter, if I did not remember the lively interest you used to take in theatrical performers.

I am, etc. etc.

"* * * *"

February 7, 1819.

FIRST FRUITS OF AUSTRALIAN POETRY.

(Sydney, New South Wales. Printed for Private Distribution. By Barron Field.)

> I first adventure; follow me who list:
> And be the second Austral harmonist.

WHOEVER thou art that hast transplanted the British wood-notes to the far-off forests which the Kangaroo haunts—whether thou art some involuntary exile that solaces his sad estrangement with recurrence to his native notes, with more wisdom than those captive Hebrews of old refused to sing their Sion songs in a strange land—or whether, as we rather suspect, thou art that valued friend of ours, who, in thy young time of life, together with thy faithful bride, thy newly " wedded flower," didst, in obedience to the stern voice of duty, quit thy friends, thy family, thy pleasing avocations, the Muses with which thou wert as deeply smitten as any, we believe, in our age and country, to go and administer tedious justice in inauspicious unliterary THIEFLAND,[1] we reclaim thee for our own, and gladly would transport thee back to thy native "fields," and studies congenial to thy habits.

We know a merry captain, and co-navigator with Cook, who prides himself upon having planted the first pun in Otaheite. It was in their own language, and the islanders first looked at him, then stared at one another, and all at once burst out into a genial laugh. It was a stranger,

---

[1] An elegant periphrasis for *the Bay*. Mr. Coleridge led us the way—" Cloudland, gorgeous land."

and as a stranger they gave it welcome. Many a quibble of their own growth, we doubt not, has since sprung from that well-timed exotic. Where puns flourish, there must be no inconsiderable advance in civilisation. The same good results we are willing to augur from this dawn of refinement at Sydney. They were beginning to have something like a theatrical establishment there, which we are sorry to hear has been suppressed; for we are of opinion with those who think that a taste for such kind of entertainments is one remove at least from profligacy, and that Shakspere and Gay may be as safe teachers of morality as the ordinary treatises which assume to instil that science. We have seen one of their play-bills (while the thing was permitted to last), and were affected by it in no ordinary degree, particularly in the omission of the titles of honour, which in this country are condescendingly conceded to the players. In their Dramatis Personæ, *Jobson* was played by Smith; *Lady Loverule*, Jones; *Nell*, Wilkinson; gentlemen and lady performers alike curtailed of their fair proportions. With a little patronage, we prophesy, that in a very few years the histrionic establishment of Sydney would have risen in respectability; and the humble performers would, by tacit leave or open permission, have been allowed to use the same encouraging affixes to their names, which dignify their prouder brethren and sisters in the mother country. What a moral advancement, what a lift in the scale, to a Braham or a Stephens of New South Wales, to write themselves *Mr.* and *Miss !* The King here has it not in his power to do so much for a commoner, no, not though he dub him a Duke.

The " First Fruits " consist of two poems. The first celebrates the plant *epacris grandiflora ;* but we are no botanists, and perhaps there is too much matter mixed up in it from the *Midsummer Night's Dream* to please some readers. The thefts are indeed so open and palpable, that we almost recur to our first surmise, that the author must be some unfortunate wight, sent on his travels for plagiarisms of a more serious complexion. But the old matter and the new blend kindly together, and must, we hope, have proved right acceptable to more than one

>   ———Among the fair
> Of that young land of Shakspere's tongue.

We select for our readers the second poem; and are mistaken if it does not relish of the graceful hyperboles of our elder writers. We can conceive it to have been written by Andrew Marvell, supposing him to have been banished to Botany Bay, as he did, we believe, once meditate a voluntary exile to Bermuda. See his fine poem, "Where the remote Bermudas ride."

THE GENTLE GIANTESS.

The widow Blacket, of Oxford, is the largest female I ever had the pleasure of beholding. There may be her parallel upon the earth; but surely I never saw it. I take her to be lineally descended from the maid's aunt of Brainford, who caused Master Ford such uneasiness. She hath Atlantean shoulders; and, as she stoopeth in her gait,—with as few offences to answer for in her own particular as any one of Eve's daughters,—her back seems broad enough to bear the blame of all the peccadilloes that have been committed since Adam. She girdeth her waist—or what she is pleased to esteem as such—nearly up to her shoulders; from beneath which that huge dorsal expanse, in mountainous declivity, emergeth. Respect for her alone preventeth the idle boys, who follow her about in shoals, whenever she cometh abroad, from getting up and riding. But her presence infallibly commands a reverence. She is indeed, as the Americans would express it, something awful. Her person is a burthen to herself no less than to the ground which bears her. To her mighty bone, she had a pinguitude withal, which makes the depth of winter to her the most desirable season. Her distress in the warmer solstice is pitiable. During the months of July and August, she usually renteth a cool cellar, where ices are kept, whereinto she descendeth when Sirius rageth. She dates from a hot Thursday,—some twenty-five years ago. Her apartment in summer is pervious to the four winds. Two doors, in north and south direction, and two windows, fronting the rising and the setting sun, never closed, from every cardinal point catch the contributory breezes. She loves to enjoy what she calls a quadruple draught. That must be a shrewd zephyr that can escape her. I owe a painful face-ache, which oppresses me at this moment, to a cold caught, sitting by her, one day in last July, at this receipt of coolness. Her fan, in ordinary, resembleth a banner spread, which she keepeth continually on the alert to detect the least breeze. She possesseth an active and gadding mind, totally incommensurate with her person. No one delighteth more than herself in country exercises and pastimes. I have passed many an agreeable holiday with her in her favourite park at Woodstock. She performs her part in these delightful ambulatory excursions by the aid of a portable garden-chair. She setteth out with you at a fair footgallop, which she keepeth up till you are both well-breathed, and then reposeth she for a few seconds. Then she is up again for a hundred paces or so, and again resteth; her movements, on these sprightly occasions, being something between walking and flying. Her great weight seemeth to propel her forward, ostrich-fashion. In this kind of relieved marching, I have traversed with her many scores of acres on those well-wooded and well-watered domains. Her delight at Oxford is in the public walks and gardens, where, when the weather is not too oppressive, she passeth much of her valuable time. There is a bench at Maudlin, or rather situated between the frontiers of that and ——'s College (some litigation, latterly, about repairs, has vested the property of it finally in ——'s), where, at the hour of noon, she is ordinarily to be found sitting,—so she calls it by courtesy,—but, in fact, pressing and breaking of it down with her enormous settlement; as both those foundations,—who, however, are good-natured enough to wink at it,—have found, I believe, to their cost. Here she taketh the fresh air, principally at vacation-times, when the walks are freest from interruption of the younger fry of students. Here she passeth her idle hours, not idly, but generally accompanied with a book, —blessed if she can but intercept some resident Fellow (as usually there are some of that brood left behind at these periods), or stray Master of Arts (to most of them she is better known than their dinner bell), with whom she may confer upon any curious topic of literature. I have seen these shy gownsmen, who truly set but a very slight value upon female conversation, cast a hawk's eye upon her from the length of Maudlin Grove, and warily glide off into another walk,—true monks as they are; and urgently neglecting the delicacies of her polished converse for their own perverse and uncommunicating solitariness! Within-doors, her principal diversion is music, vocal and instrumental; in both which she is no mean professor. Her voice is wonderfully fine; but till I got used to it, I confess it staggered me. It is, for all the world, like that of a piping bullfinch; while, from her size and stature, you would expect notes to drown the deep organ. The shake, which most fine singers reserve for the close or cadence, by some unaccountable flexibility, or tremulousness of pipe, she carrieth quite through the composition; so that her time, to a common air or ballad, keeps double motion, like the earth,— running the primary circuit of the tune, and still revolving upon its own axis. The effect, as I said before, when you are used to it, is as agreeable as it is altogether new and surprising. The spacious apartment of her outward frame lodgeth a soul in all respects disproportionate. Of more than mortal make, she evinceth withal a trembling sensibility, a yielding infirmity of purpose, a quick susceptibility to reproach, and all the train of diffident and blushing virtues, which for their habitation usually seek out a feeble frame, an attenuated and meagre constitution. With more than man's bulk, her humours and occupations are eminently feminine. She sighs,—being six feet high. She languisheth,—being two feet wide. She worketh slender sprigs upon the delicate muslin,—her fingers being capable of moulding a Colossus. She sippeth her wine out of her glass daintily—her capacity being that of a tun of Heidelberg. She goeth mincingly with those feet of hers, whose solidity need not fear the black ox's pressure. Softest and largest of thy sex, adieu! By what parting attribute may I salute thee, last and best of the Titanesses,—Ogress, fed with milk instead of blood; not least, or least handsome, among Oxford's stately structures,—Oxford, who, in its deadest time of vacation, can never properly be said to be empty, having thee to fill it.

ON A PASSAGE IN "THE TEMPEST."

As long as I can remember the play of *The Tempest*, one passage in it has always set me upon wondering. It has puzzled me beyond measure. In vain I strove to find the meaning of it. I seemed doomed to cherish infinite, hopeless curiosity.

It is where Prospero, relating the banishment of Sycorax from Argier, adds :—

—— For one thing that she did,
They would not take her life.

How have I pondered over this when a boy! How have I longed for some authentic memoir of the witch to clear up the obscurity! Was the story extant in the chronicles of Algiers? Could I get at it by some fortunate introduction to the Algerine ambassador? Was a voyage thither practicable? The Spectator, I knew, went to Grand Cairo only to measure the pyramid. Was not the object of my quest of at least as much importance? The blue-eyed hag! could *she* have done anything good or meritorious? might that succubus relent? then might there be hope for the Devil. I have often admired since that none of the commentators have boggled at this passage; how they could swallow this camel,—such a tantalising piece of obscurity, such an abortion of an anecdote.

At length I think I have lighted upon a clue which may lead to show what was passing in the mind of Shakspere when he dropped this imperfect rumour. In the "Accurate Description of Africa, by John Ogilby (folio), 1670," page 230, I find written as follows. The marginal title to the narrative is, "Charles the Fifth besieges Algier":—

"In the last place, we will briefly give an account of the Emperor Charles the Fifth, when he besieged this city: and of the great loss he suffered therein.

"This prince, in the year one thousand five hundred forty-one, having embarqued upon the sea an army of twenty-two thousand men aboard eighteen galleys, and an hundred tall ships, not counting the barques and shallops, and other small boats, in which he had engaged the principal of the Spanish and Italian nobility, with a good number of the Knights of Malta; he was to land on the coasts of Barbary, at a cape called Matifou. From this place unto the city of Algier, a flat shore or strand extends itself for about four leagues, the which is exceeding favourable to galleys. There he put ashore with his army, and in a few days caused a fortress to be built, which unto this day is called the castle of the Emperor.

"In the meantime the city of Algier took the alarm, having in it at that time but eight hundred Turks, and six thousand Moors, poor-spirited men, and unexercised in martial affairs; besides it was at that time fortified only with walls, and had no outworks: insomuch that by reason of its weakness, and the great forces of the Emperor, it could not in appearance escape taking. In fine, it was attempted with such order, that the army came up to the very gates, where the Chevalier de Savignac, a Frenchman by nation, made himself remarkable above all the rest by the miracles of his valour. For having repulsed the Turks, who, having made a sally at the gate called Babason, and there desiring to enter along with them, when he saw that they shut the gate upon him, he ran his poniard into the same, and left it sticking deep therein. They next fell to battering the city by the force of cannon; which the assailants so weakened, that in that great extremity the defendants lost their courage, and resolved to surrender.

"But as they were thus intending, there was a witch of the town, whom the history does not name, which went to seek out Assam Aga, that commanded within, and prayed him to make it good yet nine days longer with assurance, that within that time he should infallibly see Algier delivered from that siege, and the whole army of the enemy dispersed so that Christians should be as cheap as birds. In a word, the thing did happen in the manner as foretold; for upon the twenty-first day of October, in the same year, there fell a continual rain upon the land, and so furious a storm at sea, that one might have seen ships hoisted into the clouds, and in one instant again precipitated into the bottom of the water: insomuch that that same dreadful tempest was followed with the loss of fifteen galleys, and above an hundred other vessels; which was the cause why the Emperor, seeing his army wasted by the bad weather, pursued by a famine, occasioned by wrack of his ships, in which was the greatest part of his victuals and ammunition, he was constrained to raise the siege, and set sail for Sicily, whither he retreated with the miserable reliques of his fleet.

"In the meantime that witch being acknowledged the deliverer of Algier, was richly remunerated, and the credit of her charms authorised. So that ever since, witchcraft hath been very freely tolerated; of which the chief of the town, and even those who are esteemed to be of greatest sanctity among them, such as are the Marabous, a religious order of their sects, do for the most part make profession of it, under a goodly pretext of certain revelations which they say they have had from their prophet, Mahomet.

"And hereupon those of Algier, to palliate the shame and the reproaches that are thrown upon them for making use of a witch in the danger of this siege, do say that the loss of the forces of Charles V. was caused by a prayer of one of their Marabous, named Cidy Utica, which was at that time in great credit, not under the notion of a magician, but for a person of a holy life. Afterwards in remembrance of their success, they have erected unto him a small mosque without the Babason gate, where he is buried, and in which they keep sundry lamps burning in honour of him: nay, they sometimes repair thither to make their *sala*, for a testimony of greater veneration."

Can it be doubted, for a moment, that the dramatist had come fresh from reading some *older narrative* of this deliverance of Algier by a witch, and transferred the merit of the deed to his Sycorax, exchanging only the "rich remuneration," which did not suit his purpose, to the simple pardon of her life? Ogilby wrote in 1670; but the authorities to which he refers for his account of Barbary are Johannes de Leo, or Africanus, Louis Marmol, Diego de Haedo, Johannes Gramaye, Braeves, Cel. Curio, and Diego de Torres, names totally unknown to me, and to which I beg leave to refer the curious reader for his fuller satisfaction.

LETTER TO AN OLD GENTLEMAN WHOSE EDUCATION HAS BEEN NEGLECTED.

To the Editor of the London Magazine.

DEAR SIR,—I send you a bantering "Epistle to an Old Gentleman whose Education is supposed to have been neglected." Of course, it was *suggested* by some letters of your admirable Opium-Eater, the discontinuance of which has caused so much regret to myself in common with most of your readers. You will do me injustice by supposing that, in the remotest degree, it was my intention to ridicule those papers. The fact is, the most serious things may give rise to an innocent burlesque; and, the more serious they are, the fitter they become for that purpose. It is not to be supposed that Charles Cotton did not entertain a very high regard for Virgil, notwithstanding he travestied that poet. Yourself can testify the deep respect I have always held for the profound learning and penetrating genius of our friend. Nothing upon earth would give me greater pleasure than to find that he has not lost sight of his entertaining and instructive purpose.

I am, dear Sir, yours and *his* sincerely,

ELIA.

MY DEAR SIR,—The question which you have done me the honour to propose to me, through the medium of our common friend, Mr. Grierson, I shall endeavour to answer with as much exactness as a limited observation and experience can warrant.

You ask,—or rather Mr. Grierson, in his own interesting language, asks for you,—" Whether a person at the age of sixty-three, with no more proficiency than a tolerable knowledge of most of the characters of the English alphabet at first sight amounts to, by dint of persevering application and good masters, a docile and ingenuous disposition on the part of the pupil always presupposed,—may hope to arrive, within a presumable number of years, at that degree of attainments which shall entitle the possessor to the character, which you are on so many accounts justly desirous of acquiring, of a *learned man*."

This is fairly and candidly stated,—only I could wish that on one point you had been a little more explicit. In the meantime, I will take it for granted, that by a "knowledge of the alphabetic characters" you confine your meaning to the single powers only, as you are silent on the subject of the diphthongs and harder combinations.

Why, truly, sir, when I consider the vast circle of sciences,—it is not here worth while to trouble you with the distinction between learning and science, which a man must be understood to have made the tour of in these days, before the world will be willing to concede to him the title which you aspire to,—I am almost disposed to reply to your inquiry by a direct answer in the negative.

However, where all cannot be compassed, a great deal that is truly valuable may be accomplished. I am unwilling to throw out any remarks that should have a tendency to damp a hopeful genius; but I must not, in fairness, conceal from you that you have much to do. The consciousness of difficulty is sometimes a spur to exertion. Rome—or rather, my dear sir, to borrow an illustration from a place as yet more familiar to you, Rumford—Rumford was not built in a day.

Your mind as yet, give me leave to tell you, is in the state of a sheet of white paper. We must not blot or blur it over too hastily. Or, to use an opposite simile, it is like a piece of parchment all bescrawled and bescribbled over with characters of no sense or import, which we must carefully erase and remove before we can make way for the authentic characters or impresses which are to be substituted in their stead by the corrective hand of science.

Your mind, my dear sir, again, resembles that same parchment, which we will suppose a little hardened by time and disuse. We may apply the characters; but are we sure that the ink will sink?

You are in the condition of a traveller that has all his journey to begin. And, again, you are worse off than the traveller which I have supposed; for you have already lost your way.

You have much to learn, which you have never been taught; and more, I fear, to unlearn, which you have been taught erroneously. You have hitherto, I dare say, imagined that the sun moves round the earth. When you shall have mastered the true solar system, you will have quite a different theory upon that point, I assure you. I mention but this instance. Your own experience, as knowledge advances, will furnish you with many parallels.

I can scarcely approve of the intention, which Mr. Grierson informs me you have contemplated, of entering yourself at a common seminary, and working your way up from the lower to the higher forms with the children. I see more to admire in the modesty than in the expediency of such a resolution. I own I cannot reconcile myself to the spectacle of a gentleman at your time of life, seated, as must be your case at first, below a tyro of four or five, for at that early age the rudiments of education usually commence in this country. I doubt whether more might not be lost in the point of fitness than would be gained in the advantages which you propose to yourself by this scheme.

You say you stand in need of emulation; that this incitement is nowhere to be had but at a public school;

that you should be more sensible of your progress by comparing it with the daily progress of those around you. But have you considered the nature of emulation, and how it is sustained at these tender years which you would have to come in competition with? I am afraid you are dreaming of academic prizes and distinctions. Alas! in the university for which you are preparing, the highest medal would be a silver penny; and you must graduate in nuts and oranges.

I know that Peter, the Great Czar—or Emperor—of Muscovy, submitted himself to the discipline of a dockyard at Deptford, that he might learn, and convey to his countrymen, the noble art of shipbuilding. You are old enough to remember him, or at least the talk about him. I call to mind also other great princes, who, to instruct themselves in the theory and practice of war, and set an example of subordination to their subjects, have condescended to enrol themselves as private soldiers; and, passing through the successive ranks of corporal, quartermaster, and the rest, have served their way up to the station at which most princes are willing enough to set out,—of general and commander-in-chief over their own forces. But—besides that there is oftentimes great sham and pretence in their show of mock humility—the competition which they stooped to was with their coevals, however inferior to them in birth. Between ages so very disparate as those which you contemplate, I fear there can no salutary emulation subsist.

Again: in the other alternative, could you submit to the ordinary reproofs and discipline of a dayschool? Could you bear to be corrected for your faults? Or how would it look to see you put to stand, as must be the case sometimes, in a corner?

I am afraid the idea of a public school in your circumstances must be given up.

But is it impossible, my dear sir, to find some person of your own age,—if of the other sex, the more agreeable, perhaps,—whose information, like your own, has rather lagged behind his years, who should be willing to set out from the same point with yourself; to undergo the same tasks?—thus at once inciting and sweetening each other's labours in a sort of friendly rivalry. Such a one, I think, it would not be difficult to find in some of the western parts of this island,—about Dartmoor for instance.

Or what if, from your own estate,—that estate, which, unexpectedly acquired so late in life, has inspired into you this generous thirst after knowledge,—you were to select some elderly peasant, that might best be spared from the land, to come and begin his education with you, that you might till, as it were, your minds together,— one whose heavier progress might invite, without a fear of discouraging, your emulation? We might then see— starting from an equal post—the difference of the clownish and the gentle blood.

A private education, then, or such a one as I have been describing, being determined on, we must in the next place look out for a preceptor; for it will be some time before either of you, left to yourselves, will be able to assist the other to any great purpose in his studies.

And now, my dear sir, if, in describing such a tutor as I have imagined for you, I use a style a little above the familiar one in which I have hitherto chosen to address you, the nature of the subject must be my apology. *Difficile est de scientiis inscienter loqui;* which is as much as to say, that, "in treating of scientific matters, it is difficult to avoid the use of scientific terms." But I shall endeavour to be as plain as possible. I am not going to present you with the *ideal* of a pedagogue as it may exist in my fancy, or has possibly been realised in the persons of Buchanan and Busby. Something less than perfection will serve our turn. The scheme which I propose in this first or introductory letter has reference to the first four or five years of your education only; and in enumerating the qualifications of him that should undertake the direction of your studies, I shall rather point out the *minimum*, or *least*, that I shall require of him, than trouble you in the search of attainments neither common nor necessary to our immediate purpose.

He should be a man of deep and extensive knowledge. So much at least is indispensable. Something older than yourself, I could wish him, because years add reverence.

To his age and great learning, he should be blessed with a temper and a patience willing to accommodate itself to the imperfections of the slowest and meanest capacities. Such a one, in former days, Mr. Hartlib appears to have been; and such, in our days, I take Mr. Grierson to be: but our friend, you know, unhappily, has other engagements. I do not demand a consummate grammarian; but he must be a thorough master of vernacular orthography, with an insight into the accentualities and punctualities of modern Saxon, or English. He must be competently instructed (or how shall he instruct you?) in the tetralogy, or first four rules, upon which not only arithmetic, but geometry, and the pure mathematics themselves, are grounded. I do not require that he should have measured the globe with Cook or Ortelius; but it is desirable that he should have a general knowledge (I do not mean a very nice or pedantic one) of the great division of the earth into four parts, so as to teach you readily to name the quarters. He must have a genius capable in some degree of soaring to the upper element, to deduce from thence the not much dissimilar computation of the cardinal points, or hinges, upon which those invisible phenomena, which naturalists agree to term *winds*, do perpetually shift and turn. He must instruct you, in imitation of the old Orphic fragments (the mention of which has possibly escaped you), in numeric and harmonious responses, to deliver the number of solar revolutions within which each of the twelve periods, into which the *Annus Vulgaris*, or common year, is divided, doth usually complete and terminate itself. The intercalaries and other subtle problems he will do well to omit, till riper years and course of study shall have rendered you more capable thereof. He must be capable of embracing all history, so as, from the countless myriads of individual men who have peopled this globe of earth,— *for it is a globe*,—by comparison of their respective births, lives, deaths, fortunes, conduct, prowess, etc., to pronounce, and teach you to pronounce, dogmatically and catechetically, who was the richest, who was the strongest, who was the wisest, who was the meekest, man that ever lived; to the facilitation of which solution, you will readily conceive, a smattering of biography would in no inconsiderable degree conduce. Leaving the dialects of men (in one of which I shall take leave to suppose you by this time at least superficially instituted), you will learn to ascend with him to the contemplation of that unarticulated language which was before the written tongue; and, with the aid of the elder Phrygian or Æsopic key, to interpret the sounds by which the animal tribes communicate their minds, evolving moral instruction with delight from the dialogue of cocks, dogs, and foxes. Or, marrying theology with verse, from whose mixture a beautiful and healthy offspring may be expected, in your own native accents (but purified), you will keep time together to the profound harpings of the more modern or Wattsian hymnics.

Thus far I have ventured to conduct you to a "hill-side whence you may discern the right path of a virtuous and noble education; laborious, indeed, at the first ascent, but else so smooth, so green, so full of goodly prospects and melodious sounds on every side, that the harp of Orpheus was not more charming."[1]

With my best respects to Mr. Grierson when you see him, I remain, my dear Sir, your obedient servant,

ELIA.

---

[1] Milton's "Tractate on Education," addressed to Mr. Hartlib.

BIOGRAPHICAL MEMOIR OF MR. LISTON.

THE subject of our Memoir is lineally descended from Johan de L'Estonne (see "Domesday Book," where he is so written), who came in with the Conqueror, and had lands awarded him at Lupton Magna, in Kent. His particular merits or services, Fabian, whose authority I chiefly follow, has forgotten, or perhaps thought it immaterial, to specify. Fuller thinks that he was standard-bearer to Hugo de Agmondesham, a powerful Norman baron, who was slain by the hand of Harold himself at the fatal battle of Hastings. Be this as it may, we find a family of that name flourishing some centuries later in that county. John Delliston, knight, was High Sheriff for Kent, according to Fabian, *quinto Henrici Sexti;* and we trace the lineal branch flourishing downwards,— the orthography varying, according to the unsettled usage of the times, from Delleston to Leston or Liston, between which it seems to have alternated, till, in the latter end of the reign of James I., it finally settled into the determinate and pleasing dissyllabic arrangement which it still retains. Aminadab Liston, the eldest male representative of the family of that day, was of the strictest order of Puritans. Mr. Foss, of Pall Mall, has obligingly communicated to me an undoubted tract of his, which bears the initials only, A. L., and is entitled, "The Grinning Glass, or Actor's Mirrour; wherein the vituperative Visnomy of Vicious Players for the Scene is as virtuously reflected back upon their mimetic Monstrosities as it has viciously (hitherto) vitiated with its vile Vanities her Votarists." A strange title, but bearing the impress of those absurdities with which the title-pages of that pamphlet-spawning age abounded. The work bears date 1617. It preceded the "Histriomastix" by fifteen years; and, as it went before it in time, so it comes not far short of it in virulence. It is amusing to find an ancestor of Liston's thus bespattering the players at the commencement of the seventeenth century:—

"Thinketh He" (the actor), "with his costive countenances, to wry a sorrowing soul out of her anguish, or by defacing the divine denotement of destinate dignity (daignely described in the face humane and no other) to reinstamp the Paradice-plotted similitude with a novel and naughty approximation (not in the first intention) to those abhorred and ugly God-forbidden correspondences, with flouting Apes' jeering gibberings, and Babion babbling-like, to hoot out of countenance all modest measure, as if our sins were not sufficing to stoop our backs without He wresting and crooking his members to mistimed mirth (rather malice) in deformed fashion, leering when he should learn, prating for praying, goggling his eyes (better upturned for grace), whereas in Paradice (if we can go thus high for His professions) that devilish Serpent appeareth his undoubted Predecessor, first induing a mask like some roguish roistering Roscius (I spit at them all) to beguile with stage shows the gaping Woman, whose Sex hath still chiefly upheld these Mysteries, and are voiced to be the chief Stage-haunters, where, as I am told, the custom is commonly to mumble (between acts) apples, not ambiguously derived from that pernicious Pippin (worse in effect than the Apples of Discord), whereas sometimes the hissing sounds of displeasure, as I hear, do lively reintonate that snake-taking-leave, and diabolical goings off, in Paradice."

The Puritanic effervescence of the early Presbyterians appears to have abated with time, and the opinions of the more immediate ancestors of our subject to have subsided at length into a strain of moderate Calvinism.

Still a tincture of the old leaven was to be expected among the posterity of A. L.

Our hero was an only son of Habakkuk Liston, settled as an Anabaptist minister upon the patrimonial soil of his ancestors. A regular certificate appears, thus entered in the Church-book at Lupton Magna:—"*Johannes, filius Habakkuk et Rebeccæ Liston, Dissentientium, natus quinto Decembri,* 1780, *baptizatus sexto Februarii sequentis; Sponsoribus J. et W. Woollaston, unâ cum Maria Merryweather.*" The singularity of an Anabaptist minister conforming to the child-rites of the Church would have tempted me to doubt the authenticity of this entry, had I not been obliged with the actual sight of it by the favour of Mr. Minns, the intelligent and worthy parish clerk of Lupton. Possibly some expectation in point of worldly advantages from some of the sponsors might have induced this unseemly deviation, as it must have appeared, from the practice and principles of that generally rigid sect. The term *Dissentientium* was possibly intended by the orthodox clergyman as a slur upon the supposed inconsistency. What, or of what nature, the expectations we have hinted at may have been, we have now no means of ascertaining. Of the Woollastons no trace is now discoverable in the village. The name of Merryweather occurs over the front of a grocer's shop at the western extremity of Lupton.

Of the infant Liston we find no events recorded before his fourth year, in which a severe attack of the measles bid fair to have robbed the rising generation of a fund of innocent entertainment. He had it of the confluent kind, as it is called; and the child's life was for a week or two despaired of. His recovery he always attributes (under Heaven) to the humane interference of one Dr. Wilhelm Richter, a German empiric, who, in this extremity, prescribed a copious diet of *sauer-kraut*, which the child was observed to reach at with avidity, when other food repelled him; and from this change of diet his restoration was rapid and complete. We have often heard him name the circumstance with gratitude; and it is not altogether surprising that a relish for this kind of aliment, so abhorrent and harsh to common English palates, has accompanied him through life. When any of Mr. Liston's intimates invite him to supper, he never fails of finding, nearest to his knife and fork, a dish of *sauer-kraut.*

At the age of nine, we find our subject under the tuition of the Rev. Mr. Goodenough (his father's health not permitting him probably to instruct him himself), by whom he was inducted into a competent portion of Latin and Greek, with some mathematics, till the death of Mr. Goodenough, in his own seventieth, and Master Liston's eleventh year, put a stop for the present to his classical progress.

We have heard our hero, with emotions which do his heart honour, describe the awful circumstances attending the decease of this worthy old gentleman. It seems they had been walking out together, master and pupil, in a fine sunset to the distance of three-quarters of a mile west of Lupton, when a sudden curiosity took Mr. Goodenough to look down upon a chasm, where a shaft had been lately sunk in a mining speculation (then projecting, but abandoned soon after, as not answering the promised success, by Sir Ralph Shepperton, knight, and member for the county). The old clergyman leaning over, either with incaution or sudden giddiness (probably a mixture of both), suddenly lost his footing, and, to use Mr. Liston's phrase, disappeared, and was doubtless broken into a thousand pieces. The sound of his head, etc., dashing successively upon the projecting masses of the chasm, had such an effect upon the child, that a serious sickness ensued; and, even for many years after his recovery, he was not once seen so much as to smile.

The joint death of both his parents, which happened not many months after this disastrous accident, and were probably (one or both of them) accelerated by it, threw our youth upon the protection of his maternal great-aunt,

Mrs. Sittingbourn. Of this aunt we have never heard him speak but with expressions amounting almost to reverence. To the influence of her early counsels and manners he has always attributed the firmness with which, in maturer years, thrown upon a way of life commonly not the best adapted to gravity and self-retirement, he has been able to maintain a serious character, untinctured with the levities incident to his profession. Ann Sittingbourn (we have seen her portrait by Hudson) was stately, stiff, tall, with a cast of features strikingly resembling the subject of this memoir. Her estate in Kent was spacious and well-wooded; the house one of those venerable old mansions which are so impressive in childhood, and so hardly forgotten in succeeding years. In the venerable solitudes of Charnwood, among thick shades of the oak and beech (this last his favourite tree) the young Liston cultivated those contemplative habits which have never entirely deserted him in after years. Here he was commonly in the summer months to be met with, with a book in his hand,—not a play-book,— meditating. Boyle's "Reflections" was at one time the darling volume; which, in its turn, was superseded by Young's "Night Thoughts," which has continued its hold upon him through life. He carries it always about him; and it is no uncommon thing for him to be seen, in the refreshing intervals of his occupation, leaning against a side-scene, in a sort of Herbert-of-Cherbury posture, turning over a pocket-edition of his favourite author.

But the solitudes of Charnwood were not destined always to obscure the path of our young hero. The premature death of Mrs. Sittingbourn, at the age of seventy, occasioned by incautious burning of a pot of charcoal in her sleeping-chamber, left him in his nineteenth year nearly without resources. That the stage at all should have presented itself as an eligible scope for his talents, and, in particular, that he should have chosen a line so foreign to what appears to have been his turn of mind, may require some explanation.

s

At Charnwood, then, we behold him, thoughtful, grave, ascetic. From his cradle averse to flesh-meats and strong drink; abstemious even beyond the genius of the place, and almost in spite of the remonstrances of his great-aunt, who, though strict, was not rigid,—water was his habitual drink, and his food little beyond the mast and beech-nuts of his favourite groves. It is a medical fact that this kind of diet, however favourable to the contemplative powers of the primitive hermits, etc., is but ill-adapted to the less robust minds and bodies of a later generation. Hypochondria almost constantly ensues. It was so in the case of the young Liston. He was subject to sights, and had visions. Those arid beech-nuts, distilled by a complexion naturally adust, mounted into an occiput already prepared to kindle by long seclusion and the fervour of strict Calvinistic notions. In the glooms of Charnwood he was assailed by illusions similar in kind to those which are related of the famous Anthony of Padua. Wild antic faces would ever and anon protrude themselves upon his sensorium. Whether he shut his eyes, or kept them open, the same illusions operated. The darker and more profound were his cogitations, the droller and more whimsical became the apparitions. They buzzed about him thick as flies, flapping at him, flouting him, hooting in his ear, yet with such comic appendages, that what at first was his bane became at length his solace; and he desired no better society than that of his merry phantasmata. We shall presently find in what way this remarkable phenomenon influenced his future destiny.

On the death of Mrs. Sittingbourn we find him received into the family of Mr. Willoughby, an eminent Turkey merchant, resident in Birchin Lane, London. We lose a little while here the chain of his history,—by what inducements this gentleman was determined to make him an inmate of his house. Probably he had had some personal kindness for Mrs. Sittingbourn formerly; but, however it was, the young man was here treated more like a son than a clerk, though he was nominally but the latter. Different avocations, the change of scene, with that alternation of business and recreation which in its greatest perfection is to be had only in London appear to have weaned him in a short time from the hypochondriacal affections which had beset him at Charnwood.

In the three years which followed his removal to Birchin Lane, we find him making more than one voyage to the Levant, as chief factor for Mr. Willoughby at the Porte. We could easily fill our biography with the pleasant passages which we have heard him relate as having happened to him at Constantinople; such as his having been taken up on suspicion of a design of penetrating the seraglio, etc.; but, with the deepest convincement of this gentleman's own veracity, we think that some of the stories are of that whimsical, and others of that romantic nature, which, however diverting, would be out of place in a narrative of this kind, which aims not only at strict truth, but at avoiding the very appearance of the contrary.

We will now bring him over the seas again, and suppose him in the counting-house in Birchin Lane, his protector satisfied with the returns of his factorage, and all going on so smoothly, that we may expect to find Mr. Liston at last an opulent merchant upon 'Change, as it is called. But see the turns of destiny! Upon a summer's excursion into Norfolk, in the year 1801, the accidental sight of pretty Sally Parker, as she was called (then in the Norwich company), diverted his inclinations at once from commerce; and he became, in the language of commonplace biography, stage-struck. Happy for the lovers of mirth was it that our hero took this turn; he might else have been to this hour that unentertaining character, a plodding London merchant.

We accordingly find him shortly after making his *début*, as it is called, upon the Norwich boards, in the season of that year, being then in the twenty-second year of his age. Having a natural bent to tragedy, he chose the part of Pyrrhus, in the *Distressed Mother*, to Sally

Parker's Hermione. We find him afterwards as Barnwell, Altamont, Chamont, etc.; but, as if Nature had destined him to the sock, an unavoidable infirmity absolutely discapacitated him for tragedy. His person, at this latter period of which I have been speaking, was graceful, and even commanding; his countenance set to gravity: he had the power of arresting the attention of an audience at first sight almost beyond any other tragic actor. But he could not hold it. To understand this obstacle, we must go back a few years to those appalling reveries at Charnwood. Those illusions, which had vanished before the dissipation of a less recluse life and more free society, now in his solitary tragic studies, and amid the intense calls upon feeling incident to tragic acting, came back upon him with tenfold vividness. In the midst of some most pathetic passage (the parting of Jaffier with his dying friend, for instance), he would suddenly be surprised with a fit of violent horse-laughter. While the spectators were all sobbing before him with emotion, suddenly one of those grotesque faces would peep out upon him, and he could not resist the impulse. A timely excuse once or twice served his purpose, but no audiences could be expected to bear repeatedly this violation of the continuity of feeling. He describes them (the illusions) as so many demons haunting him, and paralysing every effect. Even now, I am told, he cannot recite the famous soliloquy in *Hamlet*, even in private, without immoderate bursts of laughter. However, what he had not force of reason sufficient to overcome, he had good sense enough to turn into emolument, and determined to make a commodity of his distemper. He prudently exchanged the buskin for the sock, and the illusions instantly ceased; or, if they occurred for a short season, by their very co-operation added a zest to his comic vein,—some of his most catching faces being (as he expresses it) little more than transcripts and copies of those extraordinary phantasmata.

We have now drawn out our hero's existence to the

period when he was about to meet, for the first time, the sympathies of a London audience. The particulars of his success since have been too much before our eyes to render a circumstantial detail of them expedient. I shall only mention that Mr. Willoughby, his resentments having had time to subside, is at present one of the fastest friends of his old renegade factor; and that Mr. Liston's hopes of Miss Parker vanishing along with his unsuccessful suit to Melpomene, in the autumn of 1811 he married his present lady, by whom he has been blessed with one son, Philip, and two daughters, Ann and Augustina.

AUTOBIOGRAPHY OF MR. MUNDEN.

HARK'EE, Mr. Editor. A word in your ear. They tell me you are going to put me in print,—in print, sir; to publish my life. What is my life to you, sir? What is it to you whether I ever lived at all? My life is a very good life, sir. I am insured in the Pelican, sir. I am three-score years and six,—six, mark me, sir; but I can play Polonius, which, I believe, few of your corre— correspondents can do, sir. I suspect tricks, sir: I smell a rat; I do, I do. You would cog the die upon us; you would, you would, sir. But I will forestall you, sir. You would be deriving me from William the Conqueror, with a murrain to you. It is no such thing, sir. The town shall know better, sir. They begin to smoke your flams, sir. Mr. Liston may be born where he pleases, sir; but I will not be born at Lup—Lupton Magna for anybody's pleasure, sir. My son and I have looked over the great map of Kent together, and we can find no such place as you would palm upon us, sir; palm upon us, I say. Neither Magna nor Parva, as my son says, and he knows Latin, sir; Latin. If you write my life true, sir, you must set down, that I, Joseph Munden, comedian, came into the world upon Allhallows Day, Anno Domini, 1759—1759; no sooner nor later, sir; and I saw the first light—the first light, remember, sir, at Stoke Pogis —Stoke Pogis, *comitatu* Bucks, and not at Lup—Lup Magna, which I believe to be no better than moonshine —moonshine; do you mark me, sir? I wonder you can put such flim-flams upon us, sir; I do, I do. It does

not become you, sir; I say it,—I say it. And my father
was an honest tradesman, sir: he dealt in malt and hops,
sir; and was a corporation-man, sir; and of the Church
of England, sir, and no Presbyterian; nor Ana—Anabaptist, sir; however you may be disposed to make
honest people believe to the contrary, sir. Your bams
are found out, sir. The town will be your stale-puts no
longer, sir; and you must not send us jolly fellows, sir,—
we that are comedians, sir,—you must not send us into
groves and char—charnwoods a-moping, sir. Neither
charns, nor charnel-houses, sir. It is not our constitution,
sir: I tell it you—I tell it you. I was a droll dog from
my cradle. I came into the world tittering, and the
midwife tittered, and the gossips spilt their caudle with
tittering; and, when I was brought to the font, the
parson could not christen me for tittering. So I was
never more than half baptised. And, when I was little
Joey, I made 'em all titter; there was not a melancholy
face to be seen in Pogis. Pure nature, sir. I was born
a comedian. Old Screwup, the undertaker, could tell you,
sir, if he were living. Why, I was obliged to be locked
up every time there was to be a funeral at Pogis. I was
—I was, sir? I used to *grimace* at the mutes, as he
called it, and put 'em out with my mops and my mows,
till they couldn't stand at a door for me. And when I
was locked up, with nothing but a cat in my company, I
followed my bent with trying to make her laugh; and
sometimes she would, and sometimes she would not.
And my schoolmaster could make nothing of me: I had
only to thrust my tongue in my cheek—in my cheek,
sir, and the rod dropped from his fingers; and so my
education was limited, sir. And I grew up a young
fellow, and it was thought convenient to enter me upon
some course of life that should make me serious; but it
wouldn't do, sir. And I was articled to a drysalter. My
father gave forty pounds premium with me, sir. I can
show the indent—dent—dentures, sir. But I was born
to be a comedian, sir: so I ran away, and listed with the

players, sir: and I topt my parts at Amersham and Gerrard's Cross, and played my own father to his face, in his own town of Pogis, in the part of Gripe, when I was not full seventeen years of age; and he did not know me again, but he knew me afterwards; and then he laughed, and I laughed, and, what is better, the drysalter laughed, and gave me up my articles for the joke's sake: so that I came into court afterwards with clean hands—with clean hands—do you see, sir?

[Here the manuscript becomes illegible for two or three sheets onwards, which we presume to be occasioned by the absence of Mr. Munden, jun., who clearly transcribed it for the press thus far. The rest (with the exception of the concluding paragraph, which is seemingly resumed in the first handwriting) appears to contain a confused account of some lawsuit, in which the elder Munden was engaged; with a circumstantial history of the proceedings of a case of breach of promise of marriage, made to or by (we cannot pick out which) Jemima Munden, spinster; probably the comedian's cousin, for it does not appear he had any sister; with a few dates, rather better preserved, of this great actor's engagements,—as "Cheltenham (spelt Cheltnam), 1776;" "Bath, 1779;" "London, 1789;" together with stage anecdotes of Messrs. Edwin, Wilson, Lee, Lewis, etc.; over which we have strained our eyes to no purpose, in the hope of presenting something amusing to the public. Towards the end, the manuscript brightens up a little, as we said, and concludes in the following manner:—]

——stood before them for six and thirty years [we suspect that Mr. Munden is here speaking of his final leave-taking of the stage], and to be dismissed at last. But I was heart-whole to the last, sir. What though a few drops did course themselves down the old veteran's cheeks: who could help it, sir? I was a giant that night, sir; and could have played fifty parts, each as arduous as Dozy. My faculties were never better, sir. But I was to be laid upon the shelf. It did not suit the public to laugh with their old servant any longer, sir. [Here some moisture has blotted a sentence or two.] But I can play Polonius still, sir; I can, I can. Your servant, sir, JOSEPH MUNDEN.

REFLECTIONS IN THE PILLORY.

About the year 18—, one R——d, a respectable London merchant (since dead) stood in the pillory for some alleged fraud upon the revenue. Among his papers were found the following "Reflections," which we have obtained by favour of our friend Elia, who knew him well, and had heard him describe the train of his feelings, upon that trying occasion, almost in the words of the manuscript. Elia speaks of him as a man (with the exception of the peccadillo aforesaid) of singular integrity in all his private dealings, possessing great suavity of manner, with a certain turn for humour. As our object is to present human nature under every possible circumstance, we do not think that we shall sully our pages by inserting it.—Editor.

Scene,—*Opposite the Royal Exchange.*
Time,—*Twelve to One, Noon.*

Ketch, my good fellow, you have a neat hand. Prithee adjust this new collar to my neck gingerly. I am not used to these wooden cravats. There, softly, softly. That seems the exact point between ornament and strangulation. A thought looser on this side. Now it will do. And have a care, in turning me, that I present my aspect due vertically. I now face the orient. In a quarter of an hour I shift southward,—do you mind?—and so on till I face the east again, travelling with the sun. No half-points, I beseech you,—NN. by W., or any such elaborate niceties. They become the shipman's card, but not this mystery. Now leave me a little to my own reflections.

Bless us, what a company is assembled in honour of me! How grand I stand here! I never felt so sensibly before the effect of solitude in a crowd. I muse in solemn silence upon that vast miscellaneous rabble in the pit there. From my private box I contemplate, with mingled pity and wonder, the gaping curiosity of those underlings. There are my Whitechapel supporters. Rosemary Lane has emptied herself of the very flower of her citizens to grace my show. Duke's Place sits desolate. What is there in my face, that strangers should come so far from the east to gaze upon it? [*Here an egg narrowly misses him.*] That offering was well meant, but not so cleanly executed. By the tricklings, it should not be either myrrh or frankincense. Spare your presents, my friends: I am noways mercenary. I desire no missive tokens of your approbation. I am past those valentines. Bestow these coffins of untimely chickens upon mouths that water for them. Comfort your addle spouses with them at home, and stop the mouths of your brawling brats with such Olla Podridas; they have need of them. [*A brick is let fly.*] Discase not, I pray you, nor dismantle your rent and ragged tenements, to furnish me with architectural decorations, which I can excuse. This fragment might have stopped a flaw against snow comes. [*A coal flies.*] Cinders are dear, gentlemen. This nubbling might have helped the pot boil, when your dirty cuttings from the shambles at three-halfpence a pound shall stand at a cold simmer. Now, south about, Ketch. I would enjoy Australian popularity.

What, my friends from over the water! Old benchers —files of a day—ephemeral Romans—welcome! Doth the sight of me draw souls from limbo? Can it dispeople purgatory?—Ha!

What am I, or what was my father's house, that I should thus be set up a spectacle to gentlemen and others?

Why are all faces, like Persians at the sunrise, bent singly on mine alone? I was wont to be esteemed an ordinary visnomy, a quotidian merely. Doubtless these assembled myriads discern some traits of nobleness, gentility, breeding, which hitherto have escaped the common observation, —some intimations, as it were, of wisdom, valour, piety, and so forth. My sight dazzles; and, if I am not deceived by the too-familiar pressure of this strange neckcloth that envelopes it, my countenance gives out lambent glories. For some painter now to take me in the lucky point of expression!—the posture so convenient!—the head never shifting, but standing quiescent in a sort of natural frame. But these artisans require a westerly aspect. Ketch, turn me.

Something of St. James's air in these my new friends. How my prospects shift and brighten! Now, if Sir Thomas Lawrence be anywhere in that group, his fortune is made for ever. I think I see some one taking out a crayon. I will compose my whole face to a smile, which yet shall not so predominate but that gravity and gaiety shall contend, as it were,—you understand me? I will work up my thoughts to some mild rapture,—a gentle enthusiasm,—which the artist may transfer, in a manner, warm to the canvas. I will inwardly apostrophise my tabernacle.

Delectable mansion, hail! House not made of every wood! Lodging that pays no rent; airy and commodious; which, owing no window-tax, art yet all casement, out of which men have such pleasure in peering and overlooking, that they will sometimes stand an hour together to enjoy thy prospects! Cell, recluse from the vulgar! Quiet retirement from the great Babel, yet affording sufficient glimpses into it! Pulpit, that instructs without note or sermon-book; into which the preacher is inducted without tenth or first-fruit! Throne, unshared and single, that disdainest a Brentford competitor! Honour without co-rival! Or hearest thou, rather, magnificent theatre, in which the spectator comes to see and to be seen? From thy giddy heights I look down upon the common herd, who stand with eyes upturned, as if a winged messenger hovered over them; and mouths open as if they expected manna. I feel, I feel, the true episcopal yearnings. Behold in me, my flock, your true overseer! What though I cannot lay hands, because my own are laid; yet I can mutter benedictions. True *otium cum dignitate!* Proud Pisgah eminence! pinnacle sublime! O Pillory! 'tis thee I sing! Thou younger brother to the gallows, without his rough and Esau palms, that with ineffable contempt surveyest beneath thee the grovelling stocks, which claim presumptuously to be of thy great race! Let that low wood know that thou art far higher born. Let that domicile for groundling rogues and base earth-kissing varlets envy thy preferment, not seldom fated to be the wanton baiting-house, the temporary retreat, of poet and of patriot. Shades of Bastwick and of Prynne hover over thee,—Defoe is there, and more greatly daring Shebbeare,—from their (little more elevated) stations they look down with recognitions. Ketch, turn me.

I now veer to the north. Open your widest gates, thou proud Exchange of London, that I may look in as proudly! Gresham's wonder, hail! I stand upon a level with all your kings. They and I, from equal heights, with equal superciliousness, o'erlook the plodding money-hunting tribe below, who, busied in their sordid speculations, scarce elevate their eyes to notice your ancient, or my recent, grandeur. The second Charles smiles on me from three pedestals![1] He closed the Exchequer: I cheated the Excise. Equal our darings, equal be our lot.

Are those the quarters? 'tis their fatal chime. That

---

[1] A statue of Charles II., by the elder Cibber, adorns the front of the Exchange. He stands also on high, in the train of his crowned ancestors, in his proper order, *within* that building. But the merchants of London, in a superfetation of loyalty, have, within a few years, caused to be erected another effigy of him on the ground in the centre of the interior. We do not hear that a fourth is in contemplation.

the ever-winged hours would but stand still! but I must descend—descend from this dream of greatness. Stay, stay, a little while, importunate hour-hand! A moment or two, and I shall walk on foot with the undistinguished many. The clock speaks one. I return to common life. Ketch, let me out.

THE LAST PEACH.

I AM the miserablest man living. Give me counsel, dear Editor. I was bred up in the strictest principles of honesty, and have passed my life in punctual adherence to them. Integrity might be said to be ingrained in our family. Yet I live in constant fear of one day coming to the gallows.

Till the latter end of last autumn I never experienced these feelings of self-mistrust which ever since have embittered my existence. From the apprehension of that unfortunate man,[1] whose story began to make so great an impression upon the public about that time, I date my horrors. I never can get it out of my head that I shall some time or other commit a forgery, or do some equally vile thing. To make matters worse, I am in a banking-house. I sit surrounded with a cluster of banknotes. These were formerly no more to me than meat to a butcher's dog. They are now as toads and aspics. I feel all day like one situated amidst gins and pitfalls. Sovereigns, which I once took such pleasure in counting out; and scraping up with my little tin shovel (at which I was the most expert in the banking-house), now scald my hands. When I go to sign my name, I set down that of another person, or write my own in a counterfeit character. I am beset with temptations without motive. I want no more wealth than I possess. A more contented being than myself, as to money matters, exists not. What should I fear?

[1] Fauntleroy.

When a child, I was once let loose, by favour of a nobleman's gardener, into his lordship's magnificent fruit-garden, with full leave to pull the currants and the gooseberries; only I was interdicted from touching the wall-fruit. Indeed, at that season (it was the end of autumn), there was little left. Only on the south wall (can I forget the hot feel of the brickwork?) lingered the one last peach. Now, peaches are a fruit which I always had, and still have, an almost utter aversion to. There is something to my palate singularly harsh and repulsive in the flavour of them. I know not by what demon of contradiction inspired, but I was haunted by an irresistible desire to pluck it. Tear myself as often as I would from the spot, I found myself still recurring to it; till maddening with desire (desire I cannot call it), with wilfulness rather,—without appetite,—against appetite, I may call it,—in an evil hour, I reached out my hand and plucked it. Some few raindrops just then fell; the sky (from a bright day) became overcast; and I was a type of our first parents, after the eating of that fatal fruit. I felt myself naked and ashamed, stripped of my virtue, spiritless. The downy fruit, whose sight rather than savour had tempted me, dropped from my hand never to be tasted. All the commentators in the world cannot persuade me but that the Hebrew word, in the second chapter of Gensis, translated "apple," should be rendered "peach." Only this way can I reconcile that mysterious story.

Just such a child at thirty am I among the cash and valuables, longing to pluck, without an idea of enjoyment further. I cannot reason myself out of these fears: I dare not laugh at them. I was tenderly and lovingly brought up. What then? Who that in life's entrance had seen the babe F———, from the lap stretching out his little fond mouth to catch the maternal kiss, could have predicted, or as much as imagined, that life's very different exit? The sight of my own fingers torments me; they seem so admirably constructed for—pilfering. Then that jugular vein which I have in common———; in an emphatic sense may I say with David, I am "fearfully made." All my mirth is poisoned by these unhappy suggestions. If, to dissipate reflection, I hum a tune, it changes to the "Lamentations of a Sinner." My very dreams are tainted. I awake with a shocking feeling of my hand in some pocket.

Advise me, dear Editor, on this painful heart-malady. Tell me, do you feel anything allied to it in yourself? Do you never feel an itching, as it were,—a *dactylomania*,—or am I alone? You have my honest confession. My next may appear from Bow Street.

THE ILLUSTRIOUS DEFUNCT.

SINCE writing this article, we have been informed that the object of our funeral oration is not definitively dead, but only moribund. So much the better: we shall have an opportunity of granting the request made to Walter by one of the children in the wood, and "kill him two times." The Abbé de Vertot having a siege to write, and not receiving the materials in time, composed the whole from his invention. Shortly after its completion, the expected documents arrived, when he threw them aside, exclaiming, "You are of no use to me now: I have carried the town."

> Nought but a blank remains, a dead void space,
> A step of life that promised such a race.—DRYDEN.

Napoleon has now sent us back from the grave sufficient echoes of his living renown: the twilight of posthumous fame has lingered long enough over the spot where the sun of his glory set; and his name must at length repose in the silence, if not in the darkness, of night. In this busy and evanescent scene, other spirits of the age are rapidly snatched away, claiming our undivided sympathies and regrets, until in turn they yield to some newer and more absorbing grief. Another name is now added to the list of mighty departed,—a name whose influence upon the hopes and fears, the fates and fortunes, of our countrymen, has rivalled, and perhaps eclipsed, that of the defunct "child and champion of Jacobinism," while it is associated with all the sanctions of legitimate government, all the sacred authorities of social order and our most holy religion. We speak of one, indeed, under whose warrant heavy and incessant contributions were imposed upon our fellow-citizens, but who exacted nothing without the signet and the sign-manual of most devout Chancellors of the Exchequer. Not to dally longer with the sympathies of our readers, we think it right to premonish them that we are composing an epicedium upon no less distinguished a personage than the Lottery, whose last breath, after many penultimate puffs, has been sobbed forth by sorrowing contractors, as if the world itself were about to be converted into a blank. There is a fashion of eulogy, as well as of vituperation; and, though the Lottery stood for some time in the latter predicament, we hesitate not to assert that *multis ille bonis flebilis occidit.* Never have we joined in the senseless clamour which condemned the only tax whereto we became voluntary contributors,—the only resource which gave the stimulus without the danger or infatuations of gambling; the only alembic which in these plodding days sublimised our imaginations, and filled them with more delicious dreams than ever flitted athwart the sensorium of Alnaschar.

Never can the writer forget, when, as a child, he was hoisted upon a servant's shoulder in Guildhall, and looked down upon the installed and solemn pomp of the then drawing Lottery. The two awful cabinets of iron, upon whose massy and mysterious portals the royal initials were gorgeously emblazoned, as if, after having deposited the unfulfilled prophecies within, the king himself had turned the lock, and still retained the key in his pocket; the blue-coat boy, with his naked arm, first converting the invisible wheel, and then diving into the dark recess for a ticket; the grave and reverend faces of the commissioners eyeing the announced number; the scribes below calmly committing it to their huge books; the anxious countenances of the surrounding populace; while the giant figures of Gog and Magog, like presiding deities, looked down with a grim silence upon the whole proceeding,—constituted altogether a scene, which, combined with the sudden wealth supposed to be lavished from those inscrutable wheels, was well calculated to impress the imagination of a boy with reverence and amazement. Jupiter, seated between the two fatal urns of good and evil, the blind goddess with her cornucopia, the Parcæ wielding the distaff, the thread of life, and the abhorred shears, seemed but dim and shadowy abstractions of mythology, when I had gazed upon an assemblage exercising, as I dreamt, a not less eventful power, and all presented to me in palpable and living operation. Reason and experience, ever at their old spiteful work of catching and destroying the bubbles which youth delighted to follow, have indeed dissipated much of this illusion ; but my mind so far retained the influence of that early impression, that I have ever since continued to deposit my humble offerings at its shrine, whenever the ministers of the Lottery went forth with type and trumpet to announce its periodical dispensations ; and though nothing has been doled out to me from its undiscerning coffers but blanks, or those more vexatious tantalisers of the spirit denominated small prizes, yet do I hold myself largely indebted to this most generous diffuser of universal happiness. Ingrates that we are ! are we to be thankful for no benefits that are not palpable to sense, to recognise no favours that are not of marketable value, to acknowledge no wealth unless it can be counted with the five fingers ? If we admit the mind to be the sole depository of genuine joy, where is the bosom that has not been elevated into a temporary Elysium by the magic of the Lottery ? Which of us has not converted his ticket, or even his sixteenth share of one into a nest-egg of Hope, upon which he has sate brooding in the secret roosting-places of his heart, and hatched it into a thousand fantastical apparitions ?

What a startling revelation of the passions if all the aspirations engendered by the Lottery could be made manifest! Many an impecuniary epicure has gloated over his locked-up warrant for future wealth, as a means of realising the dream of his namesake in the "Alchemist:"

"My meat shall all come in in Indian shells," etc.

Many a doting lover has kissed the scrap of paper whose promissory shower of gold was to give up to him his otherwise unattainable Danaë: Nimrods have transformed the same narrow symbol into a saddle, by which they have been enabled to bestride the backs of peerless hunters; while nymphs have metamorphosed its Protean form into—

"Rings, gauds, conceits,
Knacks, trifles, nosegays, sweetmeats,"

and all the braveries of dress, to say nothing of the obsequious husband, the two footman'd carriage, and the opera box. By the simple charm of this numbered and printed rag, gamesters have, for a time at least, recovered their losses: spendthrifts have cleared off mortgages from their estates; the imprisoned debtor has leapt over his lofty boundary of circumscription and restraint, and revelled in all the joys of liberty and fortune; the cottage-walls have swelled out into more goodly proportion than those of Baucis and Philemon; poverty has tasted the luxuries of competence; labour has lolled at ease in a perpetual armchair of idleness; sickness has been bribed into banishment; life has been invested with new charms; and death deprived of its former terrors. Nor have the affections been less gratified than the wants, appetites, and ambitions of mankind. By the conjurations of the same potent spell, kindred have lavished anticipated benefits upon one another, and charity upon all. Let it be termed a delusion,—a fool's paradise is better than the wise man's Tartarus; be it branded as an ignis-fatuus, —it was at least a benevolent one, which, instead of beguiling its followers into swamps, caverns, and pitfalls, allured them on with all the blandishments of enchantment to a garden of Eden,—an ever-blooming Elysium of delight. True, the pleasures it bestowed were evanescent: but which of our joys are permanent? and who so inexperienced as not to know that anticipation is always of higher relish than reality, which strikes a balance both in our sufferings and enjoyments? "The fear of ill exceeds the ill we fear;" and fruition, in the same proportion, invariably falls short of hope. "Men are but children of a larger growth," who may amuse themselves for a long time in gazing at the reflection of the moon in the water; but, if they jump in to grasp it, they may grope for ever, and only get the farther from their object. He is the wisest who keeps feeding upon the future, and refrains as long as possible from undeceiving himself by converting his pleasant speculations into disagreeable certainties.

The true mental epicure always purchased his ticket early, and postponed inquiry into its fate to the last possible moment, during the whole of which intervening period he had an imaginary twenty thousand locked up in his desk: and was not this well worth all the money? Who would scruple to give twenty pounds interest for even the ideal enjoyment of as many thousands during two or three months? *Crede quod habes, et habes;* and the usufruct of such a capital is surely not dear at such a price. Some years ago, a gentleman in passing along Cheapside saw the figures 1069, of which number he was the sole proprietor, flaming on the window of a lottery-office as a capital prize. Somewhat flurried by this discovery, not less welcome than unexpected, he resolved to walk round St. Paul's that he might consider in what way to communicate the happy tidings to his wife and family; but, upon re-passing the shop he observed that the number was altered to 10,069, and, upon inquiry, had the mortification to learn that his ticket was a blank, and had only been stuck up in the window by a mistake of the clerk. This effectually calmed his agitation; but he always speaks of himself as having once possessed twenty thousand pounds, and maintains that his ten-minutes' walk round St. Paul's was worth ten times the purchase-money of the ticket. A prize thus obtained has, moreover, this special advantage,—it is beyond the reach of fate; it cannot be squandered; bankruptcy cannot lay siege to it; friends cannot pull it down, nor enemies blow it up; it bears a charmed life, and none of woman born can break its integrity, even by the dissipation of a single fraction. Show me the property in these perilous times, that is equally compact and impregnable. We can no longer become enriched for a quarter of an hour; we can no longer succeed in such splendid failures; all our chances of making such a miss have vanished with the last of the Lotteries.

Life will now become a flat, prosaic routine of matter-of-fact; and sleep itself erst so prolific of numerical configurations and mysterious stimulants to lottery adventure, will be disfurnished of its figures and figments. People will cease to harp upon the one lucky number suggested in a dream, and which forms the exception, while they are scrupulously silent upon the ten thousand falsified dreams which constitute the rule. Morpheus will stifle Cocker with a handful of poppies, and our pillows will be no longer haunted by the book of numbers.

And who, too, shall maintain the art and mystery of puffing, in all its pristine glory, when the lottery professors shall have abandoned its cultivation? They were the first, as they will assuredly be the last, who fully developed the resources of that ingenious art; who cajoled and decoyed the most suspicious and wary reader into a perusal of their advertisements by devices of endless variety and cunning; who baited their lurking schemes with midnight murders, ghost-stories, crim-cons, bon-mots, balloons, dreadful catastrophies, and every diversity of joy and sorrow, to catch newspaper-gudgeons. Ought not such talents to be encouraged? Verily the abolitionists have much to answer for!

And now, having established the felicity of all those

who gained imaginary prizes, let us proceed to show that the equally numerous class who were presented with real blanks have not less reason to consider themselves happy. Most of us have cause to be thankful for that which is bestowed! but we have all, probably, reason to be still more grateful for that which is withheld, and more especially for our being denied the sudden possession of riches. In the Litany, indeed, we call upon the Lord to deliver us "in all time of our wealth;" but how few of us are sincere in deprecating such a calamity! Massinger's Luke, and Ben Jonson's Sir Epicure Mammon, and Pope's Sir Balaam, and our own daily observation, might convince us that the Devil "now tempts by making rich, not making poor." We may read in the *Guardian* a circumstantial account of a man who was utterly ruined by gaining a capital prize; we may recollect what Dr. Johnson said to Garrick, when the latter was making a display of his wealth at Hampton Court—"Ah, David, David! these are the things that make a death-bed terrible;" we may recall the Scripture declaration, as to the difficulty a rich man finds in entering the kingdom of Heaven; and, combining all these denunciations against opulence, let us heartily congratulate one another upon our lucky escape from the calamity of a twenty or thirty thousand pound prize! The fox in the fable, who accused the unattainable grapes of sourness, was more of a philosopher than we are generally willing to allow. He was an adept in that species of moral alchemy which turns everything to gold, and converts disappointment itself into a ground of resignation and content. Such we have shown to be the great lesson inculcated by the Lottery, when rightly contemplated; and, if we might parody M. de Châteaubriand's jingling expression,—"*Le Roi est mort: vive le Roi !*"—we should be tempted to exclaim, "The Lottery is no more: long live the Lottery!"

THE RELIGION OF ACTORS.

THE world has hitherto so little troubled its head upon the points of doctrine held by a community which contributes in other ways so largely to its amusement, that, before the late mischance of a celebrated tragic actor, it scarce condescended to look into the practice of any individual player, much less to inquire into the hidden and abscondite springs of his actions. Indeed, it is with some violence to the imagination that we conceive of an actor as belonging to the relations of private life, so closely do we identify these persons in our mind with the characters which they assume upon the stage. How oddly does it sound, when we are told that the late Miss Pope, for instance,—that is to say, in our notion of her *Mrs. Candour*,—was a good daughter, an affectionate sister, and exemplary in all the parts of domestic life! With still greater difficulty can we carry our notions to church, and conceive of Liston kneeling upon a hassock, or Munden uttering a pious ejaculation,—"making mouths at the invisible event." But the times are fast improving; and, if the process of sanctity begun under the happy auspices of the present licencer go on to its completion, it will be as necessary for a comedian to give an account of his faith as of his conduct. Fawcett must study the five points; and Dicky Suett, if he were alive, would have to rub up his catechism. Already the effects of it begin to appear. A celebrated performer has thought fit to oblige the world with a confession of his faith,—or Br———'s *Religio Dramatici*. This gentleman, in his laudable attempt to shift from his person the obloquy of

Judaism, with a forwardness of a new convert, in trying to prove too much, has, in the opinion of many, proved too little. A simple declaration of his Christianity was sufficient; but, strange to say, his apology has not a word about it. We are left to gather it from some expressions which imply that he is a Protestant; but we did not wish to inquire into the niceties of his orthodoxy. To his friends of the *old persuasion* the distinction was impertinent; for what cares Rabbi Ben Kimchi for the differences which have split our novelty? To the great body of Christians that holds the Pope's supremacy— that is to say, to the major part of the Christian world —his religion will appear as much to seek as ever. But perhaps he conceived that all Christians are Protestants, as children and the common people call all, that are not animals, Christians. The mistake was not very considerable in so young a proselyte, or he might think the general (as logicians speak) involved in the particular. All Protestants are Christians; but I am a Protestant; *ergo*, etc.: as if a marmoset, contending to be a man, overleaping that term as too generic and vulgar, should at once roundly proclaim himself to be a gentleman. The argument would be, as we say, *exabundanti*. From whichever course this *excessus in terminis* proceeded, we can do no less than congratulate the general state of Christendom upon the accession of so extraordinary a convert. Who was the happy instrument of the conversion, we are yet to learn: it comes nearest to the attempt of the late pious Dr. Watts to Christianise the Psalms of the Old Testament. Something of the old Hebrew raciness is lost in the transfusion; but much of its asperity is softened and pared down in the adaptation.

The appearance of so singular a treatise at this conjuncture has set us upon an inquiry into the present state of religion upon the stage generally. By the favour of the Churchwardens of St. Martin's in the Fields, and St. Paul's, Covent Garden, who have very readily, and with great kindness, assisted our pursuit, we are enabled to lay before the public the following particulars. Strictly speaking, neither of the two great bodies is collectively a religious institution. We expected to find a chaplain among them, as at St. Stephen's and other Court establishments; and were the more surprised at the omission, as the last Mr. Bengough at the one house, and Mr. Powell at the other, from a gravity of speech and demeanour, and the habit of wearing black at their first appearances in the beginning of the *fifth* or the conclusion of the *fourth* act, so eminently pointed out their qualifications for such office. These corporations, then, being not properly congregational, we must seek the solution of our question in the tastes, attainments, accidental breeding, and education of the individual members of them. As we were prepared to expect, a majority at both houses adhere to the religion of the Church Established,—only that at one of them a strong leaven of Roman Catholicism is suspected; which, considering the notorious education of the manager at a foreign seminary, is not so much to be wondered at. Some have gone so far as to report that Mr. T——y, in particular, belongs to an order lately restored on the Continent. We can contradict this: that gentleman is a member of the Kirk of Scotland: and his name is to be found, much to his honour, in the list of seceders from the congregation of Mr. Fletcher. While the generality, as we have said, are content to jog on in the safe trammels of national orthodoxy, symptoms of a sectarian spirit have broken out in quarters where we should least have looked for it. Some of the ladies at both houses are deep in controverted points. Miss F——e, we are credibly informed, is a *Sub-* and Madame V—— a *Supra*-Lapsarian. Mr. Pope is the last of the exploded sect of the Ranters. Mr. Sinclair has joined the Shakers. Mr. Grimaldi sen., after being long a Jumper, has lately fallen into some whimsical theories respecting the fall of man; which he understands, not of an allegorical, but a *real tumble,* by which the whole body of humanity became, as it were, lame to the performance of good works. Pride he will have to be nothing but a stiff neck; irresolution, the nerves shaken; an inclination to sinister paths, crookedness of the joints; spiritual deadness, a paralysis; want of charity, a contraction in the fingers; despising of government, a broken head; the plaster, a sermon; the lint to bind it up, the text; the probers, the preachers; a pair of crutches, the old and new law; a bandage, religious obligation: a fanciful mode of illustration, derived from the accidents and habits of his past calling *spiritualised*, rather than from any accurate acquaintance with the Hebrew text, in which report speaks him but a raw scholar. Mr. Elliston, from all we can learn, has his religion yet to choose; though some think him a Muggletonian.

THE MONTHS.

RUMMAGING over the contents of an old stall at a half *book*, half *old-iron shop*, in an alley leading from Wardour Street to Soho Square, yesterday, I lit upon a ragged duodecimo which had been the strange delight of my infancy, and which I had lost sight of for more than forty years,—the "Queen-like Closet, or Rich Cabinet;" written by Hannah Woolly, and printed for R. C. and T. S., 1681; being an abstract of receipts in cookery, confectionery, cosmetics, needlework, morality, and all such branches of what were then considered as female accomplishments. The price demanded was sixpence, which the owner (a little squab duodecimo character himself) enforced with the assurance that his "own mother should not have it for a farthing less." On my demurring at this extraordinary assertion, the dirty little vendor reinforced his assertion with a sort of oath, which seemed more than the occasion demanded: "And now," said he, "I have put my soul to it." Pressed by so solemn an asseveration, I could no longer resist a demand which seemed to set me, however unworthy, upon a level with its dearest relations; and depositing a tester, I bore away the tattered prize in triumph. I remember a gorgeous description of the twelve months of the year, which I thought would be a fine substitute for those poetical descriptions of them which your "Every Day Book" had nearly exhausted out of Spenser. This will be a treat, thought I, for friend Hone. To memory they seemed no less fantastic and splendid than the other. But what are the mistakes of childhood! On reviewing them, they turned out to be only a set of commonplace receipts for working the seasons, months, heathen gods and goddesses, etc., in *samplers!* Yet, as an instance of the homely occupation of our great grandmothers, they may be amusing to some readers. "I have seen," says the notable Hannah Woolly, "such Ridiculous things done in work, as it is an abomination to any Artist to behold. As for example: You may find, in some Pieces, *Abraham* and *Sarah*, and many other Persons of Old time, Clothed as they go nowadays, and truly sometimes worse; for they most resemble the Pictures on Ballads. Let all Ingenious Women have regard, that when they work any Image, to represent it aright. First, let it be Drawn well, and then observe the Directions which are given by Knowing Men. I do assure you, I never durst work any Scripture Story without informing myself from the Ground of it; nor any other Story, or single Person without informing myself both of the Visage and Habit; as followeth:—

"If your work *Jupiter, the Imperial feigned God*, he must have long, Black Curled hair, a Purple Garment trimmed with Gold, and sitting upon a golden throne, with bright yellow Clouds about him."

THE TWELVE MONTHS OF THE YEAR.

March. Is drawn in Tawny, with a fierce aspect; a Helmet upon his head, and leaning on a Spade; and a Basket of Garden-Seeds in his left hand, and in his Right hand the sign of *Aries;* and Winged.

April. A young Man in Green, with a Garland of Myrtle and Hawthorn-buds; Winged; in one hand Primroses and Violets, in the other the Sign *Taurus.*

May. With a Sweet and lovely Countenance: clad in a Robe of White and Green, embroidered with several Flowers; upon his Head a garland of all manner of roses; on the one hand a Nightingale, in the other a Lute. His sign must be *Gemini.*

June. In a Mantle of dark Grass-green; upon his

Head a garland of Bents, Kings-cups, and Maiden-hair; in his Left hand an Angle, with a box of Cantharides; in his Right, the Sign *Cancer;* and upon his arms a Basket of seasonable Fruits.

July. In a Jacket of light Yellow, eating Cherries; with his Face and Bosom Sun-burnt! on his Head a wreath of Centaury and wild Thyme; a Scythe on his shoulder, and a bottle at his girdle; carrying the Sign *Leo.*

August. A Young Man of fierce and Choleric aspect, in a Flame-coloured garment; upon his head a garland of Wheat and Rye; upon his Arm a Basket of all manner of ripe Fruits; at his Belt a Sickle; his Sign *Virgo.*

September. A merry and cheerful Countenance, in a Purple Robe; upon his Head a Wreath of red and white Grapes; in his Left hand a handful of Oats; withal carrying a Horn of Plenty, full of all manner of ripe Fruits; in his right hand the sign *Libra.*

October. In a Garment of Yellow and Carnation; upon his head a garland of Oak-leaves with Acorns; in his right hand the sign *Scorpio;* in his Left hand a Basket of Medlars, Services, and Chestnuts, and any other Fruits then in Season.

November. In a Garment of Changeable Green and Black; upon his Head a garland of Olives, with the Fruit in his Left hand; Bunches of Parsnips and Turnips in his Right; his Sign *Sagittarius.*

December. A horrid and fearful aspect, clad in Irish rags, or coarse frieze girt unto him; upon his Head three or four Night-Caps, and over them a Turkish Turban; his Nose red, his Mouth and Beard clogged with icicles; at his back a bundle of holly, ivy, or mistletoe; holding in furred mittens the sign of *Capricornus.*

January. Clad all in White, as the Earth looks with the Snow, blowing his nails; in his left arm a billet; the sign *Aquarius* standing by his side.

February. Clothed in a dark Sky-colour, carrying in his Right hand the sign *Pisces.*

The following receipt "To dress up a chimney very fine for the summer-time, as I have done many, and they have been liked very well," may not be unprofitable to the housewives of this century :—

"First, take a pack-thread, and fasten it even to the inner part of the Chimney, so high as that you can see no higher as you walk up and down the House. You must drive in several Nails to hold up all your work. Then get good store of old green Moss from Trees, and melt an equal proportion of beeswax and rosin together; and, while it is hot, dip the wrong ends of the moss in it, and presently clap it upon your pack-thread, and press it down hard with your hand. You must make haste, else it will cool before you can fasten it, and then it will fall down. Do so all around where the packthread goes; and the next row you must join to that, so that it may seem all in one: thus do till you have finished it down to the bottom. Then take some other kind of Moss, of a whitish colour and stiff, and of several sorts or kinds, and place that upon the other, here and there carelessly, and in some places put a good deal, and some a little; then any kind of fine snail-shells, in which the snails are dead, and little toad-stools, which are very old, and look like velvet, or *any other thing that was old and pretty:* place it here and there as your fancy serves, and fasten all with Wax and Rosin. Then, for the hearth of your chimney, you may lay some Orpan-Sprigs in order all over, and it will grow as it lies; and, according to the season, get what flowers you can, and stick in as if they grew, and a few sprigs of Sweet-Brier; the flowers you must renew every week; but the moss will last all the Summer, till it will be time to make a fire; and the orpan will last near two Months. A Chimney thus done doth grace a Room exceedingly."

One phrase in the above should particularly recommend it to such of your female readers as, in the nice language of the day, have done growing some time,—" little toad-stools, etc., and anything that is *old and pretty.*" Was ever antiquity so smoothed over? The culinary recipes have nothing remarkable in them, except the costliness of them. Everything (to the meanest meats) is sopped in claret, steeped in claret, basted with claret, as if claret were as cheap as ditch-water. I remember Bacon recommends opening a turf or two in your garden walks, and pouring into each a bottle of claret, to recreate the sense of smelling, being no less grateful than beneficial. We hope the Chancellor of the Exchequer will attend to this in his next reduction of French wines, that we may once more water our gardens with right Bourdeaux. The medical recipes are as whimsical as they are cruel. Our ancestors were not at all effeminate on this head. Modern sentimentalists would shrink at a cock plucked and bruised in a mortar alive to make a cullis, or a live mole baked in an oven (*be sure it be alive*) to make a powder for consumption. But the whimsicalest of all are the directions to servants (for this little book is a compendium of all duties): the footman is seriously admonished not to stand lolling against his master's chair while he waits at table; for "to lean on a chair when they wait, is a particular favour shown to any superior servant, as the chief gentleman, or the waiting-woman when she rises from the table." Also he must not "hold the plates before his mouth to be defiled with his breath, nor touch them on the right [inner] side." Surely Swift must have seen this little treatise.

REMINISCENCE OF
SIR JEFFERY DUNSTAN.

To your account of Sir Jeffery Dunstan, in columns 829-30 (where, by an unfortunate erratum, the effigies of *two Sir Jefferys* appear, when the uppermost figure is clearly meant for Sir Harry Dimsdale), you may add that the writer of this has frequently met him in his latter days, about 1790 or 1791, returning in an evening, after his long day's itineracy, to his domicile,—a wretched shed in the most beggarly purlieu of Bethnal Green, a little on this side the Mile-end Turnpike. The lower figure in that leaf most correctly describes his then appearance, except that no graphic art can convey an idea of the general squalour of it, and of his bag (his constant concomitant) in particular. Whether it contained "old wigs" at that time, I know not; but it seemed a fitter repository for bones snatched out of kennels than for any part of a gentleman's dress, even at second-hand.

The Ex-member for Garrat was a melancholy instance of a great man whose popularity is worn out. He still carried his sack; but it seemed a part of his identity rather than an implement of his profession; a badge of past grandeur: could anything have divested him of *that*, he would have shown a "poor forked animal" indeed. My life upon it, it contained no curls at the time I speak of. The most decayed and spiritless remnants of what was once a peruke would have scorned the filthy case; would absolutely have "burst its cerements." No: it was empty, or brought home bones, or a few cinders, possibly. A strong odour of burnt bones, I remember, blended with the scent of horse-flesh seething into dog's meat, and only relieved a little by the breathings of a few brick-kilns, made up the atmosphere of the delicate suburban spot which this great man had chosen for the last scene of his earthly vanities. The cry of "old wigs" had ceased with the possession of any such fripperies: his sack might have contained not unaptly a little mould to scatter upon that grave to which he was now advancing; but it told of vacancy and desolation. His quips were silent too, and his brain was empty as his sack: he slank along, and seemed to decline popular observation. If a few boys followed him, it seemed rather from habit than any expectation of fun.

> Alas! how changed from *him*,
> The life of humour, and the soul of whim,
> Gallant and gay on Garrat's hustings proud!

But it is thus that the world rewards its favourites in decay. What faults he had, I know not. I have heard something of a peccadillo or so. But some little deviation from the precise line of rectitude might have been winked at in so tortuous and stigmatic a frame. Poor Sir Jeffery! it were well if some M.P.'s in earnest had passed their parliamentary existence with no more offences against integrity than could be laid to thy charge! A fair dismissal was thy due, not so unkind a degradation; some little snug retreat, with a bit of green before thine eyes, and not a burial alive in the fetid beggaries of Bethnal. Thou wouldst have ended thy days in a manner more appropriate to thy pristine dignity, installed in munificent mockery (as in mock honours you had lived),—a poor Knight of Windsor!

Every distinct place of public speaking demands an oratory peculiar to itself. The forensic fails within the walls of St. Stephen. Sir Jeffery was a living instance of this; for, in the flower of his popularity, an attempt was made to bring him out upon the stage (at which of the winter theatres I forget, but I well remember the anecdote) in the part of *Doctor Last*. The announcement drew a crowded house; but, notwithstanding infinite tutoring,—by Foote or Garrick, I forget which,—when the curtain drew up, the heart of Sir Jeffery failed, and he faltered on, and made nothing of his part, till the hisses of the house at last, in very kindness, dismissed him from the boards. Great as his parliamentary eloquence had shown itself, brilliantly as his off-hand sallies had sparkled on a hustings, they here totally failed him. Perhaps he had an aversion to borrowed wit, and, like my Lord Foppington, disdained to entertain himself (or others) with the forced products of another man's brain. Your man of quality is more diverted with the natural sprouts of his own.

CAPTAIN STARKEY.

(*To the Editor of Hone's Every-Day Book.*)

DEAR SIR,—I read your account of this unfortunate being, and his forlorn piece of self-history, with that smile of half-interest which the Annals of Insignificance excite, till I came to where he says, "I was bound apprentice to Mr. William Bird, an eminent writer, and teacher of languages and mathematics," etc.; when I started as one does on the recognition of an old acquaintance in a supposed stranger. This, then, was that Starkey of whom I have heard my sister relate so many pleasing anecdotes; and whom, never having seen, I yet seem almost to remember. For nearly fifty years, she had lost all sight of him; and, behold! the gentle Usher of her youth, grown into an aged Beggar, dubbed with an opprobrious title to which he had no pretensions; an object and a May-game! To what base purposes may we not return! What may not have been the meek creature's sufferings,—what his wanderings,—before he finally settled down in the comparative comfort of an old Hospitaller of the Almonry of Newcastle? And is poor Starkey dead?—

I was a scholar of that "eminent writer" that he speaks of; but Starkey had quitted the school about a year before I came to it. Still the odour of his merits had left a fragrancy upon the recollection of the elder pupils. The schoolroom stands where it did, looking into a discoloured, dingy garden in the passage leading from Fetter Lane into Bartlett's Buildings. It is still a school, though the main prop, alas! has fallen so ingloriously;

and bears a Latin inscription over the entrance in the lane, which was unknown in our humbler times. Heaven knows what "languages" were taught in it then! I am sure that neither my sister nor myself brought any out of it, but a little of our native English. By "mathematics," reader, must be understood "ciphering." It was, in fact, a humble day-school, at which reading and writing were taught to us boys in the morning; and the same slender erudition was communicated to the girls, our sisters, etc., in the evening. Now, Starkey presided, under Bird, over both establishments. In my time, Mr. Cook, now or lately a respectable singer and performer at Drury Lane Theatre, and nephew to Mr. Bird, had succeeded to him. I well remember Bird. He was a squat, corpulent, middle-sized man, with something of the gentleman about him, and that peculiar mild tone—especially while he was inflicting punishment—which is so much more terrible to children than the angriest looks and gestures. Whippings were not frequent; but, when they took place, the correction was performed in a private room adjoining, where we could only hear the plaints, but saw nothing. This heightened the decorum and the solemnity. But the ordinary chastisement was the bastinado, a stroke or two on the palm with that almost obsolete weapon now,—the ferule. A ferule was a sort of flat ruler, widened, at the inflicting end, into a shape resembling a pear,—but nothing like so sweet, with a delectable hole in the middle to raise blisters, like a cupping-glass. I have an intense recollection of that disused instrument of torture, and the malignancy, in proportion to the apparent mildness, with which its strokes were applied. The idea of a rod is accompanied with something ludicrous; but by no process can I look back upon this blister-raiser with anything but unmingled horror. To make him look more formidable,—if a pedagogue had need of these heightenings,—Bird wore one of those flowered Indian gowns formerly in use with schoolmasters,. the strange figures upon which we used to interpret into hieroglyphics of pain and suffering. But, boyish fears apart, Bird, I believe, was, in the main, a humane and judicious master.

Oh, how I remember our legs wedged into those uncomfortable sloping desks, where we sat elbowing each other; and the injunctions to attain a free hand, unattainable in that position; the first copy I wrote after, with its moral lesson, "Art improves Nature;" the still earlier pot-hooks and the hangers, some traces of which I fear may yet be apparent in this manuscript; the truant looks side-long to the garden, which seemed a mockery of our imprisonment; the prize for best spelling which had almost turned my head, and which, to this day, I cannot reflect upon without a vanity, which I ought to be ashamed of; our little leaden inkstands, not separately subsisting, but sunk into the desks; the bright, punctually-washed morning fingers, darkening gradually with another and another ink-spot! What a world of little associated circumstances, pains, and pleasures, mingling their quotas of pleasure, arise at the reading of those few simple words,—"Mr. William Bird, an eminent writer, and teacher of languages and mathematics, in Fetter Lane, Holborn!"

Poor Starkey, when young, had that peculiar stamp of old-fashionedness in his face which makes it impossible for a beholder to predicate any particular age in the object. You can scarce make a guess between seventeen and seven-and-thirty. This antique cast always seems to promise ill-luck and penury. Yet it seems he was not always the abject thing he came to. My sister, who well remembers him, can hardly forgive Mr. Thomas Ranson for making an etching so unlike her idea of him when he was a youthful teacher at Mr. Bird's school. Old age and poverty—a life-long poverty, she thinks—could at no time have so effaced the marks of native gentility which were once so visible in a face otherwise strikingly ugly, thin, and care-worn. From her recollections of him, she thinks that he would have wanted bread before he would have begged or borrowed a halfpenny. "If any of the girls," she says, "who were my school-fellows, should be reading, through their aged spectacles, tidings from the dead, of their youthful friend Starkey, they will feel a pang, as I do, at having teased his gentle spirit." They were big girls, it seems—too old to attend his instructions with the silence necessary; and, however old age and a long state of beggary seems to have reduced his writing faculties to a state of imbecility, in those days his language occasionally rose to the bold and figurative; for, when he was in despair to stop their chattering, his ordinary phrase was, "Ladies, if you will not hold your peace, not all the powers in heaven can make you." Once he was missing for a day or two: he had run away. A little old unhappy-looking man brought him back,—it was his father,—and he did no business in the school that day, but sat moping in a corner, with his hands before his face; and the girls, his tormentors, in pity for his case, for the rest of that day forbore to annoy him. "I had been there but a few months," adds she, "when Starkey, who was the chief instructor of us girls, communicated to us a profound secret,—that the tragedy of *Cato* was shortly to be acted by the elder boys, and that we were to be invited to the representation." That Starkey lent a helping hand in fashioning the actors, she remembers; and, but for his unfortunate person, he might have had some distinguished part in the scene to enact. As it was, he had the arduous task of prompter assigned to him, and his feeble voice was heard clear and distinct, repeating the text during the whole performance. She describes her recollection of the cast of characters, even now, with a relish. Martia, by the handsome Edgar Hickman, who afterwards went to Africa, and of whom she never afterwards heard tidings; Lucia, by Master Walker, whose sister was her particular friend: Cato, by John Hunter, a masterly declaimer, but a plain boy, and shorter by the head than his two sons in the scene, etc. In conclusion, Starkey appears to have been one of those mild spirits, which, not originally deficient in understanding, are crushed by penury into dejection and feebleness. He might have proved a useful adjunct, if not an ornament, to society, if Fortune had taken him into a very little fostering; but, wanting that, he became a captain,—a byword,—and lived and died a broken bulrush.

THE ASS.

Mr. Collier, in his "Poetical Decameron" (Third Conversation), notices a tract printed in 1595, with the author's initials only, A.B., entitled "The Noblenesse of the Asse; a work rare, learned, and excellent." He has selected the following pretty passage from it: "He (the ass) refuseth no burden: he goes whither he is sent, without any contradiction. He lifts not his foote against any one; he bytes not; he is no fugitive, nor malicious affected. He doth all things in good sort, and to his liking that hath cause to employ him. If strokes be given him, he cares not for them; and, as our modern poet singeth,—

> "'Thou wouldst (perhaps) he should become thy foe,
> And to that end dost beat him many times:
> He cares not for himselfe, much less thy blow.'"[1]

Certainly Nature, foreseeing the cruel usage which this useful servant to man should receive at man's hand, did prudently in furnishing him with a tegument impervious to ordinary stripes. The malice of a child or a weak hand can make feeble impressions on him. His back offers no mark to a puny foeman. To a common whip or switch his hide presents an absolute insensibility. You might as well pretend to scourge a schoolboy with a tough pair of leather breeches on. His jerkin is well

---

[1] Who this modern poet was, says Mr. C—, is a secret worth discovering. The woodcut on the title of the Pamphlet is—an Ass with a wreath of laurel round his neck.

fortified; and therefore the costermongers, "between the years 1790 and 1800," did more politicly than piously in lifting up a part of his upper garment. I well remember that beastly and bloody custom. I have often longed to see one of those refiners in discipline himself at the cart's tail, with just such a convenient spot laid bare to the tender mercies of the whipster. But, since Nature has resumed her rights, it is to be hoped that this patient creature does not suffer to extremities; and that, to the savages who still belabour his poor carcass with their blows (considering the sort of anvil they are laid upon), he might in some sort, if he could speak, exclaim with the philosopher, "Lay on: you beat but upon the case of Anaxarchus."

Contemplating this natural safeguard, this fortified exterior, it is with pain I view the sleek, foppish, combed, and curried person of this animal as he is disnaturalised at watering-places, etc., where they affect to make a palfrey of him. Fie on all such sophistications! It will never do, Master Groom. Something of his honest, shaggy exterior will still peep up in spite of you,—his good, rough, native, pine-apple coating. You cannot "refine a scorpion into a fish, though you rinse it and scour it with ever so cleanly cookery."[1]

The modern poet quoted by A.B. proceeds to celebrate a virtue for which no one to this day had been aware that the ass was remarkable:—

> " One other gift this beast hath as his owne,
> Wherewith the rest could not be furnishèd;
> On man himself the same was not bestowne:
> To wit,—on him is ne'er engenderèd
> The hateful vermine that doth teare the skin,
> And to the bode [body] doth make his passage in."

And truly, when one thinks on the suit of impenetrable armour with which Nature (like Vulcan to another Achilles) has provided him, these subtle enemies to *our* repose would have shown some dexterity in getting into

[1] Milton from memory.

his quarters. As the bogs of Ireland by tradition expel toads and reptiles, he may well defy these small deer in his fastnesses. It seems the latter had not arrived at the exquisite policy adopted by the human vermin "between 1790 and 1800."

But the most singular and delightful gift of the Ass, according to the writer of this pamphlet, is his *voice*, the "goodly, sweet, and continual brayings" of which, "whereof they forme a melodious and proportionable kinde of musicke," seem to have affected him with no ordinary pleasure. "Nor thinke I," he adds, "that any of our immoderate musicians can deny but that their song is full of exceeding pleasure to be heard; because therein is to be discerned both concord, discord, singing in the meane, the beginning to sing in large compasse, then following into rise and fall, the halfe-note, whole note, musicke of five voices, firme singing by four voices, three together, or one voice and a halfe. Then their variable contrarities amongst them, when one delivers forth a long tenor or a short, the pausing for time, breathing in measure, breaking the minim or very least moment of time. Last of all, to heare the musicke of five or six voices chaunged to so many of asses is amongst them to heare a song of world without end."

There is no accounting for ears, or for that laudable enthusiasm with which an author is tempted to invest a favourite subject with the most incompatible perfections: I should otherwise, for my own taste, have been inclined rather to have given a place to these extraordinary musicians at that banquet of nothing-less-than-sweet-sounds, imagined by old Jeremy Collier (Essays, 1698, part ii. on Music), where, after describing the inspiriting effects of martial music in a battle, he hazards an ingenious conjecture, whether a sort of *anti-music* might not be invented, which should have quite the contrary effect of "sinking the spirits, shaking the nerves, curdling the blood, and inspiring despair and cowardice and consternation. 'Tis probable," he says, "the roaring of lions, the warbling of cats and screech-owls, together with a mixture of the howling of dogs, judiciously imitated and compounded, might go a great way in this invention." The dose, we confess, is pretty potent, and skilfully enough prepared. But what shall we say to the Ass of Silenus, who, if we may trust to classic lore, by his own proper sounds, without thanks to cat or screech-owl, dismayed and put to rout a whole army of giants? Here was *anti-music* with a vengeance; a whole *Pan-Dis-Harmonicon* in a single lungs of leather!

But I keep you trifling too long on this Asinine subject. I have already passed the *Pons Asinorum*, and will desist, remembering the old pedantic pun of Jem Boyer, my schoolmaster,—

"Ass *in præsenti* seldom makes a WISE MAN *in futuro.*"

IN RE SQUIRRELS.

What is gone with the Cages with the climbing Squirrel, and bells to them, which were formerly the indispensable appendage to the outside of a tinman's shop, and were, in fact, the only Live Signs? One, we believe, still hangs out on Holborn; but they are fast vanishing with the good old modes of our ancestors. They seem to have been superseded by that still more ingenious refinement of modern humanity,—the treadmill; in which *human* squirrels still perform a similar round of ceaseless, unprogressive clambering, which must be nuts to them.

We almost doubt the fact of the teeth of this creature being so purely orange-coloured as Mr. Urban's correspondent gives out. One of our old poets—and they were pretty sharp observers of Nature—describes them as brown. But perhaps the naturalist referred to meant "of the colour of a Maltese Orange,"[1] which is rather more obfuscated than your fruit of Seville or St. Michael's, and may help to reconcile the difference. We cannot speak from observation; but we remember at school getting our fingers into the orangery of one of these little

[1] Fletcher in the "Faithful Shepherdess." The satyr offers to Clorin—

> "Grapes whose lusty blood
> Is the learned poet's good,—
> Sweeter yet did never crown
> The head of Bacchus; nuts more brown
> Than the squirrels' teeth that crack them."

gentry (not having a due caution of the traps set there), and the result proved sourer than lemons. The author of the "Task" somewhere speaks of their anger as being "insignificantly fierce;" but we found the demonstration of it on this occasion quite as significant as we desired, and have not been disposed since to look any of these "gift horses" in the mouth. Maiden aunts keep these "small deer," as they do parrots, to bite people's fingers, on purpose to give them good advice "not to adventure so near the cage another time." As for their "six quavers divided into three quavers and a dotted crotchet," I suppose they may go into Jeremy Bentham's next budget of fallacies, along with the "melodious and proportionable kinde of musicke" recorded, in your last number, of another highly-gifted animal.

DEFOE'S SECONDARY NOVELS.

It has happened not seldom that one work of some author has so transcendently surpassed in execution the rest of his compositions, that the world has agreed to pass a sentence of dismissal upon the latter, and to consign them to total neglect and oblivion. It has done wisely in this not to suffer the contemplation of excellences of a lower standard to abate or stand in the way of the pleasure it has agreed to receive from the masterpiece.

Again: it has happened, that from no inferior merit of execution in the rest, but from superior good fortune in the choice of its subject, some single work shall have been suffered to eclipse and cast into shade the deserts of its less fortunate brethren. This has been done with more or less injustice in the case of the popular allegory of Bunyan, in which the beautiful and scriptural image of a pilgrim or wayfarer (we are all such upon earth), addressing itself intelligibly and feelingly to the bosoms of all, has silenced, and made almost to be forgotten, the more awful and scarcely less tender beauties of the "Holy War made by Shaddai upon Diabolus," of the same author, —a romance less happy in its subject, but surely well worthy of a secondary immortality. But in no instance has this excluding partiality been exerted with more unfairness than against what may be termed the secondary novels or romances of Defoe.

While all ages and descriptions of people hang delighted over the "Adventures of Robinson Crusoe," and shall continue to do so, we trust while the world lasts, how few comparatively will bear to be told that there exist other fictitious narratives by the same writer,—four of them at least of no inferior interest, except what results from a less felicitous choice of situation! "Roxana," "Singleton," "Moll Flanders," "Colonel Jack," are all genuine offspring of the same father. They bear the veritable impress of Defoe. An unpractised midwife that would not swear to the nose, lip, forehead, and eye of every one of them! They are, in their way, as full of incident, and some of them every bit as romantic; only they want the uninhabited island, and the charm that has bewitched the world, of the striking solitary situation.

But are there no solitudes out of the cave and the desert? or cannot the heart in the midst of crowds feel frightfully alone? Singleton on the world of waters, prowling about with pirates less merciful than the creatures of any howling wilderness,—is he not alone, with the faces of men about him, but without a guide that can conduct him through the mists of educational and habitual ignorance, or a fellow-heart that can interpret to him the new-born yearnings and aspirations of unpractised penitence? Or when the boy Colonel Jack, in the loneliness of the heart (the worst solitude), goes to hide his ill-purchased treasure in the hollow tree by night, and miraculously loses, and miraculously finds it again,— whom hath he there to sympathise with him? or of what sort are his associates?

The narrative manner of Defoe has a naturalness about it beyond that of any other novel or romance writer. His fictions have all the air of true stories. It is impossible to believe, while you are reading them, that a real person is not narrating to you everywhere nothing but what really happened to himself. To this the extreme *homeliness* of their style mainly contributes. We use the word in its best and heartiest sense,—that which comes *home* to the reader. The narrators everywhere are chosen from low life, or have had their origin in it: therefore they tell their own tales (Mr. Coleridge has anticipated us in this

x

remark), as persons in their degree are observed to do, with infinite repetition, and an overacted exactness, lest the hearer should not have minded, or have forgotten, some things that had been told before. Hence the emphatic sentences marked in the good old (but deserted) Italic type; and hence, too, the frequent interposition of the reminding old colloquial parenthesis, "I say," "Mind," and the like, when the story-teller repeats what, to a practised reader, might appear to have been sufficiently insisted upon before: which made an ingenious critic observe, that his works, in this kind, were excellent reading for the kitchen. And, in truth, the heroes and heroines of Defoe can never again hope to be popular with a much higher class of readers than that of the servant-maid or the sailor. Crusoe keeps its rank only by tough prescription. Singleton, the pirate; Colonel Jack, the thief; Moll Flanders, both thief and harlot; Roxana, harlot and something worse,—would be startling ingredients in the bill of fare of modern literary delicacies. But, then, what pirates, what thieves, and what harlots, are *the thief, the harlot,* and *the pirate* of Defoe! We would not hesitate to say, that in no other book of fiction, where the lives of such characters are described, is guilt and delinquency made less seductive, or the suffering made more closely to follow the commission, or the penitence more earnest or more bleeding, or the intervening flashes of religious visitation upon the rude and uninstructed soul more meltingly and fearfully painted. They, in this, come near to the tenderness of Bunyan; while the livelier pictures and incidents in them, as in Hogarth or in Fielding, tend to diminish the fastidiousness to the concerns and pursuits of common life which an unrestrained passion for the ideal and the sentimental is in danger of producing.

RECOLLECTIONS OF
A LATE ROYAL ACADEMICIAN.

WHAT Apelles was to the *Grecian Alexander*, the same to the *Russian* was the late G— D—. None but Apelles might attempt the lineaments of the world's conqueror; none but our Academician could have done justice to the lines of the Czar and his courtiers. There they hang, the labour of ten plodding years, in an endless gallery, erected for the nonce, in the heart of Imperial Petersburgh—eternal monuments of barbarian taste submitted to half civilised cunning—four hundred fierce Half-Lengths, all male, and all military; like the pit in a French theatre, or the characters in Timon as it was last acted, with never a woman among them. Chaste sitters to Vandyke, models of grace and womanhood; and thou Dame Venetia Digby, fairest among thy fair compeers at Windsor, hide your pure pale cheeks, and cool English beauties, before this suffocating horde of Scythian riflers, this male chaos! Your cold oaken frames shall wane before the gorgeous gildings,

> With Tartar faces throng'd, and horrent uniforms.

One emperor contended for the monopoly of the *ancient;* two were competitors at once for the pencil of the *modern Apelles*. The Russian carried it against the Haytian by a single length. And if fate, as it was at one time nearly arranged, had wafted D. to the shores of Hayti—with the same complacency, in his art, with which he persisted in daubing in, day after day, his frozen Muscovites, he would have sate down for life to smutch in upon canvas the faces of blubber-lipped sultanas, or the whole male retinue of the dingy court of Christophe. For in truth a choice of subjects was the least of D.'s care. A Goddess from Cnidus, or from the Caffre coast, was equal to him; Lot or Lot's wife; the charming widow H., or her late husband.

My acquaintance with D. was in the outset of his art, when the graving tools, rather than the pencil, administered to his humble wants. Those implements, as is well known, are not the most favourable to the cultivation of that virtue, which is esteemed next to godliness. He might "wash his hands in innocency," and so metaphorically "approach an altar;" but his material puds were anything but fit to be carried to church. By an ingrained economy in soap—if it was not for pictorial effect rather—he would wash (on Sundays) the inner oval, or portrait, as it may be termed, of his countenance, leaving the unwashed temples to form a natural black frame round the picture, in which a dead white was the predominant colour. This, with the addition of green spectacles made necessary by the impairment, which his graving labours by day and night (for he was ordinarily at them for sixteen hours out of the twenty-four) had brought upon his visual faculties, gave him a singular appearance, when he took the air abroad; insomuch, that I have seen a crowd of young men and boys following him along Oxford Street with admiration not without shouts; even as the Youth of Rome, we read in Vasari, followed the steps of Raphael with acclamations for his genius, and for his beauty, when he proceeded from his workshop to chat with Cardinals and Popes at the Vatican.

The family of D. were not at this time in affluent circumstances. His father, a clever artist, had outlived the style of art in which he excelled most of his contemporaries. He, with the father of the celebrated Morland, worked for the shop of Carrington and Bowles, which exists still for the poorer sort of caricatures, on the north side of St. Paul's Church Yard. They did clever things in colours. At an inn in Reading a screen is still preserved, full of their labours; but the separate portions of either artist are now undistinguishable. I remember a Mother teaching her Child to read (B. Barton has a copy of it); a Laundress washing; a young Quaker, a beautiful subject. But the flower of their forgotten productions hangs still at a public-house on the left hand, as thou arrivest, reader, from the now Highgate archway, at the foot of the descent where Crouch End begins, on thy road to green Hornsey. Turn in, and look at it, for the sight is well worth a cup of excusatory cyder. In the parlour to the right you will find it—an antiquated subject—a damsel sitting at her breakfast table in a gown of the flowered chintz of our grandmothers, with a tea-service before her of the *same pattern*. The effect is most delicate. Why have these harmonies—these *agrémens*—no place in the works of modern art?

With such niceties in his calling D. did not much trouble his head, but, after an ineffectual experiment to reconcile his eye-sight with his occupation, boldly quitted it, and dashed into the beaten road of common-place portraiture in oil. The Hopners, and the Lawrences, were his Vandykes, and his Velasquezes; and if he could make anything like them, he insured himself immortality. With such guides he struggled on through laborious nights and days, till he reached the eminence he aimed at—of mediocrity. Having gained that summit, he sate down contented. If the features were but cognoscible, no matter whether the flesh resembled flesh, or oil-skin. For the thousand tints—the grains—which in life diversify the nose, the chin, the cheek—which a Reynolds can but coarsely counterfeit—he cared nothing at all about them. He left such scrupulosities to opticians and anatomists. If the features were but there, the character of course could not be far off. A lucky hit which he made in painting the very *dress* of a dressy lady—Mrs. W—e—, whose handsome countenance also, and tall elegance of shape, were too palpable entirely to escape under any masque of oil, with which even D. could overlay them—brought to him at once an influx of sitters, which almost rivalled the importunate calls upon Sir Thomas. A portrait he *did* soon after, of the Princess Charlotte, clenched his fame. He proceeded Academician. At that memorable conjuncture of time it pleased the Allied Sovereigns to visit England.

I called upon D. to congratulate him upon a crisis so doubly eventful. His pleasant housekeeper seemed embarrassed; owned that her master was alone. But could he be spoken with? With some importunity I prevailed upon her to usher me into his painting-room. It was in Newman Street. At his easel stood D., with an immense spread of canvas before him, and by his side a—live goose. I inquired into this extraordinary combination. Under the rose he informed me, that he had undertaken to paint a transparency for Vauxhall, against an expected visit of the Allied Sovereigns to that place. I smiled at an engagement so derogatory to his new-born honours; but a contempt of small gains was never one of D.'s foibles. My eyes beheld crude forms of warriors, kings, rising under his brush upon this interminable stretch of cloth. The Wolga, the Don, and the Nieper, were there, or their representative River Gods; and Father Thames clubbed urns with the Vistula. Glory with her dazzling eagle was not absent, nor Fame, nor Victory. The shade of Rubens might have evoked the mighty allegories. But what was the Goose? He was evidently *sitting* for a something.

D. at last informed me, that having fixed upon a group of rivers, he could not introduce the Royal Thames without his *swans*. That he had inquired the price of a live swan, and it being more than he was prepared to give for it, he had bargained with the poulterer for the *next thing to it;* adding significantly, that it would do to roast, after it had served its turn to paint swans by. *Reader, this is a true story.*

So entirely devoid of imagination, or any feeling for his high art, was this *Painter*, that for the few historical pictures he attempted, any sitter might sit for any character. He took once for a subject *The Infant Hercules*. Did he choose for a model some robust antique? No. He did not even pilfer from Sir Joshua, who was nearer to his own size. But from a *show* he hired to sit to him a child in years indeed (though no Infant), but in fact a precocious *Man*, or human portent, that was disgustingly exhibiting at that period; a thing to be strangled. From this he formed *his* Infant Hercules. In a scriptural flight he next attempted a Samson in the lap of Dalilah. A Dalilah of some sort was procurable for love or money, but who should stand for the Jewish Hercules? He hired a tolerably stout porter, with a thickish head of hair, curling in yellowish locks, but lithe—much like a wig. And these were the robust strengths of Samson.

I once was a witness to a *family scene* in his painting closet, which I had entered rather abruptly, and but for his encouragement, should as hastily have retreated. He stood with displeased looks eyeing a female relative—whom I had known under happier auspices—that was kneeling at his feet with a baby in her arms, with her eyes uplifted and suppliant. Though I could have previously sworn to the virtue of Miss ———, yet casual slips have been known. There are such things as families disgraced, where least you would heve expected it. The child *might* be———; I had heard of no wedding—I was the last person to pry into family secrets—when D. relieved my uneasy cogitations by explaining, that the innocent, good-humoured creature before me (such as she ever was, and is now that she is married) with a baby borrowed from a public-house, was acting Andromache to *his* Ulysses, for the purpose of transferring upon canvas a tender situation from the Troades of Seneca.

On a subsequent occasion I knocked at D.'s door. I

had chanced to have been in a dreamy humour previously. I am not one that often poetises, but I had been musing —coxcombically enough in the heart of Newman Street, Oxford Road—upon Pindus, and the Aonian Maids. The Lover of Daphne was in my mind—when, answering to my summons, the door opened, and there stood before me, laurel-crowned, the God himself, unshorn Apollo. I was beginning to mutter apologies to the Celestial Presence— when on the thumb of the right hand of the Delian (his left held the harp) I spied a palette, such as painters carry, which immediately reconciled me to the whimsical transformation of my old acquaintance—with his own face, certainly any other than Grecianesque—into a temporary image of the oracle-giver of Delphos. To have impersonated the Ithacan was little : he had been just sitting for a God.—It would be no incurious inquiry to ascertain what the *minimum* of the faculty of imagination, ever supposed essential to painters along with poets, is, that, in these days of complaints of want of patronage towards the fine arts, suffices to dub a man a R——l A————n.

Not only had D. no imagination to guide him in the treatment of such subjects, but he had no relish for high art in the productions of the great masters. He turned away from them as from something foreign and irrelative to him, and his calling. He knew he had neither part nor portion in them. Cozen him into the Stafford or the Angerstein Gallery, he involuntarily turned away from the Baths of Diana—the Four Ages of Guercino— the Lazarus of Piombo—to some pretty piece of *modern art* that had been inconsistently thrust into the collection through favour. On that he would dwell and pore, blind as the dead to the delicacies that surrounded him. There he might learn something. There he might pilfer a little. There was no grappling with Titian or Angelo.

The narrowness of his domestic habits to the very last, was the consequence of his hard bringing up, and unexpected emergence into opulence. While rolling up to the ears in Russian roubles, a penny was still in his eyes the same important thing, which it had with some reason seemed to be, when a few shillings were his daily earnings. When he visited England a short time before his death, he reminded an artist of a commission, which he had executed for him in Russia, the package of which was "still unpaid." At this time he was not unreasonably supposed to have realised a sum little short of half a million sterling. What became of it was never known; what gulf, or what Arctic *vorago*, sucked it in, his acquaintance in those parts have better means of guessing, than his countrymen. It is certain that few of the latter were anything the better for it.

It was before he expatriated himself, but subsequently to his acquisition of pictorial honours in this country, that he brought home two of his brother Academicians to dine with him. He had given no orders extraordinary to his housekeeper. He trusted, as he always did, to her providing. She was a shrewd lass, and knew, as we say, a bit of her master's mind.

It had happened that on the day before, D. passing near Clare Market by one of those open shambles, where tripe and cow-heel are exposed for sale, his eye was arrested by the sight of some tempting flesh *rolled up*. It is a part of the intestines of some animal, which my olfactory sensibilities never permitted me to stay long enough to inquire the name of. D. marked the curious involutions of the unacquainted luxury; the harmony of its colours—a *sable vert*—pleased his eye; and, warmed with the prospect of a new flavour, for a few farthings he bore it off in triumph to his housekeeper. It so happened that his day's dinner was provided, so the cooking of the novelty was for that time necessarily suspended.

Next day came. The hour of dinner approached. His visitors, with no very romantic anticipations, expected a plain meal at least; they were prepared for no new dainties; when, to the astonishment of them, and almost of D. himself, the purchase of the preceding day was served up piping hot—the cook declaring, that she did not know well what it was, for "her master always marketed." His guests were not so happy in their ignorance. They kept dogs.

I will do D. the justice to say, that on such occasions he took what happened in the best humour possible. He had no *false modesty*—though I have generally observed, that persons, who are quite deficient in that *mauvaise honte*, are seldon over-troubled with the quality itself, of which it is the counterfeit.

By what arts, with *his* pretensions, D. contrived to wriggle himself into a seat in the Academy, I am not acquainted enough with the intrigues of that body (more involved than those of an Italian conclave) to pronounce. It is certain, that neither for love to him, nor out of any respects to his talents, did they elect him. Individually he was obnoxious to them all. I have heard that, in his passion for attaining this object, he went so far as to go down upon his knees to some of the members, whom he thought least favourable, and beg their suffrage with many tears.

But *death*, which extends the measure of a man's stature to appearance; and *wealth*, which men worship in life and death, which makes giants of punies, and enbalms insignificance; called around the exequies of this pigmy Painter the rank, the riches, the fashion of the world. By Academic hands his pall was borne; by the carriages of nobles of the land, and of ambassadors from foreign powers, his bier was followed; and St. Paul's (O worthy casket for the shrine of such a Zeuxis) now holds—ALL THAT WAS MORTAL OF G. D.

REMARKABLE CORRESPONDENT.

(To the Editor of the Every-Day Book.)

Sir—I am the youngest of Three hundred and sixty-six brethren—there are no fewer of us—who have the honour, in the words of the good old song, to call the Sun our Dad. You have done the rest of our family the favour of bestowing an especial compliment upon each member of it individually—I mean as far as you have gone : for it will take you some time before you can make your bow all round—and I have no reason to think it is your intention to neglect any of us but poor Me. Some you have hung round with flowers ; others you have made fine with martyrs' palms and saintly garlands. The most insignificant of us you have sent away pleased with some fitting apologue or pertinent story. What have I done that you dismiss me without mark or attribute? What though I make my public appearance seldomer than the rest of my brethren? I thought that angels' visits had been accounted the more precious for their very rarity. Reserve was always looked upon as dignified. I am seen but once for four times that my brethren obtrude themselves ; making their presence cheap and contemptible in comparison with the state which I keep.

Am I not a Day (when I do come) to all purposes, as much as any of them. Decompose me, anatomise me ; you will find that I am constituted like the rest. Divide me into twenty-four, and you will find that I cut up into as many goodly hours (or main limbs) as the rest. I too have my arteries and pulses, which are the minutes and the seconds.

It is hard to be dis-familied thus, like Cinderella in her rags and ashes, while her sisters flaunted it about in cherry-coloured ribbons and favours. My brethren, forsooth, are to be dubbed; one *Saint* Day; another *Pope* Day; a third *Bishop* Day; the least of them is *Squire* Day, or *Mr.* Day, while I am—plain Day. Our house, Sir, is a very ancient one, and the least of us is too proud to put up with an indignity. What though I am but a younger brother in some sense—for the youngest of my brethren is by some thousand years my senior—yet I bid fair to inherit as long as any of them, while I have the Calendar to show; which, you must understand, is our Title Deeds.

Not content with slurring me over with a bare and naked acknowledgment of my occasional visitation in prose, you have done your best to deprive me of my verse honours. In column 310 of your Book, you quote an antique scroll, leaving out the last couplet, as if on purpose to affront me. "Thirty days hath September" —so you transcribe very faithfully for four lines, and most invidiously suppress the exceptive clause :—

> "Except in Leap Year, that's the time
> When February's days hath twenty and——."

I need not set down the rhyme which should follow; I dare say you know it very well, though you were pleased to leave it out. These indignities demand reparation. While you have time it will be well for you to make the *amende honorable*. Ransack your stories, learned Sir, I pray of you, for some attribute, biographical, anecdotical, or floral, to invest me with. Did nobody die, or nobody flourish—was nobody born—upon any of my periodical visits to this globe? Does the world stand still as often as I vouchsafe to appear? Am I a blank in the Almanac? Alms for oblivion? If you don't find a flower at least to grace me with (a Forget-Me-Not would cheer me in my present obscurity), I shall prove the worst day to you you ever saw in your life : and your work, instead of the title it now vaunts, must be content (every fourth year at least) to go by the lame appellation of, The Every-Day-but-one-Book.

Yours, as you treat me,

TWENTY-NINTH OF FEBRUARY.

THE HUMBLE PETITION OF AN UNFORTUNATE DAY.

(To the Editor of the Every-Day Book.)

Sir—I am a poor wronged *Day*. I appeal to you as the general patron of the family of the *Days*. The candour with which you attended to the expostulations of a poor relative of ours—a sort of cousin thrice removed[1]—encourages me to hope that you will listen to the complaint of a *Day* of rather more consequence. I am the *Day*, Sir, upon which it pleased the course of Nature that your Gracious Sovereign should be born. As such, before his accession, I was always observed and honoured. But since that happy event, in which naturally none had a greater interest than myself, a flaw has been discovered in my title. My lustre has been eclipsed, and—to use the words of one of your own poets—

"I fade into the light of common *Day!*"

It seems that about that time an Impostor crept into Court, who has the effrontery to usurp my honours, and to style herself the *King's Birthday*, upon some shallow pretence, that, being *St. George's Day*, she must needs be *King George's Day* also. *All Saints' Day* we have heard of, and *All Souls' Day* we are willing to admit; but does it follow that this foolish *Twenty-third of April* must be *All Georges' Day*, and enjoy a monopoly of the whole name, from George of Cappadocia to George of Leyden, and from George-a-Green down to George Dyer?

[1] Twenty-ninth day of February.

It looks a little oddly that I was discarded not long after the discussions of a set of men and measures, with whom I have nothing in common. I hope no whisperer has insinuated into the ears of Royalty, as if I were anything whiggishly inclined, which, in my heart I abhor, all these kinds of Revolutions, by which I am sure to be the greatest sufferer.

I wonder my shameless rival can have the face to let the Tower and Park guns proclaim so many big thundering fibs as they do upon her Anniversary—making your Sovereign to be older than he really is by an hundred and odd *days*, which is no great compliment, one would think. Consider if this precedent for ante-dating of Births should become general, what confusion it must make in the Parish Registers; what crowds of young heirs we should have coming of age before they are one-and-twenty, with numberless similar grievances. If these chops and changes are suffered, we shall have *Lord Mayor's Day* eating her custard unauthentically in *May*, and *Guy Faux* preposterously blazing twice over in the Dog *Days*.

I humbly submit that it is not within the prerogatives of Royalty itself to be born twice over. We have read of the supposititious births of princes, but where are the evidences of this first birth? Why are not the nurses in attendance, the midwife, etc., produced?—the silly story has not so much as a Warming-pan to support it.

My legal advisers, to comfort me, tell me that I have the right on my side; I am the true Birth-*Day*, and the other *Day* is only kept. But what consolation is this to me, as long as this naughty-*kept-creature* keeps me out of my dues and privileges?

Pray take my unfortunate case into your consideration, and see that I am restored to my lawful Rejoicings, Firings, Bon-firings, Illuminations, etc.

And your Petitioner shall ever pray.

TWELFTH DAY OF AUGUST.

MRS. GILPIN RIDING TO EDMONTON.

>Then Mrs. Gilpin sweetly said
>　Unto her children three,
>"I'll clamber o'er this stile so high,
>　And you'll climb after me."
>But having climbed unto the top,
>　She could no further go:
>But sate to every passer by
>　A spectacle and show:
>Who said "Your spouse and you this day
>　Will show your horsemanship;
>And if you stay till he comes back,
>　Your horse will need no whip."

THE sketch here engraved (probably from the poet's friend, Romney), was found with the above three stanzas in the handwriting of Cowper, among the papers of the late Mrs. Unwin. It is to be regretted that no more was found of this little *Episode*, as it evidently was intended to be, in the "Diverting History of Johnny Gilpin." It is to be supposed that Mrs. Gilpin, in the interval between dinner and tea, finding the time to hang upon her hands, during her husband's involuntary excursion, rambled out with the children into the fields at the back of the Bell (as what could be more natural?); and at one of these high awkward stiles, for which Edmonton is so proverbially famed, the embarrassment represented, so mystifying to a substantial City madam, might have happened; a predicament which leaves her in a state which is the very Antipodes to that of her too-locomotive husband. In fact, she rides a restive horse. Now I talk of Edmonton stiles, I must speak a little about those of Enfield, its next neighbour, which are so ingeniously contrived—every rising bar to the top becoming more protuberant than the one under it—that it is impossible for any Christian climber to get over without bruising his (or her) shins as many times as there are bars. These inhospitable invitations to a flayed skin are planted so thickly too, and are so troublesomely importunate at every little paddock here, that this, with more propriety than Thebes of old, might be entitled Hecatompolis : the Town of the Hundred Gates or *Stiles*.

A SOJOURNER AT ENFIELD.

July 16, 1827.

SATURDAY NIGHT.

THERE is a Saturday night—I speak not to the admirers of Burns—erotically or theologically considered; HIS of the "Cotter's" may be a very charming picture, granting it to be but half true. Nor speak I now of the Saturday Night at Sea, which Dibdin hath dressed up with a gusto more poignant to the mere nautical palate of un-Calvinised South Britons. Nor that it is marketing night with the pretty tripping servant-maids all over London, who with judicious and economic eye, select the white and well-blown fillet, that the blue-aproned contunder of the calf can safely recommend as "prime veal," and which they are to be sure not to over-brown on the morrow. Nor speak I of the hard-handed Artisan, who on this night receives the pittance which is to furnish the neat Sabbatical dinner—not always reserved with Judaical rigour for that laudable purpose, but broken in upon, perchance, by inviting pot of ale, satisfactory to the present orifice. These are alleviatory, care-consoling. But the Hebdomadal Finale which I contemplate hath neither comfort nor alleviation in it; I pronounce it, from memory, altogether punitive, and to be abhorred. It is—Saturday Night to the School-boy!

Cleanliness, saith some sage man, is next to Godliness. It may be; but how it came to sit so very near, is the marvel. Methinks some of the more human virtues might have put in for a place before it. Justice—Humanity—Temperance—are positive qualities; the courtesies and little civil offices of life, had I been Master of the Ceremonies to that Court, should have sate above the salt in preference to a mere negation. I confess there is something wonderfully refreshing, in warm countries, in the act of ablution. Those Mahometan washings—how cool to the imagination! but in all these superstitions, the action itself, if not the duty, is voluntary. But to be washed perforce; to have a detestable flannel rag soaked in hot water, and redolent of the very coarsest coarse soap, ingrained with hard beads for torment, thrust into your mouth, eyes, nostrils—positively Burking you, under pretence of cleansing—substituting soap for dirt, the worst dirt of the two—making your poor red eyes smart all night, that they might look out brighter on the Sabbath morn (for their clearness was the effect of pain more than cleanliness), could this be true religion?

The tender mercies of the wicked are cruel. I am always disposed to add, so are those of Grandmothers. *Mine*—the Print has made her look rather too young—had never-failing pretexts of tormenting children for their good. I was a chit then; and I well remember when a fly had got into a corner of my eye, and I was complaining of it to her, the old lady deliberately pounded two ounces or more of the finest loaf sugar that could be got, and making me hold open the eye as wide as I could (all innocent of her purpose), she blew from delicate white paper, with a full breath, the whole saccharine contents into the part afflicted, saying, "There,—now the fly is out!" 'Twas most true: a legion of blue-bottles, with the prince of flies at their head, must have dislodged with the torrent and deluge of tears which followed. I kept my own counsel, and my fly in my eye when I had got one, in future, without troubling her dulcet applications for the remedy. Then her medicine case was a perfect magazine of tortures for infants. She seemed to have no notion of the comparatively tender drenches which young internals require: her potions were anything but milk for babes. Then her sewing up of a cut finger—pricking a whitloe before it was ripe, because she could not see well, with the aggravation of the pitying tone she did it in!

But of all her nostrums (rest her soul!), nothing came up to the Saturday Night's flannel, that rude fragment of a Witney blanket (Wales spins none so coarse), thrust into the corners of a weak child's eye with soap that might have absterged an Ethiop, whitened the hands of Duncan's She-murderer, and scoured away Original Sin itself. A faint image of my penance you see in the Print—but the Artist has sunk the flannel—the Age, I suppose, is too nice to bear it: and he has faintly shadowed the expostulatory suspension of the razor-strap in the hand of my Grandfather, when my pains and clamours had waxed intolerable. Peace to the Shades of them both! And if their well-meaning souls had need of cleansing when they quitted earth, may the process of it have been milder than that of my old Purgatorial Saturday Night's path to the Sabbatical rest of the morrow! NEPOS.

THOUGHTS ON PRESENTS OF GAME, &c.

"WE love to have our friend in the country sitting thus at our table *by proxy;* to apprehend his presence (though a hundred miles may be between us) by a turkey, whose goodly aspect reflects to us his 'plump corpusculum;' to taste him in grouse or woodcock; to feel him gliding down in the toast peculiar to the latter; to concorporate him in a slice of Canterbury brawn. This is indeed to have him within ourselves; to know him intimately; such participation is methinks *unitive,* as the old theologians phrase it."—*Last Essays of Elia.*

"Elia presents his acknowledgments to his 'Correspondent Unknown,' for a basket of prodigiously fine game. He takes for granted that so amiable a character must be a reader of the *Athenæum,* else he had meditated a notice in the *Times.* Now if this friend had consulted the Delphic oracle for a present suited to the palate of Elia, he could not have hit upon a morsel so acceptable. The birds he is barely thankful for; pheasants are poor *fowls* disguised in fine feathers; but a hare roasted hard and brown, with gravy and melted butter!—Old Mr. Chambers, the sensible clergyman in Warwickshire, whose son's acquaintance has made many hours happy in the life of Elia, used to allow a pound of Epping to every hare. Perhaps that was over-doing it. But, in spite of the note of Philomel, who, like some fine poets, that think no scorn to adopt plagiarisms from an humble brother, reiterates every Spring her cuckoo cry of 'Jug, Jug, Jug,' Elia pronounces that a hare, to be truly palated, must be roasted. Jugging sophisticates her. In *our* way it eats so 'crips,' as Mrs. Minikin says. Time was, when Elia was not arrived at his taste, that he preferred to all luxuries a roasted pig. But he disclaims all such green-sickness appetites in future, though he hath to acknowledge the receipt of many a delicacy in that kind from correspondents—good, but mistaken men—in consequence of their erroneous supposition that he had carried up into mature life the prepossessions of childhood. From the worthy Vicar of Enfield he acknowledges a tithe contribution of extraordinary sapor. The ancients must have loved hares; else why adopt the word *lepores* (obviously from *lepus*) but for some subtle analogy between the delicate flavour of the latter and the finer relishes of wit in what we most poorly translate *pleasantries*. The fine madnesses of the poet are the very decoction of his diet. Thence is he hare-brained. Harum-scarum is a libellous unfounded phrase, of modern usage. 'Tis true the hare is the most circumspect of animals, sleeping with her eye open. Her ears, ever erect, keep them in that wholesome exercise which conduces them to form the very tit-bit of the admirers of this noble animal. Noble will I call her, in spite of her detractors, who from occasional demonstrations of the principle of self-preservation (common to all animals), infer in her a defect of heroism. Half a hundred horsemen, with thrice the number of dogs, scour the country in pursuit of puss across three counties; and because the well-flavoured beast, weighing the odds, is willing to evade the hue and cry (with her delicate ears shrinking perchance from discord), comes the grave naturalist, Linnæus perchance, or Buffon, and gravely sets down the hare as a timid animal. Why Achilles, or Bully Dawson, would have declined the preposterous combat.

"In fact, how light of digestion we feel after a hare! How tender its processes after swallowing! What chyle it promotes! How ethereal! as if its living celerity were a type of its nimble coursing through the animal juices.

The notice might be longer. It is intended less as a Natural History of the Hare than a cursory thanks to the country 'good Unknown.' The hare has many friends, but none sincerer than ELIA."

Nov. 30, 1834.

A POPULAR FALLACY,
THAT A DEFORMED PERSON IS A LORD.

AFTER a careful perusal of the most approved works that treat of nobility, and of its origin in these realms in particular, we are left very much in the dark as to the original patent in which this branch of it is recognised. Neither Camden in his "Etymologie and Original of Barons," nor Dugdale in his "Baronage of England," nor Selden (a more exact and laborious inquirer than either) in his "Titles of Honour," affords a glimpse of satisfaction upon the subject. There is an heraldic term, indeed, which seems to imply gentility, and the right to coat-armour (but nothing further), in persons thus qualified. But the *sinister bend* is more probably interpreted by the best writers on this science, of some irregularity of birth than of bodily conformation. Nobility is either hereditary or by creation, commonly called patent. Of the former kind, the title in question cannot be, seeing that the notion of it is limited to a personal distinction which does not necessarily follow in the blood. Honours of this nature, as Mr. Anstey very well observes, descend, moreover, in a *right line*. It must be by patent, then, if any thing. But who can show it? How comes it to be dormant? Under what king's reign is it patented? Among the grounds of nobility cited by the learned Mr. Ashmole, after "Services in the Field or in the Council Chamber," he judiciously sets down "Honours conferred by the sovereign out of mere benevolence, or as favouring one subject rather than another for some likeness or conformity observed (or but supposed) in him to the royal nature," and instances the graces showered upon Charles Brandon, who, "in his goodly person being thought not a little to favour the port and bearing of the king's own majesty, was by that sovereign, King Henry the Eighth, for some or one of these respects, highly promoted and preferred." Here, if anywhere, we thought we had discovered a clue to our researches. But after a painful investigation of the rolls and records under the reign of Richard the Third, or "Richard Crouchback," as he is more usually designated in the chronicles,—from a traditionary stoop or gibbosity in that part,—we do not find that that monarch conferred any such lordships as are here pretended, upon any subject or subjects, on a simple plea of "conformity" in that respect to the "royal nature." The posture of affairs, in those tumultuous times preceding the battle of Bosworth, possibly left him at no leisure to attend to such niceties. Further than his reign we have not extended our inquiries, the kings of England who preceded or followed him being generally described by historians to have been of straight and clean limbs, the "natural derivative," says Daniel,[1] "of high blood, if not its primitive recommendation to such ennoblement, as denoting strength and martial prowess,—the qualities set most by in that fighting age." Another motive, which inclines us to scruple the validity of this claim, is the remarkable fact, that none of the persons in whom the right is supposed to be vested do ever insist upon it themselves. There is no instance of any of them "suing his patent," as the law-books call it; much less of his having actually stepped up into his proper seat, as, so qualified, we might expect that some of them would have had the spirit to do, in the House of Lords. On the contrary, it seems to be a distinction thrust upon them. "Their title of 'lord,'" says one of their own body, speaking of the common people, "I never much

[1] History of England, *Temporibus Edwardi Primi et sequentibus.*

valued, and now I entirely despise; and yet they will force it upon me as an honour which they have a right to bestow, and which I have none to refuse."[1] Upon a dispassionate review of the subject, we are disposed to believe that there is no right to the peerage incident to mere bodily configuration; that the title in dispute is merely honorary, and depending upon the breath of the common people, which in these realms is so far from the power of conferring nobility, that the ablest constitutionalists have agreed in nothing more unanimously than in the maxim, that "the king is the sole fountain of honour."

[1] Hay on Deformity.

CHARLES LAMB'S AUTOBIOGRAPHY.

CHARLES LAMB, born in the Inner Temple, 10th February, 1775; educated in Christ's Hospital; afterwards a clerk in the Accountants' Office, East India House; pensioned off from that service, 1825, after thirty-three years' service; is now a gentleman at large; can remember few specialties in his life worth noting, except that he once caught a swallow flying (*teste suâ manu*). Below the middle stature; cast of face slightly Jewish, with no Judaic tinge in his complexional religion; stammers abominably, and is therefore more apt to discharge his occasional conversation in a quaint aphorism, or a poor quibble, than in set and edifying speeches; has consequently been libelled as a person always aiming at wit; which, as he told a dull fellow that charged him with it, is at least as good as aiming at dulness. A small eater, but not drinker; confesses a partiality for the production of the juniper-berry; was a fierce smoker of tobacco, but may be resembled to a volcano burnt out, emitting only now and then a casual puff. Has been guilty of obtruding upon the public a tale, in prose, called "Rosamund Gray;" a dramatic sketch, named "John Woodvil;" a "Farewell Ode to Tobacco," with sundry other poems, and light prose matter, collected in two slight crown octavos, and pompously christened his works, though in fact they were his recreations; and his true works may be found on the shelves of Leadenhall Street, filling some hundred folios. He is also the true Elia, whose Essays are extant in a little volume, published a year or two since, and rather better known from that name without a meaning than from any thing he has done, or can hope to do, in his own. He was also the first to draw the public attention to the old English dramatists, in a work called "Specimens of English Dramatic Writers who lived about the Time of Shakspeare," published about fifteen years since. In short, all his merits and demerits to set forth would take to the end of Mr. Upcott's book, and then not be told truly.

He died 18 , much lamented.

Witness his hand,

CHARLES LAMB.

18*th April* 1827.

LETTER OF ELIA
TO ROBERT SOUTHEY, ESQ.

SIR—You have done me an unfriendly office, without perhaps much considering what you were doing. You have given an ill name to my poor lucubrations. In a recent paper on Infidelity, you usher in a conditional commendation of them with an exception; which, preceding the encomium, and taking up nearly the same space with it, must impress your readers with the notion, that the objectional parts in them are at least equal in quantity to the pardonable. The censure is in fact the criticism; the praise—a concession merely. Exceptions usually follow, to qualify praise or blame. But there stands your reproof, in the very front of your notice, in ugly characters, like some bugbear, to frighten all good Christians from purchasing. Through you I become an object of suspicion to preceptors of youth, and fathers of families. "*A book which wants only a sounder religious feeling, to be as delightful as it is original.*" With no further explanation, what must your readers conjecture, but that my little volume is some vehicle for heresy or infidelity? The quotation which you honour me by subjoining, oddly enough, is of a character which bespeaks a temperament in the writer the very reverse of *that* your reproof goes to insinuate. Had you been taxing me with superstition, the passage would have been pertinent to the censure. Was it worth your while to go so far out of your way to affront the feelings of an old friend, and commit yourself by an irrelevant quotation, for the pleasure of reflecting upon a poor child, an exile at Genoa?

I am at a loss what particular essay you had in view (if my poor ramblings amount to that appellation) when you were in such a hurry to thrust in your objection, like bad news, foremost.—Perhaps the paper on "Saying Graces" was the obnoxious feature. I have endeavoured there to rescue a voluntary duty—good in place, but never, as I remember, literally commanded—from the charge of an undecent formality. Rightly taken, sir, that paper was not against Graces, but Want of Grace; not against the ceremony, but the carelessness and slovenliness so often observed in the performance of it.

Or was it *that* on the "New Year"—in which I have described the feelings of the merely natural man, on a consideration of the amazing change, which is supposable to take place on our removal from this fleshly scene? If men would honestly confess their misgivings (which few men will) there are times when the strongest Christian of us, I believe, has reeled under questions of such staggering obscurity. I do not accuse you of this weakness. There are some who tremblingly reach out shaking hands to the guidance of Faith—others who stoutly venture into the dark (their Human Confidence their leader, whom they mistake for Faith); and, investing themselves beforehand with cherubic wings, as they fancy, find their new robes as familiar, and fitting to the supposed growth and stature in godliness, as the cast they left off yesterday—some whose hope totters upon crutches—others who stalk into futurity upon stilts.

The contemplation of a Spiritual World,—which, without the addition of a misgiving conscience, is enough to shake some natures to their foundation—is smoothly got over by others, who shall float over the black billows in their little boat of No-Distrust, as unconcernedly as over a summer sea. The difference is chiefly constitutional.

One man shall love his friends and his friends' faces; and, under the uncertainty of conversing with them again, in the same manner and familiar circumstances of sight, speech, etc., as upon earth—in a moment of no irreverent weakness — for a dream-while—no more— would be almost content, for a reward of a life of virtue (if he could ascribe such acceptance to his lame performances), to take up his portion with those he loved, and was made to love, in this good world, which he knows— which was created so lovely, beyond his deservings. Another, embracing a more exalted vision—so that he might receive indefinite additaments of power, knowledge, beauty, glory, etc.—is ready to forego the recognition of humbler individualities of earth, and the old familiar faces. The shapings of our heavens are the modifications of our constitutions; and Mr. Feeble Mind, or Mr. Great Heart, is born in every one of us.

Some (and such have been accounted the safest divines) have shrunk from pronouncing upon the final state of any man; nor dare they pronounce the case of Judas to be desperate. Others (with stronger optics), as plainly as with the eye of flesh, shall behold a *given king* in bliss, and a *given chamberlain* in torment; even to the eternising of a cast of the eye in the latter, his own self-mocked and good-humouredly-borne deformity on earth, but supposed to aggravate the uncouth and hideous expression of his pangs in the other place. That one man can presume so far, and that another would with shuddering disclaim such confidences, is, I believe, an effect of the nerves purely.

If, in either of these papers, or elsewhere, I have been betrayed into some levities—not affronting the sanctuary, but glancing perhaps at some of the outskirts and extreme edges, the debatable land between the holy and profane regions—(for the admixture of man's inventions, twisting themselves with the name of religion itself has artfully made it difficult to touch even the alloy, without, in some men's estimation, soiling the fine gold)—if I have sported within the purlieus of serious matter—it was, I dare say, a humour—be not startled, sir,—which I have unwittingly derived from yourself. You have all your life been making a jest of the Devil. Not of the scriptural meaning of that dark essence—personal or allegorical; for the nature is nowhere plainly delivered. I acquit you of intentional irreverence. But indeed you have made wonderfully free with, and been mighty pleasant upon, the popular idea and attributes of him. A Noble Lord, your brother Visionary, has scarcely taken greater liberties with the material keys, and merely Catholic notion of St. Peter. You have flattered him in prose; you have chanted him in goodly odes. You have been his Jester; volunteer Laureate, and self-elected Court Poet to Beelzebub.

You have never ridiculed, I believe, what you thought to be religion, but you are always girding at what some pious, but perhaps mistaken folks, think to be so. For this reason, I am sorry to hear that you are engaged upon a life of George Fox. I know you will fall into the error of intermixing some comic stuff with your seriousness. The Quakers tremble at the subject in your hands. The Methodists are as shy of you, upon account of *their* founder. But, above all, our Popish brethren are most in your debt. The errors of that Church have proved a fruitful source to your scoffing vein. Their Legend has been a Golden one to you. And here your friends, sir, have noticed a notable inconsistency. To the imposing rites, the solemn penances, devout austerities of that communion; the affecting though erring piety of their hermits; the silence and solitude of the Chartreux—their crossings, their holy waters—their Virgin, and their saints—to these, they say, you have been indebted for the best feelings, and the richest imagery, of your epic poetry. You have drawn copious drafts upon Loretto. We thought at one time you were going post to Rome—but that in the facetious commentaries, which it is your custom to append so plentifully, and (some say) injudiciously, to your loftiest performances in this kind, you spurn the uplifted toe, which you but just now seemed to court; leave his holiness in the lurch; and show him a fair pair of Protestant heels under your Romish vestment. When we think you already at the wicket, suddenly a violent cross wind blows you transverse—

> "Ten thousand leagues awry.
> ————Then might we see
> Cowls, hoods, and habits, with their wearers, tost
> And flutter'd into rags; then reliques, beads,
> Indulgences, dispenses, pardons, bulls,
> The sport of winds."

You pick up pence by showing the hallowed bones, shrine, and crucifix; and you take money a second time by exposing the trick of them afterwards. You carry your verse to Castle Angelo for sale in a morning; and, swifter than a pedlar can transmute his pack, you are at Canterbury with your prose ware before night.

Sir, is it that I dislike you in this merry vein? The very reverse. No countenance becomes an intelligent jest better than your own. It is your grave aspect, when you look awful upon your poor friends, which I would deprecate.

In more than one place, if I mistake not, you have been pleased to compliment me at the expense of my companions. I cannot accept your compliment at such a price. The upbraiding a man's poverty naturally makes him look about him to see whether he be so poor indeed as he is presumed to be. You have put me upon counting my riches. Really, Sir, I did not know I was so wealthy in the article of friendships. There is ———, and ———, whom you never heard of, but exemplary characters both, and excellent church-goers; and N., mine and my father's friend for nearly half a century; and the enthusiast for Wordsworth's poetry, T.N.T., a little tainted with Socinianism, it is to be feared, but constant in his attachments, and a capital critic; and ———, a sturdy old Athanasian, so that sets all to rights again; and W., the light, and warm-as-light-hearted, Janus of the *London;* and the translator of Dante, still a curate, modest and amiable C.; and Allan C., the large-hearted Scot; and P——r, candid and affectionate as his own poetry; and A——p, Coleridge's friend; and G——n, his more than friend; and Coleridge himself, the same to me still, as in those old evenings, when we used to sit and speculate (do you remember them, Sir?) at our old Salutation tavern, upon Pantisocracy and golden days to come on earth; and W——th (why, sir, I might drop my rent-roll here, such goodly farms and manors have I reckoned up already. In what possession has not this last name alone estated me?—but I will go on)—and M——, the noble-minded kinsman, by wedlock, of W——th; and H. C. R., unwearied in the offices of a friend; and Clarkson, almost above the narrowness of that relation, yet condescending not seldom heretofore from the labours of his world-embracing charity to bless my humble roof; and the gall-less and single-minded Dyer; and the high-minded associate of Cook, the veteran Colonel, with his lusty heart still sending cartels of defiance to old Time; and, not least, W.A., the last and steadiest left to me of that little knot of whist-players, that used to assemble weekly, for so many years, at the Queen's Gate (you remember them, Sir?) and called Admiral Burney friend.

I will come to the point at once. I believe you will not make many exceptions to my associates so far. But I have purposely omitted some intimacies, which I do not yet repent of having contracted, with two gentlemen diametrically opposed to yourself in principles. You will understand me to allude to the authors of "Rimini" and of the "Table Talk." And first of the former.—

It is an error more particularly incident to persons of the correctest principles and habits, to seclude themselves from the rest of mankind, as from another species, and form into knots and clubs. The best people, herding thus exclusively, are in danger of contracting a narrowness. Heat and cold, dryness and moisture, in the natural world do not fly asunder, to split the globe into sectarian parts and separations; but mingling, as they best may, correct the malignity of any single predominance. The analogy holds, I suppose, in the moral world. If all the good people were to ship themselves off to Terra Incognita, what, in humanity's name, is to become of the refuse? If the persons, whom I have chiefly in view, have not pushed matters to this extremity yet, they carry them as far as they can go. Instead of mixing with the infidel and the freethinker—in the room of opening a negotiation, to try at least to find out at which gate the error entered—they huddle close together, in a weak fear of infection, like that pusillanimous underling in Spenser—

> "This is the wandering wood, this Error's den;
> A monster vile, whom God and man does hate:
> Therefore, I rede, beware." Fly, fly, quoth then
> The fearful Dwarf.

And, if they be writers in orthodox journals, addressing themselves only to the irritable passions of the unbeliever, they proceed in a safe system of strengthening the strong hands, and confirming the valiant knees; of converting the already converted, and proselyting their own party. I am the more convinced of this from a passage in the very Treatise which occasioned this letter. It is where, having recommended to the doubter the writings of Michaelis and Lardner, you ride triumphantly over the necks of all infidels, sceptics, and dissenters, from this time to the world's end, upon the wheels of two unanswerable deductions. I do not hold it meet to set down, in a Miscellaneous Compilation like this, such religious words as you have thought fit to introduce into the pages of a petulant literary journal. I therefore beg leave to substitute *numerals*, and refer to the *Quarterly Review* (for January) for filling of them up. "Here," say you "as in the history of 7, if these books are authentic, the events which they relate must be true; if they were written by 8, 9 is 10 and 11." Your first deduction, if it means honestly, rests upon two identical propositions; though I suspect an unfairness in one of the terms, which this would not be quite the proper place for explicating. At all events, *you* have no cause to triumph; you have not been proving the premises, but refer for satisfaction therein to very long and laborious works, which may well employ the sceptic a twelve-month or two to digest, before he can possibly be ripe for your conclusion. When he has satisfied himself about the premises, he will concede to you the inference, I dare say, most readily. But your latter deduction, viz., that because 8 has written a book concerning 9, therefore 10 and 11 was certainly his meaning, is one of the most extraordinary conclusions *per saltum* that I have had the good fortune to meet with. As far as 10 is verbally asserted in the writings, all sects must agree with you; but you cannot be ignorant of the many various ways in which the doctrine of the * * * * has been understood, from a low figurative expression (with the Unitarians) up to the most mysterious actuality; in which highest sense alone you and your church take it. And for 11, that there is *no other possible conclusion*—to hazard this in the face of so many thousands of Arians and Socinians, etc., who have drawn so opposite a one, is such a piece of theological hardihood, as, I think, warrants me in concluding that, when you sit down to pen theology, you do not at all consider your opponents, but have in your eye, merely and exclusively, readers of the same way of thinking with yourself, and therefore have no occasion to trouble yourself with the quality of the logic to which you treat them.

Neither can I think, if you had had the welfare of the poor child—over whose hopeless condition you whine so lamentably and (I must think) unseasonably—seriously at heart, that you could have taken the step of sticking him up *by name*—T. H., is as good as *naming* him—to perpetuate an outrage upon the parental feelings, as long as the *Quarterly Review* shall last. Was it necessary to specify an individual case, and give to Christian compassion the appearance of a personal attack? Is this the way to conciliate unbelievers, or not rather to widen the breach irreparably?

I own I could never think so considerably of myself as to decline the society of an agreeable or worthy man upon difference of opinion only. The impediments and the facilitations to a sound belief are various and inscrutable as the heart of man. Some believe upon weak principles; others cannot feel the efficacy of the strongest. One of the most candid, most upright, and single-meaning men I ever knew, was the late Thomas Holcroft. I believe he never said one thing, and meant another, in his life; and, as near as I can guess, he never acted otherwise than with the most scrupulous attention to conscience. Ought we to wish the character false, for the sake of a hollow compliment to Christianity?

Accident introduced me to the acquaintance of Mr. L. H.—and the experience of his many friendly qualities confirmed a friendship between us. You who have been misrepresented yourself, I should hope, have not lent an idle ear to the calumnies which have been spread abroad respecting this gentleman. I was admitted to his household for some years, and do most solemnly aver that I believe him to be in his domestic relations as correct as any man. He chose an ill-judged subject for a poem, the peccant humours of which have been visited on him tenfold by the artful use, which his adversaries have made, of an *equivocal term*. The subject itself was started by Dante, but better because brieflier treated of. But the crime of the lovers, in the Italian and the English poet, with its aggravated enormity of circumstance, is not of a kind (as the critics of the latter well knew) with those conjunctions, for which Nature herself has provided no excuse, because no temptation. It has nothing in common with the black horrors, sung by Ford and Massinger. The familiarising of it in the tale and fable may be for that reason incidentally more contagious. In spite of Rimini, I must look upon its author as a man of taste and a poet. He is better than so; he is one of the most cordial-minded men I ever knew, and matchless as a fireside companion. I mean not to affront or wound your feelings when I say that in his more genial moods he has often reminded me of you. There is the same air of mild dogmatism—the same condescending to a boyish sportiveness—in both your conversations. His handwriting is so much the same with your own, that I have opened more than one letter of his, hoping, nay, not doubting, but it was from you, and have been disappointed (he will bear with my saying so) at the discovery of my error. L. H. is unfortunate in holding some loose and not very definite speculations (for at times I think he hardly knows whither his premises would carry him) on marriage— the tenets, I conceive, of the "Political Justice" carried a little farther. For anything I could discover in his practice, they have reference, like those, to some future possible condition of society, and not to the present times. But neither for these obliquities of thinking (upon which my own conclusions are as distant as the poles asunder)— nor for his political asperities and petulances, which are wearing out with the heats and vanities of youth—did I select him for a friend; but for qualities which fitted him for that relation. I do not know whether I flatter myself with being the occasion, but certain it is, that, touched with some misgivings for sundry harsh things which he had written aforetime against our friend C., before he left this country, he sought a reconciliation with that gentleman (himself being his own introducer), and found it.

L. H. is now in Italy; on his departure to which land, with much regret I took my leave of him and his little family—seven of them, Sir, with their mother—and as kind a set of little people (T. H. and all), as affectionate children as ever blessed a parent. Had you seen them, Sir, I think you could not have looked upon them as so many little Jonases—but rather as pledges of the vessel's safety, that was to bear such a freight of love.

I wish you would read Mr. H.'s lines to that same T. H., "six years old, during a sickness:"—

> " Sleep breathes at last from out thee,
> My little patient boy——."

(they are to be found on the 47th page of "Foliage") —and ask yourself how far they are out of the spirit of Christianity. I have a letter from Italy, received but the other day, into which L. H. has put as much heart, and as many friendly yearnings after old associates, and native country, as, I think, paper can well hold. It would do you no hurt to give that the perusal also.

From the *other gentleman* I neither expect nor desire (as he is well assured) any such concessions as L. H. made to C. What hath soured him, and made him to suspect his friends of infidelity towards him, when there was no such matter, I know not. I stood well with him for fifteen years (the proudest of my life), and have ever spoken my full mind of him to some, to whom his panegyric must naturally be least tasteful. I never in thought swerved from him, I never betrayed him, I never slackened in my admiration of him; I was the same to him (neither better nor worse), though he could not see it, as in the days when he thought fit to trust me. At this instant he may be preparing for me some compliment, above my deserts, as he has sprinkled many such among his admirable books, for which I rest his debtor; or, for anything I know, or can guess to the contrary, he may be about to read a lecture on my weaknesses. He is welcome to them (as he was to my humble hearth), if they can divert a spleen, or ventilate a fit of sullenness. I wish he would not quarrel with the world at the rate he does; but the reconciliation must be effected by himself, and I despair of living to see that day. But protesting against much that he has written, and some things which he chooses to do; judging him by his conversation which I enjoyed so long, and relished so deeply; or by his books, in those places where no clouding passion intervenes—I should belie my own conscience, if I said less, than that I think W. H. to be, in his natural and healthy state, one of the wisest and finest spirits breathing. So far from being ashamed of that intimacy, which was betwixt us, it is my boast that I was able for so many years to have preserved it entire; and I think I shall go to my grave without finding or expecting to find, such another companion. But I forget my manners—you will pardon me, Sir—I return to the correspondence.

Sir, you were pleased (you know where) to invite me to a compliance with the wholesome forms and doctrines of the Church of England. I take your advice with as much kindness as it was meant. But I must think the invitation rather more kind than seasonable. I am a Dissenter. The last sect, with which you can remember me to have made common profession, were the Unitarians. You would think it not very pertinent, if (fearing that all was not well with you) I were gravely to invite you (for a remedy) to attend with me a course of Mr. Belsham's Lectures at Hackney. Perhaps I have scruples to some of your forms and doctrines. But if I come, am I secure of civil treatment? The last time I was in any of your places of worship was on Easter Sunday last. I had the satisfaction of listening to a very sensible sermon of an argumentative turn, delivered with great propriety by one of your bishops. The place was Westminster Abbey. As such religion as I have, has always acted on me more by way of sentiment than argumentative process, I was not unwilling, after sermon ended, by no unbecoming transition, to pass over to some serious feelings, impossible to be disconnected from the sight of those old tombs, etc. But, by whose order I know not, I was debarred that privilege even for so short a space as a few minutes; and turned, like a dog, or some profane person, out into the common street; with feelings, which I could not help, but not very congenial to the day or discourse.

I do not know that I shall ever venture myself again into one of your churches.

You had your education at Westminster; and doubtless among those dim aisles and cloisters, you must have gathered much of that devotional feeling in those young years, on which your purest mind feeds still—and may it feed! The antiquarian spirit, strong in you, and gracefully blending ever with the religious, may have been sown in you among those wrecks of splendid mortality. You owe it to the place of your education; you owe it to your learned fondness for the architecture of your ancestors; you owe it to the venerableness of your ecclesiastical establishment, which is daily lessened and called in question through these practices—to speak aloud your sense of them; never to desist raising your voice against them, till they be totally done away with and abolished; till the doors of Westminster Abbey be no longer closed against the decent, though low-in-purse enthusiast, or blameless devotee, who must commit an injury against his family economy, if he would be indulged with a bare admission within its walls. You owe it to the decencies, which you wish to see maintained in its impressive services, that our Cathedral be no longer an object of inspection to the poor at those times only, in which they must rob from their attendance on the worship every minute which they can bestow upon the fabric. In vain the public prints have taken up this subject, in vain such poor nameless writers as myself express their indignation. A word from you, Sir—a hint in your Journal—would be sufficient to fling open the doors of the Beautiful Temple again, as we can remember them when we were boys. At that time of life, what would the imaginative faculty (such as it is) in both of us, have suffered, if the entrance to so much reflection had been obstructed by the demand of so much silver!—If we had scraped it up to gain an occasional admission (as we certainly should have done) would the sight of those old tombs have been as impressive to us (while we had been weighing anxiously prudence against sentiment) as when the gates stood open, as those of the adjacent Park; when we could walk in at any time, as the mood brought us, for a shorter or a longer time, as that lasted? Is the being shown over a place the same as silently for ourselves detecting the genius of it? In no part of our beloved Abbey now can a person find entrance (out of service time) under the sum of *two shillings*. The rich and the great will smile at the anticlimax, presumed to lie in those two short words. But you can tell them, Sir, how much quiet worth, how much capacity for enlarged feeling, how much taste and genius, may coexist, especially in youth, with a purse incompetent to this demand. A respected friend of ours, during his late visit to the metropolis, presented himself for admission to Saint Paul's. At the same time a decently clothed man, with as decent a wife, and child, were bargaining for the same indulgence. The price was only two-pence each person. The poor but decent man hesitated, desirous to go in; but there were three of them, and he turned away reluctantly. Perhaps he wished to have seen the tomb of Nelson. Perhaps the Interior of the Cathedral was his object. But in the state of his finances, even sixpence might reasonably seem too much. Tell the Aristocracy of the country (no man can do it more impressively); instruct them of what value these insignificant pieces of money, these minims to their sight, may be to their humbler brethren. Shame these Sellers out of the Temple. Show the poor that you can sometimes think of them in some other light than as mutineers and malcontents. Conciliate them by such kind methods to their superiors, civil and ecclesiastical. Stop the mouths of the railers; and suffer your old friends, upon the old terms, again to honour and admire you. Stifle not the suggestions of your better nature with the pretext, that an indiscriminate admission would expose the Tombs to violation. Remember your boy days. Did you ever see or hear of a mob in the Abbey, while it was free to all?

Did the rabble come there, or trouble their heads about such speculations? It is all that you can do to drive them into your churches; they do not voluntarily offer themselves. They have, alas! no passion for antiquities; for tomb of king or prelate, sage or poet. If they had, they would be no longer the rabble.

For forty years that I have known the Fabric, the only well-attested charge of violation adduced, has been —a ridiculous dismemberment committed upon the effigy of that amiable spy Major André. And is it for this— the wanton mischief of some school-boy, fired perhaps with raw notions of Transatlantic Freedom — or the remote possibility of such a mischief occurring again, so easily to be prevented by stationing a constable within the walls, if the vergers are incompetent to the duty— is it upon such wretched pretences, that the people of England are made to pay a new Peter's Pence, so long abrogated; or must content themselves with contemplating the ragged Exterior of their Cathedral? The mischief was done about the time that you were a scholar there. Do you know anything about the unfortunate relic? Can you help us in this emergency to find the nose? or can you give Chantrey a notion (from memory) of its pristine life and vigour? I am willing for peace's sake to subscribe my guinea towards the restoration of the lamented feature.—I am, Sir, your humble Servant,

ELIA.

TABLE-TALK, AND FRAGMENTS OF CRITICISM.

IT is a desideratum in works that treat *de re culinariâ*, that we have no *rationale* of sauces, or theory of mixed flavours: as to show why cabbage is reprehensible with roast beef, laudable with bacon; why the haunch of mutton seeks the alliance of currant-jelly, the shoulder civilly declineth it; why loin of veal (a pretty problem), being itself unctuous, seeketh the adventitious lubricity of melted butter,—and why the same part in pork, not more oleaginous, abhorreth from it; why the French bean sympathises with the flesh of deer; why salt fish points to parsnip, brawn makes a dead-set at mustard; why cats prefer valerian to heart's-ease, old ladies *vice versâ*,—though this is rather travelling out of the road of the dietetics, and may be thought a question more curious than relevant; why salmon (a strong sapor *per se*) fortifieth its condition with the mighty lobster-sauce, whose embraces are fatal to the delicater relish of the turbot; why oysters in death rise up against the contamination of brown sugar, while they are posthumously amorous of vinegar, why the sour mango and the sweet jam by turns court and are accepted by the compliable mutton-hash,—she not yet decidedly declaring for either. We are as yet but in the empirical stage of cookery. We feed ignorantly, and want to be able to give a reason of the relish that is in us; so that, if Nature should furnish us with a new meat, or be prodigally pleased to restore the phœnix, upon a *given* flavour, we might be able to pronounce instantly, on philosophical principles, what the sauce to it should be,—what the curious adjuncts.

The greatest pleasure I know is to do a good action by stealth, and to have it found out by accident.

'Tis unpleasant to meet a beggar. It is painful to deny him; and, if you relieve him, it is so much out of your pocket.

Men marry for fortune, and sometimes to please their fancy; but, much oftener than is suspected, they consider what the world will say of it,—how such a woman in their friends' eyes will look at the head of a table. Hence we see so many insipid beauties made wives of, that could not have struck the particular fancy of any man that had any fancy at all. These I call *furniture wives;* as men buy *furniture pictures,* because they suit this or that niche in their dining-parlours.

Your universally cried-up beauties are the very last choice which a man of taste would make. What pleases all, cannot have that individual charm which makes this or that countenance engaging to you, and to you only perhaps, you know not why. What gained the fair Gunnings titled husbands, who, after all, turned out very sorry wives? Popular repute.

It is a sore trial when a daughter shall marry against her father's approbation. A little hard-heartedness, and aversion to a reconcilement, is almost pardonable. After all, Will Dockwray's way is, perhaps, the wisest. His best-loved daughter made a most imprudent match; in fact, eloped with the last-man in the world that her father would have wished her to marry. All the world said that he would never speak to her again. For months she durst not write to him, much less come near him. But, in a casual rencounter, he met her in the streets of Ware,—Ware, that will long remember the mild virtues of William Dockwray, Esq. What said the parent to his disobedient child, whose knees faltered under her at the sight of him? "Ha, Sukey! is it you?" with that benevolent aspect with which he paced the streets of Ware, venerated as an angel: "come and dine with us on Sunday." Then turning away, and again turning back, as if he had forgotten something, he added, "And, Sukey, do you hear?—bring your husband with you." This was all the reproof she ever heard from him. Need it be added, that the match turned out better for Susan than the world expected?

The vices of some men are magnificent. Compare the amours of Henry the Eighth and Charles the Second. The Stuart had mistresses: the Tudor *kept* wives.

"We read the 'Paradise Lost' as a task," says Dr. Johnson. Nay, rather as a celestial recreation, of which the dullard mind is not at all hours alike recipient. "Nobody ever wished it longer;" nor the moon rounder, he might have added. Why, 'tis the perfectness and completeness of it which makes us imagine that not a line could be added to it, or diminished from it, with advantage. Would we have a cubit added to the stature of the Medicean Venus? Do we wish her taller?

Amidst the complaints of the wide spread of infidelity among us, it is consolatory that a sect has sprung up in the heart of the metropolis, and is daily on the increase, of teachers of that healing doctrine which Pope upheld, and against which Voltaire directed his envenomed wit: we mean those practical preachers of optimism, or the belief that *whatever is is best;* the cads of omnibuses, who from their little back pulpits, not once in three or four hours, as those proclaimers of "God and his prophet" in Mussulman countries, but every minute, at the entry or exit of a brief passenger, are heard, in an almost prophetic tone, to exclaim (Wisdom crying out, as it were, in the streets), "ALL'S RIGHT!"

Advice is not so commonly thrown away as is imagined. We seek it in difficulties. But, in common speech, we are apt to confound with it *admonition;* as when a friend reminds one that drink is prejudicial to the health, etc. We do not care to be told of that which we know better than the good man that admonishes. M—— sent to his friend L——, who is no water-drinker, a twopenny tract "Against the Use of Fermented Liquors." L—— acknowledged the obligation, as far as to *twopence.* Penotier's advice was the safest, after all:—

"I advised him"—

But I must tell you. The dear, good-meaning, no-thinking creature had been dumfounding a company of us with a detail of inextricable difficulties, in which the circumstances of an acquaintance of his were involved. No clew of light offered itself. He grew more and more misty as he proceeded. We pitied his friend, and thought,—

"God help the man so rapt in Error's endless maze!"

when, suddenly brightening up his placid countenance, like one that had found out a riddle, and looked to have the solution admired,—

"At last," said he, "I advised him"—

Here he paused, and here we were again interminably thrown back. By no possible guess could any of us aim at the drift of the meaning he was about to be delivered of.

"I advised him," he repeated, "to have some *advice* upon the subject."

A general approbation followed; and it was unanimously agreed, that, under all the circumstances of the case, no sounder or more judicious counsel could have been given.

A laxity pervades the popular use of words.

Parson W—— is not quite so continent as Diana, yet prettily dissembleth his frailty. Is Parson W——, therefore, a *hypocrite?* I think not. Where the concealment of a vice is less pernicious than the barefaced publication of it would be, no additional delinquency is incurred in the secrecy. Parson W—— is simply an immoral clergyman. But if Parson W—— were to be for ever haranguing on the opposite virtue; choosing for his perpetual text, in preference to all other pulpit-topics, the remarkable resistance recorded in the 39th of Exodus; dwelling, moreover, and dilating upon it, —then Parson W—— might be reasonably suspected of hypocrisy. But Parson W—— rarely diverteth into such line of argument, or toucheth it briefly. His ordinary topics are fetched from "obedience to the powers that are," "submission to the civil magistrate in all commands that are not absolutely unlawful;" on which he can delight to expatiate with equal fervour and sincerity.

Again: to *despise* a person is properly to *look down* upon him with none or the least possible emotion; but when Clementina, who has lately lost her lover, with bosom heaving, eyes flashing, and her whole frame in agitation, pronounces with a peculiar emphasis that she "*despises* the fellow," depend upon it that he is not quite so despicable in her eyes as she would have us imagine.

One more instance. If we must naturalise that portentous phrase, *a truism*, it were well that we limited the use of it. Every commonplace or trite observation is not a truism. For example: A good name helps a man on in the world. This is nothing but a simple truth, however hackneyed. It has a distinct subject and predicate. But when the thing predicated is involved in the term of the subject, and so necessarily involved that by no possible conception they can be separated, then it becomes a truism; as to say, "A good name is a proof of a man's estimation in the world." We seem to be saying something, when we say nothing. I was describing to F—— some knavish tricks of a mutual friend of ours. "If he did so and so," was the reply, "he cannot be an honest man." Here was a genuine truism, truth upon truth, inference and proposition identical, or rather a dictionary definition usurping the place of an inference.

We are ashamed at sight of a monkey,—somehow as we are shy of poor relations.

C—— imagined a Caledonian compartment in Hades, where there should be fire without sulphur.

Absurd images are sometimes irresistible. I will mention two,—an elephant in a coach-office gravely coming to have his trunk booked; a mermaid over a fish-kettle cooking her own tail.

It is the praise of Shakspeare, with reference to the playwriters his contemporaries, that he has so few revolting characters. Yet he has one that is singularly mean and disagreeable,—the King in "Hamlet." Neither has he characters of insignificance, unless the phantom that stalks over the stage as Julius Cæsar, in the play of that name, may be accounted one. Neither has he envious characters, excepting the short part of Don John, in "Much Ado about Nothing." Neither has he unentertaining characters, if we except Parolles, and the little that there is of the Clown in "All's Well that Ends Well."

Is it possible that Shakspeare should never have read Homer, in Chapman's version at least? If he had read it, could he mean to *travesty* it in the parts of those big boobies, Ajax and Achilles? Ulysses, Nestor, and Agamemnon are true to their parts in the "Iliad:" they are gentlemen at least. Thersites, though unamusing, is fairly deducible from it. Troïlus and Cressida are a fine graft upon it. But those two big bulks—

It would settle the dispute as to whether Shakspeare intended Othello for a jealous character, to consider how differently we are affected towards him and towards Leontes in the "Winter's Tale." Leontes *is* that character. Othello's fault was simply credulity.

> "*Lear.* Who are you?
> Mine eyes are none of the best. I'll tell you straight.
> Are you not Kent?
>   *Kent.* The same; your servant Kent.
> Where is your servant Caius?
>   *Lear.* 'Twas a good fellow, I can tell you that;
> He'd strike, and quickly too: he is dead and rotten.
>   *Kent.* No, my good lord: I am the very man—
>   *Lear.* I'll see that straight—
>   *Kent.* That from your first of difference and decay
> Have followed your sad steps.
>   *Lear.* You are welcome hither.
>   *Albany.* He knows not what he says; and vain is it
> That we present us to him.
>   *Edgar.* Look up, my lord.
>   *Kent.* Vex not his ghost. Oh! let him pass. He hates him
> That would upon the rack of this rough world
> Stretch him out longer."

So ends "King Lear," the most stupendous of the Shakspearian dramas; and Kent, the noblest feature of the conceptions of his divine mind. This is the magnanimity of authorship, when a writer, having a topic presented to him, fruitful of beauties for common minds, waives his privilege, and trusts to the judicious few for understanding the reason of his abstinence. What a pudder would a common dramatist have raised here of a reconciliation-scene, a perfect recognition, between the assumed Caius and his master!—to the suffusing of many fair eyes, and the moistening of cambric handkerchiefs. The old dying king partially catching at the truth, and immediately lapsing into obliviousness, with the high-minded carelessness of the other to have his services appreciated,—as one that—

> "Served not for gain,
> Or followed out of form,"—

are among the most judicious, not to say heart-touching, strokes in Shakspeare.

Allied to this magnanimity it is, where the pith and point of an argument, the amplification of which might compromise the modesty of the speaker, is delivered briefly, and, as it were, *parenthetically;* as in those few but pregnant words, in which the man in the old "Nut-brown Maid" rather intimates than reveals his unsuspecting high birth to the woman:—

> "Now understand, to Westmoreland,
> *Which is my heritage,*
> I will you bring, and with a ring,
> By way of marriage,
> I will you take, and lady make."

Turn we to the version of it, ten times diluted, of dear Mat. Prior,—in his own way unequalled, and a poet now-a-days too much neglected. "In me," quoth Henry, addressing the astounded Emma,—with a flourish and an attitude, as we may conceive,—

> "In me behold the potent Edgar's heir,
> Illustrious earl! him terrible in war,
> Let Loire confess."

And with a deal of skimble-skamble stuff, as Hotspur would term it, more, presents the lady with a full and true enumeration of his papa's rent-roll in the fat soil by Deva.

But, of all parentheses (not to quit the topic too suddenly), commend me to that most significant one, at the commencement of the old popular ballad of "Fair Rosamond:"—

> "When good King Henry ruled this land,
> The second of that name,"

Now mark,—

> "(Besides the Queen) he dearly loved
> A fair and comely dame."

There is great virtue in this *besides.*

The different way in which the same story may be told by different persons was never more strikingly illustrated than by the manner in which the celebrated Jeremy Collier has described the effects of Timotheus' music upon Alexander, in the second part of his Essays. We all know how Dryden has treated the subject. Let us now hear his great contemporary and antagonist: "Timotheus, a Grecian," says Collier, "was so great a master, that he could make a man storm and swagger like a tempest; and then, by altering the notes and the time, he could take him down again, and sweeten his humour in a trice. One time, when Alexander was at dinner, the man played him a Phrygian air. The prince immediately rises, snatches up his lance, and puts himself into a posture of fighting; and the retreat was no sooner sounded by the change of the harmony, but his arms were grounded, and his fire extinct; and he sat down as orderly as if he had come from one of Aristotle's lectures. I warrant you, Demosthenes would have been flourishing about such business a long hour, and may be not have done it neither. But Timotheus had a nearer cut to the soul: he could neck a passion at a stroke, and lay it asleep. Pythagoras once met with a parcel of drunken fellows, who were likely to be troublesome enough. He presently orders music to play grave, and chops into a Dorian. Upon this they all threw away their garlands, and were as sober and as shamefaced as one would wish." It is evident that Dryden in his inspired ode, and Collier in all this pudder of prose, meant the same thing. But what a work does the latter make with his "necking a passion at his stroke," "making a man storm and swagger like a tempest," and then "taking him down, and sweeting his humour in a trice"! What in Dryden is "softly sweet in Lydian measures," Collier calls "chopping into a Dorian." This Collier was the same, who, in his Biographical Dictionary, says of Shakspeare, that "though his genius generally was jocular, and inclining to festivity, yet *he could when he pleased be as serious as anybody.*"

Oh the comfort of sitting down heartily to an old folio, and thinking surely that the next hour or two will be your own!—and the misery of being defeated by the useless call of somebody, who is come to tell you that he has just come from hearing Mr. Irving! What is that to you? Let him go home, and digest what the good man has said. You are at your chapel, in your oratory.

My friend Hume (not M.P.) has a curious manuscript in his possession, the original draught of the celebrated "Beggar's Petition" (who cannot say by heart the "Beggar's Petition"?) as it was written by some school-usher (as I remember), with corrections interlined from the pen of Oliver Goldsmith. As a specimen of the doctor's improvement, I recollect one most judicious alteration:—

"A pampered menial drove me from the door,"

It stood originally,—

"A livery servant drove me," etc.

Here is an instance of poetical or artificial language properly substituted for the phrase of common conversation; against Wordsworth.

Our ancestors, the noble old Puritans of Cromwell's day, could distinguish between a day of religious rest and a day of recreation; and while they exacted a vigorous abstinence from all amusements (even to walking out of nursery-maids with their charges in the fields) upon the Sabbath, in lieu of the superstitious observance of the saints' days, which they abrogated, they humanely gave to the apprentices and poorer sort of people every alternate Thursday for a day of entire sport and recreation. A strain of piety and policy to be commended above the profane mockery of the Stuarts and their "Book of Sports."

I was once amused—there is a pleasure in *affecting* affectation — at the indignation of a crowd that was justling in with me at the pit-door of Covent Garden Theatre to have a sight of Master Betty—then at once in his dawn and his meridian—in Hamlet. I had been invited quite unexpectedly to join a party whom I met near the door of the play-house; and I happened to have in my hand a large octavo of Johnson and Steevens' "Shakspeare," which, the time not admitting of my carrying it home, of course went with me to the theatre. Just in the very heat and pressure of the doors opening, —the rush, as they term it,—I deliberately held the volume over my head, open at the scene in which the young Roscius had been most cried up, and quietly read by the lamplight. The clamour became universal. "The affectation of the fellow!" cried one. "Look at that gentleman *reading*, papa!" squeaked a young lady, who, in her admiration of the novelty, almost forgot her fears. I read on. "He ought to have his book knocked out of his hand!" exclaimed a pursy cit, whose arms were too fast pinioned to his side to suffer him to execute his kind intention. Still I read on, and, till the time came to pay my money, kept as unmoved as Saint Anthony at his holy offices, with the satyrs, apes, and hobgoblins moping, and making mouths at him, in the picture; while the good man sits as undisturbed at the sight as if he were sole tenant of the desert. The individual rabble (I recognised more than one of their ugly faces) had damned a slight piece of mine but a few nights since; and I was determined the culprits should not a second time put me out of countenance.

We are too apt to indemnify ourselves for some characteristic excellence we are kind enough to concede to a great author by denying him every thing else. Thus Donne and Cowley, by happening to possess more wit, and faculty of illustration, than other men, are supposed to have been incapable of nature or feeling: they are usually opposed to such writers as Shenstone and Parnell; whereas, in the very thickest of their conceits,—in the bewildering mazes of tropes and figures,—a warmth of soul and generous feeling shines through, the "sum" of which, "forty thousand" of those natural poets, as they are called, "with all their quantity," could not make up.

"Pray God, your honour relieve me," said a poor beads-woman to my friend L—— one day : "I have seen better days."—"So have I, my good woman," retorted he, looking up at the welkin, which was just then threatening a storm ; and the jest (he will have it) was as good to the beggar as a tester.

It was, at all events, kinder than consigning her to the stocks or the parish beadle.

But L—— has a way of viewing things in a paradoxical light on some occasions.

I have in my possession a curious volume of Latin verses, which I believe to be unique. It is entitled. *Alexandri Fultoni Scoti Epigrammatorum libri quinque*, It purports to be printed at Perth, and bears date 1679. By the appellation which the author gives himself in the preface, *hypodidasculus*, I suppose him to have been an usher at some school. It is no uncommon thing now-a-days for persons concerned in academies to affect a literary reputation in the way of their trade. The "master of a seminary for a limited number of pupils at Islington" lately put forth an edition of that scarce tract, "The Elegy in a Country Churchyard" (to use his own words), with notes and headlines! But to our author. These epigrams of Alexander Fulton, Scotchman, have little remarkable in them besides extreme dulness and insipidity; but there is one, which, by its being marshalled in the front of the volume, seems to have been the darling of its parent, and for its exquisite flatness, and the surprising strokes of an anachronism with which it is pointed, deserves to be rescued from oblivion. It is addressed, like many of the others to a fair one :—

AD MARIULAM SUAM AUTOR.

" Miserunt bella olim Helenæ decor atque venustas
Europen inter frugiferamque Asiam.
Tam bona, quam tu, tam prudens, sin illa fuisset,
Ad lites issent Africa et America!"

Which, in humble imitation of mine author's peculiar poverty of style, I have ventured thus to render into English :—

THE AUTHOR TO HIS MOGGY.

"For Love's illustrious cause, and Helen's charms,
All Europe and all Asia rushed to arms.
Had she with these thy polished sense combined,
All Afric and America had joined!"

The happy idea of an American war undertaken in the cause of beauty ought certainly to recommend the author's memory to the countrymen of Madison and Jefferson; and the bold anticipation of the discovery of that continent in the time of the Trojan War is a flight beyond the Sibyl's books.

ELIA TO HIS CORRESPONDENTS.

A WRITER, whose real name, it seems, is *Boldero*, but who has been entertaining the town for the last twelve months with some very pleasant lucubrations under the assumed signature of *Leigh Hunt*,[1] in his "Indicator" of the 31st January last has thought fit to insinuate that I, *Elia*, do not write the little sketches which bear my signature in this magazine, but that the true author of them is a Mr. L———b. Observe the critical period at which he has chosen to impute the calumny,—on the very eve of the publication of our last number,—affording no scope for explanation for a full month; during which time I must needs lie writhing and tossing under the cruel imputation of nonentity. Good Heavens! that a plain man must not be allowed *to be*—

They call this an age of personality; but surely this spirit of anti-personality (if I may so express it) is something worse.

Take away my moral reputation,—I may live to discredit that calumny; injure my literary fame,—I may write that up again: but, when a gentleman is robbed of his identity, where is he?

Other murderers stab but at our existence, a frail and perishing trifle at the best: but here is an assassin who aims at our very essence; who not only forbids us *to*

---

[1] Clearly a fictitious appellation; for, if we admit the latter of these names to be in a manner English, what is *Leigh?* Christian nomenclature knows no such.

be any longer, but *to have been* at all. Let our ancestors look to it.

Is the parish register nothing? Is the house in Princes Street, Cavendish Square, where we saw the light six and forty years ago, nothing? Were our progenitors from stately Genoa, where we flourished four centuries back, before the barbarous name of Boldero[1] was known to a European mouth, nothing? Was the goodly scion of our name, transplanted into England in the reign of the seventh Henry, nothing? Are the archives of the steelyard, in succeeding reigns (if haply they survive the fury of our envious enemies), showing that we flourished in prime repute, as merchants, down to the period of the Commonwealth, nothing!

"Why, then the world, and all that's in't, is nothing;
The covering sky is nothing; Bohemia nothing."

I am ashamed that this trifling writer should have power to move me so.

A CORRESPONDENT, who writes himself Peter Ball, or Bell,—for his handwriting is as ragged as his manners,—admonishes me of the old saying, that some people (under a courteous periphrasis, I slur his less ceremonious epithet) had need have good memories. In my "Old Benchers of the Inner Temple," I have delivered myself, and truly, a Templar born. Bell clamours upon this, and thinketh that he hath caught a fox. It seems that in a former paper, retorting upon a weekly scribbler who had called my good identity in question (see Postscript to my "Chapter on Ears"), I profess myself a native of some spot near Cavendish Square, deducing my remoter origin from Italy. But who does not see, except this tinkling cymbal, that, in that idle fiction of Genoese ancestry, I was answering a

[1] It is clearly of Transatlantic origin.

fool according to his folly,—that Elia there expresseth himself ironically as to an approved slanderer, who hath no right to the truth, and can be no fit recipient of it? Such a one it is usual to leave to his delusions; or, leading him from error still to contradictory error, to plunge him (as we say) deeper in the mire, and give him line till he suspend himself. No understanding reader could be imposed upon by such obvious rodomontade to suspect me for an alien, or believe me other than English.

To a second correspondent, who signs himself "A Wiltshire Man," and claims me for a countryman upon the strength of an equivocal phrase in my "Christ's Hospital," a more mannerly reply is due. Passing over the Genoese fable, which Bell makes such a ring about, he nicely detects a more subtle discrepancy, which Bell was too obtuse to strike upon. Referring to the passage, I must confess, that the term "native town," applied to Calne, *primâ facie* seems to bear out the construction which my friendly correspondent is willing to put upon it. The context too, I am afraid, a little favours it. But where the words of an author, taken literally, compared with some other passage in his writings, admitted to be authentic, involve a palpable contradiction, it hath been the custom of the ingenuous commentator to smooth the difficulty by the supposition that in the one case an allegorical or tropical sense was chiefly intended. So, by the word "native," I may be supposed to mean a town where I might have been born, or where it might be desirable that I should have been born, as being situate in wholesome air, upon a dry, chalky soil, in which I delight; or a town with the inhabitants of which I passed some weeks, a summer or two ago, so agreeably, that they and it became in a manner native to me. Without some such latitude of interpretation in the present case, I see not how we can avoid falling into a gross error in physics, as to conceive that a gentleman may be born in two places, from which all modern and ancient testimony is alike abhorrent. Bacchus cometh the nearest to it, whom I remember Ovid to have honoured with the epithet "twice born."[1] But, not to mention that he is so called (we conceive) in reference to the places *whence* rather than the places *where* he was delivered,—for, by either birth, he may probably be challenged for a Theban,—in a strict way of speaking, he was a *filius femoris* by no means in the same sense as he had been before a *filius alvi;* for that latter was but a secondary and tralatitious way of being born, and he but a denizen of the second house of his geniture. Thus much by way of explanation was thought due to the courteous "Wiltshire Man."

To "Indagator," "Investigator," "Incertus," and the rest of the pack, that are so importunate about the true localities of his birth,—as if, forsooth, Elia were presently about to be passed to his parish,—to all such churchwarden critics he answereth, that, any explanation here given notwithstanding, he hath not so fixed his nativity (like a rusty vane) to one dull spot, but that, if he seeth occasion, or the argument shall demand it, he will be born again, in future papers, in whatever place, and at whatever period, shall seem good unto him.

"Modò me Thebis, modò Athenis."

---

[1] "Imperfectus adhuc infans genetricis ab alvo
Eripitur patrioque tener (si credere dignum)
Insuitur femori. . . .
Tutaque bis geniti sunt incunabula Bacchi."
Metamorph., lib. iii.

ON THE DEATH OF COLERIDGE.

WHEN I heard of the death of Coleridge, it was without grief. It seemed to me that he long had been on the confines of the next world,—that he had a hunger for eternity. I grieved then that I could not grieve. But, since, I feel how great a part he was of me. His great and dear spirit haunts me. I cannot think a thought, I cannot make a criticism on men and books, without an ineffectual turning and reference to him. He was the proof and touchstone of all my cogitations. He was a Grecian (or in the first form) at Christ's Hospital, where I was Deputy-Grecian; and the same subordination and deference to him I have preserved through a life-long acquaintance. Great in his writings, he was greatest in his conversation. In him was disproved that old maxim, that we should allow every one his share of talk. He would talk from morn to dewy eve, nor cease till far midnight; yet who ever would interrupt him? who would obstruct that continuous flow of converse, fetched from Helicon or Zion? He had the tact of making the unintelligible seem plain. Many who read the abstruser parts of his "Friend" would complain that his words did not answer to his spoken wisdom. They were identical. But he had a tone in oral delivery which seemed to convey sense to those who were otherwise imperfect recipients. He was my fifty-years-old friend without a dissension. Never saw I his likeness, nor probably the world can see again. I seem to love the house he died at more passionately than when he lived. I love the faithful Gillmans more than while they exercised their virtues towards him living. What was his mansion is consecrated to me a chapel.

EDMONTON, *Nov.* 21, 1834.

PROLOGUES, EPILOGUES, AND MISCELLANEOUS VERSE.

PROLOGUE TO COLERIDGE'S TRAGEDY OF "REMORSE."

THERE are, I am told, who sharply criticise
Our modern theatres' unwieldy size.
We players shall scarce plead guilty to that charge,
Who think a house can never be too large:
Grieved when a rant, that's worth a nation's ear,
Shakes some prescribed Lyceum's petty sphere;
And pleased to mark the grin from space to space
Spread epidemic o'er a town's broad face.
O might old Betterton or Booth return
To view our structures from their silent urn,
Could Quin come stalking from Elysian glades,
Or Garrick get a day-rule from the shades,
Where now, perhaps, in mirth which spirits approve,
He imitates the ways of men above,
And apes the actions of our upper coast,
As in his days of flesh he play'd the ghost:
How might they bless our ampler scope to please,
And hate their own old shrunk-up audiences.
Their houses yet were palaces to those
Which Ben and Fletcher for their triumphs chose.
Shakespeare, who wish'd a kingdom for a stage,
Like giant pent in disproportion'd cage,
Mourn'd his contracted strengths and crippled rage.

He who could tame his vast ambition down
To please some scatter'd gleanings of a town,
And if some hundred auditors supplied
Their meagre meed of claps, was satisfied,
How had he felt, when that dread curse of Lear's
Had burst tremendous on a thousand ears,
While deep-struck wonder from applauding bands
Return'd the tribute of as many hands!
Rude were his guests; he never made his bow
To such an audience as salutes us now.
He lack'd the balm of labour, female praise.
Few ladies in his time frequented plays,
Or came to see a youth with awkward art
And shrill sharp pipe burlesque the woman's part.
The very use, since so essential grown,
Of painted scenes, was to his stage unknown.
The air-blest castle, round whose wholesome crest,
The martlet, guest of summer, chose her nest—
The forest walks of Arden's fair domain,
Where Jaques fed his solitary vein,—
No pencil's aid as yet had dared supply,
Seen only by the intellectual eye.
Those scenic helps, denied to Shakespeare's page,
Our Author owes to a more liberal age.
Nor pomp nor circumstance are wanting here;
'Tis for himself alone that he must fear.
Yet shall remembrance cherish the just pride,
That (be the laurel granted or denied)
He first essay'd in this distinguish'd fane
Severer muses and a tragic strain.

PROLOGUE TO GODWIN'S TRAGEDY "ANTONIO."

" LADIES, ye've seen how Guzman's consort died,
Poor victim of a Spanish brother's pride,
When Spanish honour through the world was blown,
And Spanish beauty for the best was known.[1]
In that romantic, unenlightened time,
A *breach of promise*[2] was a sort of crime—
Which of you handsome English ladies here,
But deem the penance bloody and severe?
A whimsical old Saragossa[3] fashion,
That a dead father's dying inclination
Should *live* to thwart a living daughter's passion[4]
Unjustly on the sex *we*[5] men exclaim,
Rail at *your*[6] vices, and commit the same;—
Man is a promise-breaker from the womb,
And goes a promise-breaker to the tomb—
What need we instance here the lover's vow,
The sick Man's purpose, or the great man's bow?[7]
The truth by few examples best is shown—
Instead of many which are better known,
Take poor Jack Incident, that's dead and gone.
Jack, of dramatic genius justly vain,
Purchased a renter's share at Drury Lane;
A prudent man in every other matter,
Known at his club-room for an honest hatter;
Humane and courteous, led a civil life,
And has been seldom known to beat his wife;
But Jack is now grown quite another man,
Frequents the green-room, knows the plot and plan
   Of each new piece,
And has been seen to talk with Sheridan!
In at the play-house just at six he pops,

---

[1] "Four *easy* lines."   [2] "For which the *heroine died*."
[3] In *Spain!!*   [4] Two *neat* lines.   [5] Or *you*.
[6] Or *our*, as *they* have altered it.   [7] Antithesis!!—C. L.

And never quits it till the curtain drops,
Is never absent on the *author's night*,
Knows actresses and actors too——by sight;
So humble, that with Suett he'll confer,
Or take a pipe with plain Jack Bannister;
Nay, with an author has been known so free,
He once suggested a catastrophe—
In short, John dabbled till his head was turn'd:
His wife remonstrated, his neighbours mourned,
His customers were dropping off apace,
And Jack's affairs began to wear a piteous face.
One night his wife began a curtain lecture:
'My dearest Johnny, husband, spouse, protector,
Take pity on your helpless babes and me,
Save us from ruin, you from bankruptcy—
Look to your business, leave these cursed plays,
And try again your old industrious ways.'
Jack, who was always scar'd at the Gazette,
And had some bits of skull uninjured yet,
Promis'd amendment, vow'd his wife spake reason,
'He would not see another play that season.'
Three stubborn fortnights Jack his promise kept,
Was late and early in his shop, eat, slept,
And walk'd and talk'd, like ordinary men;
No *wit*, but John the hatter once again—
Visits his club: when lo! one *fatal night*
His wife with horror viewed the well-known sight—
John's *hat*, *wig*, *snuff-box*—well she knew his tricks—
And Jack decamping at the hour of six.
Just at the counter's edge a playbill lay,
Announcing that 'Pizarro' was the play—
'O Johnny, Johnny, this is your old doing.'
Quoth Jack, 'Why what the devil storm's a-brewing?
About a harmless play why all this fright?
I'll go and see it, if it's but for spite—
Zounds, woman! Nelson's[1] to be there to-night.'"

---

[1] "A good clap-trap. Nelson has exhibited two or three times at both theatres—and advertised himself."—C. L.

PROLOGUE TO FAULKENER:
A TRAGEDY BY WILLIAM GODWIN, 1807.

An Author who has given you all delight
Furnished the tale our stage presents to-night.
Some of our earliest tears he taught to steal
Down our young cheeks, and forced us first to feel.
To solitary shores whole years confined,
Who has not read how pensive Crusoe pined?
Who, now grown old, that did not once admire
His goat, his parrot, his uncouth attire,
The stick, due notched, that told each tedious day
That in the lonely island wore away?
Who has not shuddered, where he stands aghast
At sight of human footsteps in the waste?
Or joyed not, when his trembling hands unbind
Thee, Friday, gentlest of the savage kind?
The genius who conceived that magic tale
Was skilled by native pathos to prevail.
His stories, though rough-drawn and framed in haste,
Had that which pleased our homely grandsires' taste.
His was a various pen, that freely roved
Into all subjects, was in most approved.
Whate'er the theme, his ready muse obeyed—
Love, Courtship, Politics, Religion, Trade—
Gifted alike to shine in every sphere,
Novelist, Historian, Poet, Pamphleteer.

In some blest interval of party-strife,
He drew a striking sketch from private life,
Whose moving scenes of intricate distress
We try to-night in a dramatic dress:
A real story of domestic woe,
That asks no aid from music, verse, or show,
But trusts to truth, to Nature, and D foe.

EPILOGUE TO "THE WIFE: A TALE OF MANTUA," BY JAMES SHERIDAN KNOWLES.

WHEN first our bard his simple will express'd
That I should in his heroine's robes be dress'd,
My fears were with my vanity at strife,
How I could act that untried part—"a wife."
But Fancy to the Grison hills me drew
Where Mariana like a wild-flower grew,
Nursing her garden-kindred: so far I
Liked her condition, willing to comply
With that sweet single life: when, with a cranch,
Down came that thundering, crashing avalanche,
Startling my mountain-project! "Take this spade,"
Said Fancy then, "dig low, adventurous maid,
For hidden wealth." I did; and, Ladies, lo!
Was e'er romantic female's fortune so,
To dig a life-warm lover from the snow?
   A wife and princess see me next, beset
With subtle toils, in an Italian net,
While knavish courtiers, stung with rage or fear,
Distill'd lip-poison in a husband's ear.
I ponder'd on the boiling Southern vein;
Racks, cords, stilettoes, rush'd upon my brain!
By poor, good, weak Antonio, too, disown'd—
I dream'd each night I should be Desdemona'd,
And, being in Mantua, thought upon the shop
Whence fair Verona's youth his breath did stop:
And what if Leonardo, in foul scorn,
Some lean apothecary should suborn
To take my hated life? A "tortoise" hung
Before my eyes, and in my ears scaled "alligators rung."
But *my* Othello, to his vows more zealous—
Twenty Iagos could not make *him* jealous!
   New raised to reputation, and to life—
At your commands behold me, without strife,
Well-pleased, and ready to repeat—the "Wife."

TO THOMAS STOTHARD, R.A., ON HIS ILLUSTRATIONS OF THE POEMS OF MR. ROGERS.

Consummate Artist, whose undying name
With classic Rogers shall go down to fame,
Be this thy crowning work! In my young days
How often have I with a child's fond gaze
Pored on the pictured wonders thou hadst done:
Clarissa mournful, and prim Grandison!
All Fielding's, Smollett's heroes, rose to view;
I saw, and I believed the phantoms true.
But, above all, that most romantic tale
Did o'er my raw credulity prevail,
Where Glums and Gawries wear mysterious things,
That serve at once for jackets and for wings.
Age, that enfeebles other men's designs,
But heightens thine, and thy free draught refines.
In several ways distinct you make us feel—
Graceful as Raphael, as Watteau *genteel*.
Your lights and shades, as Titianesque, we praise;
And warmly wish you Titian's length of days.

TO CLARA N.

The Gods have made me most unmusical,
With feelings that respond not to the call
Of stringèd harp or voice—obtuse and mute
To hautboy, sackbut, dulcimer, and flute;
King David's lyre, that made the madness flee
From Saul, had been but a jew's-harp to me:
Theorbos, violins, French horns, guitars,
Leave in my wounded ears inflicted scars;
I hate those trills, and shakes, and sounds that float
Upon the captive air; I know no note,

Nor ever shall, whatever folks may say,
Of the strange mysteries of *Sol* and *Fa*;
I sit at oratorios like a fish,
Incapable of sound, and only wish
The thing was over. Yet do I admire,
O tuneful daughter of a tuneful sire,
Thy painful labours in a science, which
To your deserts I pray may make you rich
As much as you are loved, and add a grace
To the most musical Novello race.
Women lead men by the nose, some cynics say;
You draw them by the ear—a delicater way.

TO MY FRIEND THE INDICATOR.

YOUR easy Essays indicate a flow,
Dear friend, of brain which we may elsewhere seek;
And to their pages I and hundreds owe,
That Wednesday is the sweetest of the week.
Such observation, wit, and sense, are shown,
We think the days of Bickerstaff return'd;
And that a portion of that oil you own,
In his undying midnight lamp which burn'd.
I would not lightly bruise old Priscian's head
Or wrong the rules of grammar understood;
But, with the leave of Priscian be it said,
The *Indicative* is your *Potential Mood*.
Wit, poet, prose-man, party-man, translator—
H[unt], your best title yet is *Indicator*.

SAINT CRISPIN TO MR. GIFFORD.

ALL unadvised and in an evil hour,
Lured by aspiring thoughts, my son, you daft
The lowly labours of the " Gentle Craft "

For lowly toils, which blood and spirits sour.
All things, dear pledge, are not in all men's power;
The wiser sort of shrub affects the ground;
The sweet content of mind is oftener found
In cobbler's parlour than in critic's bower.
The sorest work is what doth cross the grain;
And better to this hour you had been plying
The obsequious awl, with well-wax'd finger flying,
Than ceaseless thus to till a thankless vein:
Still teasing muses, which are still denying;
Making a stretching-leather of your brain.

St. Crispin's Eve.

IN TABULAM EXIMII PICTORIS R. B. HAYDONI IN QUA JUDAEI ADVENIENTE DOMINO PALMAS IN VIA PROSTERNENTES MIRA ARTE DEPINGUNTUR.

QUID vult Iste Equitans? et quid velit ista virorum
Palmifera ingens turba et vox tremebunda Hosanna?
Hosanna Christo semper, semperque canamus.
Palma fuit senior Pictor celeberrimus olim;
Sed palmam cedat, modo si foret ille superstes
Palma Haydone tibi: tu palmas omnibus aufers.
Palma negata macrum, donataque reddit opimum
Si simul incipiat cum fama increscere corpus
Tu cito pinguesces, fies et, amicule, obesus.
Affectant lauros pictores atque poetæ,
Sin laurum invideant (sed quis tibi?) laurigerentes
Pro lauro palma viridanti tempora cinge.

Carolagnulus.

TRANSLATION OF THE ABOVE.

WHAT rider's that? and who those myriads bringing
Him on his way, with palms, Hosanna singing?
Hosanna to Christ! Heaven, Earth, shall still be ringing.

In days of old, Old Palma won renown :
But Palma's self must yield the painter's crown,
Haydon, to thee : Thy palms put every other down.

If Flaccus' sentence with the truth agree,
That palms awarded make men plump to be,
Friend Horace, Haydon soon shall match in bulk with
    thee.

Painters with poets for the laurel vie ;
But should the laureate band thy claims deny,
Wear thou thine own green palm, Haydon, triumphantly.

POLITICAL SQUIBS, EPIGRAMS, ETC.

TO SIR JAMES MACKINTOSH.

Though thou'rt like Judas, an apostate black,
In the resemblance one thing thou dost lack;
When he had gotten his ill-purchased pelf,
He went away, and wisely hanged himself.
This thou may'st do at last; yet much I doubt,
If thou hast any *bowels* to gush out!

THE TRIUMPH OF THE WHALE.

Io! Pæan! Io! sing,
To the finny people's king.
Not a mightier whale than this
In the vast Atlantic is;
Not a fatter fish than he
Flounders round the Polar sea.
See his blubber!—at his gills
What a world of drink he swills!
From his trunk, as from a spout,
Which next moment he pours out.
    Such his person.—Next declare,
Muse, who his companions are:—
Every fish of generous kind
Scuds aside, or slinks behind:
But about his presence keep
All the monsters of the deep;

Mermaids, with their tails and singing,
His delighted fancy stinging;
Crooked dolphins, they surround him;
Dog-like seals, they fawn around him;
Following hard, the progress mark
Of the intolerant salt-sea shark:
For his solace and relief
Flat fish are his courtiers chief;
Last, and lowest in his train,
Ink-fish (libellers of the main)
Their black liquor shed in spite:
(Such on earth *the things that write*.)
In his stomach, some do say,
No good thing can ever stay:
Had it been the fortune of it
To have swallow'd that old prophet,
Three days there he'd not have dwell'd,
But in one have been expell'd.
Hapless mariners are they,
Who beguiled (as seamen say)
Deeming him some rock or island,
Footing sure, safe spot, and dry land,
Anchor in his scaly rind—
Soon the difference they find;
Sudden, plumb! he sinks beneath them,—
Does to ruthless seas bequeath them!

    Name or title what has he?
Is he Regent of the Sea?
From this difficulty free us,
Buffon, Banks, or sage Linnæus.
With his wondrous attributes
Say what appellation suits?
By his bulk, and by his size,
By his oily qualities,
This (or else my eyesight fails),
This should be the Prince of W*h*ales.

R. ET R.

THE THREE GRAVES.

CLOSE by the ever-burning brimstone beds
Where Bedloe, Oates, and Judas hide their heads,
I saw great Satan like a Sexton stand
With his intolerable spade in hand
Digging three graves. Of coffin shape they were,
For those who coffinless must enter there
With unblest rites. The shrouds were of that cloth
Which Clotho weaveth in her blackest wrath:
The dismal tinct oppress'd the eye that dwelt
Upon it long, like darkness to be felt.
The pillows to these baleful beds were toads,
Large, living, livid, melancholy loads,
Whose softness shock'd. Worms of all monstrous size
Crawl'd round; and one, upcoil'd, which never dies.
A doleful bell, inculcating despair,
Was always ringing in the heavy air;
And all about the detestable pit
Strange headless ghosts, and quarter'd forms did flit;
Rivers of blood from dripping traitors spilt,
By treachery slung from poverty to guilt.
I ask'd the fiend for whom those rites were meant?
"These graves," quoth he, "when life's brief oil is spent,
When the dark night comes, and they're sinking bedwards,
I mean for Castles, Oliver, and Edwards."

R. ET R.

EPIGRAM.

WRITTEN IN THE LAST REIGN.

YE Politicians, tell me, pray,
Why thus with woe and care rent?
This is the worst that you can say,
Some wind has blown the *Wig* away,
And left the *Hair Apparent*.   R. ET R.

LINES.

SUGGESTED BY A SIGHT OF WALTHAM CROSS.

POINT still the spots, to hallow'd wedlock dear,
Where rested on its solemn way the bier,
That bore the bones of Edward's Elinor
To mix with Royal dust at Westminster.—
Far different rites did thee to dust consign,
Duke Brunswick's daughter, princely Caroline,
A hurried funeral, and a banish'd grave,
High-minded wife! were all that thou couldst have.
Grieve not, great ghost, nor count in death thy losses;
Thou in thy life-time had'st thy share of *crosses*.

"ONE DIP."

MUCH speech obscures the sense; the soul of wit
Is brevity: our tale one proof of it.
Poor Balbulus, a stammering invalid,
Consults the doctors, and by them is bid
To try sea-bathing, with this special heed,
" One dip was all his malady did need;
More than that one his certain death would be."
Now who so nervous or so shook as he,
For Balbulus had never dipped before?
Two well-known dippers, at the Broadstairs' shore,
Stout sturdy churls, have stript him to the skin,
And naked, cold, and shivering plunge him in.
Soon he emerges with scarce breath to say,
" I'm to be dip-dip-dipt——." "We know it," they
Reply. Expostulation seemed in vain,
And over ears they souse him in again;
And up again he rises; his words trip,
And falter as before, Still " dip-dip-dip "—
And in he goes again with furious plunge,
Once more to rise; when with a desperate lunge

At length he bolts these words out, "*only once!*"
The villains crave his pardon.   Had the dunce
But aimed at these bare words the rogues had found him;
But striving to be prolix, they half-drowned him.

H——Y.

SATAN IN SEARCH OF A WIFE.

DEDICATION.

To delicate bosoms, that have sighed over the *Loves of the Angels*, this poem is with tenderest regard consecrated. It can be no offence to you, dear ladies, that the author has endeavoured to extend the dominion of your darling passion; to show love triumphant in places, to which his advent has been never yet suspected. If one Cecilia drew an Angel down, another may have leave to attract a spirit upwards; which, I am sure, was the most desperate adventure of the two. Wonder not at the inferior condition of the agent; for, if King Cophetua wooed a beggar-maid, a greater king need not scorn to confess the attractions of a fair tailor's daughter. The more disproportionate the rank, the more signal is the glory of your sex. Like that of Hecate, a triple empire is now confessed your own. Nor Heaven, nor Earth, nor deepest tracts of Erebus, as Milton hath it, have power to resist your sway. I congratulate your last victory. You have fairly made an honest man of the Old One; and, if your conquest is late, the success must be salutary. The new Benedick has employment enough on his hands to desist from dabbling with the affairs of poor mortals; he may fairly leave human nature to herself; and we may sleep for one while at least secure from the attacks of this hitherto restless Old Bachelor. It remains to be seen, whether the world will be much benefited by the change in his condition.

PART THE FIRST.

I.

THE Devil was sick and queasy of late,
   And his sleep and his appetite fail'd him;
His ears they hung down, and his tail it was clapp'd
Between his poor hoofs, like a dog that's been rapp'd—
   None knew what the devil ail'd him.

II.

He tumbled and toss'd on his mattress o' nights,
    That was fit for a fiend's disportal;
For 'twas made of the finest of thistles and thorn,
Which Alecto herself had gather'd in scorn
    Of the best down beds that are mortal.

III.

His giantly chest in earthquakes heaved,
    With groanings corresponding;
And mincing and few were the words he spoke,
While a sigh, like some delicate whirlwind, broke
    From a heart that seem'd desponding.

IV.

Now the Devil an old wife had for his dam.
    I think none e'er was older:
Her years—old Parr's were nothing to them;
And a chicken to her was Methusalem,
    You'd say, could you behold her.

V.

She remember'd Chaos a little child,
    Strumming upon hand organs;
At the birth of Old Night a gossip she sat,
The ancientest there, and was godmother at
    The christening of the Gorgons.

VI.

Her bones peep'd through a rhinoceros' skin,
    Like a mummy's through its cerement;
But she had a mother's heart, and guess'd
What pinch'd her son; whom she thus address'd
    In terms that bespoke endearment.

VII.

" What ails my Nicky, my darling Imp,
    My Lucifer bright, my Beelze?

  My Pig, my Pug-with-a-curly-tail,
  You are not well. Can a mother fail
   To see *that* which all Hell see ?'

VIII.

" O mother dear, I am dying, I fear ;
  Prepare the yew, and the willow,
And the cypress black : for I get no ease
By day or by night for the cursed fleas
  That skip about my pillow."

IX.

" Your pillow is clean, and your pillow-beer,
  For I wash'd 'em in Styx last night, son,
And your blankets both, and dried them upon
The brimstony banks of Acheron—
  It is not the *fleas* that bite, son."

X.

" O I perish of cold these bitter sharp nights,
  The damp like an ague ferrets ;
The ice and the frost hath shot into the bone ;
And I care not greatly to sleep alone
  O' nights—for the fear of spirits."

XI.

" The weather is warm, my own sweet boy,
  And the nights are close and stifling ;
And for fearing of spirits, you cowardly elf—
Have you quite forgot you're a spirit yourself ?
  Come, come, I see you are trifling.

XII.

" I wish my Nicky is not in love—"
 " O mother, you have nick'd it—"
And he turn'd his head aside with a blush—
Not red hot pokers or crimson plush,
  Could half so deep have prick'd it.

XIII.

"These twenty thousand good years or more,"
    Quoth he, "on this burning shingle
I have led a lonesome bachelor's life,
Nor known the comfort of babe or wife—
    'Tis a long time to live single."

XIV.

Quoth she, "If a wife is all you want,
    I shall quickly dance at your wedding.
I am dry nurse, you know, to the female ghosts—"
And she call'd up her charge, and they came in hosts
    To do the old beldam's bidding:

XV.

All who in their lives had been servants of sin—
    Adulteress, wench, virago—
And murd'resses old that had pointed the knife
Against a husband's or father's life,
    Each one a she Iago.

XVI.

First Jezebel came—no need of paint
    Or dressing to make her charming;
For the blood of the old prophetical race
Had heighten'd the natural flush of her face
    To a pitch 'bove rouge or carmine.

XVII.

Semiramis there low tender'd herself,
    With all Babel for a dowry:
With Helen, the flower and the bane of Greece—
And bloody Medea next offer'd her fleece,
    That was of Hell the houri.

XVIII.

Clytemnestra, with Joan of Naples, put in;
    Cleopatra, by Antony quicken'd;

Jocasta, that married where she should not,
Came hand in hand with the daughters of Lot,
   'Till the Devil was fairly sicken'd.

XIX.

For the Devil himself, a devil as he is,
   Disapproves unequal matches.
" O mother," he cried, " despatch them hence ;
No spirit—I speak it without offence—
   Shall have me in her hatches."

XX.

With a wave of her wand they all were gone !
   And now came out the slaughter :
" 'Tis none of these that can serve my turn ;
For a wife of flesh and blood I burn—
   I'm in love with a tailor's daughter.

XXI.

" 'Tis she must heal the wounds that she made,
   'Tis she must be my physician.
O parent mild, stand not my foe— "
For his mother had whisper'd something low
   About " matching beneath his condition."

XXII.

" And then we must get paternal consent,
   Or an unblest match may vex ye."
" Her father is dead ; I fetch'd him away,
In the midst of his goose last Michaelmas day—
   He died of an apoplexy.

XXIII.

" His daughter is fair, and an only heir—
   With her I long to tether—
He has left her his *hell*, and all that he had ;
The estates are contiguous, and I shall be mad
   'Till we lay our two hells together."

XXIV.

" But how do you know the fair maid's mind ?"
   Quoth he, "Her loss was but recent ;
And I could not speak *my* mind, you know,
Just when I was fetching her father below—
   It would have been hardly decent.

XXV.

" But a leer from her eye, where Cupids lie,
   Of love gave proof apparent ;
And, from something she dropp'd, I shrewdly ween'd,
In her heart she judged that a *living Fiend*
   Was better than a *dead Parent*.

XXVI.

" But the time is short ; and suitors may come
   While I stand here reporting ;
Then make your son a bit of a beau,
And give me your blessing before I go
   To the other world a-courting."

XXVII.

" But what will you do with your horns, my son ?
   And that tail—fair maids will mock it—"
" My tail I will dock—and as for the horn,
Like husbands above, I think no scorn
   To carry it in my pocket."

XXVIII.

" But what will you do with your feet, my son ?"
   " Here are stockings fairly woven :
My hoofs I will hide in silken hose ;
And cinnamon-sweet are my pettitoes—
   Because, you know, they are *cloven*."

XXIX.

" Then take a blessing, my darling son,"
   Quoth she and kissed him civil—

Then his neckcloth she tied; and when he was drest
From top to toe in his Sunday's best,
  He appear'd a comely devil.

XXX.

So his leave he took: but how he fared
  In his courtship—barring failures—
In a Second Part you shall read it soon,
In a brand-new song, to be sung to the tune
  Of the "Devil among the Tailors."

THE SECOND PART,

CONTAINING THE COURTSHIP AND THE WEDDING.

I.

WHO is she that by night from her balcony looks
  On a garden where cabbage is springing?
'Tis the tailor's fair lass, that we told of above;
She muses by moonlight on her true love;
  So sharp is Cupid's stinging.

II.

She has caught a glimpse of the Prince of the Air
  In his Luciferian splendour,
And away with coyness and maiden reserve!
For none but the Devil her turn will serve,
  Her sorrows else will end her.

III.

She saw when he fetch'd her father away,
  And the sight no whit did shake her;
For the Devil may sure with his own make free—
And "it saves besides," quoth merrily she,
  "The expense of an undertaker.

IV.

"Then come, my Satan, my darling Sin,
  Return to my arms, my Hell beau;
My Prince of Darkness, my crow-black dove—"
And she scarce had spoke, when her own true love
  Was kneeling at her elbow!

V.

But she wist not at first that this was he,
  That had raised such a boiling passion;
For his old costume he had laid aside,
And was come to court a mortal bride
  In a coat-and-waistcoat fashion.

VI.

She miss'd his large horns, and she miss'd his fair tail,
  That had hung so retrospective;
And his raven plumes, and some other marks
Regarding his feet, that had left their sparks
  In a mind but too susceptive:

VII.

And she held it scorn that a mortal born
  Should the Prince of Spirits rival,
To clamber at midnight her garden fence—
For she knew not else by what pretence
  To account for his arrival.

VIII.

"What thief art thou," quoth she, "in the dark
  That stumblest here presumptuous?
Some Irish adventurer I take you to be—
A foreigner, from your garb I see,
  Which besides is not over sumptuous."

IX.

Then Satan, awhile dissembling his rank,
  A piece of amorous fun tries:

Quoth he, "I'm a Netherlander born;
Fair virgin, receive not my suit with scorn;
I'm a Prince in the Low Countries—

X.

"Though I travel *incog.* From the Land of Fog
    And Mist I am come to proffer
My crown and my sceptre to lay at your feet;
It is not every day in the week you may meet,
    Fair maid, with a Prince's offer."

XI.

"Your crown and your sceptre I like full well,
    They tempt a poor maiden's pride, sir;
But your lands and possessions—excuse if I'm rude—
Are too far in a northerly latitude
    For me to become your bride, sir.

XII.

"In that aguish clime I should catch my death,
    Being but a raw new-comer—"
Quoth he, "We have plenty of fuel stout;
And the fires, which I kindle, never go out
    By winter, nor yet by summer.

XIII.

"I am Prince of Hell, and Lord Paramount
    Over monarchs there abiding.
My groom of the stables is Nimrod old;
And Nebuchadnazor my stirrups must hold,
    When I go out a-riding.

XIV.

"To spare your blushes, and maiden fears,
    I resorted to these inventions—
But, imposture, begone; and avaunt, disguise!"
And the Devil began to swell and rise
    To his own diabolic dimensions.

XV.

Twin horns from his forehead shot up to the moon,
    Like a branching stag in Arden;
Dusk wings through his shoulders with eagle's strength
Push'd out; and his train lay floundering in length
    An acre beyond the garden.—

XVI.

To tender hearts I have framed my lay—
    Judge ye, all love-sick maidens,
When the virgin saw in the soft moonlight,
In his proper proportions, her own true knight,
    If she needed long persuadings.

XVII.

Yet a maidenly modesty kept her back,
    As her sex's art had taught her:
For "the biggest fortunes," quoth she, "in the land
Are not worthy," then blush'd, "of your Highness's hand,
    Much less a poor tailor's daughter.

XVIII.

"There's the two Miss Crockfords are single still,
    For whom great suitors hunger;
And their father's hell is much larger than mine."
Quoth the Devil, "I've no such ambitious design,
    For their dad is an old fishmonger;

XIX.

"And I cannot endure the smell of fish—
    I have taken an anti-bias
To their livers, especially since the day
That the Angel smoked my cousin away
    From the chaste spouse of Tobias.

XX.

"Had my amorous kinsman much longer stay'd,
    The perfume would have scal'd his obit;

For he had a nicer nose than the wench,
Who cared not a pin for the smother and stench,
   In the arms of the son of Tobit."

XXI.

"I have read it," quoth she, "in Apocryphal Writ—"
   And the Devil stoop'd down and kiss'd her;
Not Jove himself, when he courted in flame,
On Semele's lips, the love-scorch'd dame,
   Impress'd such a burning blister.

XXII.

The fire through her bones and her vitals shot—
   "O, I yield, my winsome marrow—
I am thine for life"—and black thunders roll'd—
And she sank in his arms through the garden mould,
   With the speed of a red-hot arrow.

XXIII.

Merrily, merrily, ring the bells
   From each Pandemonian steeple;
For the Devil hath gotten his beautiful bride,
And a wedding dinner he will provide,
   To feast all kinds of people.

XXIV.

Fat bulls of Basan are roasted whole,
   Of the breed that ran at David;
With the flesh of goats, on the sinister side,
That shall stand apart, when the world is tried;
   Fit meat for souls unsavèd!

XXV.

The fowl from the spit were the Harpies' brood,
   Which the bard sang near Cremona,
With a garnish of bats in their leathern wings imp'd;
And the fish was—two delicate slices crimp'd,
   Of the whale that swallow'd Jonah.

XXVI.

Then the goblets were crown'd, and a health went round
    To the bride, in a wine like scarlet;
No earthly vintage so deeply paints,
For 'twas dash'd with a tinge from the blood of the saints
    By the Babylonian Harlot.

XXVII.

No Hebe fair stood cup-bearer there,
    The guests were their own skinkers;
But Bishop Judas first blest the can,
Who is of all Hell Metropolitan,
    And kiss'd it to all the drinkers.

XXVIII.

The feast being ended, to dancing they went,
    To music that did produce a
Most dissonant sound, while a hellish glee
Was sung in parts by the Furies Three;
    And the Devil took out Medusa.

XXIX.

But the best of the sport was to hear his old dam,
    Set up her shrill forlorn pipe—
How the wither'd Beldam hobbled about,
And put the rest of the company out—
    For she needs must try a hornpipe.

XXX.

But the heat, and the press, and the noise, and the din,
    Were so great, that, howe'er unwilling,
Our reporter no longer was able to stay,
But came in his own defence away,
    And left the bride quadrilling.

NOTES.

Mrs. Leicester's School (p. 1).—London, printed for M. J. Godwin, at the Juvenile Library, No. 41 Skinner Street, 1807. The joint composition of Charles and Mary Lamb, the three stories, *Maria Howe*, *Susan Yates*, and *Arabella Hardy*, being by Charles, and the remainder by Mary. No mention is to be found in Lamb's letters of the origin of this work; but it was certainly written at the suggestion of Godwin, for his series of Children's books. It is interesting to trace in the scenes and incidents of the various stories recollections of the childish days of the brother and sister. The pretty village of Amwell, where the school is placed, was only some five miles from Blakesware. The story called *The Young Mahometan* contains Mary Lamb's own recollections of the old Family Seat of the Plumers, and her reference to the marble hall, the twelve Cæsars, the Hogarth prints, and the picture of the young shepherdess, may be put side by side with her brother's essay, "Blakesmoor in H——shire," and other allusions in letter and essay to the old mansion. The *Witch Aunt* (absurdly altered in modern editions to the much less expressive "Effect of Witch Stories"), is the first sketch of an experience afterwards elaborated by Lamb in the Elia Essay, *Witches and other Night Fears*. *Susan Yates*, the scene of which is laid in a village in the Lincolnshire Fens, was probably derived from the early recollections of old John Lamb, who had originally come up to London from Lincolnshire a poor boy to enter service, and who when he came in after years to live in the Temple would naturally love to compare the grotesque faces "in the round tower of the Temple Church" with those in the old Minster Church of his native county. The *Changeling* is curious as illustrating the strong Shakspearian bias of the writers, as shown in their resorting to the expedient of a play within a play, whereby to "catch the conscience" of the delinquent nurse. Perhaps the most perfect of the stories, in point of delicacy and humour, are *The Sea Voyage* of Charles and *The*

Father's Wedding-Day of Mary. It was the latter which was Walter Savage Landor's special favourite. We have Lamb's own authority for the respective authorship of the various tales. "I wrote only the *Witch Aunt;* the *First going to Church;* and the final story about 'a little Indian girl' in a ship."

The Adventures of Ulysses (p. 89).—1808. Another contribution to Godwin's Juvenile Library. Lamb writes to Manning in February 1808 :—"I have done two books since the failure of my farce; they will both be out this summer. The one is a juvenile book—'The adventures of Ulysses,' intended to be an introduction to the reading of Telemachus ! It is done out of the Odyssey, not from the Greek—I would not mislead you— nor yet from Pope's Odyssey, but from an older translation of one Chapman. The 'Shakspeare Tales' suggested the doing it." Again, in 1827, writing to Barton, he asks :—"Did you ever read my 'Adventures of Ulysses,' founded on Chapman's old translation of it, for children or men ? Chapman is divine, and my abridgment has not quite emptied him of his divinity." Traces of Chapman may be discovered in abundance in Lamb's version, extending to a repetition of misprints in Chapman which even down to the present day have not been corrected. The Homeric river-epithet "Fair-flowing" was personified by Chapman into a river goddess, which we may suppose he intended to write "Callirhoe," but which by a printer's error became "Callicoe," in which shape it strangely appears in Lamb's copy. But Lamb's Greek was not his strong point. For the rest, he frequently borrows whole lines of Chapman's version, as in the story of Æolus—

" Only he left abroad the western wind ; "

in that of Polyphemus—

" Which that abhorred No-man did put out,
Assisted by his execrable rout,"

and so forth, giving to his narrative a rhythm and diction pleasantly old-fashioned. There seems no reason why the version should not again become a favourite schoolroom story-book, and form as pleasant an introduction to the Odyssey as the Tales from Shakspeare have been, and still are, to the study of our English poet.

Guy Faux (p. 180).—(*London Magazine*, November 1823.) The latter portion of this paper first appeared in Leigh Hunt's *Reflector* in 1811, under the following title, "On the probable effects of the Gunpowder Treason in this country, if the Conspirators had accomplished their object." It began with the paragraph on p. 183, "The Gunpowder Treason was the subject," etc. etc. Lamb revived it with additions twelve years later in the *London Magazine*, à propos of an article of Hazlitt's (the "ingenious and subtle writer" alluded to) in the *Examiner* of November 1821.

On the Custom of Hissing at the Theatres (p. 192).—(The *Reflector*, No. iii., Art. xi., 1811). A reminiscence of the failure of *Mr. H.* at Drury Lane in 1806. *The Vindictive Man* was a play of Holcroft's produced in November 1806, only three weeks before Lamb's equally unsuccessful venture. The condemnation of Holcroft's play is fully and amusingly described by Lamb in a letter to Manning of December 5, 1806. Mr. De Camp, who played Goldfinch, a character revived from Holcroft's *Road to Ruin*, "was hooted, more than hissed ; hooted and bellowed off the stage before the second act was finished, so that the remainder of his part was forced to be, with some violence to the play, omitted." The play, according to Lamb, "died in part of its own weakness, and in part for being choked up with bad actors." It was acted only twice.

The Good Clerk (p. 200).—(The *Reflector*, No. iv., Art. xxiii., 1811.)

The Reynolds Gallery (p. 207).—(The *Examiner*, June 6, 1813.) An exhibition of the works of Reynolds, first suggested by a "lover of the arts" at the Royal Academy dinner in 1811. "It was warmly applauded by the Prince Regent, who was present, and who offered to contribute several works by the late president in his own possession. This commemoration of Reynolds took place in 1813, when 113 of his works were gathered together for exhibition to the public, and included some of his finest productions. It was inaugurated by a banquet at Willis's Rooms at which the Prince Regent was present, and at which all who were distinguished in position and associated with the encouragement of the arts were specially invited to attend. This was the first public exhibition of the works of any individual British artist" (Sandby's *History of the Royal Academy*. London, 1862).

Wordsworth's Excursion (p. 210).—(*Quarterly Review*, October 1814.) Jeffrey's famous notice of the *Excursion*, beginning "This will never do," appeared in the *Edinburgh Review* of November 1814, and by a happy coincidence Lamb's appeared in the corresponding number of the *Quarterly*. Just before its publication Lamb wrote to Wordsworth asking for indulgence on the ground that it was the first review he had ever written. "I hope," he says, "you will see good-will in the thing. I had a difficulty to perform not to make it all panegyric ; I have attempted to personate a mere stranger to you, perhaps with too much strangeness. But you must bear that in mind when you read it, and not think that I am in mind distant from you or your poem, but that both are close to me, among the nearest of persons and things. . . . But," he concludes, "it must speak for itself, if Gifford and his crew do not put words in its mouth, which I suspect." This ominous hint was only too literally to be fulfilled. Immediately after the appearance of the *Quarterly* Lamb wrote again to his friend, this time in dismay :—"I told you my review was a very imperfect one. But what you will see in the *Quarterly* is a spurious one, which Mr. Baviad Gifford has palmed upon it for mine. I never felt more vexed in my life than when I read it. I cannot give you an idea of what he has done to it, out of spite at me, because he once suffered me to be called a lunatic in his *Review*. The *language* he has altered throughout. Whatever inadequateness it had to its subject it was, in point of composition, the prettiest piece of prose I ever writ ; and so my sister (to whom alone I read the MS.) said. That charm, if it had any, is all gone ; more than a third of the substance is cut away, and that not all from one place, but *passim*, so as to make utter nonsense. Every warm expression is changed for a nasty cold one. I have not the cursed alteration by me ; I shall never look at it again ; but, for a specimen, I remember I had said the poet of the *Excursion* 'walks through common forests as through some Dodona or enchanted wood, and every casual bird that flits upon the boughs, like that miraculous one in Tasso, but in language more piercing than any articulate sounds, reveals to him far higher love-lays.' It is now (besides half a dozen alterations in the same half dozen lines) 'but in language more *intelligent* reveals to him ;' that is one I remember." There is much more in the same letter on the subject that will be read with interest. In spite of Gifford's alterations there are passages in the *Review*, as it appeared, that are unmistakably Lamb's, and could have been written by no other hand. The beautiful sentence about those who "never having possessed the tenderness and docility" of the childish age, "know not what the soul of a child is, how apprehensive, how imaginative, how religious," is unquestionably a "sweet forewarning" of one of the most affecting passages in the Elia Essay "New Year's Eve."

As I have elsewhere remarked, much of Lamb's praise may seem commonplace compared with the able and sympathetic Wordsworthian criticism that has been produced in the last seventy years. But, as usual, he was among the first to recognise a really good thing, while the world's eyes were still closed. It is the timeliness of his appreciation that should win our gratitude.

Theatrical Notices (p. 225).—The three following theatrical criticisms appeared in the columns of the *Examiner* with the signature, four asterisks (* * * *), adopted by Lamb in his communications to that journal. To the third of these anonymous articles (*New pieces at the Lyceum*), Leigh Hunt prefixed an editorial note, pointing to a special and distinguished authorship. He speaks of "an impudent rogue of a friend whose most daring tricks and pretences carry as good a countenance with them as virtues in any other man, and who has the face above all to be a better critic than ourselves."

The letter about Miss Kelly was originally addressed to Lamb's old schoolfellow and friend John Matthew Gutch, for a long time editor of Farley's *Bristol Journal*. Leigh Hunt prefaced the letter, in copying it into the *Examiner*, as follows:—"The reader we are sure will thank us for extracting the following observations on a favourite actress from a provincial paper, the *Bristol Journal*. We should have guessed the masterly and cordial hand that wrote them had we met with it in the East Indies. There is but one praise belonging to Miss Kelly which it has omitted and which it could not supply ; and that is, that she has had finer criticism written upon her than any performer that ever trod the stage."

First Fruits of Australian Poetry (p. 235.)—(*Examiner*, January 16, 1820.) A collection of verse, printed for private circulation, by Lamb's old friend, Barron Field, who was Judge of the Supreme Court at Sydney, New South Wales, from 1816 to 1824. The poems afterwards appeared as an appendix to a volume of geographical memoirs, published by Murray, in 1825. Compare Lamb's Elia Essay, *Distant Correspondents*.

The Gentle Giantess (p. 238).—(*London Magazine*, December 1822.) Although Lamb domiciles the widow Blacket at Oxford, her original would seem to have belonged to the sister University. It can hardly be coincidence that Lamb thus writes in the same year to Miss Wordsworth of a certain stout lady at Cambridge :—"Ask anybody you meet who is the biggest woman in Cambridge, and I'll hold you a wager they'll say Mrs. Smith. She broke down two benches in Trinity Gardens, one on the confines of St. John's, which occasioned a litigation between the Societies as to repairing it. In warm weather she retires into an ice-cellar (literally !) and dates the returns of the years from a hot Thursday some twenty years back. She sits in a room with opposite doors and windows, to let in a thorough draught, which gives her slenderer friends toothaches."

On a Passage in the Tempest (p. 242).—(*London Magazine*, November 1823.) Lamb's citation from Ogilby is no *jeu d'esprit*, but a genuine transcript. There can be little doubt that an early version of this story was known to Shakspeare. The siege of Algiers took place in 1542, and all the authorities cited by Ogilby wrote before Shakspeare's day. In company with Mr. Aldis Wright, I have referred to many of these in the Library of Trinity College Cambridge, but as yet have not found any mention of the witch incident.

Letter to an old Gentleman whose Education has been neglected (p. 250).—(*London Magazine*, January 1825.) The papers here playfully imitated are of course De Quincey's "Letters to a Young Man whose Education has been neglected," which appeared first in the *London Magazine*. Lamb has not attempted to parody more than the introductory passages of De Quincey's first letter, and here and there the solemn sententiousness of the original. The "first question" addressed to De Quincey, "Whether to you, with your purposes, and at your age of thirty-two, a residence at either of our English universities or at any foreign university can be of much service?" is very humorously paralleled by the supposed question of Lamb's correspondent "Whether a person at the age of sixty-three, with no more proficiency than a tolerable knowledge of most of the characters of the English alphabet at first sight amounts to . . . may hope to arrive, within a presumable number of years, at that degree of attainments which shall entitle the possessor to the character, which you are on so many accounts justly desirous of acquiring, of a *learned man*." Lamb writes to Miss Hutchinson that "De Quincey's parody was submitted to him before being printed, and had his *probatum*."

Biographical Memoir of Mr. Liston (p. 253).—(*London Magazine*, January 1825.) See letter of Lamb to Miss Hutchinson of January 25, 1825. "Did you read the *Memoir of Liston?* and did you guess whose it was? Of all the lies I ever put off, I value this most. It is from top to toe, every paragraph, pure invention, and has passed for gospel; has been republished in newspapers, and in the penny play-bills of the night, as an authentic account. I shall certainly go to the naughty man some day for my fibbings." So again, to Bernard Barton:— "I have caused great speculation in the dramatic (not *thy*) world by a lying 'Life of Liston,' all pure invention. The town has swallowed it, and it is copied into newspapers, play-bills, etc., as authentic. You do not know the droll, and possibly missed reading the article (in our first number, new series). A life more improbable for him to have lived would not easily be invented."

Autobiography of Mr. Munden (p. 262).—(*London Magazine*,

February 1825.) "He wrote in the same Magazine two lives of Liston and Munden which the public took for serious, and which exhibit an extraordinary jumble of imaginary facts and truth of bye-painting. Munden he made born at Stoke Pogis, the very sound of which was like the actor speaking and digging his words" (Leigh Hunt's Autobiography, chap. xvi).

Reflections in the Pillory (p. 266).—(*London Magazine*, March 1825.)

The Last Peach (p. 271).—(*London Magazine*, April 1825.) A reminiscence, apparently of the old mansion of the Plumers at Blakesware, and of Lamb's summer holiday spent there with his grandmother. See Elia Essay, *Blakesmoor in H——shire*, and my notes upon it. The "hot feel of the brickwork" is another exquisite touch to be added to the "sulky pike" and the "solitary wasp" in that delightful picture.

The Illustrious Defunct (p. 274).—(*New Monthly Magazine*, 1825.) When Lamb wrote this admirable essay, the State-lottery system was, as he says, "moribund," but not yet extinct. It came to an end in the following year. In the number of Hone's *Every-Day Book* for November 15, 1826, will be found some most amusing particulars of the event, and the expiring efforts of the ticket-sellers to advertise their wares. "Positively the last lottery that will ever be drawn in England. All lotteries end for ever, 18 October." Hone gives a copy of a pictorial advertisement, representing a fishwoman, sitting down by the side of her basket and reading a printed bill— "What's the odds?" she says, "while I am floundering here the goldfish will be gone; and as I always was a dab at hooking the right numbers, I must cast for a share of the six £30,000 on the 18th of July; for it is but 'giving a sprat to catch a herring,' as a body may say, and it is the last chance we shall have in England." In after days, Hone adds, this may be looked on with interest as a specimen of the means to which the lottery-schemers were reduced in order to attract attention to "the last."

The Religion of Actors (p. 281).—(*New Monthly Magazine*, 1826.) "A little thing without name will also be printed on the Religion of the Actors, but it is out of your way, so I recommend you, with true author's hypocrisy, to skip it" (Lamb to Bernard Barton, March, 1826).

The Months (p. 285).—(Hone's *Every-Day Book*, April 16, 1826.) Hone prefixes the following note:—"C. L., whose papers under these initials on 'Captain Starkey,' 'The Ass,' and 'Squirrels,' besides other communications are in the first volume, drops the following pleasant article 'in an hour of need.'"

"Those *Every-Day* and *Table Books* will be a treasure a hundred years hence, but they have failed to make Hone's fortune." So Lamb wrote to Southey in 1830, pleading for the struggling editor, for whom kind friends had then just opened a coffee-house in the city. It was in a like "hour of need" that Lamb had originally sent contributions to the pleasant columns of the *Every-Day Book*. Hone acknowledges his gratitude in a dedicatory letter prefixed to the completed work. "Your letter to me," he writes, "within the first two months from the commencement of the present work, approving my notice of St. Chad's Well, and your afterwards daring to publish me your 'friend' with your proper name annexed, I shall never forget. How can I forget your and Miss Lamb's sympathy and kindness when glooms overmastered me, and that your pen sparkled in the book when my mind was in clouds and darkness. These 'trifles,' as each of you would call them, are benefits scored upon my heart."

Reminiscence of Sir Jeffrey Dunstan (p. 289).—(Hone's *Every-Day Book*, June 22, 1826). The following extract from Sir Richard Phillips' *Morning's Walk to Kew* (1817), as quoted in Hone's *Every-Day Book*, forms the best explanation of Lamb's letter to the editor:—"Southward of Wandsworth a road extends nearly two miles to the village of Lower Tooting, and nearly midway are a few houses or hamlets by the side of a small common called *Garrat*, from which the road itself is called Garrat Lane. Various encroachments on this common led to an association of the neighbours, about three score years since, when they chose a president, or *mayor*, to protect their rights; and the time of their first election being the period of a new Parliament, it was agreed that the mayor should be rechosen after every general election. Some facetious members of the club gave in a few years local notoriety to this election; and when party spirit ran high in the days of *Wilkes and Liberty*, it was easy to create an appetite for a burlesque election among the lower orders of the metropolis. The publicans at Wandsworth, Tooting, Battersea, Clapham and Vauxhall, made a purse to give it character; and Mr. Foote rendered its interest universal by calling one of his inimitable farces "The Mayor of Garrat." I have indeed been told that Foote, Garrick, and Wilkes wrote some of the candidates' addresses, for the purpose of instructing the people in the corruptions which attend elections to the legislature, and of producing those reforms by means of ridicule and shame which are vainly expected from solemn appeals of argument and patriotism.

Not being able to find the members for Garrat in Beatson's political index, or in any of the court calendars, I am obliged to depend on tradition for information in regard to the early history of this famous borough. The first mayor of whom I could hear was called Sir John Harper. He filled the seat during two Parliaments, and was, it appears, a man of wit, for on a dead cat being thrown at him on the hustings, and a bystander exclaiming that it stunk worse than a fox, Sir John vociferated, "That's no wonder, for you see its a *pole*-cat."

This noted baronet was, in the metropolis, a retailer of brick-dust; and, his Garrat honours being supposed to be a means of improving his trade and the condition of his ass, many characters in similar occupations were led to aspire to the same distinctions.

He was succeeded by Sir Jeffrey Dunstan, who was returned for three parliaments, and was the most popular candidate that ever appeared on the Garrat hustings. His occupation was that of buying *old wigs*, once an article of trade like that in old clothes, but become obsolete since the full-bottomed and full-dressed wigs of both sexes went out of fashion. Sir Jeffrey usually carried his wig-bag over his shoulder, and, to avoid the charge of vagrancy, vociferated, as he passed along the street, "old wigs;" but having a person like Esop, and a countenance and manner marked by irresistible humour, he never appeared without a train of boys and curious persons whom he entertained by his sallies of wit, shrewd sayings, and smart repartees; and from whom without begging he collected sufficient to maintain his dignity as mayor and knight. He was no respecter of persons, and was so severe in his jokes on the corruptions and compromisers of power, that the street-jester was prosecuted for using what were then called seditious expressions; and, as a caricature on the times which ought never to be forgotten, he was in 1793 tried, convicted, and imprisoned! In conse-quence of this affair, and some charges of dishonesty, he lost his popularity, and at the general election for 1796 was ousted by Sir Harry Dimsdale, muffin-seller, a man as much deformed as himself. Sir Jeffrey could not long survive his fall; but in death as in life he proved a satire on the vices of the proud, for in 1797 he died—like Alexander the Great and many other heroes renowned in the historic page—"of suffocation from excessive drinking!"

Captain Starkey (p. 292).—(Hone's *Every-Day Book*, vol. i., July 21.) Under the date of 9th July Hone had published a review of the following work—"Memoirs of the Life of Benj.

Starkey, late of London, but now an inmate of the Freemen's Hospital in Newcastle. Written by himself. With a portrait of the author, and a fac-simile of his handwriting. Printed and sold by William Hall, Great Market, Newcastle, 1818." The book, the reviewer good-naturedly says, is the adventureless history of a man who did no harm in the world, and thought he had a right to live, because he was a living being. In the course of his hand-to-mouth struggle for existence, Starkey records how, at the age of fourteen, he was "bound apprentice to Mr. William Bird, an eminent writer and teacher of languages and mathematics, in Fetter Lane, Holborn." It was the mention of this, his earliest place of education, that attracted the notice of Lamb, and produced the singularly interesting contribution to his own biography contained in this letter.

The Ass (p. 297).—(Hone's *Every-Day Book*, vol. i., October 5.) Hone prefaces Lamb's contribution with the following note:—"The cantering of Tim Tims" (a correspondent who had written on the same subject a few weeks earlier) "startles him who told of his 'youthful days' at the school wherein poor Starkey cyphered part of his little life. C. L. 'getting well, but weak' from painful and severe indisposition, is 'off and away' for a short discursion. Better health to him, and good be to him all his life. Here he is."

In Re Squirrels (p. 301).—(Hone's *Every-Day Book*, vol. i., October 18.) A correspondent of the *Gentleman's Magazine*, on the seventh of the same month, had communicated his experience of these little creatures, and among other letters to Hone which it had called forth was this of Lamb's—a trifle, but rich in his peculiar humour.

Estimate of Defoe's Secondary Novels (p. 303).—Contributed by Lamb to his friend Walter Wilson's "Memoirs of the Life and Times of Daniel Defoe, 1829." The substance of a portion of it will be found in a letter of December 1822, on first hearing of Wilson's intention to undertake the work. See also another letter to Wilson, of November 15, 1829, acknowledging a present of the completed work, and saying—"I shall always feel happy in having my name go down anyhow with Defoe's and that of his historiographer. I promise myself, if not immortality, yet diuturnity of being read in consequence."

Recollections of a late Royal Academician (p. 308).—(*Englishman's Magazine*, September 1831.) George Dawe, born in London, February 8, 1781; died, October 15, 1829; buried in St. Paul's Cathedral. His chief work, after early years engaged in historical-painting, was in portrait-painting. He was engaged by the Emperor of Russia to paint his officers who had been prominent in the wars with Napoleon. For this purpose he started for Russia in January 1819, and, during a residence there of nine years, is said to have painted four hundred portraits, which decorate a large gallery in the Emperor's Palace, called the Hermitage (Redgrave's *Biographical Dictionary of British Artists*). Dawe made a large fortune, but seems to have lost it in imprudent speculations. He was made Associate of the Academy in 1809 ("By what law of association," Lamb wrote at the time, "I cannot guess"), and full Academician in 1814.

This paper was Lamb's first contribution to the *Englishman's Magazine*, when his friend Moxon became publisher of it. It was arranged that Lamb should furnish miscellaneous papers to appear under the general heading of *Peter's Net*. Lamb writes to Moxon in August 1831 on the subject of these Recollections:—"The R.A. here memorised was George Dawe, whom I knew well, and heard many anecdotes of, from Daniels and Westall, at H. Rogers's : to *each of them* it will be well to send a Magazine in my name. It will fly like wild-fire among the Royal Academicians and artists. . . . The anecdotes of G. D. are substantially true; what does Elia (or Peter) care for dates?"

Remarkable Correspondent (p. 315).—This letter, and the one that follows it, explain themselves. They appeared in Hone's *Every-Day Book* under the dates May 1 and August 12. It will be remembered that George IV. was born on August 12, 1762, but that the anniversary was always kept on the corresponding Saint's Day, that of St. George, April 23,—the day which for the same reason, oddly enough, has always been claimed for Shakspeare's birthday. To both these remonstrances Hone appended a playful reply.

Mrs. Gilpin riding to Edmonton (p. 320).—This short paper, headed by a rude woodcut of a woman in a poke-bonnet sitting on a stile, appeared in Hone's *Table-Book* (1827-28), vol. ii. The signature and the internal evidence of style would sufficiently identify the author even if Mr. Frederick Locker did not possess the original manuscript in Lamb's unmistakable handwriting. Lamb was living at Enfield at the time, and the proximity of Edmonton, combined with his own and his sister's experiences of the fields in that neighbourhood, fully account for the playful romance. It hardly needs to be said that the whole thing is invention. The suggestion that the rude woodcut, obviously by one of Hone's stock caricaturists, was "probably by the poet's friend, Romney," is a stroke of humour that could belong to no one except Charles Lamb.

Saturday Night (p. 322).—From *The Gem*, a keepsake or annual for the year 1830. The preceding volume, for 1829, had been edited by Thomas Hood, and in it had appeared a short sketch, signed with Lamb's name, but really contributed by Hood himself, as a joke in which Lamb's love of hoaxing allowed him to concur.

The present contribution was written to accompany an engraving from David Wilkie's picture, *Saturday Night*, in which a cottager appears washing her child's face, and apparently rubbing the soap and water well in with her bare hand. An old man, presumably the child's grandfather, is leisurely stropping a razor in the chimney corner. It is yet one more vivid remembrance of Lamb's childish days with his grandmother in Hertfordshire.

Thoughts on Presents of Game, etc. (p. 325).—From the *Athenæum*, November 30, 1833. Lamb's friend Chambers—who had made "many hours happy in the life of Elia"—was a fellow-clerk with him in the India House; one of the six who sat in the same compartment of the large room in the accountant's office. These compartments were called "compounds." Lamb once defined his compound, it may be remembered, as a "collection of simples."

A Popular Fallacy (p. 328).—From the *New Monthly Magazine*, June 1826. Originally intended, no doubt, to form one of the series afterwards republished in the *Last Essays of Elia*.

Charles Lamb's Autobiography (p. 331).—Appeared first in the *New Monthly Magazine* for April 1835, with the following prefatory note:—

"We have been favoured, by the kindness of Mr. Upcott, with the following sketch, written in one of his manuscript collections by Charles Lamb. It will be read with deep interest by all, but with the deepest interest by those who had the honour and happiness of knowing the writer. It is so singularly characteristic that we can scarcely persuade ourselves we do not hear it, as we read, spoken from his living lips. Slight as it is, it conveys the most exquisite and perfect notion of the personal manner and habits of our friend. For the intellectual rest we lift the veil of its noble modesty, and can even here discern them. Mark its humour, crammed into a few thinking words; its pathetic sensibility in the midst of contrast; its wit, truth, and feeling; and, above all, its fanciful retreat at the close, under a phantom cloud of death."

Mr. Upcott was Assistant Librarian of the London Institution, and one of the contributors to a *Biographical Dictionary of Living Authors of Great Britain and Ireland*, 1816. It may have been for a proposed new edition of this work that Lamb contributed this brief account of himself and estimate of his powers in 1827.

Letter of Elia to Robert Southey, Esq. (p. 333).—(*London Magazine*, October 1823.) The concluding paragraphs of this letter, under the title of "The Tombs in the Abbey," were republished by Lamb in the *Last Essays of Elia* in 1833. For the origin and history of the letter, as a whole, I may refer to my notes on that essay. The article by Southey which provoked it appeared in the *Quarterly Review* for January 1823.

A Poor Child, an Exile at Genoa.—Leigh Hunt's eldest boy, Thornton, at that time with his family in Italy. Leigh Hunt left for Italy in November 1821, and was absent from England till 1825.

I am sorry to hear that you are engaged upon a Life of George Fox.—This idea, if ever entertained by Southey, was never, I believe, carried out. His *Life of Wesley* had appeared in 1820. It was after reading this work that a Wesleyan minister is related to have murmured, as he laid it down, "Sir, thou hast nothing to draw with, and the well is deep"—a profounder criticism on Southey's capacity for dealing with such subjects than any to be found in this essay.

There is ——, and ——, whom you never heard of.—The blanks in the sentences that follow cannot all be supplied, but most of the initials belong to names easily to be identified. "N., my own and my father's friend," was Randal Norris, the Sub-Treasurer of the Inner Temple; "T. N. T.," Thomas Noon Talfourd, afterwards the judge, and Lamb's executor and biographer; "W. the light... Janus of *The London*," Wainwright, whose affected gaiety and high spirits imposed upon Lamb and many others, till convicted of forgery and murder; "modest and amiable C.," Henry Francis Cary, the translator of Dante; "Allan C.," Allan Cunningham; "P——r," Procter, better known as Barry Cornwall; "A——p," Thomas Allsop, author of the *Letters, Conversations, and Recollections of Samuel Taylor Coleridge;* "G——n," James Gillman, the surgeon, in whose house at Highgate Coleridge lived and died; "M," Mr. Monkhouse, a cousin of Mrs. Wordsworth's; "H. C. R.," Henry Crabb Robinson, in whose delightful diaries many an interesting anecdote of Lamb and Coleridge is to be found; "W. A.," William Ayrton, the musical critic, and one of the first to make the great German composers popular in this country, through that admirable work *The Musical Library*. By the courtesy of the present Mr. William Scroop Ayrton,

I possess copies of several short notes from Lamb to his father, chiefly referring to the weekly rubber, in which the Ayrtons and the Burneys took part. They are, for the most part, written in the wildest spirit of drollery. One may be given as a sample, especially as it touches a national event of July 1821 :—

"DEAR AYRTON—In consequence of the august coronation, we propose postponing (I wonder if these words ever met so close before—mark the elegancy) our Wednesday this week to Friday, when a grand rural *fête champêtre* will be given at Russell House ; the back-garden to be illuminated in honour of the late ceremony. Vivat Regina. Moriatur R—x. C. L."

The Authors of Rimini and of the Table Talk.—Leigh Hunt and William Hazlitt.

I wish you would read Mr. H.'s lines.—The first stanza runs thus :—

> " Sleep breathes at last from out thee,
>   My little patient boy ;
> And balmy rest about thee
>   Smooths off the day's annoy :
> I sit me down and think
>   Of all thy winning ways,
> Yet almost wish, with sudden shrink,
>   That I had less to praise."

I stood well with him for fifteen years.—The precise occasion of the breach between Lamb and Hazlitt it might be impossible to discover. Hazlitt was moody and sensitive, and unduly impatient of criticism. It is pleasant to know that Lamb's manly defence of his old friend in this letter had the effect of restoring their old intimacy ; and when he died, seven years later, Lamb was among the friends who were round his bed.

That amiable spy, Major André.—For an interesting account of the removal of André's remains to Westminster Abbey in 1821, see Dean Stanley's *Memorials of the Abbey*. "On the monument, in bas-relief, by Van Gelder, is to be seen the likeness of Washington receiving the flag of truce, and the letter either of André or of Clinton. Many a citizen of the great Western Republic has paused before the sight of the sad story. Often has the head of Washington or André been carried off, perhaps by republican or royalist indignation, but more probably by the pranks of Westminster boys."

On the subject of the letter generally, see letters of Lamb to Bernard Barton, July 10 and September 17, 1823 : also letter to Southey of November 21, in which the old friendly relations are once more established. "The kindness of your note has melted away the mist which was upon me. That accursed Q.R. had vexed me by a gratuitous speaking, of its own knowledge, that the "Confessions of a Drunkard" was a genuine description of the state of the writer. Little things that are not ill-meant may produce much ill. *That* might have injured me alive and dead. I am in a public office, and my life is insured. I was prepared for anger, and I thought I saw in a few obnoxious words, a hard case of repetition directed against me. I wish both Magazine and Review at the bottom of the sea. I shall be ashamed to see you, and my sister (though innocent) will be still more so; for the folly was done without her knowledge, and has made her uneasy ever since. My guardian angel was absent at that time.

Table-Talk and Fragments of Criticism (p. 348).—A portion of these were published in the *Athenæum*, January 4, 1834; the remainder are culled from very various sources.

Elia to his Correspondents (p. 361). In Leigh Hunt's *Indicator* of January 31, 1821, appeared the paragraph referred to by Lamb. It ran as follows:—

"*The Works of Charles Lamb.*—We reprint in our present number a criticism in the *Examiner* on the works of this author. He is not so much known as he is admired; but if to be admired, and more, by those who are better known have anything of the old laudatory desideratum in it, we know no man who possesses a more enviable share of praise. The truth is that Mr. Lamb in general has performed his services to the literary world so anonymously, and in his most trivial subjects has such a delicate and extreme sense of all that is human, that common readers have not been aware of half his merits, nor great numbers of his existence. When his writings were collected by the bookseller (in 1818), people of taste were asking who this Mr. Charles Lamb was that had written so well. They were answered, The man who set the critics right about the old English dramatists, and whom some of them showed at once their ingratitude and their false pretensions by abusing. Besides the work here alluded to, Mr. Lamb is the author of an interesting prose abridgment of the *Odyssey*, under the title of the Adventures of Ulysses, and has helped his sister in other little works for children (equally fit for those 'of a larger growth'), especially one called *Mrs. Leicester's School.* We believe we are taking no greater liberty with him than our motives will warrant when we add that he sometimes writes in the *London Magazine* under the signature of *Elia.*"

The second of these replies to correspondents arose out of the former. Very curious and pathetic is the reference to his alleged birthplace in Princes Street, Cavendish Square. Princes Street, *Leicester Square*, is where Mr. Bartram lived, who married Lamb's old love, Alice W——. The whole paper is a series of mystifications. Calne in Wiltshire was not the birthplace of Coleridge, whose personality Lamb adopted in the Essay on Christ's Hospital; but Coleridge did actually live at Calne for a time, in later years.

On the Death of Coleridge (p. 365).—This singularly touching confidence was first communicated to the world by Mr. John Forster, in a paper on Lamb contributed after his death to the *New Monthly Magazine* in 1835. It was thus introduced:— "Lamb never fairly recovered the death of Coleridge. He thought of little else (his sister was but another portion of himself) until his own great spirit joined his friend's. He had a habit of venting his melancholy in a sort of mirth. He would with nothing graver than a pun 'cleanse his bosom of the perilous stuff that weighed' upon it. In a jest or a few light phrases he would lay open the recesses of his heart. So in respect of the death of Coleridge. Some old friends of his saw him two or three weeks ago, and remarked the constant turning and reference of his mind. He interrupted himself and them almost every instant with some play of affected wonder or humorous melancholy on the words—'*Coleridge is dead.*' Nothing could divert him from that, for the thought of it never left him. About the same time we had written to him to request a few lines for the literary album of a gentleman who entertained a fitting admiration of his genius. It was the last request we were to make, and the last kindness we were to receive. He wrote in Mr. ——'s volume, and wrote of Coleridge. This, we believe, was the last production of his pen. A strange and not unenviable chance, which saw him at the end of his literary pilgrimage, as he had been at the beginning, in that immortal company. We are indebted, with the reader, to the kindness of our friend for permission to print the whole of what was written. It would be impertinence to offer a remark on it. Once read, its noble and affectionate tenderness will be remembered for ever."

Prologue to Coleridge's Remorse (p. 367).—Coleridge's tragedy of *Osorio*, originally written in 1797, was brought out in a revised shape, and under the name of *Remorse*, at Drury Lane in 1813. It had a run of twenty nights.

Prologue to Antonio (p. 369).—Godwin's play was produced on December 13, 1800, and hopelessly failed. See letter of Lamb to Manning, December 16, 1800. See also Mr. Kegan Paul's *Life of Godwin* for a full account of Lamb's untiring efforts in his friend's behalf. The footnotes to the prologue are, of course, Lamb's own, appended in a letter to Manning of December 13.

Prologue to Faulkener (p. 371).—The tragedy was played at Drury Lane, December 16, 1807. The subject of the play was taken from an incident in Defoe's *Roxana*. See Kegan Paul's *Life of Godwin*, ii. 162.

Epilogue to the Wife (p. 372).—Sheridan Knowles acknowledges Lamb's contribution to his drama in the preface to the published edition in 1833. The Epilogue was spoken by Miss Ellen Tree, who played the heroine.

To Clara N. (p. 373).—(*Athenæum*, July 26, 1834.) Clara Novello, the fourth daughter of Lamb's old and valued friend, Vincent Novello. When Lamb wrote this complimentary tribute, she was only sixteen years of age. She had made her first appearance in public the year before, and was already singing (in this year, 1834) at both the Philharmonic and the Ancient Concerts. Lamb had probably heard her chiefly at her father's house. Clara Novello, afterwards the Countess Gigliucci, happily still lives, to remember with pride her enthusiastic though unmusical admirer.

To my Friend, the Indicator (p. 374).—(Leigh Hunt, who brought out the periodical in question in 1819.) It took its name from a fanciful application of the following passage from a work on Natural History :—"There is a bird in the interior of Africa whose habits would rather seem to belong to the interior of Fairy-land, but they have been well authenticated. It indicates to honey-hunters where the nests of wild bees are to be found. It calls them with a cheerful cry which they answer; and, on finding itself recognised, flies and hovers over a hollow tree containing the honey. While they are occupied in collecting it, the bird goes to a little distance, where he observes all that passes; and the hunters, when they have helped themselves, take care to leave him his portion of the food. This is the Cuculus Indicator of Linnæus, otherwise called the Moroc, Bee Cuckoo, or Honey Bird."

Saint Crispin to Mr. Gifford (p. 374).—Gifford, the Editor of the *Quarterly*, was, as is well known, in early life apprenticed to a shoemaker. Lamb had a special grudge against him for mangling his review of Wordsworth's *Excursion*. See note on Lamb's review in the present volume.

In Tabulam Eximii (p. 375).—On Haydon's Picture, the Entry of Christ into Jerusalem. I have corrected the text of the Latin from the copy given in Haydon's *Memoirs*, vol. ii. p. 13. As Tom Taylor remarks, this specimen of Lamb's Latinity is more monkish than classical. He probably meant it to be so. Haydon's picture was exhibited by him in 1820. See his *Memoirs*, i. 399.

To Sir James Mackintosh (p. 377).—The unfortunate epigram that brought about the final collapse of the *Albion*. See Elia Essay, "Newspapers thirty-five years ago." The epigrams that follow will not strike the reader as having any great merit, or reason to exist. They appeared for the most part in the *Examiner*, where any stick did well enough with which to beat the Prince Regent. He tells Bernard Barton, in 1829, "Strolling to Waltham Cross the other day, I hit off these lines. It is one of the crosses which Edward I. caused to be built for his wife at every town where her corpse rested, between Northamptonshire and London." The epigram, as given in the letter, exhibits some considerable variations.

One Dip (p. 380).—Archdeacon Hessey has lately made public, for the first time, the very curious history of this little fable. It was one of two epigrams written by Lamb for Archdeacon Hessey and his brother, the late Rev. Francis Hessey, when schoolboys at *Merchant Taylors*. The subject for the Latin epigram was "Suum Cuique," and the epigram may be found in my notes to the Essay "On the Inconveniences resulting from being hanged" (*Lamb's Poems, Plays, and Miscellaneous Essays*, p. 403). The subject proposed for the English epigram was, "Brevis esse laboro," and, as Archdeacon Hessey remarks, "the adventure recorded might well have happened to Lamb himself." It should be added that the production of these epigrams being of regular and frequent recurrence, the boys were allowed and almost expected to obtain help from their friends. In previous editions of Lamb's works, the epigram will be found, with the signature "H——y," but up to the date of Archdeacon Hessey's interesting paper in the *Taylorian*, it had never been explained. "I have now before me," the Archdeacon writes, "the copies of them as they were shown up to the head-master, with the names of J. A. Hessey and F. Hessey attached to them respectively." See letter of Lamb to Southey, of May 10, 1830.

Satan in Search of a Wife (p. 381).—Originally published in a thin volume, with illustrations, by Moxon in 1831. It seems to have been the combined product of reading Moore's *Loves of the Angels* and Coleridge and Southey's *Devil's Walk*, with the crop of imitations to which the latter poem gave rise. The choosing the daughter of a tailor, as the lady who won

Satan's young affections, is due solely to the grim circumstance that the cavity beneath a tailor's shop-board, into which he lets fall the portions of cloth which form his "cabbage," is called in the strange slang of the profession, his "Hell." The verses are indeed but little worthy of their author; but they gave occasion for one of his many and familiar acts of generosity, and it is pleasant to take lèave of him with the record of it. Moxon had been forced to abandon the publication of his *Englishman's Magazine* for want of support. Lamb had written for it, and helped it in all ways he could, but in vain; and he writes to his friend, October 24, 1831, commending his prudence in not continuing the experiment longer. "To drop metaphors, I am sure you have done wisely. The very spirit of your epistle speaks that you have a weight off your mind. I have one on mine—the cash in hand, which, as —— less truly says, burns in my pocket. I feel queer at returning it (who does not?)—you feel awkward at retaking it (who ought not?) —is there no middle way of adjusting this fine embarrassment? I think I have hit upon a medium to skin the sore place over, if not quite to heal it. You hinted that there might be something under £10 by and by, accruing to me—*Devil's money* " (the allusion is to the squib now before us), " (you are sanguine, say £7 : 10s); that I entirely renounce, and abjure all future interest in; I insist upon it, and ' by him I will not name ' I won't touch a penny of it. That will split your loss one half, and leave me conscientious possessor of what I hold. Less than your assent to this, no proposal will I accept of."

THE END.

Printed by R. & R. CLARK, *Edinburgh.*

www.ingramcontent.com/pod-product-compliance
Lightning Source LLC
Chambersburg PA
CBHW032142010526
44111CB00035B/858